Focus on GRAMMAR 4

FOURTH EDITION

Marjorie Fuchs
Margaret Bonner

ALWAYS LEARNING

PEARSON

To the memory of my parents, Edith and Joseph Fuchs—MF
To my parents, Marie and Joseph Maus, and to my son, Luke Frances—MB

Focus on Grammar 4: An Integrated Skills Approach, Fourth Edition

Copyright © 2012, 2006, 2000, 1995 by Pearson Education, Inc.
All rights reserved.

Pearson Education, 10 Bank Street, White Plains, NY 10606

Staff credits: The people who made up the *Focus on Grammar 4, Fourth Edition*
team, representing editorial, production, design, and manufacturing, are Elizabeth Carlson,
Tracey Cataldo, Aerin Csigay, Dave Dickey, Christine Edmonds, Nancy Flaggman, Ann France,
Françoise Leffler, Lise Minovitz, Barbara Perez, Robert Ruvo, and Debbie Sistino.

Cover image: Shutterstock.com
Text composition: ElectraGraphics, Inc.
Text font: New Aster

Library of Congress Cataloging-in-Publication Data

Schoenberg, Irene, 1946–
    Focus on grammar. 1: an integrated skills approach / Irene E. Schoenberg, Jay Maurer.—3rd ed.
        p. cm.
    Includes index.
    ISBN 0-13-245591-9—ISBN 0-13-254647-7—ISBN 0-13-254648-5—ISBN 0-13-254649-3—
ISBN 0-13-254650-7 1. English language—Textbooks for foreign speakers. 2. English language—
Grammar—Problems, exercises, etc. I. Maurer, Jay. II. Title.
    PE1128.S3456824 2011
    428.2'4—dc22
                                                                                    2011014126

Printed in the United States of America
ISBN 10: 0-13-254649-3
ISBN 13: 978-0-13-254649-2

12 17

ISBN 10: 0-13-216936-3 (with MyLab)
ISBN 13: 978-0-13-216936-3 (with MyLab)

6 16

CONTENTS

Welcome to Focus on Grammar

Now in a new edition, the popular five-level **Focus on Grammar** course continues to provide an integrated-skills approach to help students understand and practice English grammar. Centered on thematic instruction, **Focus on Grammar** combines controlled and communicative practice with critical thinking skills and ongoing assessment. Students gain the confidence they need to speak and write English accurately and fluently.

NEW for the FOURTH EDITION

VOCABULARY

Key vocabulary is highlighted, practiced, and recycled throughout the unit.

PRONUNCIATION

Now, in every unit, pronunciation points and activities help students improve spoken accuracy and fluency.

LISTENING

Expanded listening tasks allow students to develop a range of listening skills.

UPDATED CHARTS and NOTES

Target structures are presented in a clear, easy-to-read format.

NEW READINGS

High-interest readings, updated or completely new, in a variety of genres integrate grammar and vocabulary in natural contexts.

NEW UNIT REVIEWS

Students can check their understanding and monitor their progress after completing each unit.

MyFocusOnGrammarLab

An easy-to-use online learning and assessment program offers online homework and individualized instruction anywhere, anytime.

Teacher's Resource Pack   One compact resource includes:

THE TEACHER'S MANUAL: General Teaching Notes, Unit Teaching Notes, the Student Book Audioscript, and the Student Book Answer Key.

TEACHER'S RESOURCE DISC: Bound into the Resource Pack, this CD-ROM contains reproducible Placement, Part, and Unit Tests, as well as customizable Test-Generating Software. It also includes reproducible Internet Activities and PowerPoint® Grammar Presentations.

THE *FOCUS ON GRAMMAR* APPROACH

The new edition follows the same successful four-step approach of previous editions. The books provide an abundance of both controlled and communicative exercises so that students can bridge the gap between identifying grammatical structures and using them. The many communicative activities in each Student Book provide opportunities for critical thinking while enabling students to personalize what they have learned.

- **STEP 1: GRAMMAR IN CONTEXT** highlights the target structures in realistic contexts, such as conversations, magazine articles, and blog posts.
- **STEP 2: GRAMMAR PRESENTATION** presents the structures in clear and accessible grammar charts and notes with multiple examples of form and usage.
- **STEP 3: FOCUSED PRACTICE** provides numerous and varied controlled exercises for both the form and meaning of the new structures.
- **STEP 4: COMMUNICATION PRACTICE** includes listening and pronunciation and allows students to use the new structures freely and creatively in motivating, open-ended speaking and writing activities.

Recycling

Underpinning the scope and sequence of the *Focus on Grammar* series is the belief that students need to use target structures and vocabulary many times, in different contexts. New grammar and vocabulary are recycled throughout the book. Students have maximum exposure and become confident using the language in speech and in writing.

Assessment

Extensive testing informs instruction and allows teachers and students to measure progress.

- **Unit Reviews** at the end of every Student Book unit assess students' understanding of the grammar and allow students to monitor their own progress.
- Easy to administer and score, **Part and Unit Tests** provide teachers with a valid and reliable means to determine how well students know the material they are about to study and to assess students' mastery after they complete the material. These tests can be found on MyFocusOnGrammarLab, where they include immediate feedback and remediation, and as reproducible tests on the Teacher's Resource Disc.
- **Test-Generating Software** on the Teacher's Resource Disc includes a bank of *additional* test items teachers can use to create customized tests.
- A reproducible **Placement Test** on the Teacher's Resource Disc is designed to help teachers place students into one of the five levels of the *Focus on Grammar* course.

COMPONENTS

In addition to the Student Books, Teacher's Resource Packs, and MyLabs, the complete *Focus on Grammar* course includes:

Workbooks   Contain additional contextualized exercises appropriate for self-study.

Audio Program   Includes all of the listening and pronunciation exercises and opening passages from the Student Book. Some Student Books are packaged with the complete audio program (mp3 files). Alternatively, the audio program is available on a classroom set of CDs and on the MyLab.

THE FOCUS ON GRAMMAR UNIT

Focus on Grammar introduces grammar structures in the context of unified themes. All units follow a **four-step approach**, taking learners from grammar in context to communicative practice.

STEP 1 GRAMMAR IN CONTEXT

This section presents the target structure(s) in a natural context. As students read the **high-interest texts**, they encounter the form, meaning, and use of the grammar. **Before You Read** activities create interest and elicit students' knowledge about the topic. **After You Read** activities build students' reading vocabulary and comprehension.

Vocabulary exercises improve students' command of English. Vocabulary is **recycled** throughout the unit.

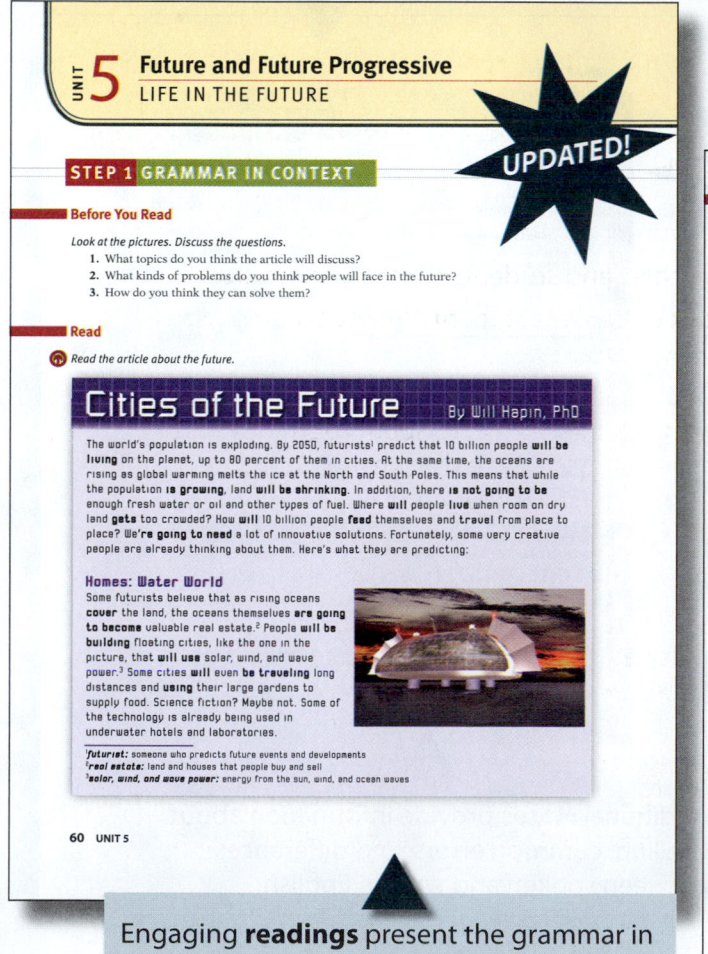

Engaging **readings** present the grammar in realistic contexts such as **magazine articles** and **blog posts**.

Reading comprehension tasks focus on the meaning of the text and draw students' attention to the target structure.

This section gives students a comprehensive and explicit overview of the grammar with detailed **Grammar Charts** and **Grammar Notes** that present the form, meaning, and use of the structure(s).

Grammar Charts present the structure in a clear, easy-to-read format.

Grammar Notes give concise, simple **explanations** and **examples** to ensure students' understanding.

Additional **Notes** provide information about spelling, common errors, and differences between spoken and written English.

REDESIGNED!

STEP 2 GRAMMAR PRESENTATION

FUTURE

Affirmative Statements	
We **are going to take**	
We **will take**	the airship at 9:00.
We **are taking**	
We **take**	

Negative Statements	
We **are not going to take**	
We **will not take**	the airship at 10:00.
We **are not taking**	
We **don't take**	

Yes / No Questions	
Is she **going to take**	
Will she **take**	the airship at 9:00?
Is she **taking**	
Does she **take**	

Short Answers			
Affirmative		Negative	
	she **is**.		she **isn't**.
Yes,	she **will**.	No,	she **won't**.
	she **is**.		she **isn't**.
	she **does**.		she **doesn't**.

Wh- Questions	
When is she **going to take**	
When **will** she **take**	the airship?
When is she **taking**	
When **does** she **take**	

FUTURE PROGRESSIVE

Statements			
Subject	Be (not) going to / Will (not)	Be + Base Form + -ing	
People	are (not) going to will (not)	be traveling	to Mars by 2050.

Yes / No Questions				
Be / Will	Subject	Going to	Be + Base Form + -ing	
Are	they	going to	be traveling	to Mars?
Will				

Short Answers			
Affirmative		Negative	
Yes,	they **are**.	No,	they're **not**.
	they **will**.		they **won't**.

Wh- Questions					
Wh- Word	Be / Will	Subject	Going to	Be + Base Form + -ing	
When	are	they	going to	be traveling	to Mars?
	will				

Future and Future Progressive   **63**

GRAMMAR NOTES

1 Use the **simple present** to describe what generally happens (but not necessarily right now).

Now
Past —X—X—X—X—X—X→ Future

People often call him George.

Use the **present progressive** to describe what is happening right now or in the extended present (for example, *nowadays, this month, these days, this year*).

Now
Past ———X———→ Future
She's studying

- People **often call** him George.
- We **never use** nicknames.
- The paper **usually arrives** at 7:00 A.M.

A: Where's Dusya?
B: At the library. She's **studying**.

A: What's Jorge **doing these days**?
B: He's **working** on a new project.

2 Remember that **non-action verbs** are NOT usually used in the progressive even when they describe a situation that exists at the moment of speaking.

Non-action verbs describe emotions (*love, hate*); mental states (*remember, understand*); wants (*need, want*); perceptions (*hear, see*); appearance (*look, seem*); and possession (*have, own*).

- I **want** to have a special name.
  NOT: I'm **wanting** to have a special name.

- I **hate** my nickname.
- **Do** you **remember** her name?
- Jan **wants** to change her name.

3 Use the **simple present** to talk about situations that are not connected to time—for example, scientific facts and physical laws.

- Water **freezes** at 0ºC (32ºF).
- The Earth **orbits** the sun.

4 The **simple present** is often used in book or movie reviews and in newspaper reports.

- This book **gives** information about names. It also **talks** about giving gifts.

5 The **present progressive** is often used with always to express a repeated action.

USAGE NOTE: We often use the present progressive to express a negative reaction to a situation.

- She's **always smiling**. That's why we call her "Sunshine." It's her nickname.
- He's **always calling** me "Sweetie." I really hate that name.

Controlled practice activities in this section lead students to master form, meaning, and use of the target grammar.

STEP 3 FOCUSED PRACTICE

EXERCISE 1: Discover the Grammar

Match the facts with the speculations and conclusions.

Facts

Speculations and Conclusions

_e_ **1.** The original title of *Chariots of the Gods?* was *Erinnerungen an die Zukunft*.

____ **2.** Erich von Däniken visited every place he described in his book.

____ **3.** In 1973, he wrote *In Search of Ancient Gods*.

____ **4.** He doesn't have a degree in archeology.

____ **5.** *Chariots of the Gods?* was published the same year as the Apollo moon landing.

____ **6.** In the 1900s, writer Annie Besant said beings from Venus helped develop culture on Earth.

____ **7.** Von Däniken's books sold millions of copies.

____ **8.** As soon as von Däniken published his book, scientists attacked his theories.

a. He must have made a lot of money.

b. He may have known about her unusual ideas.

c. He could have learned about the subject on his own.

d. He must have traveled a lot.

e. He must have written his book in German.

f. This great event had to have increased sales of the book.

g. He must not have had scientific evidence for his beliefs.

h. He might have written some other books too.

EXERCISE 2: Questions and Statements

(Grammar Notes 1–4)

Circle the correct words to complete the review of Erich von Däniken's book, Chariots of the Gods?

Who could have make / made the Nazca lines? Who
1.
could have carve / carved the Easter Island statues?
2.
According to Erich von Däniken, ancient achievements
like these are mysteries because our ancestors could not
have / had created these things on their own. His
3.
conclusion: They must / couldn't have gotten help from
4.
space visitors.

Von Däniken's readers may not realize that experiments
have contributed to our understanding of some of these
"mysteries." Von Däniken asks: How may / could the Nazcans have planned the lines from
5.
the ground? Archeologists now speculate that this civilization might have / has developed flight.
6.
They think ancient Nazcans may draw / have drawn pictures of hot-air balloons on pottery. To test
7.

"Here comes another one."

(continued on next page)

Speculations and Conclusions About the Past **275**

Discover the Grammar activities develop students' recognition and understanding of the target structure before they are asked to produce it.

An **Editing** exercise ends every Focused Practice section and teaches students to find and correct typical mistakes.

EXERCISE 6: Editing

Read this article about cars of the future. There are ten mistakes in the use of the future and future progressive. The first mistake is already corrected. Find and correct nine more.

Flying Cars

The SkyCar

Your class starts in 10 minutes, but you're stuck in traffic. Don't panic. With just a press of a button, your car will ~~lifts~~ *lift* off the ground, and you'll be on your way to school. No bad roads, no stop signs, no worries!

Welcome to the future! It seems like science fiction, but it isn't. Engineers have been working on flying cars for decades, and they have already solved many of the big challenges. They predict that we'll all be use these amazing vehicles one day.

According to *Car Trends Magazine*, one model, part car and part plane, is going be on the market in the not-so-distant future. It will look like a regular car when it's on the road, but its wings will unfold when the driver will decide to take to the skies. It will runs on the same fuel for both land and air travel, and you'll be able to keep it in your garage. (But you're still going need an airport to take off and land.)

A better model will be a vertical takeoff and landing vehicle (VTOL). You won't need to go to the airport anymore, and all controls will being automatic. Imagine this: You'll be doing your homework while your car will be getting you to school safely and on time.

And what does this future dream car cost? Well, fasten your seatbelts—the price will going to be sky-high. At first it will be about a million dollars, but after a few years, you'll be able to buy one for "only" $60,000. Don't throw away your old driver's license just yet!

A **variety of exercise types** engage students and guide them from recognition and understanding to accurate production of the grammar structures.

Future and Future Progressive **71**

STEP 4 COMMUNICATION PRACTICE

This section provides practice with the structure in **listening** and **pronunciation** exercises as well as in communicative, open-ended **speaking** and **writing** activities that move students toward fluency.

Listening activities allow students to hear the grammar in natural contexts and to practice a range of listening skills.

Pronunciation Notes and **exercises** improve students' spoken fluency and accuracy.

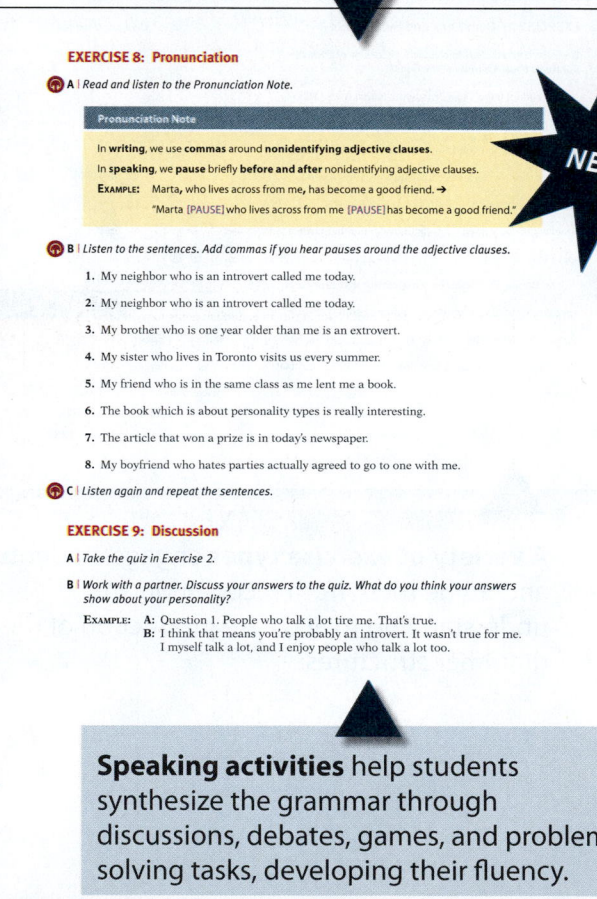

Speaking activities help students synthesize the grammar through discussions, debates, games, and problem-solving tasks, developing their fluency.

Writing activities encourage students to produce meaningful writing that integrates the grammar structure.

An **Editing Checklist** teaches students to correct their mistakes and revise their work.

Unit Reviews give students the opportunity to check their understanding of the target structure. **Answers** at the back of the book allow students to monitor their own progress.

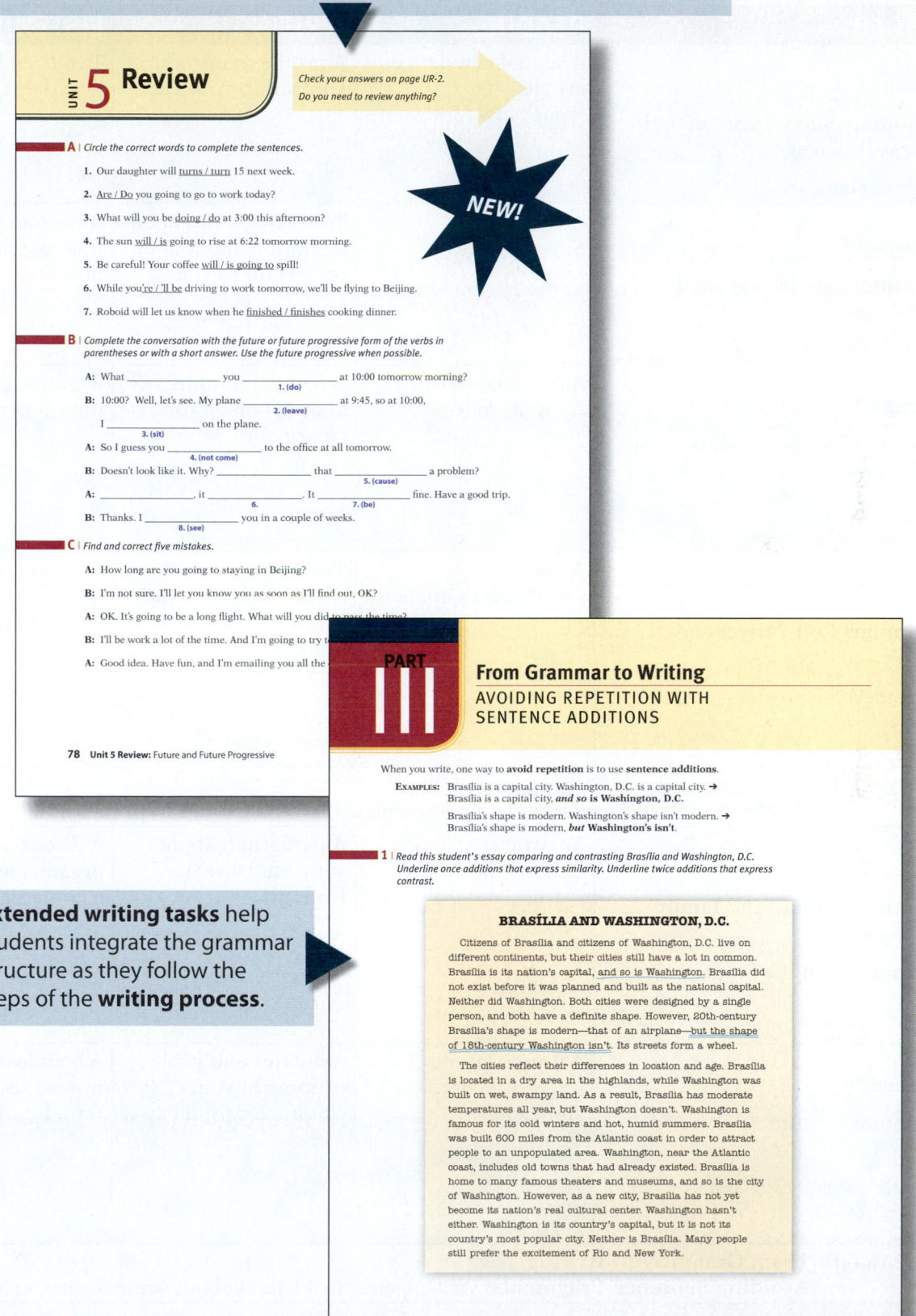

UNIT 5 **Review**

Check your answers on page UR-2.
Do you need to review anything?

NEW!

A | *Circle the correct words to complete the sentences.*

1. Our daughter will <u>turns / turn</u> 15 next week.

2. <u>Are / Do</u> you going to go to work today?

3. What will you be <u>doing / do</u> at 3:00 this afternoon?

4. The sun <u>will / is</u> going to rise at 6:22 tomorrow morning.

5. Be careful! Your coffee <u>will / is going to</u> spill!

6. While you<u>'re / 'll be</u> driving to work tomorrow, we'll be flying to Beijing.

7. Roboid will let us know when he <u>finished / finishes</u> cooking dinner.

B | *Complete the conversation with the future or future progressive form of the verbs in parentheses or with a short answer. Use the future progressive when possible.*

A: What _____ you _____ at 10:00 tomorrow morning?
     1. (do)

B: 10:00? Well, let's see. My plane _____ at 9:45, so at 10:00,
                                    2. (leave)

   I _____ on the plane.
      3. (sit)

A: So I guess you _____ to the office at all tomorrow.
                    4. (not come)

B: Doesn't look like it. Why? _____ that _____ a problem?
                                            5. (cause)

A: _____, it _____. It _____ fine. Have a good trip.
                        6.   7. (be)

B: Thanks. I _____ you in a couple of weeks.
               8. (see)

C | *Find and correct five mistakes.*

A: How long are you going to staying in Beijing?

B: I'm not sure. I'll let you know you as soon as I'll find out, OK?

A: OK. It's going to be a long flight. What will you did to pass the time?

B: I'll be work a lot of the time. And I'm going to try t...

A: Good idea. Have fun, and I'm emailing you all the...

78   Unit 5 Review: Future and Future Progressive

PART III

From Grammar to Writing

AVOIDING REPETITION WITH SENTENCE ADDITIONS

When you write, one way to **avoid repetition** is to use **sentence additions**.

EXAMPLES: Brasília is a capital city. Washington, D.C. is a capital city. →
Brasília is a capital city, *and so is* Washington, D.C.

Brasília's shape is modern. Washington's shape isn't modern. →
Brasília's shape is modern, *but Washington's isn't*.

1 | *Read this student's essay comparing and contrasting Brasília and Washington, D.C. Underline once additions that express similarity. Underline twice additions that express contrast.*

BRASÍLIA AND WASHINGTON, D.C.

Citizens of Brasília and citizens of Washington, D.C. live on different continents, but their cities still have a lot in common. Brasília is its nation's capital, <u>and so is Washington</u>. Brasília did not exist before it was planned and built as the national capital. Neither did Washington. Both cities were designed by a single person, and both have a definite shape. However, 20th-century Brasília's shape is modern—that of an airplane—<u>but the shape of 18th-century Washington isn't</u>. Its streets form a wheel.

The cities reflect their differences in location and age. Brasília is located in a dry area in the highlands, while Washington was built on wet, swampy land. As a result, Brasília has moderate temperatures all year, but Washington doesn't. Washington is famous for its cold winters and hot, humid summers. Brasília was built 600 miles from the Atlantic coast in order to attract people to an unpopulated area. Washington, near the Atlantic coast, includes old towns that had already existed. Brasília is home to many famous theaters and museums, and so is the city of Washington. However, as a new city, Brasília has not yet become its nation's real cultural center. Washington hasn't either. Washington is its country's capital, but it is not its country's most popular city. Neither is Brasília. Many people still prefer the excitement of Rio and New York.

134   PART III

Extended writing tasks help students integrate the grammar structure as they follow the steps of the **writing process**.

SCOPE AND SEQUENCE

UNIT	READING	WRITING	LISTENING
1 page 2 **Grammar:** Simple Present and Present Progressive **Theme:** Names	A school newsletter article: *What's in a Name?*	A profile to introduce yourself to your class	Two friends discussing photos
2 page 13 **Grammar:** Simple Past and Past Progressive **Theme:** First Meetings	An article: *Super Couples*	Two paragraphs about a relationship that is important to you	A woman explaining how she met her husband
3 page 26 **Grammar:** Simple Past, Present Perfect, and Present Perfect Progressive **Theme:** Hobbies and Interests	A personal website: *Jumping for Joy*	A few paragraphs about yourself for a personal website	A couple planning their honeymoon trip
4 page 38 **Grammar:** Past Perfect and Past Perfect Progressive **Theme:** Musicians	An article: *The People's Conductor*	Two paragraphs about a musician or singer	A radio host interviewing several young musicians

PART I   From Grammar to Writing, page 55
Editing for Verb Forms: Write a paragraph about a phase you went through.

UNIT	READING	WRITING	LISTENING
5 page 60 **Grammar:** Future and Future Progressive **Theme:** Life in the Future	An article: *Cities of the Future*	A paragraph about your life 10 years from now	A discussion about organizing a conference
6 page 79 **Grammar:** Future Perfect and Future Perfect Progressive **Theme:** Money and Goals	A transcript of a TV finance show: *Money Talks*	Activities and goals of some of your classmates for a class website	A couple discussing how to save money for a family vacation

PART II   From Grammar to Writing, page 96
Avoiding Sentence Fragments: Write a letter to a friend about some plans you are making.

SPEAKING	PRONUNCIATION	VOCABULARY	
Find Someone Who . . .	Stressing contrasting or new information	actually convince* institute*	style* (n) title
What About You? The first time you met someone who became influential in your life *Ask and Answer:* Important events in your life	Intonation and pauses in sentences with time clauses	couple* cover (v) influential	opponent recover* research* (n)
What About You? Talk about your hobbies and interests *Ask and Answer:* What did you plan to accomplish last week?	Reduction of *has he* ("hazee") and *did he* ("didee") *have you* ("havya") and *did you* ("didja")	celebrate engaged extreme	fantastic historic introduce
What About You? Compare your day yesterday with a classmate's *Conversation:* Talk about things you had never done before . . . *Game:* Find the Differences	Pronunciation of the contraction of *had* ('d) after pronouns and nouns	conduct* (v) contract* (n) enthusiastic	ethnic* participate* transform*
Reaching Agreement: Finding a time to get together *Discussion:* Which activities will robots be doing and not doing? *Information Gap:* Dr. Eon's Calendar	Stress for contrasting information	challenge* (n) creative* innovative*	technology* vehicle* vertical
Conversation: What will some of the people in your life have achieved by the end of this year, month, or week? *What About You?* Three goals you would like to achieve in the next five years	Reduction of *have* ("of") in the future perfect and future perfect progressive	budget (n) credit* (n) debt	minimum* purchase* (n) statistics*

* = AWL (Academic Word List) items

UNIT	READING	WRITING	LISTENING
7 page 100 **Grammar:** Negative *Yes / No* Questions and Tag Questions **Theme:** Places to Live	On-the-street interviews: *It's a Great Place to Live, Isn't It?*	An interview of a classmate about his or her city	Short conversations asking for information or looking for agreement
8 page 118 **Grammar:** Additions and Responses: *So, Too, Neither, Not either,* and *But* **Theme:** Similarities and Differences	An article: *The Twin Question: Nature or Nurture?*	Two paragraphs about two people who are close	A couple talking about their similarities and differences

PART III From Grammar to Writing, page 134
Avoiding Repetition with Sentence Additions: Write an essay of comparison and contrast.

UNIT	READING	WRITING	LISTENING
9 page 138 **Grammar:** Gerunds and Infinitives: Review and Expansion **Theme:** Fast Food	An article: *McWorld*	A short editorial about a social issue involving food	Two college students discussing their responses to a food service survey
10 page 156 **Grammar:** *Make, Have, Let, Help,* and *Get* **Theme:** Zoos and Water Parks	An article: *That's Entertainment?*	A three-paragraph essay for and against keeping animals in zoos and water parks	A student and teacher talking about a writing assignment

PART IV From Grammar to Writing, page 168
Using Parallel Forms: Gerunds and Infinitives: Write a summary of a movie, TV show, or story.

SPEAKING	PRONUNCIATION	VOCABULARY	
Information Gap: London and Vancouver *Conversation:* How well do you know your classmates?	Rising or falling intonation in tag questions	adjustment* attract bother	originally provide structure* (n)
Discussion: Are the man and woman a good match? *Picture Discussion:* Imagine the conversations of reunited twins *Find Someone Who . . .* *Compare and Contrast:* Look at pictures of a pair of twins and find their similarities and differences *What Do You Think?* Which is more important, nature or nurture?	Stress in additions and short responses of similarity and difference	coincidence* despite* factor*	identical* image* outgoing
Information Gap: The Right Job? *Questionnaire:* Compare your answers on a fast-food questionnaire with your partner's *Cross-Cultural Comparison:* Describe a food from your culture. Then choose foods to include in an international food festival. *Problem Solving:* Solutions to social problems	Intonation to express sincerity or sarcasm	appealing consequence* globe*	objection region* reliability*
Discussion: Who helped you learn something? *For or Against:* Keeping animals captive	Reductions and linking of pronouns: *let her* ("let'er"), *made him* ("made'im"), *got them* ("got'em")	complicated former humane	physical* punishment reward (n)

* = AWL (Academic Word List) items

SPEAKING	PRONUNCIATION	VOCABULARY	
Problem Solving: How would you like to change your classroom or your school? *Compare and Contrast:* Describe the differences in Before and After pictures of a room	Linking final consonant sounds to beginning vowel sounds in phrasal verbs	complex* consultant* environment*	harmful theory*
For or Against: Telemarketing calls *Discussion:* What do you think about an ad, a piece of junk mail, spam, or an Internet offer?	Stress in separable phrasal verbs	authorities* constantly* eliminate*	equivalent* identify* tactic
Discussion: What do your answers on a personality quiz mean? *Questionnaire:* A friend is someone who . . . *Quotable Quotes:* Friends and personality types	Pausing before and after nonidentifying adjective clauses	contradict* define* personality	require* sensitive unique*
What About You? Share photos of people and places with your classmates. *Quotable Quotes:* Home	Breaking long sentences into thought groups	connection generation* immigrant*	issue* poverty translation
Discussion: What do you think of a student's profile on a social networking site? *Reaching Agreement:* Designing a class website *Problem Solving:* What would you do to survive on a desert island? *For or Against:* The advantages and disadvantages of online social networking	Reductions of: *have to* ("hafta"), *have got to* ("have gotta"), *ought to* ("oughta"), *be able to* ("be able ta")	comment* (n) content (n) involved*	network* (v) privacy resource*

* = AWL (Academic Word List) items

SPEAKING	PRONUNCIATION	VOCABULARY	
Game: Find the Problems *Survey:* Sense of Obligation *Problem Solving:* What should the people have done in these situations?	Reductions of *have* in past modals: *should have* ("shoulda"), *could have* ("coulda"), *might have* ("mighta"), *ought to have* ("oughta of")	process* (n) psychology* ruined	strategy* technique* unrealistic
Picture Discussion: Speculate on what ancient objects are and how people might have used them *For or Against:* Do you agree or disagree with Erich von Däniken's theories?	Reductions of *have* in past modals: *could have* ("could of"), *may have* ("may of"), *couldn't have* ("couldn't of")	conclusion* contribute* encounter* (n)	estimate* (v) evidence* speculate*
Quotable Quotes: International proverbs *Information Gap:* The Philippines *Game:* Trivia Quiz	Stressing corrected information	decade* edition* explorer	inhabitant mission publication*
Reaching Agreement: What rules should be made for living in close quarters? *Problem Solving:* What things must be done to get a student lounge in order? *For or Against:* Spending money on space projects	Dropping the final "t" in *must be, mustn't be, couldn't be,* and *shouldn't be*	assemble* benefit* (v) cooperate*	period* perspective* undertaking*
Making Plans: A car trip to another country *Compare and Contrast:* Describe what a model had done to change her appearance *Cross-Cultural Comparison:* The types of things people do or get done to change their appearance	Contrast: Contractions of *have* in the present perfect (*She's cut her hair.*) and Uncontracted use of *have* in the passive causative (*She has her hair cut.*)	appearance event option*	permanent remove* risk (n)

* = AWL (Academic Word List) items

SPEAKING	PRONUNCIATION	VOCABULARY	
Reaching Agreement: Ordering T-shirts from a store's website *Cross-Cultural Comparison:* Shopping *Discussion:* What do you do when you want to make an important purchase? *For or Against:* Shopping in a "store with doors" and shopping online	Intonation and pauses in conditional statements	consumer* dispute (v) policy*	precaution secure* (adj) site*
Problem Solving: What are possible solutions to everyday problems? *Cross-Cultural Comparison:* Superstitions about luck	Intonation in conditional *yes / no* and *wh-* questions	anticipate* attitude* confident	insight* percent* widespread*
What About You? What would you do if . . . ? *Problem Solving:* Giving Advice *Discussion:* What three wishes would you make?	Contractions of *would* ("d") Dropping the final "t" after *wouldn't*	consent* (v) embarrassed enchanted	furious grant* (v) respond*
What About You? How a single decision or event changed your life or the life of someone you know *Problem Solving:* What would you have done in certain situations? *Discussion:* What is a situation in your life that you regret?	Reduction of *have* ("of") Contractions for: *had* ("d"), *had not* ("hadn't"), *would not* ("wouldn't"), *could not* ("couldn't")	alternate* (adj) intelligent* occur*	outcome* parallel* (adj) version*
Discussion: Is it OK to lie in certain circumstances? *Questionnaire:* Honesty *Game:* To Tell the Truth *Quotable Quotes:* Lying and telling the truth	Stress and intonation to express belief and disbelief about what someone said	average (adj) aware* justify*	majority* reveal*

* = AWL (Academic Word List) items

UNIT	READING	WRITING	LISTENING
26 page 417 **Grammar:** Indirect Speech: Tense Changes **Theme:** Extreme Weather	A news article: *The Flood of the Century*	A paragraph reporting someone else's experience with extreme weather	A winter storm warning
27 page 432 **Grammar:** Indirect Instructions, Commands, Requests, and Invitations **Theme:** Health Problems and Remedies	A radio interview: *Here's to Your Health: The Snooze News*	A paragraph about a dream	A conversation about treatment at a headache clinic
28 page 445 **Grammar:** Indirect Questions **Theme:** Job Interviews	An article: *The Stress Interview*	A report of an interview with someone working in a job that might interest you	A job interview
29 page 461 **Grammar:** Embedded Questions **Theme:** Travel Tips	An interview: *The Tip: Who? When? and How Much?*	A paragraph about a situation that confused or surprised you	A call-in radio program about tipping
PART X **From Grammar to Writing,** page 478 **Using Direct and Indirect Speech:** Write a letter of complaint.			

SPEAKING	PRONUNCIATION	VOCABULARY	
Game: Telephone *Interview:* Experiences with severe weather conditions	Stress on content words	bear (v) collapse* (v) damage (n)	evacuate optimistic restore*
Problem Solving: What advice would you give for some minor health problems? *Picture Discussion:* Which instructions did Jeff follow?	Stress in affirmative and negative indirect instructions, commands, requests, and invitations	astonishing fatigue (n) interfere	monitor* (v) persist* remedy (n)
Role Play: A Job Interview *Questionnaire:* Work Values *What About You?* A personal experience with a school or job interview	Intonation in direct and indirect *yes / no* questions	appropriate* (adj) candidate evaluation*	handle (v) potential* (adj) pressure (n)
Information Gap: Eating Out *Discussion:* What is your opinion about tipping? *What About You?* The problems you had when you did something for the first time *Role Play:* Information Please!	Intonation in direct and embedded *wh-* questions	clarify* custom depend on	logical* ordinary ultimate*

* = AWL (Academic Word List) items

ABOUT THE AUTHORS

Marjorie Fuchs has taught ESL at New York City Technical College and LaGuardia Community College of the City University of New York and EFL at the Sprach Studio Lingua Nova in Munich, Germany. She has a master's degree in Applied English Linguistics and a certificate in TESOL from the University of Wisconsin-Madison. She has authored and co-authored many widely used books and multimedia materials, notably *Crossroads, Top Twenty ESL Word Games: Beginning Vocabulary Development, Families: Ten Card Games for Language Learners, Focus on Grammar 3: An Integrated Skills Approach, Focus on Grammar 3 CD-ROM, Focus on Grammar 4 CD-ROM, Longman English Interactive 3* and *4, Grammar Express Basic, Grammar Express Basic CD-ROM, Grammar Express Intermediate, Future 1: English for Results,* and workbooks for *The Oxford Picture Dictionary High Beginning* and *Low Intermediate, Focus on Grammar 3* and *4,* and *Grammar Express Basic.*

Margaret Bonner has taught ESL at Hunter College and the Borough of Manhattan Community College of the City University of New York, at Taiwan National University in Taipei, and at Virginia Commonwealth University in Richmond. She holds a master's degree in library science from Columbia University, and she has done work toward a PhD in English literature at the Graduate Center of the City University of New York. She has authored and co-authored numerous ESL and EFL print and multimedia materials, including textbooks for the national school system of Oman, *Step into Writing: A Basic Writing Text, Focus on Grammar 3: An Integrated Skills Approach, Focus on Grammar 4 Workbook, Grammar Express Basic, Grammar Express Basic CD-ROM, Grammar Express Basic Workbook, Grammar Express Intermediate, Focus on Grammar 3 CD-ROM, Focus on Grammar 4 CD-ROM, Longman English Interactive 4,* and *The Oxford Picture Dictionary Low-Intermediate Workbook.*

ACKNOWLEDGMENTS

Before acknowledging the many people who have contributed to the fourth edition of *Focus on Grammar,* we wish to express our gratitude to those who worked on the first, second, and third editions, and whose influence is still present in the new work. Our continuing thanks to:

- **Joanne Dresner**, who initiated the project and helped conceptualize the general approach of *Focus on Grammar*

- Our editors for the first three editions: **Nancy Perry**, **Penny Laporte**, **Louisa Hellegers**, **Joan Saslow**, **Laura Le Dréan**, and **Françoise Leffler**, for helping to bring the books to fruition

- **Sharon Hilles**, our grammar consultant, for her insight and advice on the first edition

In the fourth edition, *Focus on Grammar* has continued to evolve as we update materials and respond to the valuable feedback from teachers and students who have been using the series. We are grateful to the following editors and colleagues:

- The Pearson *FOG* team, in particular **Debbie Sistino** for overseeing the project and for her down-to-earth approach based on years of experience and knowledge of the field; **Lise Minovitz** for her enthusiasm and alacrity in answering our queries; and **Rosa Chapinal** for her courteous and competent administrative support.

- **Françoise Leffler**, our multi-talented editor, for her continued dedication to the series and for helping improve *Focus on Grammar* with each new edition. With her ear for natural language, eye for detail, analytical mind, and sense of style, she is truly an editor *extraordinaire*.

- **Robert Ruvo** for piloting the book through its many stages of production

- **Irene Schoenberg** and **Jay Maurer** for their suggestions and support, and Irene for generously sharing her experience in teaching with the first three editions of this book

- **Irene Frankel** for reviewing Unit 29 and offering us some good tips of her own

- **Sharon Goldstein** for her intelligent, thoughtful, and practical suggestions

Finally, we are grateful, as always, to **Rick Smith** and **Luke Frances** for their helpful input and for standing by and supporting us as we navigated our way through our fourth *FOG*.

Reviewers

We are grateful to the following reviewers for their many helpful comments:

Aida Aganagic, Seneca College, Toronto, Canada; **Aftab Ahmed**, American University of Sharjah, Sharjah, United Arab Emirates; **Todd Allen**, English Language Institute, Gainesville, FL; **Anthony Anderson**, University of Texas, Austin, TX; **Anna K. Andrade**, ASA Institute, New York, NY; **Bayda Asbridge**, Worcester State College, Worcester, MA; **Raquel Ashkenasi**, American Language Institute, La Jolla, CA; **James Bakker**, Mt. San Antonio College, Walnut, CA; **Kate Baldrige-Hale**, Harper College, Palatine, IL; **Leticia S. Banks**, ALCI-SDUSM, San Marcos, CA; **Aegina Barnes**, York College CUNY, Forest Hills, NY; **Sarah Barnhardt**, Community College of Baltimore County, Reisterstown, MD; **Kimberly Becker**, Nashville State Community College, Nashville, TN; **Holly Bell**, California State University, San Marcos, CA; **Anne Bliss**, University of Colorado, Boulder, CO; **Diana Booth**, Elgin Community College, Elgin, IL; **Barbara Boyer**, South Plainfield High School, South Plainfield, NJ; **Janna Brink**, Mt. San Antonio College, Walnut, CA; **AJ Brown**, Portland State University, Portland, OR; **Amanda Burgoyne**, Worcester State College, Worcester, MA; **Brenda Burlingame**, Independence High School, Charlotte, NC; **Sandra Byrd**, Shelby County High School and Kentucky State University, Shelbyville, KY; **Edward Carlstedt**, American University of Sharjah, Sharjah, United Arab Emirates; **Sean Cochran**, American Language Institute, Fullerton, CA; **Yanely Cordero**, Miami Dade College, Miami, FL; **Lin Cui**, William Rainey Harper College, Palatine, IL; **Sheila Detweiler**, College Lake County, Libertyville, IL; **Ann Duncan**, University of Texas, Austin, TX; **Debra Edell**, Merrill Middle School, Denver, CO; **Virginia Edwards**, Chandler-Gilbert Community College, Chandler, AZ; **Kenneth Fackler**, University of Tennessee, Martin, TN; **Jennifer Farnell**, American Language Program, Stamford, CT; **Allen P. Feiste**, Suwon University, Hwaseong, South Korea; **Mina Fowler**, Mt. San Antonio Community College, Rancho Cucamonga, CA; **Rosemary Franklin**, University of Cincinnati, Cincinnati, OH; **Christiane Galvani**, Texas Southern University, Sugar Land, TX; **Chester Gates**, Community College of Baltimore County, Baltimore, MD; **Luka Gavrilovic**, Quest Language Studies, Toronto, Canada; **Sally Gearhart**, Santa Rosa Community College, Santa Rosa, CA; **Shannon Gerrity**, James Lick Middle School, San Francisco, CA; **Jeanette Gerrity Gomez**, Prince George's Community College, Largo, MD; **Carlos Gonzalez**, Miami Dade College, Miami, FL; **Therese Gormley Hirmer**, University of Guelph, Guelph, Canada; **Sudeepa Gulati**, Long Beach City College, Long Beach, CA; **Anthony Halderman**, Cuesta College, San Luis Obispo, CA; **Ann A. Hall**, University of Texas, Austin, TX; **Cora Higgins**, Boston Academy of English, Boston, MA; **Michelle Hilton**, South Lane School District, Cottage Grove, OR; **Nicole Hines**, Troy University, Atlanta, GA; **Rosemary Hiruma**, American Language Institute, Long Beach, CA; **Harriet Hoffman**, University of Texas, Austin, TX; **Leah Holck**, Michigan State University, East Lansing, MI; **Christy Hunt**, English for Internationals, Roswell, GA; **Osmany Hurtado**, Miami Dade College, Miami, FL; **Isabel Innocenti**, Miami Dade College, Miami, FL; **Donna Janian**, Oxford Intensive School of English, Medford, MA; **Scott Jenison**, Antelope Valley College, Lancaster, CA; **Grace Kim**, Mt. San Antonio College, Diamond Bar, CA; **Brian King**, ELS Language Center, Chicago, IL; **Pam Kopitzke**, Modesto Junior College, Modesto, CA; **Elena Lattarulo**, American Language Institute, San Diego, CA; **Karen Lavaty**, Mt. San Antonio College, Glendora, CA; **JJ Lee-Gilbert**, Menlo-Atherton High School, Foster City, CA; **Ruth Luman**, Modesto Junior College, Modesto, CA; **Yvette Lyons**, Tarrant County College, Fort Worth, TX; **Janet Magnoni**, Diablo Valley College, Pleasant Hill, CA; **Meg Maher**, YWCA Princeton, Princeton, NJ; **Carmen Marquez-Rivera**, Curie Metropolitan High School, Chicago, IL; **Meredith Massey**, Prince George's Community College, Hyattsville, MD; **Linda Maynard**, Coastline Community College, Westminster, CA; **Eve Mazereeuw**, University of Guelph, Guelph, Canada; **Susanne McLaughlin**, Roosevelt University, Chicago, IL; **Madeline Medeiros**, Cuesta College, San Luis Obispo, CA; **Gioconda Melendez**, Miami Dade College, Miami, FL; **Marcia Menaker**, Passaic County Community College, Morris Plains, NJ; **Seabrook Mendoza**, Cal State San Marcos University, Wildomar, CA; **Anadalia Mendoza**, Felix Varela Senior High School, Miami, FL; **Charmaine Mergulhao**, Quest Language Studies, Toronto, Canada; **Dana Miho**, Mt. San Antonio College, San Jacinto, CA; **Sonia Nelson**, Centennial Middle School, Portland, OR; **Manuel Niebla**, Miami Dade College, Miami, FL; **Alice Nitta**, Leeward Community College, Pearl City, HI; **Gabriela Oliva**, Quest Language Studies, Toronto, Canada; **Sara Packer**, Portland State University, Portland, OR; **Lesley Painter**, New School, New York, NY; **Carlos Paz-Perez**, Miami Dade College, Miami, FL; **Ileana Perez**, Miami Dade College, Miami, FL; **Barbara Pogue**, Essex County College, Newark, NJ; **Phillips Potash**, University of Texas, Austin, TX; **Jada Pothina**, University of Texas, Austin, TX; **Ewa Pratt**, Des Moines Area Community College, Des Moines, IA; **Pedro Prentt**, Hudson County Community College, Jersey City, NJ; **Maida Purdy**, Miami Dade College, Miami, FL; **Dolores Quiles**, SUNY Ulster, Stone Ridge, NY; **Mark Rau**, American River College, Sacramento, CA; **Lynne Raxlen**, Seneca College, Toronto, Canada; **Lauren Rein**, English for Internationals, Sandy Springs, GA; **Diana Rivers**, NOCCCD, Cypress, CA; **Silvia Rodriguez**, Santa Ana College, Mission Viejo, CA; **Rolando Romero**, Miami Dade College, Miami, FL; **Pedro Rosabal**, Miami Dade College, Miami, FL; **Natalie Rublik**, University of Quebec, Chicoutimi, Quebec, Canada; **Matilde Sanchez**, Oxnard College, Oxnard, CA; **Therese Sarkis-Kruse**, Wilson Commencement, Rochester, NY; **Mike Sfiropoulos**, Palm Beach Community College, Boynton Beach, FL; **Amy Shearon**, Rice University, Houston, TX; **Sara Shore**, Modesto Junior College, Modesto, CA; **Patricia Silva**, Richard Daley College, Chicago, IL; **Stephanie Solomon**, Seattle Central Community College, Vashon, WA; **Roberta Steinberg**, Mount Ida College, Newton, MA; **Teresa Szymula**, Curie Metropolitan High School, Chicago, IL; **Hui-Lien Tang**, Jasper High School, Plano, TX; **Christine Tierney**, Houston Community College, Sugar Land, TX; **Ileana Torres**, Miami Dade College, Miami, FL; **Michelle Van Slyke**, Western Washington University, Bellingham, WA; **Melissa Villamil**, Houston Community College, Sugar Land, TX; **Elizabeth Wagenheim**, Prince George's Community College, Lago, MD; **Mark Wagner**, Worcester State College, Worcester, MA; **Angela Waigand**, American University of Sharjah, Sharjah, United Arab Emirates; **Merari Weber**, Metropolitan Skills Center, Los Angeles, CA; **Sonia Wei**, Seneca College, Toronto, Canada; and **Vicki Woodward**, Indiana University, Bloomington, IN.

PRESENT AND PAST: REVIEW AND EXPANSION

Simple Present and Present Progressive
NAMES

Before You Read

Look at the title of the article and at the chart. Discuss the questions.

1. What do you think the title means?
2. What are some common first and last names in your native language?
3. Do you have a nickname[1]? If yes, what is it? How did you get it?

Common Last Names around the World	
ARABIC	Ali, Ahmed, Haddad
CHINESE	Zhang, Wang, Chen
ENGLISH	Smith, Jones, Williams
JAPANESE	Sato, Suzuki, Takahashi
KOREAN	Kim, Lee, Park
RUSSIAN	Ivanov, Smirnov, Vasilev
SPANISH	García, Fernandez, Lopez
TURKISH	Özkan, Akcan, Gürbüz

Read

 Read the school newsletter article about names.

What's in a Name?

 Hi. My name **is** Yevdokiya Ivanova. I**'m** from Russia, but this year I**'m living** and **working** in Canada. Yevdokiya **is** an old-fashioned name, but it**'s coming back** into style. My classmates **find** it difficult to pronounce, so they **call** me by my nickname— Dusya. In my country, people always **call** their teachers by a first and a middle name, for example, Viktor Antonovich. The middle name **comes** from the father's first name and **means** "son of Anton." We **don't use** titles like "Mr." or "Professor." Here, some teachers actually **prefer** to be called by just their first name. At first, this was very hard for me to do. It still **seems** a little disrespectful,[2] but I**'m getting** used to it.

 Hola![3] My name **is** Jorge Santiago García de Gonzalez, and I**'m** from Mexico City. I**'m studying** English here at the language institute. Jorge **is** my first, or given, name; Santiago, my middle name; García **comes** from my father (it**'s** his last name); and Gonzalez from my mother (it**'s** her last name). People often **think** my name **is** Mr. Gonzalez, but it**'s** actually Mr. García. Of course in class, everyone just **calls** me Jorge. People here **find** my name a "mouthful," but to me it **seems** perfectly normal. Some of my new friends **are trying** to convince me to call myself "George" while I**'m** here, but I **like** my name, and I **don't want** to lose my identity.

[1] *nickname:* a funny name or a shorter form of a person's first name, usually given by friends or family

[2] *disrespectful:* not polite

[3] *hola:* hello in Spanish

A | Vocabulary: *Circle the letter of the word or phrase that best completes each sentence.*

1. If a name is in **style**, many people _____ it.
   a. have
   b. don't like
   c. have to spell

2. _____ is NOT an example of a **title**.
   a. *President*
   b. *Doctor*
   c. *John*

3. A _____ is an example of an **institute**.
   a. house
   b. school
   c. park

4. If you **convince** a person, you _____ that person's opinion.
   a. ask
   b. explain
   c. change

5. If you **actually** like your name, this means you _____.
   a. didn't like it before
   b. truly like it
   c. pretend to like it

B | Comprehension: *Check (✓)* **True** *or* **False**. *Correct the false statements.*

	True	False
1. Yevdokiya is now in Russia.	☐	☐
2. Her classmates call her by her nickname.	☐	☐
3. In Russia, she calls her teacher by his first name only.	☐	☐
4. Jorge is in Mexico City.	☐	☐
5. His classmates think his name is hard to say.	☐	☐
6. He's going to change his first name.	☐	☐

SIMPLE PRESENT

Affirmative Statements

They **live** in Mexico.
She always **works** here.

Negative Statements

They **don't live** in Mexico.
She **doesn't work** here.

Yes / No Questions

Do they **live** in Mexico?
Does she **work** here?

Short Answers

Yes, they **do**.
Yes, she **does**.

No, they **don't**.
No, she **doesn't**.

Wh- Questions

Where **do** they **live**?
Why **does** she **work** so hard?
Who **teaches** that class?

PRESENT PROGRESSIVE

Affirmative Statements

They**'re living** in Mexico now.
She**'s working** here today.

Negative Statements

They **aren't living** in Mexico now.
She **isn't working** here now.

Yes / No Questions

Are they **living** in Mexico now?
Is she **working** here now?

Short Answers

Yes, they **are**.
Yes, she **is**.

No, they **aren't**.
No, she **isn't**.

Wh- Questions

Where **are** they **living** these days?
Why **is** she **working** so hard?
Who**'s teaching** that class now?

GRAMMAR NOTES

1 Use the **simple present** to describe what <u>generally happens</u> (but not necessarily right now).

Now

Past ——X——X——X——X——X——➤ Future

People often call him George.

Use the **present progressive** to describe what is happening <u>right now</u> or in the <u>extended present</u> (for example, *nowadays, this month, these days, this year*).

Now

Past ————————X————————➤ Future

She's studying.

- People *often* **call** him George.
- We *never* **use** nicknames.
- The paper *usually* **arrives** at 7:00 A.M.

A: Where's Dusya?
B: At the library. She**'s studying**.

A: What's Jorge **doing** *these days*?
B: He**'s working** on a new project.

2 Remember that **non-action verbs** are <u>NOT usually used in the progressive</u> even when they describe a situation that exists at the moment of speaking.

Non-action verbs describe emotions *(love, hate)*; mental states *(remember, understand)*; wants *(need, want)*; perceptions *(hear, see)*; appearance *(look, seem)*; and possession *(have, own)*.

- I **want** to have a special name.
  Not: I'm wanting to have a special name.

- I **hate** my nickname.
- **Do** you **remember** her name?
- Jan **wants** to change her name.

3 Use the **simple present** to talk about situations that are <u>not connected to time</u>—for example, scientific facts and physical laws.

- Water **freezes** at 0ºC (32ºF).
- The Earth **orbits** the sun.

4 The **simple present** is often used in book or movie <u>reviews</u> and in newspaper <u>reports</u>.

- This book **gives** information about names. It also **talks** about giving gifts.

5 The **present progressive** is often used with *always* to express a <u>repeated action</u>.

USAGE NOTE: We often use the present progressive to express a negative reaction to a situation.

- She**'s** *always* smiling. That's why we call her "Sunshine." It's her nickname.

- He**'s** *always* **calling** me "Sweetie." I really hate that name.

REFERENCE NOTES

For a list of **non-action verbs**, see Appendix 2 on page A-2.
For **spelling rules** on forming the **present progressive**, see Appendix 23 on page A-11.
For **spelling rules** on forming the third-person singular of the **simple present**, see Appendix 22 on page A-11.
For **pronunciation rules** for the **simple present**, see Appendix 29 on page A-14.

EXERCISE 1: Discover the Grammar

Read the book review. Circle the simple present verbs and underline the present progressive verbs.

ACROSS CULTURES

<u>Are you living</u> or working in a foreign country? (Do you worry) about making a mistake with someone's name or title? You are right to be concerned. Naming systems vary a lot from culture to culture, and people tend to have very strong feelings about their names. Well, now help is available in the form of an interesting and practical book by Terri Morrison. *Kiss, Bow, or Shake Hands: How to Do Business in Sixty Countries* gives information on cross-cultural naming customs and much more. And it's not just for businesspeople. In today's shrinking world, people are traveling abroad in record numbers. They're flying to all corners of the world, and they're exchanging emails with people they've never actually met. So, if you're doing business abroad or making friends across cultures, I recommend this book.

EXERCISE 2: Statements and Questions   *(Grammar Notes 1–3, 5)*

Complete the conversations. Use the correct form of the verbs in parentheses—the simple present or the present progressive.

A. IANTHA: Hi, I'm Iantha.

   ALAN: Nice to meet you, Iantha. I'm Alan, but my friends _____*call*_____ me Al.

   1. (call)

   Iantha is an unusual name. Where _____ it _____ from?

   2. (come)

   Is it Latin or Greek?

   IANTHA: It's Greek. It _____ "violet-colored flower."

   3. (mean)

   ALAN: That's pretty. What _____ you _____, Iantha?

   4. (do)

   IANTHA: Well, I usually _____ computer equipment, but right now

   5. (sell)

   I _____ at a flower shop. My uncle _____ it.

   6. (work)   7. (own)

   ALAN: You _____! I _____ it's true that names

   8. (joke)   9. (guess)

   _____ our lives!

   10. (influence)

B. MARIO: I _____ to find Greg Costanza. _____ you

   1. (try)

   _____ him?

   2. (know)

BELLA: Greg? Oh, you _____ Lucky. That's his nickname. Everyone
                                                3. (mean)

_____ him Lucky because he _____ things.
        4. (call)   5. (always win)

C. **LOLA:** I _____ that you and Anya _____ a baby. Have you decided
                        1. (hear)   2. (expect)

on a name yet?

VANYA: We _____ names related to music. What _____ you
                    3. (look for)

_____ "Mangena"? It means "melody" in Hebrew.
        4. (think of)

LOLA: It _____ pretty. How _____ you _____ it?
                5. (sound)   6. (spell)

D. **ROSA:** Who _____ coffee? Would you like a cup of coffee, Dr. Ho?
                        1. (want)

DR. HO: Oh. No, thanks. It _____ delicious, but I _____ coffee.
                                2. (smell)   3. (not drink)

ROSA: Well, how about a cup of tea? The water _____. By the way, Dr. Ho, why
                                                        4. (boil)

_____ water _____ so quickly here?
        5. (boil)

DR. HO: In the mountains, water _____ at a lower temperature. It's a law of nature.
                                        6. (boil)

EXERCISE 3: Editing

Read this post to a class electronic bulletin board. There are eleven mistakes in the use of the simple present and the present progressive. The first mistake is already corrected. Find and correct ten more.

www.classbulletinboard.org

CLASS BULLETIN BOARD   [Follow Ups]   [Post a Reply]   [Message Board Index]

Posted February 16, 2012, at 15:30:03

I'm writing

Hi, everybody. ~~I write~~ this note to introduce myself to you, my classmates in English 047. Our teacher is

wanting a profile from each of us. At first I was confused by this assignment because my English dictionary

is defining *profile* as "a side view of someone's head." I thought, "Why does she wants that? She sees my

head every day!" Then I saw the next definition: "a short description of a person's life and character." OK,

then. Here is my profile:

My name is Peter Holzer. Some of my friends are calling me Pay-Ha because that is how my initials

actually sounding in German. I am study English here in Miami because I want to attend the Aspen Institute

of International Leadership in Colorado. Maybe are you asking yourself, "Why he wants to leave Miami for

Colorado?" The answer is snow! I am coming from Austria, so I love to ski. It's part of my identity. In fact, my

nickname in my family is Blitz (lightning) because always I'm trying to improve my speed.

EXERCISE 4: Listening

A | *Listen to two friends discuss these photos. Then listen again and label each photo with the correct name(s) from the box.*

~~Alex~~	Bertha	"Bozo"	Karl	Red	"Sunshine"	Vicki

a. _____

d. _____

b. _____ *Alex* _____

e. _____

c. _____

f. _____ and _____

1. Nowadays, more and more people are giving boys /(girls) names like *Alex*.

2. Red got his nickname because of his <u>clothes / hair</u>.

3. Bozo <u>has / doesn't have</u> a headache.

4. Janine agrees that her cousin's photo <u>matches / doesn't match</u> her nickname.

5. Janine's friend <u>recognizes / doesn't recognize</u> Karl.

6. Vicki and Bertha are <u>mother and daughter / aunt and niece</u>.

EXERCISE 5: Pronunciation

🎧 **A** | *Read and listen to the Pronunciation Note.*

Pronunciation Note
When we **compare two things**, we put **stress** on the **information that is different**. For example, when we compare what we **usually do** with what we are **doing now**, we put stress on: • the **things we are comparing**   • **adverbs and time words** or expressions, such as *usually*, *now*, and *these days*   **EXAMPLES:** I **usually** take the **train** home, but **these days** I'm taking the **bus**.   Sara **normally washes** the dishes, but **now** she's **drying** them.

🎧 **B** | *Listen to the conversations. Put a dot (•) over the words in the answers that have the most stress.*

1. **A:** What does she drink?

   B: She often drinks coffee, but at the moment she's drinking tea.

2. **A:** Hi Tiffany. Are you making dinner now?

   B: I'm not making dinner. I'm eating dinner!

3. **A:** Where do you study?

   B: I often study at home, but these days I'm studying at the library.

4. **A:** What color jacket does she wear?

   B: She normally wears red, but right now she's wearing black.

5. **A:** What do they call him?

   B: They usually call him Bill, but today they're calling him William.

(continued on next page)

6. A: Does he speak Spanish?

   B: He doesn't speak Spanish, but he reads it very well.

7. A: How does he get to school?

   B: He generally takes the bus, but this week he's taking the train.

C | *Listen again to the conversations and repeat the answers. Then practice the conversations with a partner.*

EXERCISE 6: Find Someone Who . . .

A | *Write down your full name on a piece of paper. Your teacher will collect all the papers and redistribute them. Walk around the room. Introduce yourself to other students and try to find the person whose name you have on your piece of paper.*

> **EXAMPLE:** **A:** Hi. I'm Jelena.
> **B:** I'm Eddy.
> **A:** I'm looking for Kadin Al-Tattany. Do you know him?
> **B:** I think that's him over there. OR Sorry, I don't.

B | *When you find the person you are looking for, find out about his or her name. You can ask some of these questions:*

- What does your name mean?
- Which part of your name is your family name?
- Do you use a title? (for example, Ms., Miss, Mrs., Mr.)
- What do your friends call you?
- Do you have a nickname?
- What do you prefer to be called?
- How do you feel about your name?
- *Other:* _____

> **EXAMPLE:** **A:** What does Kadin mean?
> **B:** It means "friend" or "companion" in Arabic.
>   OR I don't actually know what it means.

You can also ask some general questions such as these:

- Where do you come from?
- Where are you living now?
- Why are you studying English?
- *Other:* _____

C | *Finally, introduce your classmate to the rest of the class.*

> **EXAMPLE:** This is Henka Krol. Henka comes from Poland.
> Her name means "ruler of the house or home."

EXERCISE 7: Writing

A | *Write a profile to introduce yourself to your class. Write about your name, your interests and hobbies, and your plans. Use the simple present and the present progressive. You can use the profile in Exercise 3 on page 7 as a model.*

EXAMPLE: My name is Thuy Nguyen, but my American friends call me Tina.

B | *Check your work. Use the Editing Checklist.*

Editing Checklist
Did you use . . . ? ☐ the simple present for things that generally happen ☐ the present progressive for things happening right now or in the extended present ☐ the simple present with non-action verbs ☐ the present progressive with ***always*** for repeated actions

Check your answers on page UR-1.

Do you need to review anything?

A | *Circle the correct words to complete the sentences.*

1. Ekaterina <u>is helping</u> / <u>helps</u> me with my Russian homework every weekend.

2. Felix <u>is working</u> / <u>works</u> on a new project these days.

3. <u>Are</u> / <u>Do</u> you ever talk on your cell phone while you're driving?

4. I don't <u>understanding</u> / <u>understand</u> what this word means. Can you explain it?

5. We <u>usually go</u> / <u>go usually</u> to the beach for vacation.

B | *Complete the conversation with the simple present or present progressive form of the verbs in parentheses.*

ANA: Hi, Kim! I _____ Jeff Goodale. Is he here?
            1. (look for)

KIM: I _____ he's here somewhere.
            2. (think)

ANA: He _____ a cell phone today, so I _____ to give him
            3. (not carry)   **4. (need)**

   a message from Lynn.

KIM: I _____ him! He _____ next to Kevin.
            5. (see)   **6. (stand)**

ANA: Jeff, hi. Call Lynn, OK? She _____ for your call right now.
                                         7. (wait)

JEFF: That _____ serious! Can I use your phone?
               8. (sound)

ANA: Sure. I _____ it's anything serious. She just _____
             9. (not believe)   **10. (want)**

   you to buy a new cell phone.

C | *Find and correct five mistakes.*

Hi Leda,

How do you do these days? We're all fine. I'm writing to tell you that we not living in

California anymore. We just moved to Oregon. Also, we expect a baby! We're looking for an

interesting name for our new daughter. Do you have any ideas? Right now, we're thinking about

Gabriella because it's having good nicknames. For example, *Gabby*, *Bree*, and *Ella* all seem good

to us. How are those nicknames sound to you? We hope you'll write soon and tell us your news.

Love,

Samantha

Simple Past and Past Progressive
FIRST MEETINGS

STEP 1 GRAMMAR IN CONTEXT

Before You Read

Look at the photos here and on the next page. Discuss the questions.

1. Which couples do you recognize?
2. What do you know about them?
3. Do you know how they met?

Read

Read the article about four famous couples.

BEARING LOIS IN HIS ARMS SUPERMAN HEADS TOWARD THE CITY — —

Superman and Lois Lane

SUPER COUPLES

Cover Story by Dennis Brooks

It's a bird, . . . it's a plane, . . . it's Superman! Disguised as Clark Kent, this world-famous character **met** Lois Lane while the two **were working** as newspaper reporters for the *Daily Planet*. At first Lane **wasn't** interested in mild-mannered[1] Kent—she **wanted** to cover stories about "The Man of Steel." In time, she **changed** her mind. When Kent **proposed**, Lane **accepted**. (And she **didn't** even **know** he **was** Superman!)

Like Superman and Lois Lane, some names just seem to belong together: Marie and Pierre Curie, Diego Rivera and Frida Kahlo, or Steffi Graf and Andre Agassi. What **were** these other super couples **doing** when they **met**? What **did** they **accomplish** together? Let's find out.

(*continued on next page*)

---

[1] *mild-mannered:* behaving in a quiet, gentle way

SUPER COUPLES

Marie and Pierre Curie

Frida Kahlo and Diego Rivera

Steffi Graf and Andre Agassi

When she **was** 24, Maria Sklodowska **left** Poland and **moved** to Paris. While she **was studying** at the Sorbonne,[2] she **met** physicist Pierre Curie. She **was planning** to return to Poland after her studies, but the two scientists **fell** in love and **got** married. While they **were raising** their daughters, they **were** also **doing** research on radioactivity. In 1903, the Curies **won** the Nobel Prize in physics. Then, in 1906, a horse-drawn carriage **hit** and **killed** Pierre while he **was** out **walking**. When Marie **recovered** from the shock, she **continued** their work. In 1911, she **received** her second Nobel Prize.

Born in Guanajuato, Mexico, in 1886, Diego Rivera **began** painting at a young age. He **became** famous for his large murals,[3] which he **painted** for universities and other public buildings. In 1922 he **met** Frida Kahlo for the first time while he **was working** on one of his murals. It **was** at the school that the 15-year-old Kahlo **was attending**. A few years later, Kahlo **was** in a serious bus accident. While she **was recovering**, she **started** painting from bed. One day she **went** to see Rivera to ask him for career advice. He **was** very impressed with her work. The two **fell** in love and **got** married. Today they are considered two of Mexico's greatest, most influential artists.

Steffi Graf first **picked up** a tennis racket when she **was** only three years old. She **went on** to become the best women's tennis player in the world—winning all four Grand Slam singles and the Olympic gold medal in a year. Her career **was going** great until she **suffered** a series of injuries while she **was playing**. She **was** also deeply shocked after a disturbed[4] fan **stabbed** her biggest opponent in an attempt to help Graf's career. But she **continued** to win many tournaments until she **retired**. She **got together** with future-husband Andre Agassi while they both **were competing** in Paris. He **was** the number 1 professional male American tennis player in the world; she **was** ranked the number 1 female German player. The superstars **started** dating and **married** a few years later.

[2] **Sorbonne:** the University of Paris, in Paris, France
[3] **mural:** a painting on a wall
[4] **disturbed:** having emotional problems

A | Vocabulary: *Complete the sentences with the words from the box.*

couple	cover	influential	opponent	recover	research

1. I was doing _____ at the university on the psychology of sports.

2. I met a very interesting _____ in my program. The three of us became good

   friends. We spent a lot of time together.

3. The woman taught me how to deal with losing to a(n) _____ on the tennis

   court. It really helped my game.

4. The man was having some psychological problems. It took him many months to

   _____ from his illness.

5. After that, he became a very _____ writer. He changed people's opinions

   about mental illness.

6. All the newspapers wanted to _____ his story.

B | Comprehension: *Circle the word that best completes each sentence.*

1. Clark Kent met Lois Lane before / during / after his time at the *Daily Planet*.

2. Lane found out Kent was Superman before / during / after Kent's marriage proposal.

3. Maria Sklodowska met Pierre Curie before / during / after her move to Paris.

4. Before / During / After her marriage, Sklodowska wanted to return to Poland.

5. Diego Rivera began painting murals before / during / after his project at the school.

6. Frida Kahlo began painting before / during / after her recovery from the bus accident.

7. Steffi Graf was injured several times before / during / after games.

8. She married Andre Agassi before / during / after the competition in Paris.

SIMPLE PAST

Affirmative Statements
Marie **studied** at the Sorbonne.

Negative Statements
Lois **didn't plan** to marry Clark at first.

Yes / No Questions	Short Answers
Did he **teach**?	**Yes**, he **did**. **No**, he **didn't**.

Wh- Questions
Where **did** they **play** tennis? Who **won**?

Simple Past and Simple Past
He **won** when he **played** there.

Simple Past and Past Progressive
She **met** him while she **was studying**.

PAST PROGRESSIVE

Affirmative Statements
She **was studying** at the Sorbonne in 1892.

Negative Statements
She **wasn't planning** to get married.

Yes / No Questions	Short Answers
Was he **doing** research?	**Yes**, he **was**. **No**, he **wasn't**.

Wh- Questions
Where **were** they **playing** tennis? Who **was winning**?

Past Progressive and Past Progressive
He **was winning** while he **was playing** there.

Past Progressive and Simple Past
She **was studying** when she **met** him.

GRAMMAR NOTES

1 Use the **simple past** to describe an action that was <u>completed</u> at a specific time in the past. The simple past focuses on the <u>completion</u> of the past action.

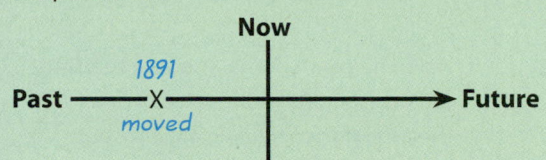

- Marie **moved** to Paris in 1891.
- The Curies **won** the Nobel Prize in 1903.
- She **researched** uranium.
 (*She completed her research.*)

2 Use the **past progressive** to describe an action that was <u>in progress</u> at a specific time in the past. The action began before the specific time and may or may not continue after the specific time. The past progressive focuses on the <u>duration</u> of the action, not its completion.

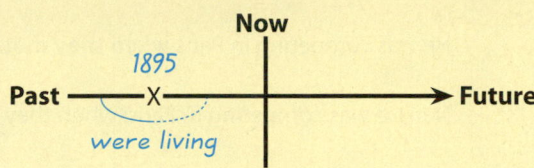

REMEMBER: Non-action verbs are NOT usually used in the progressive.

- The Curies **were living** in Paris in 1895.
- Marie **was studying** at the Sorbonne.
- During 1897, she **was researching** uranium.
 (*Her work was continuing.*)

- Marie **had** a degree in physics.
 NOT: Marie ~~was having~~ a degree in physics.

3 Use the **past progressive** with the **simple past** to talk about an action that was <u>interrupted by another action</u>. Use the simple past for the interrupting action.

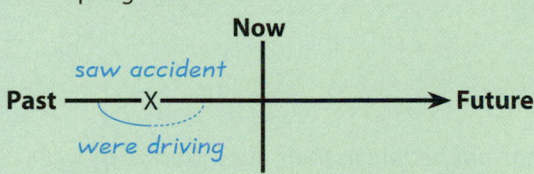

- Use **while** to introduce the **past progressive** action.
- Use **when** to introduce the **simple past** action.

- They **were driving** to work when they **saw** the accident.

- **While** he **was walking**, the car **hit** him.

- **When** the car **hit** him, he **was walking**.

4 You can use the **past progressive** with **while** or **when** to talk about two actions <u>in progress at the same time</u> in the past. Use the past progressive in both clauses.

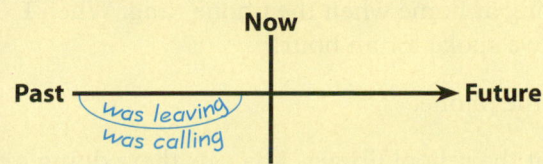

- **While** Clark **was leaving** the newsroom, Lois **was calling** the police.
- **When** Clark **was leaving** the newsroom, Lois **was calling** the police.

(continued on next page)

5 **BE CAREFUL!** Sentences with two clauses in the simple past have a very **different meaning** from sentences with one clause in the simple past and one clause in the past progressive.

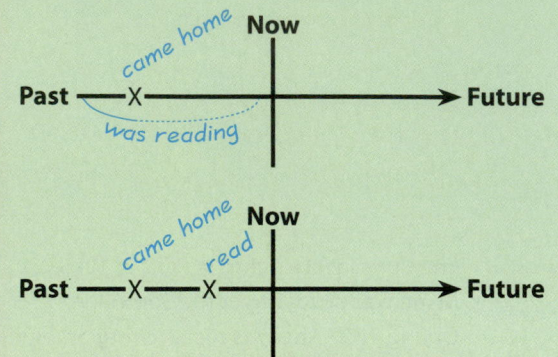

- When he **came** home, she **was reading** the newspaper.
  (*First she started reading the newspaper. Then he came home.*)

- When he **came** home, she **read** the paper.
  (*First he came home. Then she read the paper.*)

6 **REMEMBER:** The **time clause** (the part of the sentence with **when** or **while**) can come at the beginning or the end of the sentence.

Use a **comma** after the time clause when it comes at the **beginning**. Do NOT use a comma when it comes at the end.

- **When** they met, he was competing in Paris.
  OR
- He was competing in Paris **when** they met.

  NOT: He was competing in Paris͟X͟when they met.

REFERENCE NOTE
For a list of **irregular past verbs**, see Appendix 1 on page A-1.

STEP 3 FOCUSED PRACTICE

EXERCISE 1: Discover the Grammar

Read these people's descriptions of how they met important people in their lives. Decide if the statement that follows is True (T) or False (F).

1. **LUCKY:** I was riding home on my bike when I saw Elena on a park bench.

   _F_ Lucky saw Elena before he got on his bike.

2. **ROD:** I was climbing a mountain when I met my best friend, Ian.

   _____ Ian was on the mountain.

3. **MARIE:** How did I meet Philippe? I was sitting at home when the phone rang. When I answered it, it was the wrong number, but we spoke for an hour!

   _____ Marie knew Philippe before they spoke on the phone.

4. **DON:** When I first met Ana, I was working at the school library. Ana was there doing research.

   _____ Don started his library job after he met Ana.

5. TONY: How did I meet my wife? Actually, it was kind of like a blind date. My cousins invited her to dinner while I was living at their place.

_____ Tony moved in with his cousins after he met his wife.

6. MONICA: I was taking an English class while Dania was taking Spanish. We met in the hall during a break.

_____ Monica and Dania were students at the same time.

EXERCISE 2: Simple Past or Past Progressive
(Grammar Notes 1–6)

Complete the conversations. Circle the correct verbs.

A. LILY: Guess what! I was seeing / saw Andre Agassi and Steffi Graf at Club Rio last night.
1.

TONY: Really? They're such a great couple! What were / did they do / doing there?
2.   **3.**

LILY: They were dancing / danced near us on the dance floor.
4.

TONY: Wow! Were / Did you getting / get their autographs?
5.   **6.**

LILY: Yes. And then Graf was giving / gave me her pen!
7.

TONY: Awesome! Were / Did you bringing / bring it with you? I want to see it!
8.   **9.**

LILY: No. It was falling / fell out of my pocket when someone was bumping / bumped into
10.   **11.**
me. I never was finding / found it.
12.

B. TARO: What were / did you doing / do when you were spraining / sprained your wrist?
1.   **2.**   **3.**

KIWA: I was playing / played tennis with my boyfriend. We were pretending / pretended to be
4.   **5.**
Agassi and Graf. I was hurting / hurt myself while I was hitting / hit the ball!
6.   **7.**

TARO: Sounds like he's a pretty tough opponent! I hope you recover soon.

C. JASON: Are you OK, Erin? Were / Did you crying / cry?
1.   **2.**

ERIN: Yes, but how were / did you knowing / know? I wasn't crying / didn't cry when you
3.   **4.**   **5.**
were coming / came in.
6.

JASON: Your eyes are red.

ERIN: The movie *Frida* was on TV. It's about the Mexican painter Frida Kahlo.

Were you ever seeing / Did you ever see it? It's so sad. While I was watching / watched
7.   **8.**
it, I was thinking / thought about her life. She had so many physical problems and she
9.
never really was recovering / recovered from them.
10.

EXERCISE 3: Simple Past or Past Progressive

(Grammar Notes 1–6)

Complete the conversations. Use the correct form of the verbs in parentheses—simple past or past progressive.

A. **Paz:** What _____*were*_____ you _____*looking*_____ at just then? You _____.
1. (look)   2. (smile)

Eva: I _____ the video of Nicole's wedding. She _____ so happy.
3. (watch)   4. (look)

Paz: How _____ she and Matt _____?
5. (meet)

Eva: At my graduation party. Matt almost _____. He _____ a big
6. (not come)   7. (cover)

story for the newspaper. Luckily, his plans _____. The rest is history.
8. (change)

B. **Dan:** I _____ your Superman web page while I _____ the Internet.
1. (find)   2. (surf)

It's great.

Dee: Thanks. When _____ you _____ a Superman fan?
3. (become)

Dan: Years ago. I _____ a comic book when I _____ to marry Lois
4. (read)   5. (decide)

Lane! Just kidding. I _____ to *draw* Lois Lane and Superman.
6. (want)

Dee: Me too. I _____ graphic arts when I _____ my web page.
7. (study)   8. (start)

Dan: So, it seems like Superman was influential in *both* our lives!

C. **Lara:** _____ Jason _____ you when he _____ over
1. (surprise)   2. (come)

last night?

Erin: Yes! I _____ a tennis match on TV when he _____ on the
3. (watch)   4. (knock)

door. When the game _____, we _____ a delicious dinner.
5. (end)   6. (have)

And while we _____, Jason _____ me to marry him!
7. (eat)   8. (ask)

Lara: That's great. Congratulations!

EXERCISE 4: Connecting Clauses: *When* or *While*

(Grammar Notes 2–6)

*This timeline shows some important events in Monique's life. Use the timeline and the cues on the next page to write sentences about her. Use **when** or **while** and the simple past or past progressive. There is more than one way to write some of the sentences.*

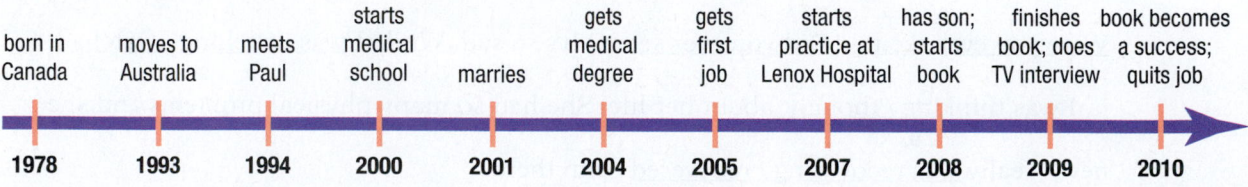

born in Canada	moves to Australia	meets Paul	starts medical school	marries	gets medical degree	gets first job	starts practice at Lenox Hospital	has son; starts book	finishes book; does TV interview	book becomes a success; quits job
1978	1993	1994	2000	2001	2004	2005	2007	2008	2009	2010

1. moves to Australia / meets Paul _She met Paul when she moved to Australia._

2. gets married / studies medicine _She got married while she was studying medicine._

3. lives in Australia / gets married _____

4. has medical degree / gets her first job _____

5. practices medicine at Lenox Hospital / has her son _____

6. writes a book / works at Lenox Hospital _____

7. does a TV interview / finishes her book _____

8. leaves her job / her book becomes a success _____

EXERCISE 5: Editing

Read Monique's email to a friend. There are eleven mistakes in the use of the simple past and the past progressive. The first mistake is already corrected. Find and correct ten more.

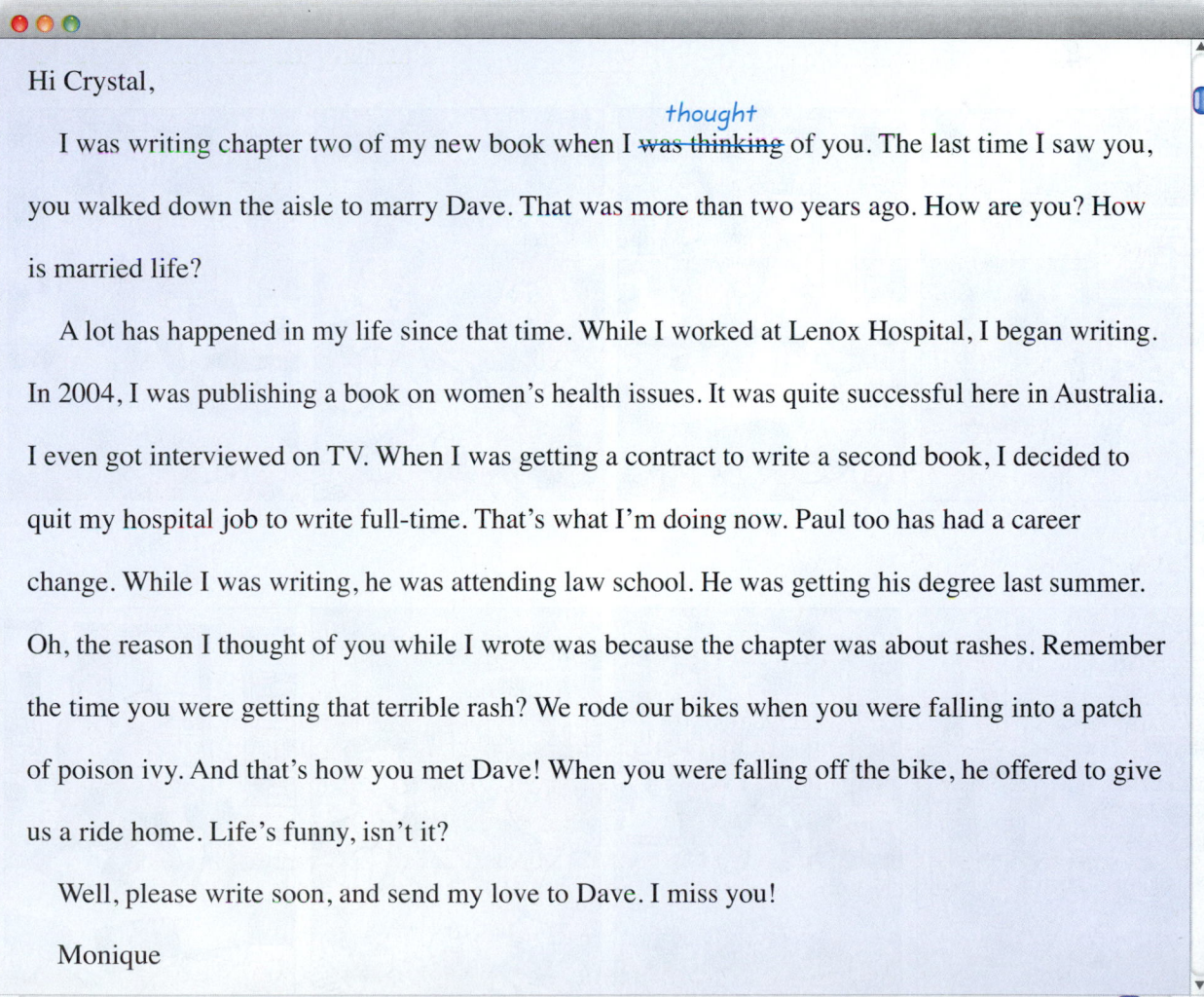

Hi Crystal,

I was writing chapter two of my new book when I ~~was thinking~~ _thought_ of you. The last time I saw you, you walked down the aisle to marry Dave. That was more than two years ago. How are you? How is married life?

A lot has happened in my life since that time. While I worked at Lenox Hospital, I began writing. In 2004, I was publishing a book on women's health issues. It was quite successful here in Australia. I even got interviewed on TV. When I was getting a contract to write a second book, I decided to quit my hospital job to write full-time. That's what I'm doing now. Paul too has had a career change. While I was writing, he was attending law school. He was getting his degree last summer. Oh, the reason I thought of you while I wrote was because the chapter was about rashes. Remember the time you were getting that terrible rash? We rode our bikes when you were falling into a patch of poison ivy. And that's how you met Dave! When you were falling off the bike, he offered to give us a ride home. Life's funny, isn't it?

Well, please write soon, and send my love to Dave. I miss you!

Monique

EXERCISE 6: Listening

A | *Look at the pictures. Then listen to a woman explain how she met her husband. Listen again and circle the letter of the series of pictures that illustrates the story.*

A.

B.

C.

| *Read the statements. Listen again and check (✓)* **True** *or* **False** *for each statement. Correct the false statements.*

	True	False
1. The couple worked for a ~~movie company~~. *newspaper*	☐	☑
2. They didn't know each other well before they got an assignment together.	☐	☐
3. They were covering a story about neighborhood crime.	☐	☐
4. They had an appointment at a coffee shop.	☐	☐
5. They were at the coffee shop for several hours.	☐	☐
6. They got married a few years after.	☐	☐

EXERCISE 7: Pronunciation

A | *Read and listen to the Pronunciation Note.*

Pronunciation Note

When a **time clause begins a sentence**:

We usually **pause** briefly at the **end of the time clause** (at the **comma** in written sentences).

EXAMPLE: While we were talking, the rain started. ➔
"While we were talking [PAUSE] the rain started."

The voice **falls** and then **rises a little** at the **end of the time clause** to show that the sentence **isn't finished**.

The voice **falls lower** at the **end of the second clause** to show that the sentence **is finished**.

EXAMPLE: While we were talking, the rain started.

B | *Listen to the sentences. Add a comma where you hear the pause at the end of each time clause. Then practice the conversations with a partner.*

1. **A:** What did you do when the rain started?

   B: When it started to rain we went inside.

2. **A:** What did you do during the storm?

   B: While it was raining we were talking.

3. **A:** What did you do after the storm?

   B: When the storm was over we left.

4. **A:** What happened while you were leaving?

   B: While we were leaving the sun came out.

5. **A:** What did you do when you got home?

   B: When we got home we turned on the TV.

6. **A:** When did you get the phone call?

   B: While I was exercising the phone rang.

EXERCISE 8: What About You?

Work in small groups. Think about the first time you met someone who became influential in your life: a best friend, teacher, boyfriend or girlfriend, husband or wife. Tell your classmates about the meeting. What were you doing? What happened then? How did that person influence your life?

> **EXAMPLE:**   I was walking to class when this guy came over and asked me for the time . . .

EXERCISE 9: Ask and Answer

Complete the timeline with some important events in your life. Include your first meeting with someone who is significant to you. Show your timeline to a classmate. Answer your classmate's questions.

Event

Year

> **EXAMPLE:**   **A:** Where did you meet your wife?
> **B:** I was studying medicine, and she was in my class.

EXERCISE 10: Writing

A | *Write two paragraphs about a relationship that is important to you. Use the simple past and past progressive. Follow these steps:*

1. In the first paragraph answer the questions:

- How did you meet?
- What were you doing when you met?
- What were your first impressions of the person?

2. In the second paragraph, describe some events in the relationship.

> **EXAMPLE:**   I met my friend Dania while I was living in Germany . . .

B | *Check your work. Use the Editing Checklist.*

Editing Checklist

Did you use . . . ?
- ☐ the simple past
- ☐ the past progressive
- ☐ *when* or *while*
- ☐ commas after time clauses at the beginning of a sentence

A | *Circle the correct words to complete the sentences.*

1. I first <u>met</u> / was meeting my wife in 2002.

2. She <u>worked</u> / was working at the museum the day I went to see a Picasso exhibit.

3. I <u>saw</u> / was seeing her as soon as I walked into the room.

4. She <u>had</u> / was having long dark hair and a beautiful smile.

5. <u>While</u> / When I had a question about a painting, I went over to speak to her.

6. The whole time she was talking, I <u>thought</u> / was thinking about asking her on a date.

7. When I left the museum, she <u>gave</u> / was giving me her phone number.

B | *Complete the conversation with the simple past or past progressive form of the verbs in parentheses.*

A: What _____ you _____ when you first _____ Ed?
            1. (do)   **2. (meet)**

B: We _____ for a bus. We started to talk, and, as they say, "The rest is history."
            3. (wait)

     What about you? How did you meet Karl?

A: Oh, Karl and I _____ in school when we _____ English. I
                        4. (meet)   **5. (study)**

     _____ him as soon as I _____ the room on the first day of class.
            6. (notice)   **7. (enter)**

B: It sounds like it was love at first sight!

C | *Find and correct six mistakes.*

It was 2005. I studied French in Paris while I met Paul. Like me, Paul was from California.

We were both taking the same 9:00 A.M. conversation class. After class we always were going

to a café with some of our classmates. One day, while we was drinking café au lait, Paul was

asking me to go to a movie with him. After that, we started to spend most of our free time

together. We really got to know each other well, and we discovered that we had a lot of similar

interests. When the course was over, we left Paris and were going back to California together.

The next year we got married!

Simple Past, Present Perfect, and Present Perfect Progressive

HOBBIES AND INTERESTS

STEP 1 GRAMMAR IN CONTEXT

Before You Read

Look at the photo. Discuss the questions.

1. What are the people doing?
2. Have you ever participated in an adventure sport?
3. What do you like to do in your free time?

Read

Read the personal website.

---

www.jumpforjoy.com

JUMPING FOR JOY

Hi, I'm Jason Barricelli. I**'ve been building** this website for a while, and now I'm almost finished. I**'ve written** this page to introduce myself.

I**'ve** always **been** a work-hard, play-hard kind of guy. I **grew up** in Perth, Australia, and my family **did** adventure sports like rock climbing. Lately, some people **have called** these activities "extreme sports," but to me they**'ve** always **seemed** like normal fun.

We've been falling for an awfully long time!

I**'ve been working** on a master's degree for a couple of years, but I still take time out to play. Since I **moved** to Sydney, I**'ve learned** how to skydive. This month, I**'ve** already **made** five jumps.

Yes, I have a social life too. In fact, last month I **got** engaged to a fantastic woman. Here's a picture of the two of us jumping together.

Joy **hasn't been skydiving** that long, but she **wanted** to celebrate our engagement with a jump.

I**'ve included** more pictures of this historic jump. Just click on the plane to continue.

Next   My Family   Other Interests   Home

A | Vocabulary: *Circle the letter of the word or phrase that best completes each sentence.*

1. Someone who is **engaged** is planning to _____.
   a. get married
   b. find a marriage partner
   c. get a master's degree

2. An example of an **extreme** sport is _____.
   a. tennis
   b. mountain biking
   c. swimming in a pool

3. One reason people **celebrate** an event is to _____.
   a. show that the event is important
   b. criticize the event
   c. help them forget the event

4. To **introduce** yourself, you can _____.
   a. leave the room
   b. explain something
   c. say your name

5. A **fantastic** person is usually _____.
   a. imaginary
   b. very special
   c. very strange

6. An **historic** event in your life is one that is very _____.
   a. important
   b. interesting
   c. dangerous

B | Comprehension: *Check (✓) the correct box for each event in Jason's life.*

	Finished	Unfinished
1. build a website	☐	☐
2. live in Perth, Australia	☐	☐
3. get a master's degree	☐	☐
4. live in Sydney, Australia	☐	☐
5. learn to skydive	☐	☐
6. get engaged	☐	☐

SIMPLE PAST

PRESENT PERFECT
PRESENT PERFECT PROGRESSIVE

Affirmative Statements
I **built** a website last month.

Affirmative Statements
I**'ve built** a website.
I**'ve been building** a website this month.

Negative Statements
She **didn't write** last week.

Negative Statements
She **hasn't written** many letters.
She **hasn't been writing** lately.

Yes / No Questions	Short Answers
Did he **move**?	**Yes**, he **did**. **No**, he **didn't**.

Yes / No Questions	Short Answers
Has he **moved**?	**Yes**, he **has**.
Has he **been living** in Perth?	**No**, he **hasn't**.

Wh- Questions
Where **did** he **work**?
Who **lived** in Perth?

Wh- Questions
Where **has** he **worked**?
Where **has** he **been working**?
Who**'s lived** in Perth?
Who**'s been living** in Perth?

GRAMMAR NOTES

1 Use the **simple past** for things that happened and were <u>completed in the past</u>.

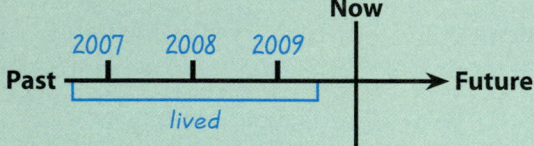

We often use <u>specific past time expressions</u> with the simple past.

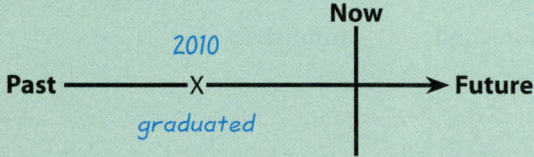

We often use **ago** with the simple past to show when something started.

- I **lived** in Perth for three years.
  (I don't live in Perth now.)

- He **graduated** *in 2010*.
- He **moved** to Sydney *last year*.

- I **moved** there *five years ago*.

2 | Use the **present perfect** or the **present perfect progressive** with *for* or *since* to talk about things that started in the past but were <u>not completed</u>. These things continue up to the present and may continue into the future.

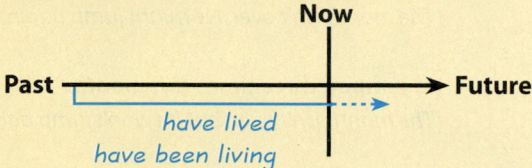

We often use verbs such as *live*, *teach*, *wear*, *work*, *study*, and *feel* in this way.

a. Use *for* + **a length of time** to show <u>how long</u> a present condition has been true.

b. Use *since* + **a point of time** to show <u>when</u> a present condition <u>started</u>.

BE CAREFUL! Do NOT use the present perfect with specific points of time (except after *since*).

REMEMBER: Non-action verbs are NOT usually used in the progressive.

- I**'ve lived** in Perth for three years. OR
- I**'ve been living** in Perth for three years.
  (*I moved to Perth three years ago, and I'm still living there today.*)

- She**'s worked** hard this week. OR
- She**'s been working** hard this week.

- He**'s lived** in Sydney **for two years**.

- He**'s been living** there **since he graduated**.

- He**'s lived** in Sydney **since 2007**.
  Nᴏᴛ: He ~~has moved~~ there in 2007.

- I**'ve known** Joy for a long time.
  Nᴏᴛ: I~~'ve been knowing~~ Joy for a long time.

---

3 | Use the **present perfect** <u>without *for* or *since*</u> to talk about things that happened at some indefinite time in the past and <u>were completed</u>.

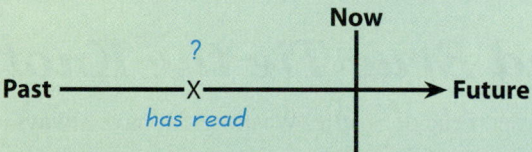

USAGE NOTE: We use the present perfect (not the past) to show that the result of the action or state is <u>important in the present</u>. The present perfect always has some connection to the present.

BE CAREFUL! *She's read a book* and *She's been reading a book* have very different meanings.

a. The **present perfect** without *for* or *since* shows that an activity is <u>finished</u>. We often say *how many* or *how many times* with this use of the present perfect.

b. The **present perfect progressive** shows that an activity is <u>unfinished</u>. We often say *how long* with the present perfect progressive.

- She**'s read** a book about skydiving.
  (*We don't know when she read the book, or the time is not important.*)

- She**'s completed** her master's degree, so she's looking for a teaching position.
  (*Because she has her master's degree, she can now look for a teaching position.*)

- She**'s read** the book.
  (*She's finished the book.*)
- She**'s read** *three books* about skydiving.
- She**'s read** that book *three times*.

- She**'s been reading** a book.
  (*She's still reading it.*)
- She**'s been reading** the book *for a week*.

(continued on next page)

4 Use the **present perfect** or the **simple past** with time expressions for <u>unfinished time periods</u> such as *today*, *this week*, *this month*, and *this year*.

a. Use the **present perfect** for things that <u>might happen again</u> in that time period.

- He's **jumped** three times *this month*.
  (*The month isn't over. He might jump again.*)

b. Use the **simple past** for things that <u>probably won't happen again</u> in that period.

- He **jumped** three times *this month*.
  (*The month isn't over, but he won't jump again.*)

BE CAREFUL! *This morning, this afternoon,* and *this evening* can be either unfinished or finished. Use the **simple past** if the time period is <u>finished</u>.

- I've **had** three cups of coffee *this morning*.
  (*It's still morning.*)
- I **had** three cups of coffee *this morning*.
  (*It's now afternoon.*)

REFERENCE NOTES
For a list of **irregular past verbs**, see Appendix 1 on page A-1.
For a list of **irregular past participles** used in forming the **present perfect**, see Appendix 1 on page A-1.

STEP 3 | FOCUSED PRACTICE

EXERCISE 1: Discover the Grammar

A | *Read this newspaper article about a wedding. Circle the simple past verbs and underline the present perfect verbs.*

Board and Eruc Tie the Knot[1]

Nancy Board and Erden Eruc of Seattle, Washington, <u>have</u> always <u>loved</u> the outdoors, so Alaska (was) a natural choice to celebrate their wedding. Nancy flew there for the June 7 ceremony, but Erden started in February and rode his bike. Then he climbed Mount Denali. Unfortunately, he ran into some bad weather, so the historic event was a week late. Nancy understood. She herself has been doing extreme sports for years.

Erden, an engineer, has earned degrees from universities in Turkey and the United States. He has been climbing since he was 11. In 2003, he left his job to begin an around-the-world trip powered only by human effort. Since then, he has been climbing, hiking, biking, and rowing his way across several continents. So far, he has climbed Mount Denali in Alaska, and he has rowed across two oceans (the Atlantic and the Pacific).

Nancy, a psychotherapist, recently founded a new business in Seattle. She and her co-founder have been using their outdoor experience to teach leadership skills to women in Australia, Canada, South Africa, and the United States.

---
[1] *tie the knot:* to get married

B | *Now read the statements and check (✓)* **True, False,** *or* **?** *(the information isn't in the article).*

	True	False	?
1. The couple's love of the outdoors began ~~after~~ *before* their wedding.	☐	☑	☐
2. They got married on June 7.	☐	☐	☐
3. Erden left for Alaska before Nancy.	☐	☐	☐
4. Nancy started adventure sports a year ago.	☐	☐	☐
5. Erden got his degree in Turkey in 1989.	☐	☐	☐
6. He started climbing at the age of 11.	☐	☐	☐
7. He started his around-the-world trip in 2003.	☐	☐	☐
8. He crossed the Pacific in a boat in 2009.	☐	☐	☐
9. Nancy started her business in 2010.	☐	☐	☐
10. She teaches leadership skills.	☐	☐	☐

EXERCISE 2: Simple Past, Present Perfect, or Present Perfect Progressive

(Grammar Notes 1–3)

Complete the article about another hobby—collecting toys. Circle the correct verbs.

MOVE OVER, BARBIE!

Ty Warner (has been making) / made toys since 1986.
 1.

In 1992, he has gotten / got the idea to make stuffed
 2.

animals that children could afford. The first nine Beanie

Babies have appeared / appeared in stores just one year
 3.

later. Pattie the Platypus and her eight companions

have sold out / sold out immediately. In the 1990s, the
 4.

fad has become / became an international craze, and
 5.

the Beanies are still popular. More than 2 billion fans have visited / have been visiting Ty's
 6.

website. The growth of eBay,[1] which has started / started around the same time as the Beanies,
 7.

has been keeping / kept the collecting craze going to this day. In fact, a few years ago, one
 8.

collector has been buying / bought a Beanie Bear on eBay for an amazing $24,000. Which
 9.

reminds me—I'd like to discuss some trades. Have you found / Have you been finding Nana
 10.

the Monkey yet?

---

[1] **eBay:** a website where people and companies can buy and sell a lot of different things

EXERCISE 3: Simple Past, Present Perfect, or Present Perfect Progressive

(Grammar Notes 1–4)

Complete the paragraphs about other people's interests. Use the correct form of the verbs in parentheses—simple past, present perfect, or present perfect progressive. Sometimes more than one answer is correct.

A. May _____has been taking_____ photos ever since her parents _____ her a camera when
        1. (take)   **2. (buy)**

she _____ only 10. At first she only _____ color snapshots of friends
        3. (be)   **4. (take)**

and family, but then she _____ to black and white. Lately she _____
                                    5. (change)   **6. (shoot)**

a lot of nature photographs. This year she _____ in three amateur photography
                                                7. (compete)

contests—and it's only April! In fact, last month she _____ second prize for her
                                                            8. (win)

nighttime photo of a lightning storm.

B. Carlos _____ playing music when he _____ an electric guitar for
            1. (begin)   **2. (get)**

his 12th birthday. He _____ playing since. In fact, the guitar _____
                        3. (not stop)   **4. (become)**

more than just a way of having some fun with his friends. Last year he _____
                                                                            5. (join)

a local band. Since then, they _____ all over town. So far this year, the band
                                    6. (perform)

_____ six concerts, and they have plans for many more.
    7. (give)

C. Kate _____ a beautiful old stamp last month. It is now part of the fantastic
            1. (find)

collection she _____ on for the past two years. At first she just _____
                    2. (work)   **3. (save)**

stamps from letters that she _____ from friends. After some time, however,
                                4. (get)

she _____ to look more actively for stamps. Lately, she _____
        5. (begin)   **6. (buy)**

them from special stores and _____ stamps with other collectors. So far she
                                7. (trade)

_____ over 200 stamps from all over the world.
    8. (find)

EXERCISE 4: Editing

Read the email message. There are nine mistakes in the use of the simple past, the present perfect, and the present perfect progressive. The first mistake is already corrected. Find and correct eight more.

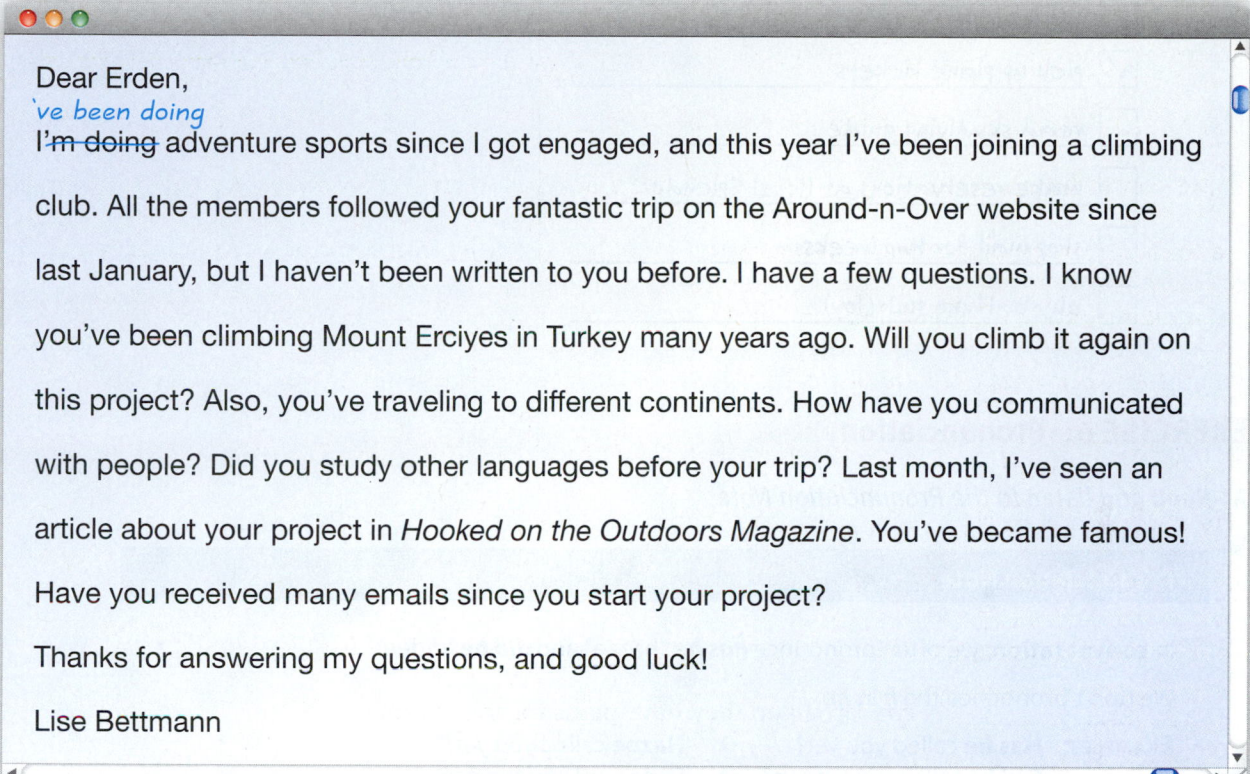

Dear Erden,

`ve been doing`
I'm doing adventure sports since I got engaged, and this year I've been joining a climbing club. All the members followed your fantastic trip on the Around-n-Over website since last January, but I haven't been written to you before. I have a few questions. I know you've been climbing Mount Erciyes in Turkey many years ago. Will you climb it again on this project? Also, you've traveling to different continents. How have you communicated with people? Did you study other languages before your trip? Last month, I've seen an article about your project in *Hooked on the Outdoors Magazine*. You've became famous!

Have you received many emails since you start your project?

Thanks for answering my questions, and good luck!

Lise Bettmann

STEP 4 COMMUNICATION PRACTICE

EXERCISE 5: Listening

A | *Jason and Joy have been planning their honeymoon trip. Read the sentences from their conversation. Then listen to their conversation. Listen again and circle the correct verbs to complete the sentences.*

1. You wouldn't believe the lines down here. I <u>waited</u> / <u>'ve been waiting</u> for 40 minutes.

2. I've <u>been getting / got</u> them on the way over here.

3. I<u>'ve read / been reading</u> it. I found some fantastic locations.

4. I <u>called / 've been calling</u> all morning, but I <u>didn't get / haven't gotten</u> through.

5. I <u>had to / 've had to</u> wait more than half an hour.

6. <u>Have you looked / Did you look</u> for a bathing suit?

B | *Now read Jason and Joy's* **To Do** *list. Which things have they already done? Check (✓) the ones you remember. Then listen again and check your answers.*

To Do

- [ ] renew passport (Jason)
- [✓] pick up plane tickets
- [ ] read skydiving guide
- [ ] make reservations at Hotel Splendor
- [ ] stop mail for two weeks
- [ ] buy bathing suit (Joy)

EXERCISE 6: Pronunciation

A | *Read and listen to the Pronunciation Note.*

> **Pronunciation Note**
>
> In **conversation**, we often pronounce **has he** "hazee" and **did he** "didee."
>
> We don't pronounce the **h** in **he**.
>
> EXAMPLES: **Has he** called you yet? → "**Hazee** called you yet?"
> **Did he** tell you the news? → "**Didee** tell you the news?"
>
> We often pronounce **have you** "havya" and **did you** "didja."
>
> EXAMPLES: **Have you** heard about Jason? → "**Havya** heard about Jason?"
> **Did you** meet Joy last night? → "**Didja** meet Joy last night?

B | *Listen to the short conversations. Then listen again and complete the conversations with the words that you hear.*

1. **A:** _____ about Jason and Joy?
   (hear)
   B: Yeah, they just got engaged. It's great.

2. **A:** _____ Joy to skydive yet?
   (teach)
   B: Yes. She's already made three jumps.

3. **A:** How _____ them?
   (meet)
   B: A friend introduced us.

4. **A:** _____ skydiving?
   (try)
   B: No, extreme sports are too dangerous.

5. A: _____?
      (graduate)

B: No. One more year to go!

6. A: _____ here from Perth?
      (move)

B: Yes. Three years ago.

7. A: _____ them a long time?
      (know)

B: No, just a couple of years.

C | *Listen again to the conversations and repeat the questions. Then practice the conversations with a partner.*

EXERCISE 7: What About You?

Work in small groups. Talk about your hobbies and interests. What have you done in the past with your hobby? What have you been doing lately? Find out about other people's hobbies.

EXAMPLE: **A:** Do you have any hobbies, Ben?
          B: Yes. My hobby has been photography since I was a kid. Recently I've been taking pictures of nature. I even won first prize in a contest last month. What about you? Do you have a hobby?
          C: I collect sneakers. I got my first pair of Nikes when I was 10, and I've been collecting different kinds of sneakers ever since. Recently I've been selling some of the older pairs on eBay. Last week I sold a really old pair of Air Jordans for $250.

EXERCISE 8: Ask and Answer

A | *What did you plan to accomplish last week? Make a list. Include things you did and things that you still haven't done. Do not check (✓) any of the items. Exchange lists with a partner.*

EXAMPLE: ☐ Organize the photos on my computer
          ☐ Research photography contests on the Internet

B | *Now ask questions about your partner's list. Check (✓) the things that your partner has already done. Answer your partner's questions about your list. When you are done, compare your answers.*

EXAMPLE: **A:** Have you organized your photos yet?
          B: Yes, I have. I organized them last week.

EXERCISE 9: Writing

A | *Write a few paragraphs about yourself for a personal website like the one on page 26. Tell about your interests and hobbies. Use the simple past, present perfect, and present perfect progressive.*

EXAMPLE: Welcome! I'm Steffie Hart. I've been living in Tokyo since 2004. I built this website to record my experience here. I've posted a lot of photos. I hope you enjoy them.

B | *Check your work. Use the Editing Checklist.*

Editing Checklist

Did you use . . . ?

☐ the simple past for things that happened and were completed in the past

☐ the present perfect and present perfect progressive with **for** and **since** for things that started in the past but were not completed

☐ the present perfect without time words for things that were completed at an indefinite past time

☐ the present perfect progressive without time words for things that continue into the present

A | *Circle the correct words to complete the sentences.*

1. Tina and Raoul <u>have gotten / got</u> married in 2009.

2. Raoul <u>lived / has been living</u> in Chile his whole life. He never wants to move.

3. Tina has lived there <u>since / for</u> 2005.

4. Last week, I <u>read / 've been reading</u> two books about South America. They were both excellent.

5. Jason has <u>been playing / played</u> basketball for an hour. He should stop and start his

   homework. Could you tell him to come in soon?

6. Where <u>has / was</u> Jena been living?

7. This year, I <u>studied / 've been studying</u> photography. I'm really enjoying my class.

B | *Complete the sentences with the simple past, present perfect, or present perfect progressive form of the verbs in parentheses.*

Lisa _____ on her stamp collection for five years, and she still enjoys it.
       1. (work)

Last year, she _____ a very valuable stamp on an old letter in her attic.
               2. (discover)

At first, she _____ it was valuable.
             3. (not know)

She _____ after she _____ some research on the Internet.
    4. (find out)   **5. (do)**

Since then, she _____ to garage sales and flea markets every weekend.
                6. (go)

She _____ another valuable stamp, but she _____ a great
    7. (not find)   **8. (have)**

time searching.

C | *Find and correct five mistakes.*

A: How long did you been doing adventure sports?

B: I've gotten interested five years ago, and I haven't stopped since then.

A: You're lucky to live here in Colorado. It's a great place for adventure sports.

   Did you live here long?

B: No, not long. I moved here last year. Before that, I've been living in Alaska.

A: I haven't go there yet, but I've heard it's great.

B: It *is* great. When you go, be sure to visit Denali National Park.

Past Perfect and Past Perfect Progressive
MUSICIANS

STEP 1 GRAMMAR IN CONTEXT

Before You Read

Look at the photo, the title, and the first paragraph of the article. Discuss the questions.

1. What is the man doing? Describe him.
2. What type of music do you like? Do you enjoy classical music? Which composers?
3. Why do you think the article is called "The People's Conductor"?

Read

 Read the article about Gustavo Dudamel.

The People's Conductor

He's young. He's exciting. He's great-looking. He's "The Dude,[1]" and he's changing the way people around the world feel about classical music.[2]

Gustavo Dudamel grew up in Barquisimeto, Venezuela. A child prodigy,[3] he **had already started** taking music lessons by the early age of four. His father played the trombone in a salsa band, and young Dudamel **had been hoping** to take up the same instrument. But his arms were too short, and so he studied the violin instead.

Dudamel soon became part of El Sistema—a free national program that teaches young Venezuelans, mostly from poor families, how to play instruments. Many of these kids **had been getting** into pretty serious trouble before participating in the program. El Sistema has transformed the lives of hundreds of thousands of them by taking them off the streets and introducing them to the power of music. "The music saved me. I'm sure of this," said Dudamel in a TV interview.

In El Sistema, Dudamel's amazing talent was obvious, and by the time he was 15, he **had become** the conductor of the Simón Bolívar National Youth Orchestra. But that wasn't the first time

[1] *dude:* a man (an informal word, used to express positive feelings about the person)
[2] *classical music:* a type of music that is considered to be important and serious and that has continuing artistic value, for example operas and symphonies
[3] *prodigy:* a very young person who has a great natural ability in a subject or skill

The People's Conductor

he **had led** an orchestra. According to Dudamel, he **had been conducting** in his imagination since he was six.

On October 3, 2009, Dudamel lifted his baton for the first time as music director of the famed Los Angeles Philharmonic. He was only 28, and he **had** just **signed** a five-year contract as conductor. Tickets for this free concert at the 18,000-seat Hollywood Bowl **had become** available two months earlier. By the time the Bowl's ticket office opened on August 1, hundreds of people **had** already **arrived**. They **had been lining up** for hours in the hot Californian sun. The tickets were gone in minutes. On October 3, that lucky audience, a mix of all ages and ethnic backgrounds, **had come** for one thing—to see "Gustavo the Great" conduct. They were not disappointed. By the end of the concert

they **had** all **risen** to their feet and **had been applauding** enthusiastically for ten minutes.

Since then Dudamel's career has continued to skyrocket[4] as he conducts orchestras all over the world. Although he has become famous, he has never forgotten his roots[5] or how his life **had been** before he learned to make music. To help other young people, he set up a program in Los Angeles modeled on El Sistema—the program that **had changed** his life. He said, "You cannot imagine how it changes the life of a kid if you put a violin or a cello or a flute in his hand. You feel you have your world . . . and it changes your life. This happened to me." Dudamel's goal is to make sure this happens to many others and to spread his love of classical music around the world.

---

[4]*skyrocket:* to improve a lot and very quickly
[5]*roots:* the connection a person feels with a place because he or she was born there or his or her family lived there

After You Read

A | Vocabulary: *Complete the sentences with the words from the box.*

conducted	contract	enthusiastic	ethnic	participated	transformed

1. The experience _____ her life. It really changed everything for her.

2. The reviewer loved the concert. He wrote a(n) _____ review about it.

3. How many times has Dudamel _____ the orchestra this season?

4. The audience was a real _____ mix. There were African Americans, Asians, Hispanics, and whites.

5. Many musicians and singers _____ in the event.

6. One violinist signed a(n) _____ with the orchestra for two years.

B | Comprehension: Put these events in Dudamel's life in the correct chronological order
(1 = first, 6 = last).

_____ He became conductor of the Simón Bolívar National Youth Orchestra.

_____ He turned four.

_____ Music saved him.

_____ He became music director of the Los Angeles Philharmonic.

_____ He started taking music lessons.

_____ He became part of El Sistema.

STEP 2 GRAMMAR PRESENTATION

PAST PERFECT

Statements				
Subject	_Had (not)_	**Past Participle**		
I You He She It We You They	had (not)	arrived	in the U.S.	by then.
		become	famous	

Contractions	
I had	= **I'd**
you had	= **you'd**
he had	= **he'd**
she had	= **she'd**
we had	= **we'd**
they had	= **they'd**
had not	= **hadn't**

Yes / No Questions				
Had	**Subject**	**Past Participle**		
Had	you he they	arrived	in the U.S.	by then?
		become	famous	

Short Answers					
Affirmative			**Negative**		
Yes,	I he they	**had.**	**No,**	I he they	**hadn't.**

Wh- Questions					
_Wh-_ **Word**		_Had_	**Subject**	**Past Participle**	
How many	concerts	**had**	he	given	by then?

PAST PERFECT PROGRESSIVE

Statements			
Subject	_Had (not) been_	**Base Form + -ing**	
I You He She It We You They	had (not) been	playing	all over the world by then.

Yes / No Questions				Short Answers					
Had	**Subject**	**Been** + Base Form + **-ing**		**Affirmative**			**Negative**		
Had	you he they	**been playing**	all over the world by then?	Yes,	I he they	**had.**	No,	I he they	**hadn't.**

Wh- Questions				
Wh- Word	**Had**	**Subject**	**Been** + Base Form + **-ing**	
How long	**had**	he	**been playing**	classical music by then?

GRAMMAR NOTES

1 Use the **past perfect** to show that something <u>happened before a specific time</u> in the past.

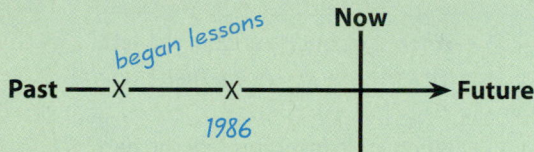

The focus is often on the <u>completion</u> of an action.

- **By 1986**, Dudamel **had begun** violin lessons.
- **It was 2004.** He **had been** a conductor for several years.

- **By 2010,** Kato **had conducted** Beethoven's Ninth Symphony for the first time.

2 Use the **past perfect progressive** to show that an action was in <u>progress before a specific time</u> in the past. It possibly continued after that specific time. The focus is on the <u>continuation</u> of the action, not the end result.

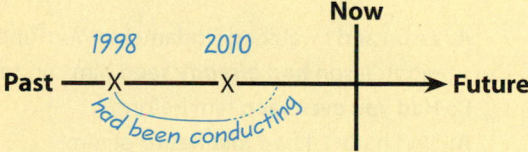

USAGE NOTE: We also use the **past perfect progressive** for <u>finished</u> actions that had <u>just ended</u>. You can often still see the results of the action.

REMEMBER: Non-action verbs are NOT usually used in the progressive.

- **By 2010**, Kato **had been conducting** an orchestra for 12 years.
  (She was still conducting in 2010, and possibly continued to conduct.)

- She was out of breath. It was clear that she **had been running**.
  (She was no longer running when I saw her.)

- It was 2008. He **had been** a conductor for several years.
  NOT: He ~~had been being~~ a conductor for several years.

(continued on next page)

3 Use the **past perfect** and the **past perfect progressive** with the **simple past** to show a relationship between two past events.

a. Use the **past perfect** or the **past perfect progressive** for the <u>earlier event</u>. Use the **simple past** for the <u>later time or event</u>.

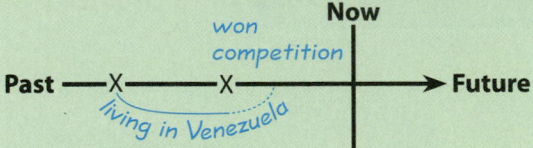

b. When the <u>time relationship between two past events is clear</u> (as with *before*, *after*, and *as soon as*), we often use the **simple past for both events**.

BE CAREFUL! In sentences with *when*, notice the difference in meaning between the **simple past** and the **past perfect**.

- He **had been living** in Venezuela when he **won** a competition in Germany.
  (He was living in Venezuela. During that time, he won a competition in Germany.)

- *After* Dudamel **had joined** El Sistema, he **studied** the violin.
  OR
- *After* Dudamel **joined** El Sistema, he **studied** the violin.

- *When* the concert ended, she **left**.
  (First the concert ended. Then she left.)

- *When* the concert ended, she **had left**.
  (First she left. Then the concert ended.)

4 We often use the **past perfect** and the **past perfect progressive** with *by* + **time or event**, or *by the time* + **time clause**.

We usually use the **simple past** in the **time clause** for the later time or event.

Use *already*, *yet*, *ever*, *never*, and *just* with the **past perfect** to emphasize which event <u>happened first</u>.

BE CAREFUL! Do NOT put an adverb between the **main verb** and a **direct object**.

- *By 2006*, Gustavo **had gotten** married.
- *By the time we got tickets*, we **had been waiting** in line for an hour.

A: Jason and I watched Dudamel on YouTube last night. Jason **had *already* seen** him conduct.
B: **Had** you *ever* **seen** him before?
A: No, I hadn't. I **had *just* heard** of him!

- I hadn't **seen him *yet***. OR I hadn't ***yet* seen him**.
  NOT: I hadn't ~~seen *yet* him~~.

REFERENCE NOTES
For a list of **irregular past participles**, see Appendix 1 on page A-1.
For **spelling rules for progressive forms**, see Appendix 23 on page A-11.

EXERCISE 1: Discover the Grammar

*Read each numbered situation. Decide if the description that follows is **True (T)** or **False (F)**.*
*If there is not enough information to know, write a question mark **(?)**.*

1. The talk show host invited the musician on her show because he had won a competition.

   __F__ The musician won the competition after his appearance on the show.

2. Before the break, the musician had been explaining why he had chosen to play the violin.

   _____ The musician's explanation was finished.

3. It was 4:00 P.M. They had been selling tickets for an hour.

   _____ They were still selling tickets at 4:05.

4. When I found my seat, the concert started.

   _____ First the concert started. Then I found my seat.

5. When I found my seat, the concert had started.

   _____ First the concert started. Then I found my seat.

6. When I saw Mei Ling, she was very enthusiastic. She had been rehearsing with Dudamel.

   _____ She wasn't rehearsing when I saw her.

7. By the end of the concert, the audience had fallen in love with Dudamel.

   _____ The audience fell in love with Dudamel after the concert.

EXERCISE 2: Past Perfect: Statements with *Already* and *Yet*   (Grammar Notes 1, 4)

Look at some important events in Gustavo Dudamel's career. Then complete the sentences.
*Use the past perfect with **already** or **not yet**.*

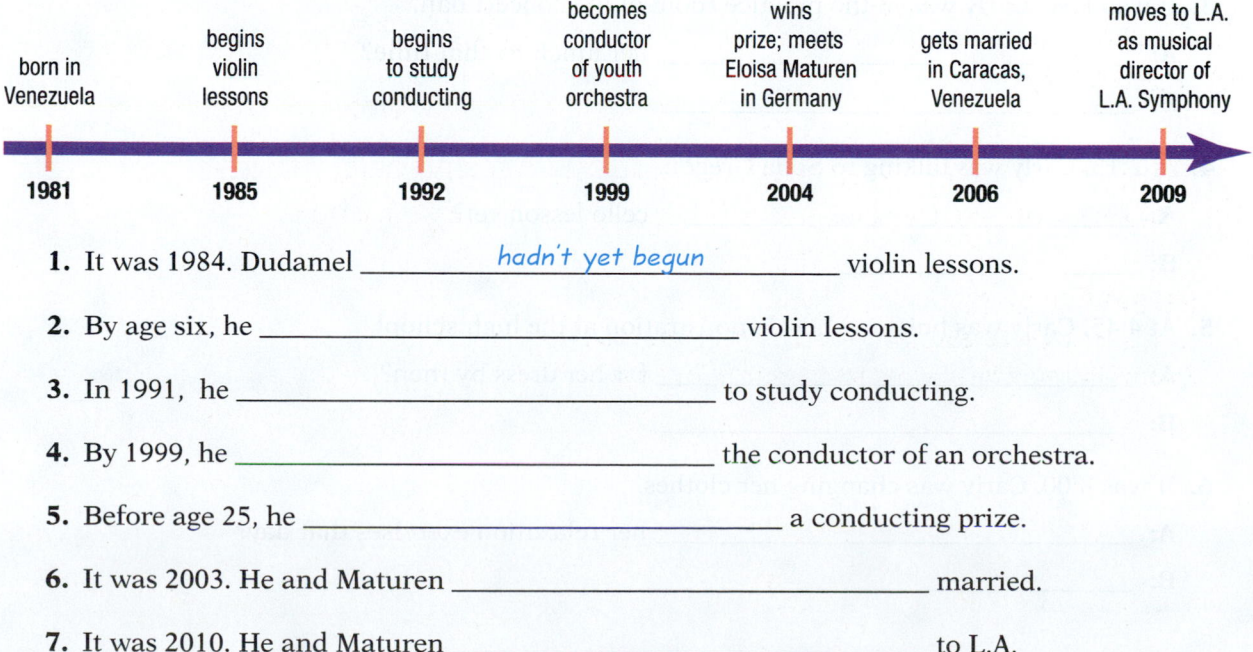

born in Venezuela	begins violin lessons	begins to study conducting	becomes conductor of youth orchestra	wins prize; meets Eloisa Maturen in Germany	gets married in Caracas, Venezuela	moves to L.A. as musical director of L.A. Symphony
1981	1985	1992	1999	2004	2006	2009

1. It was 1984. Dudamel _____*hadn't yet begun*_____ violin lessons.

2. By age six, he _____ violin lessons.

3. In 1991, he _____ to study conducting.

4. By 1999, he _____ the conductor of an orchestra.

5. Before age 25, he _____ a conducting prize.

6. It was 2003. He and Maturen _____ married.

7. It was 2010. He and Maturen _____ to L.A.

EXERCISE 3: Past Perfect: Questions and Short Answers

(Grammar Note 1)

Carly plays cello in an orchestra. Read her diary notes. Then complete the questions about her day and give short answers. Use the past perfect.

> DATE: Thursday, May 18, 2012
>
> 8:30 took yoga class at the gym
>
> 10:00 started rehearsing at the concert hall for Saturday's concert
>
> 12:30 ate lunch
>
> 2:30 had cello lesson with Sofia Gregor
>
> 4:00 gave cello demonstration at Performing Arts High School
>
> 6:00 shopped for dress for Saturday night's concert
>
> 7:30 did relaxation exercises
>
> 8:30 ordered takeout
>
> 11:00 fell asleep—forgot to eat!

1. It was 9:30 A.M. Carly was at the gym.

   A: _____ *Had she taken* _____ her yoga class yet?

   B: _____ *Yes, she had.* _____

2. At 10:00, Carly was at the concert hall.

   A: _____ for Saturday's concert yet?

   B: _____

3. It was 1:30. Carly was in the practice room of the concert hall.

   A: _____ her lunch by that time?

   B: _____

4. At 2:15, Carly was talking to Sofia Gregor.

   A: _____ cello lesson yet?

   B: _____

5. At 4:45, Carly was finishing her demonstration at the high school.

   A: _____ for her dress by then?

   B: _____

6. It was 8:00. Carly was changing her clothes.

   A: _____ her relaxation exercises that day?

   B: _____

7. At 10:00 Carly was listening to a CD of her last performance.

A: _____ takeout yet?

B: _____

8. It was 11:00. Carly was sleeping.

A: _____ her dinner yet?

B: _____

EXERCISE 4: Past Perfect Progressive: Statements

(Grammar Note 2)

Gustavo Dudamel was a musical child prodigy. Complete the information about two other prodigies. Use the past perfect progressive form of the verbs in parentheses.

AKRIT JASWAL has been called "the world's smartest boy" and "the Mozart

of modern medicine." By the age of six, he _____*had*_____ already

_____*been reading*_____ Shakespeare in his native village in northern India. Even
      1. (read)

more amazing, he _____ medical textbooks on his own. He
      2. (study)

_____ even _____ surgeries at local hospitals.
            3. (observe)

Then at age seven, he operated on a young girl whose hand had been severely injured in a fire. The

operation, which he performed for free in his home, was a success, and Jaswal became famous. His

family _____ that their son could start medical school when he was eight, but he had
      4. (hope)

to wait three years before he enrolled at Punjab University—the youngest student ever admitted.

Jaswal's dream is to someday find a cure for cancer.

JUDIT POLGAR is known as the strongest female chess player who has ever

lived. In 1991, she became the youngest Grandmaster ever at age 15, not

surprising since she _____ the game since she was five years old.
      5. (play)

For five years, she _____ games against older chess masters. By
      6. (win)

age 20, Polgar was ranked the 10th best player in the world—the first woman to

achieve a rating in the top 10. In 2002, she defeated Garry Kasparov, the highest rated player in the

world. It was a great personal victory. She had lost to Kasparov in 1994, and she _____
                                                7. (wait)

to try again. In 2000, Polgar married Gusztav Font. Font, a veterinarian, _____
                                                8. (treat)

Polgar's dog when the two met. Between 2004 and 2007, the couple had two children, and Polgar

competed less often. Because she _____ as much, her rank dropped to 20th, but by
      9. (not compete)

2008, Polgar was playing for Hungary in the Olympics, her career back on track.

EXERCISE 5: Past Perfect Progressive: Questions

(Grammar Note 4)

*A talk-show host is trying to get some background information on violinist Mei Ling before her interview. Use **before** or **when** and the words in parentheses to write questions with the past perfect progressive.*

1. Mei Ling quit her old job to play full-time.

   What kind of work had she been doing when she quit her job to play full-time?

   (what kind of work / she / do)

2. She signed a contract with the L.A. Philharmonic.

   _____

   (she / live in Los Angeles)

3. She gave her first solo performance.

   _____

   (she / practice long)

4. She won first prize in the Paganini Violin Competition.

   _____

   (she / compete a long time)

5. Her bow[1] broke during the concert.

   _____

   (how long / she / play)

6. They took pictures of her in front of her home.

   _____

   (the newspaper reporters / follow her)

7. She married the conductor Lorenzo Russo.

   _____

   (how long / they / date)

8. Mei Ling and her husband moved to Rome.

   _____

   (where / they / live)

[1] ***bow:*** a long thin piece of wood with strings stretched tightly from one end to the other used for playing string instruments, such as the violin

EXERCISE 6: Past Perfect and Past Perfect Progressive

(Grammar Notes 1–4)

Complete this report on El Sistema. Use the past perfect or past perfect progressive form of the verbs in the boxes. Use the progressive form when possible. Some verbs can be used more than once.

come up	help	observe	receive	show up	teach

It was 1975. José Antonio Abreu ___*had received*___ his degree in economics and
                        1.

_____ economics at Simón Bolívar University for years. As an economist, he
   2.

_____ the poverty he saw around him. As a trained musician, he _____

3.   **4.**

with a creative solution—a music program for children. El Sistema began in a parking garage in

1975. Abreu remembers the first night of the program. Only 11 children _____,

5.

but, Abreu says, he still felt it was the start of something very big. It was. By 2009, Abreu

_____ many prizes for his work, and he _____ hundreds of thousands

6.   **7.**

of Venezuela's kids turn their lives around with music.

arrest	be	hope	live	work

Gustavo Dudamel, now a world-famous conductor, _____ one of those kids. He, in

8.

turn, has established similar organizations, such as The Youth Orchestra of Los Angeles. Canadian

singer Measha Brueggersgosman participated in the project, and in October 2009 the kids attended

Dudamel's concert at the Hollywood Bowl. They were wildly enthusiastic. "A lot of the people . . .

_____ never _____ to a classical music concert before. . . .They were

9.

crying and screaming," she recalls. But Dudamel is only one of El Sistema's success stories. Here

are just two more out of thousands: At age nine, Edicson Ruiz _____ at a Caracas

10.

supermarket to help support his family. El Sistema helped him put down the supermarket packages

and pick up the bow. He is now a successful double bass player with the Berlin Philarmonie. And

then there's Lennar Acosta. Before he got his clarinet, Acosta _____ a life of crime.

11.

Police _____ already _____ the troubled youth nine times for robbery

12.

and drug use. But thanks to El Sistema, he traded in his gun for a musical instrument, and today he

is a clarinetist at the Caracas Youth Orchestra.

   This is what José Antonio Abreu _____ to accomplish when he began El Sistema

13.

more than three decades ago. For Abreu, music has always been more than just an art form. He calls

it a "weapon against poverty" and a way to change lives.

Dudamel and the Simón Bolívar Youth Orchestra

EXERCISE 7: Time Clauses

(Grammar Note 4)

A talk-show host is interviewing violinist Mei Ling about her career. Complete the interview. Determine the correct order of the sentences in parentheses and use the past perfect or past perfect progressive to express the event that occurred first. Use the progressive form when possible.

HOST: When did you decide to play the violin professionally?

LING: (I made up my mind to play professionally. / I was 10.)

By the time _____*I was 10, I had made up my mind to play professionally*_____.
1.

HOST: How did you get your first paying job?

LING: (I was performing with a group at college. / My professor recommended me.)

_____ when _____.
2.

The job was with an opera company.

HOST: That was lucky! Did you work there for a long time?

LING: No. (The company closed. / I was working there for only a month.)

After _____,
3.

_____.

HOST: Did you find another job performing?

LING: Yes, but not for a while. (I was teaching in a community music program. / City Orchestra called me.)

Before _____ , _____.
4.

(I almost decided to stop performing. / I loved working with those kids.)

_____ because
5.

_____.

HOST: Do you still keep in touch with the community program?

LING: Oh, sure. (We were planning an orchestra for the kids. / I left.)

_____ when
6.

_____. I still want to do that.

Read this article about a singer. There are eight mistakes in the use of the past perfect and the past perfect progressive. The first mistake is already corrected. Find and correct seven more.

A Diva¹ with a Difference

Measha Brueggergosman was born in 1977 in New Brunswick, Canada. Her first-grade teacher urged Brueggergosman's parents to give her music lessons. They did, and by age 15, she ~~had been deciding~~ *had decided* on a singing career. Not growing up in a large cultural center, she didn't have the chance to attend concerts or the opera. However, by the time she enrolled at the University of Toronto, she listening to classical music on the radio for years, and she participated in her church's music program since she was a child.

After receiving her degree in Toronto, Brueggergosman moved to Düsseldorf, Germany, to study. By age 25, she had been performing internationally for several years and had won a number of important prizes. One enthusiastic judge said she'd never been meeting so young a singer with such perfect vocal control.

By her 30th birthday, Brueggergosman has become both a classical music sensation² and a popular celebrity. A diva with a Facebook fan club, she had been developed her own unique fashion style. She had also appearing on popular TV shows. Things had been going along fine when, in June 2009, she experienced a health crisis that led to emergency surgery. She had to cancel many performances, but she recovered in time to sing at the *Bienvenido Dudamel!* concert in L.A. four months later. When she took the stage at the Hollywood Bowl, it was clear why the soprano had been made such an impression on critics and audiences for the last 10 years. They had all fallen in love with her style as well as her beautiful voice. Brava Brueggergosman!

---

¹**diva:** a very successful female opera singer
²**sensation:** something or someone that causes a lot of excitement or interest

EXERCISE 9: Listening

A | *A radio host is interviewing several young musicians. Read the sentences. Then listen to the interview. Listen again and circle the words you hear.*

1. **Julio:** I'd / (I hadn't) really been planning to study the trombone.

2. **Marta:** We'd / We hadn't been playing in the same orchestra.

3. **Klaus:** He'd / He hadn't gotten us tickets for a concert.

4. **Ling:** I'd / I hadn't been dreaming of getting a violin of my own.

5. **Antonio:** I'd / I hadn't been doing my schoolwork.

B | *Read the statements. Then listen again to the interview and check (✓) **True** or **False**. Correct the false statements.*

	True	False
1. Before Julio started lessons, he'd wanted to play the ~~trombone~~. *flute*	☐	☑
2. Maria and Julio were good friends before the concert in Berlin.	☐	☐
3. Klaus had seen Dudamel conduct many times before the concert in Caracas.	☐	☐
4. Ling decided she wanted a violin before she turned 10.	☐	☐
5. After Antonio started making music, he spent less time hanging out with his friends.	☐	☐

EXERCISE 10: Pronunciation

A | *Read and listen to the Pronunciation Note.*

Pronunciation Note

In conversation, we often use the contraction **'d** for **had** in the **past perfect** or **past perfect progressive**.

After **pronouns** (except **it**), we pronounce **'d** as /**d**/.

Example: **We had** been there before.   →   "**We'd** been there before."

After **it** and **nouns** we pronounce **'d** as a short extra syllable /əd/.

Examples: **It had** been a great concert.   →   "**It'd** been a great concert."
                 My **friends had** enjoyed it a lot.   →   "My **friends'd** enjoyed it a lot."
                 Rosa had been rehearsing for weeks.   →   "**Rosa'd** been rehearsing for weeks."

We do NOT usually write the contraction **'d** after a noun or it. We write *friends had* and *it had* (Not: ~~friends'd~~ or ~~it'd~~).

1. **A:** We'd been standing in line for hours.
   B: Yes. But it had been worth it.

2. **A:** Maria had come late.
   B: I know. Her seat had been taken.

3. **A:** I'd seen him conduct twice before.
   B: It was the first time my son had seen him.

4. **A:** The concert had been sold out.
   B: People had come from all over.

5. **A:** The day had been perfect.
   B: The audience had loved the performance.

C | *Practice the conversations with a partner.*

EXERCISE 11: What About You?

Think about what you did yesterday. Indicate whether it was or wasn't a busy day. Complete the sentences. Then compare your day with a classmate's.

EXAMPLE: **A:** By 9:00 A.M., I'd already been practicing the piano for two hours. What about you?
B: By 9:00 A.M., I hadn't even gotten up!

Yesterday was / wasn't a busy day for me.

1. By 9:00 A.M., _____ .

2. By the time I got to work / school, _____ .

3. By the time I had lunch, _____ .

4. By the time I left work / school, _____ .

5. By the time I had dinner, _____ .

6. By 9:00 P.M., I _____ .

7. By the time I went to bed, I had done so much / little that I felt _____ .

EXERCISE 12: Conversation

Work in small groups. Talk about things you had never done before you began living here (or before a certain year). Possible topics: music, food, sports, clothing, entertainment, transportation.

EXAMPLE: **A:** Before I went to the Dudamel concert in Los Angeles, I wasn't really enthusiastic about classical music.
B: Me neither. I'd only listened to popular music.
C: I'd never been to a classical concert before.

EXERCISE 13: Game: Find the Differences

Work with a partner. Look at the two pictures. There are eleven differences in the pictures.
Find and discuss them. Use **by** *+ past perfect in your discussion.*

4:00 P.M.

6:00 P.M.

EXAMPLE: **A:** At 4:00 the woman wasn't wearing a sweater. By 6:00 she had put her sweater on.
B: And the boy had fallen asleep.

EXERCISE 14: Writing

A | *Find information in the library or on the Internet about the life and career of a musician or singer that you like. Make a timeline using seven or eight events in the artist's life and career.*

B | *Write two paragraphs about the artist you researched. For example, the first paragraph could be about the person's career. The second could be about the artist's personal life. Use the timeline to help you write sentences in the past perfect and past perfect progressive. If you can, download a photo of the artist for your essay.*

EXAMPLE: Vanessa-Mae only uses her first name professionally. She was born in Singapore on October 27. By age five, she had been playing the piano for two years. By the time she was a teenager, she had already made three classical recordings . . .

C | *Check your work. Use the Editing Checklist.*

Editing Checklist

Did you use . . . ?
- ☐ the past perfect and the past perfect progressive
- ☐ the past perfect for things that began before a specific past time
- ☐ the past perfect progressive for things that were in progress before a specific past time
- ☐ time clauses to show the relationship between past events
- ☐ adverbs to emphasize the first event

4 Review

Check your answers on page UR-1.

Do you need to review anything?

A | Circle the correct words to complete the sentences.

1. By the time I was 10, I got / had gotten my first violin.

2. It was 2007. I have been studying / had been studying the violin for two years by then.

3. By 2010, I had graduated / had been graduating from Juilliard School of Music.

4. After I finished school, I moved / had been moving to Los Angeles.

5. I had given / hadn't given a concert yet.

B | Complete the interview with the simple past, past perfect, or past perfect progressive form of the verbs in parentheses. Use the past perfect progressive when possible.

A: You're only 25. How long _____ you _____ the violin when you
                                        1. (play)

    _____ the Philharmonic Orchestra?
    2. (join)

B: Ten years. By the time I was 13, I _____ to become a professional,
                                     3. (decide)

    and I _____ for three hours a day. My father was a musician, and he
        4. (practice)

    _____ me to play the piano too.
    5. (teach)

A: _____ you _____ to this country yet?
                6. (come)

B: Yes. We _____ already _____ here. We _____ here for a year.
                        7. (move)   **8. (live)**

A: Well, congratulations on winning the grand prize. Were you surprised?

B: Very! I _____ it, and I was very excited.
    9. (not expect)

C | Find and correct six mistakes.

When five-year-old Sarah Chang enrolled in the Juilliard School of Music, she has already been playing the violin for more than a year. Her parents, both musicians, had been moving from Korea to further their careers. They had gave their daughter a violin as a fourth birthday present, and Sarah had been practiced hard since then. By seven, she already performed with several local orchestras. A child prodigy, Sarah became the youngest person to receive the Hollywood Bowl's Hall of Fame Award. She had already been receiving several awards including the Nan Pa Award—South Korea's highest prize for musical talent.

From Grammar to Writing
EDITING FOR VERB FORMS

When a paragraph includes more than one time frame (both present and past, for example), use correct verb forms to keep your meaning clear. You should also use **transitional words and phrases** such as *one day*, *now*, *at that time*, and *since then* to **signal a change in time**.

     SIMPLE PAST   PRESENT PERFECT
EXAMPLE: I **decided** to change my behavior. I **have been** much happier. ➔
      One day I **decided** to change my behavior. *Since then* I **have been** much happier.

1 | *Complete the student's paragraph about a phase in her life (a temporary period when she had particular kinds of behavior and feelings). Use the correct form of the verbs in parentheses.*

MY "STUPID" PHASE

Today my friends _____*think*_____ of me as a serious student,
         1. (think)

but they _____ about my "stupid" phase. Until two years
    2. (not know)

ago, I _____ mostly about clothes and makeup, and I usually
    3. (think)

_____ people by their appearance and possessions. In that
   4. (judge)

period of my life, my friends and I always _____ in
              5. (speak)

stereotyped phrases. We _____ "Hel-LO?" when something
       6. (say)

_____ obvious, and "Whatever" when we _____ about
  7. (seem)   **8. (not care)**

something. I never _____ any of my friends to realize that I
       9. (want)

_____ interested in school. Sometimes I _____ the
  10. (be)   **11. (read)**

newspaper secretly and _____ to be unprepared for tests.
        12. (pretend)

One day, my older brother _____ into my room while I
         13. (come)

_____ a serious novel. No one _____ ever
  14. (read)

_____ me do that before even though I _____ an
  15. (see)   **16. (be)**

avid reader for years. He thought I _____ to be interested
          17. (pretend)

                 (continued on next page)

---

in the book in order to impress a new boyfriend. I _____
18. (get)

angry when he _____ at me, so I _____ a
19. (laugh)   20. (make)

decision. I _____ hiding my real interests. Since that day, I
21. (stop)

_____ my news magazines proudly and _____
22. (carry)   23. (express)

opinions in class. For the last two years I _____ for tests
24. (prepare)

openly. Now I _____ for college, and I _____
25. (apply)   26. (feel)

proud of being a good student.

2 | Look at the paragraph in Exercise 1. Find the transitional words and phrases that signal a change in time.

1. the simple present to the simple past _____ *Until two years ago* _____

2. the simple past to the present perfect (progressive) _____

3. the present perfect (progressive) to the present progressive _____

3 | Complete the chart with information from the paragraph in Exercise 1.

Paragraph Section	Information	Form of the Verb
Topic Sentence • what the writer is like now	*a serious student*	*simple present*
Body of the Paragraph • habits and feelings the writer had during the phase		
• the event that ended the phase		
• behavior since the phase ended		
Conclusion • the results of the change		

4 | Before you write . . .
1. Work with a partner. Discuss a phase that each of you has experienced.
2. Make a chart like the one in Exercise 3 about your own phase.

5 | Write a paragraph about a phase you went through. Use information from the chart you made in Exercise 4. Remember to use transitional words or phrases when you shift from one time to another.

6 | *Exchange paragraphs with a different partner. Underline the verbs in your partner's paragraph. Circle the transitional words and phrases. Write a question mark (?) where something seems wrong or missing. Then answer the following questions.*

	Yes	No
1. Does each verb correctly express the time the author is writing about?	☐	☐
2. Is each verb formed correctly?	☐	☐
3. Are the shifts from one time to another time clearly marked with transitional words or phrases?	☐	☐

7 | *Work with your partner. Discuss each other's editing questions from Exercise 6. Then rewrite your own paragraph and make any necessary corrections.*

FUTURE: REVIEW AND EXPANSION

Future and Future Progressive
LIFE IN THE FUTURE

Before You Read

Look at the pictures. Discuss the questions.

1. What topics do you think the article will discuss?
2. What kinds of problems do you think people will face in the future?
3. How do you think they can solve them?

Read

Read the article about the future.

Cities of the Future   By Will Hapin, PhD

The world's population is exploding. By 2050, futurists[1] predict that 10 billion people **will be living** on the planet, up to 80 percent of them in cities. At the same time, the oceans are rising as global warming melts the ice at the North and South Poles. This means that while the population **is growing**, land **will be shrinking**. In addition, there **is not going to be** enough fresh water or oil and other types of fuel. Where **will** people **live** when room on dry land **gets** too crowded? How **will** 10 billion people **feed** themselves and **travel** from place to place? We**'re going to need** a lot of innovative solutions. Fortunately, some very creative people are already thinking about them. Here's what they are predicting:

Homes: Water World

Some futurists believe that as rising oceans **cover** the land, the oceans themselves **are going to become** valuable real estate.[2] People **will be building** floating cities, like the one in the picture, that **will use** solar, wind, and wave power.[3] Some cities **will** even **be traveling** long distances and **using** their large gardens to supply food. Science fiction? Maybe not. Some of the technology is already being used in underwater hotels and laboratories.

[1]**futurist:** someone who predicts future events and developments
[2]**real estate:** land and houses that people buy and sell
[3]**solar, wind, and wave power:** energy from the sun, wind, and ocean waves

Food: The Sky's the Limit

According to the United Nations Food and Agriculture Organization, the world **is going to need** 70 percent more food by 2050. This **will require** additional farmland equal to the size of Brazil. Where **will** we **find** it? Dr. Dickson Despommier, a professor at Columbia University, says urban farmers **will be growing** food on vertical farms, and that "sky farms" in New York **will produce** enough chicken, vegetables, and fruit to feed Manhattan. Instead of fuel-guzzling[4] farm machines, farmers **will be using** robots for difficult and dangerous work. The farms **will** also **save** energy because food **won't be traveling** into the city by truck from distant farms.

Travel: Back to the Future?

More than 50 years ago, luxurious airships—large "balloons" filled with helium[5]—carried passengers around Europe and across the Atlantic. However, after one terrible accident, people stopped traveling in them. Now, with fuel becoming more expensive, airships are coming back. A Spanish company is developing a solar-powered airship that **will fly** on sunshine during the day and **use** fuel only at night. Commuters **will be taking** airships to work, and the company predicts many other uses for the vehicles. For example, disaster relief organizations, such as the Red Cross and Red Crescent Societies, **will be using** them as flying hospitals to help earthquake and storm victims.

Earth and Beyond: The Space Elevator

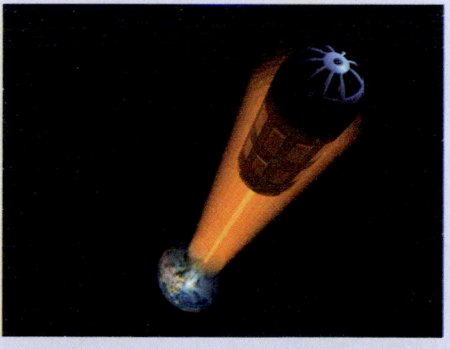

What **will** vacationers of the future **do** when they **need** a break from their crowded cities? They**'ll** just **hop** on the space elevator—a "ribbon" from the Earth that **will carry** people into space. This amazing idea was first proposed in 1895 by Russian scientist Konstantin Tsiolkovsky. Now, new technology and materials are turning the elevator into a reality. Supporters of the idea claim the elevators **are going to make** space travel cheap and safe. By the end of the century, they say, tourists **will be visiting** sky hotels and even **traveling** to the Moon, Mars, and beyond. Next stop, the 10,000th floor!

The future **is coming**, with all its opportunities and challenges. **Will** we **be** ready? With enough imagination and hard work, we **will be**!

---

[4]*fuel-guzzling:* using too much fuel. *Guzzle* means "to drink large amounts of something."
[5]*helium:* a gas that is lighter than air, often used to make balloons and airships float in the air

A | Vocabulary: *Circle the letter of the word or phrase that best completes each sentence.*

1. A **creative** or **innovative** plan is _____.

   a. new

   b. old

   c. easy

2. **Technology** is the _____ we use to do things.

   a. money and skills

   b. machines and knowledge

   c. people and animals

3. A _____ is NOT usually **vertical**.

   a. tall building

   b. tree

   c. desktop

4. A(n) _____ is an example of a **vehicle**.

   a. accident

   b. automobile

   c. hospital

5. A **challenge** is a task that is _____.

   a. new and difficult

   b. easy and safe

   c. in the far future

B | Comprehension: *Which of these statements are true* **Now***? Which will be true only in the* **Future***? Check (✓) the correct boxes.*

	Now	Future
1. The world's population is growing fast.	☐	☐
2. People are living on floating cities.	☐	☐
3. Tourists are staying in underwater hotels.	☐	☐
4. Sky farms are using robots as workers.	☐	☐
5. A company is building a solar-powered airship.	☐	☐
6. People are riding an elevator into space.	☐	☐

FUTURE

Affirmative Statements	
We **are going to take**	
We **will take**	the airship at 9:00.
We **are taking**	
We **take**	

Negative Statements	
We **are not going to take**	
We **will not take**	the airship at 10:00.
We **are not taking**	
We **don't take**	

Yes / No Questions	
Is she **going to take**	
Will she **take**	the airship at 9:00?
Is she **taking**	
Does she **take**	

Short Answers				
Affirmative			**Negative**	
	she **is.**			she **isn't.**
Yes,	she **will.**	**No,**		she **won't.**
	she **is.**			she **isn't.**
	she **does.**			she **doesn't.**

Wh- Questions	
When **is** she **going to take**	
When **will** she **take**	the airship?
When **is** she **taking**	
When **does** she **take**	

FUTURE PROGRESSIVE

Statements			
Subject	*Be (not) going to / Will (not)*	*Be* + Base Form + *-ing*	
People	are (not) going to will (not)	be traveling	to Mars by 2050.

Yes / No Questions				
Be / Will	Subject	*Going to*	*Be* + Base Form + *-ing*	
Are	they	going to	be traveling	to Mars?
Will				

Short Answers				
Affirmative		**Negative**		
Yes,	they **are.**	**No,**	they**'re not.**	
	they **will.**		they **won't.**	

Wh- Questions					
Wh- Word	*Be / Will*	Subject	*Going to*	*Be* + Base Form + *-ing*	
When	are	they	going to	be traveling	to Mars?
	will				

GRAMMAR NOTES

1 There are several ways to talk about the **future**. You can use:
- *be going to*
- *will*
- **present progressive**
- **simple present**

Now

Past ——————+————X————→ Future

take

tomorrow

USAGE NOTE: Sometimes only one form of the future is appropriate, but in many cases more than one form is possible.

- **I'm going to take** the airship tomorrow.
- It**'ll be** a nice trip.
- It**'s leaving** from Barcelona.
- It **takes off** at 9:00 A.M.

---

2 To talk about **facts** or things you are certain will happen in the future, use *be going to* or *will*.

- The sun **is going to rise** at 6:43 tomorrow.
  OR
- The sun **will rise** at 6:43 tomorrow.

---

3 To make **predictions** about things you are quite sure will happen in the future, use *be going to* or *will*.

BE CAREFUL! Use *be going to* (not *will*) when something that you <u>see right now</u> makes you almost certain an event is going to happen.

- I think people **are going to use** robots for a lot of tasks.
  OR
- I think people **will use** robots for a lot of tasks.

- Look! That robot**'s going to** serve our coffee! Not: That robot'll serve . . .

---

4 To talk about future **plans** or things you have already decided, use *be going to* or the **present progressive**.

USAGE NOTE: We often use the **present progressive** for plans that are <u>already arranged</u>.

- **I'm going to fly** to Tokyo next week.
  OR
- **I'm flying** to Tokyo next week.
  Not: I'll fly to Tokyo next week.

- **I'm flying** to Tokyo next week. I already have a ticket.

---

5 For **quick decisions** (made as you are speaking), or to make **offers** or **promises**, use *will*.

QUICK DECISION:
A: The Robot Show is opening next week.
B: Sounds interesting. I think I**'ll go**.

OFFER OR PROMISE:
A: I'd like to go too, but I don't have a ride.
B: I**'ll drive** you, but I'd like to leave by 7:00.
A: No problem. I**'ll be** ready.

| **6** | To talk about **scheduled future events** (timetables, programs, schedules), use the **simple present**.
We often use verbs such as *leave*, *start*, *end*, and *begin* this way. | • The airship **leaves** at 9:00 A.M.
• The conference **starts** tomorrow morning. |

| **7** | Use the **future progressive** with **be going to** or **will** to talk about actions that will be in progress at a specific time in the future.

Now
tomorrow
Past ──────X────→ Future
fly to Tokyo | • At this time tomorrow, I**'m going to be flying** to Tokyo.
OR
• At this time tomorrow, I**'ll be flying** to Tokyo. |

USAGE NOTES:

a. We often use the **future progressive** instead of the future to make a question about someone's plans <u>more polite</u>.

• When **are** you **going to hand in** your paper? *(teacher to student)*
• When **will** you **be grading** our tests? *(student to teacher)*

b. People often use the **future progressive** to ask indirectly for a favor. This makes the request <u>more polite</u>.

• **Will** you **be going** by the post office tomorrow? I need some stamps.

| **8** | In sentences with a **future time clause**: | **MAIN CLAUSE**   **TIME CLAUSE** |

a. Use the future or the future progressive in the main clause.

• I**'ll call** when the robot **finishes** the laundry.

b. Use the **simple present** or the **present progressive** in the **time clause**.

• I**'ll be eating** while he **is dusting**.

BE CAREFUL! Do NOT use the future or the future progressive in the time clause.

• I'll be making lunch while the robot **is cleaning**.
NOT: I'll be making lunch while the robot ~~will be cleaning~~.

EXERCISE 1: Discover the Grammar

A | *Dr. Will Hapin just met his friend Dr. Nouvella Eon at a conference. Read the conversation and underline all the verbs that refer to the future.*

HAPIN: Nouvella! It's nice to see you. <u>Are you presenting</u> a paper today?

EON: Hi, Will! Yes. In fact my talk starts at two o'clock.

HAPIN: Oh, I think I'll go. What do you plan to talk about? Will you be discussing robots?

EON: Yes. I'm focusing on personal robots for household work. My talk is called "Creative Uses of Home Robots."

HAPIN: *I* want one of those! But seriously, you promised me an interview on personal robots. Will you be getting some free time in the next few weeks?

EON: I'm not sure. I'll get back to you, OK?

HAPIN: Great! Where's your son, by the way? Is he with you?

EON: No. Rocky stays in Denver with his grandparents in the summer. I'm going to visit him right after the conference. He'll be 10 years old in a few days. I can't believe it!

HAPIN: It's his birthday, huh? Here, take this little model of the flying car for him.

EON: Oh, he's going to love this! Thanks, Will. So, what are you working on these days?

HAPIN: Well, *Futurist Magazine* just published my story on cities of the future. And I'm still with the World Future Association. In fact, I'm speaking at a news conference next month about the space elevator.

EON: That'll be exciting! Good luck with it!

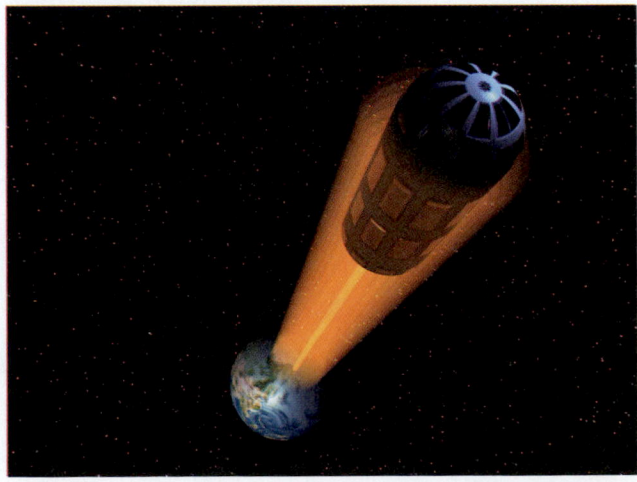

The space elevator

B | Complete the chart. List the 12 future verb forms in Part A. Then check (✓) the correct column for each form.

	Facts	Predictions	Plans	Quick Decisions	Offers and Promises	Schedules
1. Are you presenting			✓			
2.						
3.						
4.						
5.						
6.						
7.						
8.						
9.						
10.						
11.						
12.						

EXERCISE 2: Forms of the Future

(Grammar Notes 1–6)

Complete these conversations. Circle the correct words.

1. **EON:** Which projects <u>do you report</u> / <u>are you going to report</u> on?

   HAPIN: I haven't decided for sure. Probably flying cars.

2. **HAPIN:** Look at those dark clouds!

   EON: Yes. It looks like <u>it's raining</u> / <u>it's going to rain</u> any minute.

3. **EON:** I'd better get back to my hotel room before it starts to rain. Call me, OK?

   HAPIN: OK. <u>I'm talking</u> / <u>I'll talk</u> to you later.

4. **DESK:** Dr. Eon, your son just called.

   EON: Oh, good. I think <u>I'll call</u> / <u>I'm calling</u> him back right away.

5. **EON:** Hi, honey. How's it going?

   ROCKY: Great. And guess what? <u>I go</u> / <u>I'm going</u> fishing with Grandpa tomorrow.

6. **EON:** Have fun, but don't forget. You still have to finish that paper.

   ROCKY: I know, Mom. <u>I send</u> / <u>I'm sending</u> it to my teacher tomorrow. I already discussed it with her.

7. **ROCKY:** How's the conference?

   EON: Good. <u>I'm giving</u> / <u>I'll give</u> my talk this afternoon.

(continued on next page)

8. Rocky: Good luck. When <u>are you / will you be</u> here?

Eon: Tomorrow. The airship <u>lands / will land</u> at 7:00, so <u>I see / I'll see</u> you about 8:00.

9. Rocky: Great! <u>Are we going / Do we go</u> to the car show on my birthday?

Eon: Sure! Oh, and Will gave me something for you. I think <u>you like / you're going to like</u> it.

EXERCISE 3: Future Progressive
(Grammar Note 7)

Will Hapin is interviewing Nouvella Eon. Complete the interview. Use the future progressive form of the words in parentheses and short answers.

Hapin: You've been presenting a lot of papers recently. _____*Will*_____ you _____*be going*_____
1. (will / go)

to the robotics conference in Tokyo next month?

Eon: _____*Yes, I will*_____. But I _____. The Japanese are doing very innovative
2. **3. (won't / present)**

things with personal robotics, and I _____ every lecture possible.
4. (be going to / attend)

Hapin: Why all the excitement? What _____ robots _____ for us?
5. (be going to / do)

Eon: A lot! Oh, personal robots _____ still _____ the elderly
6. (be going to / help)

and people with disabilities. But the new 'bots _____ our lives
7. (will / improve)

in a lot of other ways too. They _____ complicated recipes.
8. (will / cook)

They _____ music and other creative tasks. So, _____ you
9. (will / perform)

_____ one for your family, Will?
10. (be going to / buy)

Hapin: _____ . They look too much like machines to me. _____ their appearance
11.

_____?
12. (be going to / change)

Eon: _____—and very soon. Companies are starting to meet that challenge now. In
13.

just a couple of years, they _____ 'bots that look just like humans—
14. (will / sell)

and show human emotions.

Hapin: Amazing! Well, thanks for the interview, Nouvella. Oh! Look at the time. This afternoon I

_____ the new flying car. You should see it. The technology is really
15. (be going to / test)

amazing.

Eon: I'd love to! _____ you be _____ by the university?
16. (will / drive)

Hapin: Sure. Why don't I give you a lift?

EXERCISE 4: Future Progressive: Affirmative and Negative Statements *(Grammar Note 7)*

Dr. Eon's family uses a robot for household chores. Look at Asimo the Robot's schedule for tomorrow. Write sentences using the words in parentheses and the future progressive.

TOMORROW

8:00	make breakfast
9:00	vacuum
10:00	dust
11:00	shop for food
12:00	do laundry
12:30	make lunch
1:00	recycle the garbage
2:00	pay bills
3:00	give Dr. Eon a massage
5:00	make dinner
6:00	play chess with Rocky

1. *At 8:05 Asimo won't be vacuuming. He'll be making breakfast.*
   (8:05 / vacuum)

2. *At 9:05 he'll be vacuuming.*
   (9:05 / vacuum)

3. _____
   (10:05 / dust)

4. _____
   (11:05 / do laundry)

5. _____
   (12:05 / shop for food)

6. _____
   (1:05 / recycle the garbage)

7. _____
   (2:05 / pay bills)

8. _____
   (3:05 / give Dr. Eon a massage)

9. _____
   (5:05 / make dinner)

10. _____
   (6:05 / play cards with Rocky)

EXERCISE 5: Future Progressive Statements and Time Clauses

(Grammar Notes 7–8)

Complete the ad for a getaway[1] in space with the verbs in parentheses. In sentences with time clauses, use the future progressive in the main clause. Use the simple present or the present progressive in the time clause.

The Sky's Not the Limit

Need a break? Call today and in just a few days, you ___*'ll be traveling*___ skyward for a
                                      1. (travel)

week at Starburst Suites Hotel. No rockets necessary—our comfortable modern elevator

_____ you quietly into space while everyone else _____
    2. (lift)   **3. (be)**

stuck in the crowds and noise back on Earth. While you _____ a meal on
                                           4. (enjoy)

this luxurious vehicle, a friendly flight robot _____ amazing views of our
                                      5. (point out)

planet from space. And before you _____ it, you _____ to
                          6. (know)   **7. (get ready)**

check into your hotel for a week of fun "near the Sun." After you _____,
                                           8. (unpack)

you _____ the other guests for a tour. Do you love sunsets? You're in luck!
    9. (join)

You _____ 16 of them every day from the hotel's huge windows. Do you
    10. (watch)

prefer adventure? Picture this! While other guests _____ in the spa, you
                                           11. (relax)

_____ your spacesuit for a
    12. (put on)

walk under the stars.

    So call for a reservation. Once aboard, we

guarantee it—you _____ about
                  13. (not think)

anything except returning again and again

and again . . .

---
[1] **getaway:** a short vacation trip

EXERCISE 6: Editing

Read this article about cars of the future. There are ten mistakes in the use of the future and future progressive. The first mistake is already corrected. Find and correct nine more.

Flying Cars

The SkyCar

Your class starts in 10 minutes, but you're stuck in traffic. Don't panic. With just a press of a button, your car will ~~lifts~~ *lift* off the ground, and you'll be on your way to school. No bad roads, no stop signs, no worries!

Welcome to the future! It seems like science fiction, but it isn't. Engineers have been working on flying cars for decades, and they have already solved many of the big challenges. They predict that we'll all be use these amazing vehicles one day.

According to *Car Trends Magazine*, one model, part car and part plane, is going be on the market in the not-so-distant future. It will look like a regular car when it's on the road, but its wings will unfold when the driver will decide to take to the skies. It will runs on the same fuel for both land and air travel, and you'll be able to keep it in your garage. (But you're still going need an airport to take off and land.)

A better model will be a vertical takeoff and landing vehicle (VTOL). You won't need to go to the airport anymore, and all controls will being automatic. Imagine this: You'll be doing your homework while your car will be getting you to school safely and on time.

And what does this future dream car cost? Well, fasten your seatbelts—the price will going to be sky-high. At first it will be about a million dollars, but after a few years, you'll be able to buy one for "only" $60,000. Don't throw away your old driver's license just yet!

EXERCISE 7: Listening

A | *Four members of the Mars Association are trying to organize a conference on Venus. Read the statements. Then listen to their conversation. Listen again and check (✓)* **True** *or* **False**. *Correct the false statements.*

		True	False
1.	Skyler ~~has~~ *hasn't* made all of his summer plans.	☐	☑
2.	Jarek is taking a summer vacation.	☐	☐
3.	Lorna needs to give her boss two or more weeks' notice before taking time off.	☐	☐
4.	A lot of tourists from other planets will be visiting Earth.	☐	☐
5.	Zindra is spending most of the summer at home.	☐	☐
6.	Zindra won't be doing any research this summer.	☐	☐

B | *Listen again to the conversation. Mark the chart below to help you figure out when everyone will be available.*

	July				August			
Weeks:	1	2	3	4	1	2	3	4
Skyler							X	X
Jarek								
Lorna								
Zindra								

When they're all available: _____

X = not available

EXERCISE 8: Pronunciation

A | *Read and listen to the Pronunciation Note.*

Pronunciation Note

When we **contrast information**, we **stress** the words with the **information**.

                 •   •

EXAMPLES: I won't be **traveling** next summer. I'll be **studying**.

                    •   •

        Noor won't be **home** on Monday. She'll be in the **office**.

Listen to the short conversations. Put a dot (•) over the words in the answers that have the most stress.

1. **A:** Will Jason be running this morning?

   B: No, he won't be running. He'll be swimming.

2. **A:** Will you be leaving for vacation next month?

   B: No, I won't be leaving for vacation, but I'll be leaving for a business trip.

3. **A:** Ana will be going into the office tomorrow. Say hi for me.

   B: Oh, she won't be going into the office tomorrow. She'll be working in the library.

4. **A:** Are you going to be working on the weekend?

   B: We'll be working Saturday, but we won't be working Sunday.

5. **A:** Will you be visiting your family in Toronto next summer?

   B: Well, I'll be visiting my sister. But my brother isn't there now.

6. **A:** Will your study group be meeting this summer?

   B: We'll be meeting in August. In July a lot of people will be on vacation.

C Listen again to the conversations and repeat the answers. Then practice the conversations with a partner.

EXERCISE 9: Reaching Agreement

Complete the schedule. Write all your plans for next week. Then work with a partner. Without showing each other your schedules, find a time to get together. Then discuss your plans. Use different forms of the future.

EXAMPLE:
    A: What are you doing on Tuesday morning?
    B: I'm going to see the Robot Show at the Science Museum.
    A: I'll go with you. I'll be free at 11:00.
    B: Great. The coffee shop opens at 10:00. Want to meet for coffee first?

	MONDAY	TUESDAY	WEDNESDAY	THURSDAY	FRIDAY
9:00					
11:00					
1:00					
3:00					
5:00					
7:00					

EXERCISE 10: Discussion

Robots will be doing many things in the near future. Look at the list of activities and decide which ones you think robots will or won't be doing. In small groups, share and explain your opinions. Do you think robots will be doing too much for humans? Why?

- answer the phone
- drive cars
- find information on the Internet
- go shopping
- guide vacation tours
- have a conversation
- invent new technology
- make dinner
- paint pictures
- plant gardens
- play musical instruments
- report the news
- take a vacation
- take care of children
- teach English
- teach themselves new skills
- write letters
- write the laws

EXAMPLE: **A:** I don't think robots will be teaching English, but they will be taking care of children. Children will think they're fun—like big toys.

B: I don't agree. I think it's a bad idea. Children need human contact to help them develop emotional security.

C: Do you think robots will be driving cars?

EXERCISE 11: Information Gap: Dr. Eon's Calendar

Work in pairs (A and B). **Student B,** *go to page 77 and follow the instructions there.* **Student A,** *complete Dr. Eon's calendar below. Get information from Student B. Ask questions and fill in the calendar. Answer Student B's questions.*

EXAMPLE:
A: What will Dr. Eon be doing on Sunday the first?
B: She'll be flying to Tokyo. What about on the second? Will she be taking the day off?
A: No, she'll be meeting with Dr. Kato.

FEBRUARY						2115
SUNDAY	**MONDAY**	**TUESDAY**	**WEDNESDAY**	**THURSDAY**	**FRIDAY**	**SATURDAY**
1 fly to Tokyo	2 meet with Dr. Kato	3	4	5	6	7
8 take Bullet Train to Osaka	9 sightseeing	10	11	12	13	14
15 fly home	16	17	18 attend energy seminar	19	20	21 shop with Rocky and Asimo
22	23	24	25	26	27	28 take shuttle to Mars

When you are finished, compare calendars. Do they have the same information?

EXERCISE 12: Writing

A | *Write a paragraph about your life 10 years from now. What will you be doing for a living? What kind of family life will you have? What hobbies will you be enjoying? What will you do to achieve these things? Use the future and future progressive.*

EXAMPLE: In 10 years, I will be working for the space program. I am going to be planning the first colony on Mars. First I'll graduate from college. . . .

B | *Check your work. Use the Editing Checklist.*

Editing Checklist

Did you use . . . ?
- [ ] *be going to* or *will* for facts and predictions
- [ ] *be going to* or the present progressive for plans
- [ ] the simple present for scheduled future events
- [ ] the future progressive for actions that will be in progress at a specific time in the future
- [ ] the simple present or the present progressive in time clauses

Student B, complete Dr. Eon's calendar below. Answer Student A's questions. Then ask Student A questions and fill in the information.

EXAMPLE: **A:** What will Dr. Eon be doing on Sunday the first?
                B: She'll be flying to Tokyo. What about on the second? Will she be taking the day off?
                A: No, she'll be meeting with Dr. Kato.

FEBRUARY						2115
SUNDAY	MONDAY	TUESDAY	WEDNESDAY	THURSDAY	FRIDAY	SATURDAY
1 fly to Tokyo	**2** *meet with Dr. Kato*	**3** attend World Future Conference	**4** ⟶	**5**	**6**	**7** ⟶
8	**9** ⟶	**10**	**11**	**12** fly to Denver	**13** visit Mom and Dad	**14** ⟶
15	**16** give speech at Harvard University	**17** meet with Dr. Rover	**18** ⟶	**19**	**20** ⟶	**21**
22 relax!	**23** work at home ⟶	**24**	**25**	**26**	**27** ⟶	**28**

When you are finished, compare calendars. Do they have the same information?

Check your answers on page UR-2.

Do you need to review anything?

A | *Circle the correct words to complete the sentences.*

1. Our daughter will <u>turns / turn</u> 15 next week.

2. <u>Are / Do</u> you going to go to work today?

3. What will you be <u>doing / do</u> at 3:00 this afternoon?

4. The sun <u>will / is</u> going to rise at 6:22 tomorrow morning.

5. Be careful! Your coffee <u>will / is going to</u> spill!

6. While you<u>'re / 'll be</u> driving to work tomorrow, we'll be flying to Beijing.

7. Roboid will let us know when he <u>finished / finishes</u> cooking dinner.

B | *Complete the conversation with the future or future progressive form of the verbs in parentheses or with a short answer. Use the future progressive when possible.*

A: What _____ you _____ at 10:00 tomorrow morning?
                                              1. (do)

B: 10:00? Well, let's see. My plane _____ at 9:45, so at 10:00,
                                                2. (leave)

    I _____ on the plane.
       3. (sit)

A: So I guess you _____ to the office at all tomorrow.
               4. (not come)

B: Doesn't look like it. Why? _____ that _____ a problem?
                                      5. (cause)

A: _____, it _____. It _____ fine. Have a good trip.
                        6.   **7. (be)**

B: Thanks. I _____ you in a couple of weeks.
         8. (see)

C | *Find and correct five mistakes.*

A: How long are you going to staying in Beijing?

B: I'm not sure. I'll let you know you as soon as I'll find out, OK?

A: OK. It's going to be a long flight. What will you did to pass the time?

B: I'll be work a lot of the time. And I'm going to try to sleep.

A: Good idea. Have fun, and I'm emailing you all the office news. I promise.

UNIT 6 — Future Perfect and Future Perfect Progressive

MONEY AND GOALS

STEP 1 GRAMMAR IN CONTEXT

Before You Read

Look at the photos and the information for each person. Discuss the questions.

1. What are some good and bad uses of their credit cards?
2. How does money management help people reach their goals?
3. What do you think the show is about?

Read

Read the transcript of a personal finance TV show.

MONEY TALKS

Debbie Hart, age 20
Number of credit cards: 3
Used for: movies, CDs, clothes
Balance: $2,500

Sung Park, age 18
Number of credit cards: 5
Used for: textbooks, car repairs
Balance: $1,750

Jeff Hassad, age 22
Number of credit cards: 1
Used for: eating out, entertainment
Balance: $600

Trudy: Hi, everyone. I'm Trudy Norman and you're watching *Money Talks*. We've taken the show on the road —to college campuses—and by the end of tonight's *Money Talks*, we**'ll have been traveling** for a month, and we**'ll have been** in 22 cities in that time!

I love bringing the show to colleges because good money management is such an important goal for people starting out in life. In fact, it's almost as important as getting your degree. It just makes sense —if you're managing your money well, your other goals are going to be much easier to reach.

Tonight we're at Gibson College in Nebraska, and we have students Debbie Hart, Sung Park, and Jeff Hassad on our panel. Our topic is credit cards.

(continued on next page)

To get started, let me give you some shocking[1] statistics. A typical college freshman **will have gotten** eight credit card offers by the end of the first semester. For today's freshman, a lot of the offers will include gifts—from pizzas to iPods. So it's not surprising that many students accept at least some of those offers. In fact, by graduation, the average student in the United States **will have tripled** the number of cards in his or her wallet.

Sung: That's true. When I first got here, I only had one credit card. Then I started receiving all these emails and even phone calls with credit card offers. Finally, I thought, "Why not?" Now I have five cards.

Trudy: The national average for college students is 4.7 cards, so you're not alone. And it isn't only the number of credit cards that increases. So does the amount you owe. If you're like many students, you**'ll have doubled** your credit card debt by graduation. The average student's debt **will have grown** to $4,138 by the time he or she graduates.

Debbie: My problem is, it's too easy just to take out my card when I see something I want. Then, when I get my bill, I**'ll have charged** more than I can pay for. I'm carrying a pretty big balance right now.

Trudy: Did you know that people who always use credit cards spend more? Create a budget and start using cash—by next year you**'ll have spent** 12 percent less! And you **won't have been paying** interest on your purchases. But if you must charge, you should also start paying more than the minimum every month, even if it's only $20 more.

Debbie: How much can an extra $20 help?

Trudy: A lot. Suppose you're a freshman and you owe $1,000 on your card at 15 percent interest. Pay an extra $20 every month, and by the time you graduate, you**'ll have** already **become** debt-free! And you**'ll have been saving** interest charges the whole time. On the other hand, if you only pay the minimum, you'll be paying for 15 years, and at the end, you**'ll have spent** $1,122.78 in interest. Everything you bought on that card **will have cost** twice as much as the actual price.

Jeff: I hear what you're saying. By the end of this school year, I**'ll have been paying** interest for nine months on pizzas I ate last September! But are you saying students shouldn't use credit cards?

Trudy: That's not realistic,[2] is it? No, I'm saying one card is enough. And use it for essentials,[3] not for pizza and cool shoes.

Sung: My brother didn't have a credit card in college. When he graduated, he had a hard time getting one.

Trudy: Good point, Sung. It's hard to get credit when you have no credit history. Getting your first credit card as a student, when it's easier, can be a good idea. Use it wisely, and by graduation you**'ll have earned** a good credit rating, and that will be very useful when you're starting out.

That's all for tonight. Remember, guys, you're going to be doing a lot in the next few years. Don't let poor money management hold you back, and keep you from reaching your goals. See you next week on *Money Talks*.

---

[1] *shocking:* very upsetting and surprising
[2] *realistic:* practical or sensible
[3] *essentials:* things that are necessary

After You Read

A | Vocabulary: *Circle the letter of the word or phrase that best completes each sentence.*

1. A **budget** is a _____ for saving money.
   a. reason
   b. book
   c. plan

2. If you buy something on **credit**, you pay for it _____.
   a. now
   b. later
   c. with cash

3. A **debt** is money that you _____.
   a. save
   b. owe
   c. earn

4. If you pay the **minimum** amount, you pay the _____ amount.
   a. exact
   b. most
   c. least

5. **Statistics** are _____ that give information about people and activities.
   a. numbers
   b. students
   c. books

6. A **purchase** is something that you _____.
   a. borrow
   b. buy
   c. return

B | Comprehension: *Check (✓)* **True** *or* **False**. *Correct the false statements.*

	True	False
1. The show was traveling two months ago.	☐	☐
2. Many students get eight credit card offers in their first semester of college.	☐	☐
3. Many students have twice as much credit card debt after four years.	☐	☐
4. People who pay with credit cards spend more.	☐	☐
5. Jeff has already paid interest for nine months on pizzas he ate last September.	☐	☐
6. It's never a good idea to use a credit card when you're a student.	☐	☐

FUTURE PERFECT

Statements			
Subject	***Will (not)***	***Have* + Past Participle**	
I You He She It We They	**will (not)**	**have earned**	interest by then.

Yes / No Questions			
Will	**Subject**	***Have* + Past Participle**	
Will	I she they	**have earned**	interest by then?

Short Answers					
Affirmative			**Negative**		
Yes,	you she they	**will (have).**	**No,**	you she they	**won't (have).**

Wh- Questions				
***Wh-* Word**	***Will***	**Subject**	***Have* + Past Participle**	
How much	**will**	I she they	**have earned**	by then?

FUTURE PERFECT PROGRESSIVE

Statements			
Subject	**Will (not)**	**Have been + Base Form + -ing**	
I You He She It We They	**will (not)**	**have been earning**	interest for a month.

Yes / No Questions			
Will	**Subject**	**Have been + Base Form + -ing**	
Will	I she they	**have been earning**	interest for a month?

Short Answers					
Affirmative			**Negative**		
Yes,	you she they	**will (have).**	**No,**	you she they	**won't (have).**

Wh- Questions				
Wh- Word	**Will**	**Subject**	**Have been + Base Form + -ing**	
How long	**will**	I she they	**have been earning**	interest?

GRAMMAR NOTES

1 Use the **future perfect** to show that something will happen before a specific time in the future.

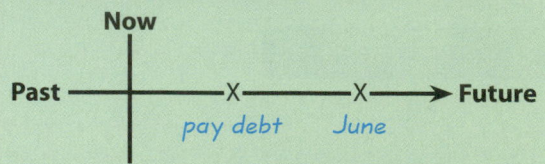

The focus is often on the completion of an action.

- **By June**, he **will have paid** his debt.
- She**'ll have bought** a new car **by May**.
- I**'ll have been** in college for a year **by then**.
- We**'ll have saved** enough **by then**.

2 Use the **future perfect progressive** to show that an action will be in progress until a specific time in the future. It may continue after that specific time. The focus is on the continuation of the action, not the end result.

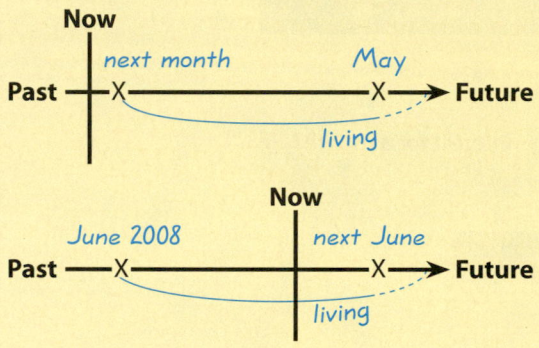

Notice that the action may start sometime in the future or it may have already started.

REMEMBER: Non-action verbs are NOT usually used in the progressive.

A: You're buying a house in L.A. next month? Great! Can I visit in May?
B: Sure. By then, we**'ll have been living** there for three months.

- They moved to Atlanta in June 2008. So by next June, they**'ll have been living** there for three years.

- By May, he**'ll have owned** that car for five years. NOT: By May, he'll have ~~been owning~~ that car for five years.

3 Use the **future perfect** or the **future perfect progressive** with the **simple present** to show the relationship between two future events.

Use the **future perfect** or the **future perfect progressive** for the earlier event. Use the **simple present** for the later time or event.

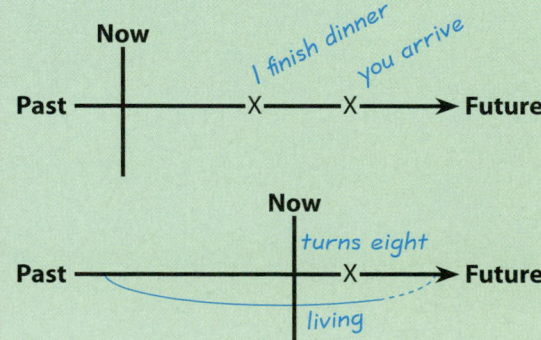

- By the time you **arrive**, I **will have finished** dinner. (*First I'll finish dinner. Then you'll arrive*) NOT: By the time you ~~will~~ arrive, I will have finished dinner.

- When my daughter **turns** eight, we **will have been living** here for 10 years. (*First we'll live here 10 years, then my daughter will turn eight.*)

<table>
<tr>
<td>**4**</td>
<td>We often use the **future perfect** and the **future perfect progressive** with **by** + **time or event** or **by the time** + **time clause**.

We often use **already** and **yet** with the **future perfect** to emphasize which event will <u>happen first</u>.</td>
<td>• **By 2013**, he**'ll have saved** $1,000.
• He **won't have saved** $5,000 **by the time he graduates**.

• By 9:00, we**'ll** **already** **have finished** dinner.
• We **won't have washed** the dishes **yet**.</td>
</tr>
</table>

STEP 3 FOCUSED PRACTICE

EXERCISE 1: Discover the Grammar

Read each numbered statement. Circle the letter of the sentence that is similar in meaning.

1. By next year, Trudy will have been doing her show *Money Talks* for five years.

    a. Trudy will stop doing her show this year.

    (b.) Next year, Trudy can celebrate the fifth anniversary of *Money Talks*.

2. By this time tomorrow, I'll have decided which car to buy.

    a. I know which car I'm going to buy.

    b. I haven't decided yet.

3. By the time you get home, we'll have finished studying.

    a. You will get home while we are studying.

    b. You will get home after we finish studying.

4. By 2017, we'll have been working in this office for eight years.

    a. We'll move to another office before 2017.

    b. We'll be in the same office in 2017.

5. They won't have finished taping *Money Talks* by 10:00.

    a. They will still be taping at 10:00.

    b. They will finish taping at 10:00.

6. They will have finished Trudy's *Money* newsletter by 5:00.

    a. They'll be finished by 5:00.

    b. They'll still be working at 5:00.

EXERCISE 2: Future Perfect

Debbie has a lot of goals. Look at the timeline. Write sentences describing what Debbie Hart **will have done** *or* **won't have done** *by the year 2015.*

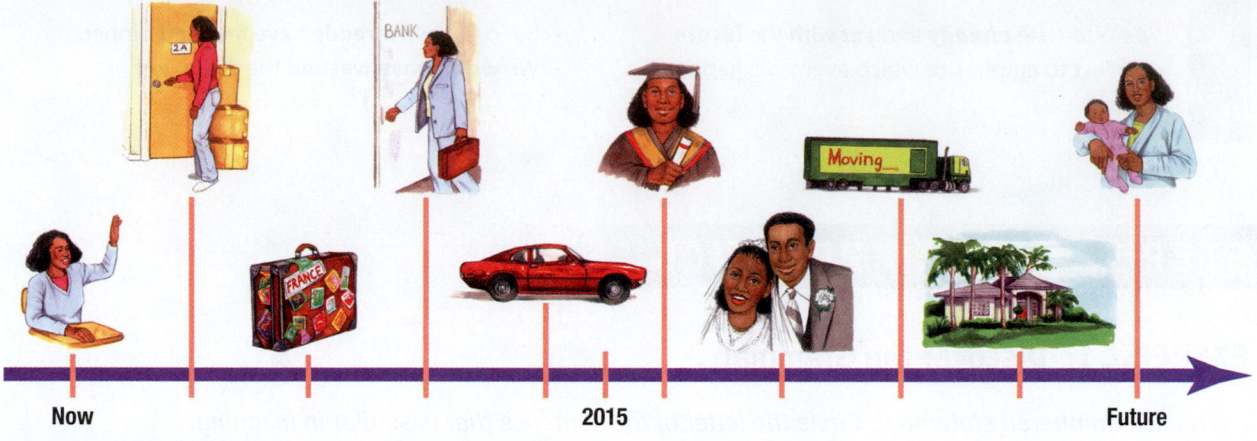

Now   2015   Future

1. (start college)

    By 2015, Debbie will have started college.

2. (get married)

_____

3. (move into an apartment)

_____

4. (move to Miami)

_____

5. (spend a summer in France)

_____

6. (start working at a bank)

_____

7. (buy a used car)

_____

8. (buy a house)

_____

9. (graduate from college)

_____

10. (become a parent)

_____

EXERCISE 3: Time Clauses with *Already* and *Yet*

(Grammar Notes 1, 3–4)

Read Debbie's goals. What will or won't she have achieved by the time the first event occurs? Use the information in the timeline from Exercise 2. Write sentences using **already** *and* **yet**.

1. (move into an apartment / start college)

    By the time Debbie moves into an apartment, she'll have already started college.

2. (move into an apartment / get married)

    _____

3. (start college / buy a used car)

    _____

4. (graduate from college / move into an apartment)

    _____

5. (spend a summer in France / find a job at a bank)

    _____

6. (graduate from college / spend a summer in France)

    _____

7. (get married / graduate from college)

    _____

8. (move to Miami / buy a home)

    _____

9. (become a parent / graduate from college)

    _____

10. (buy a home / become a parent)

    _____

EXERCISE 4: Future Perfect or Future Perfect Progressive

(Grammar Notes 1–4)

Ask and answer questions about these people's accomplishments. Choose between the future perfect and the future perfect progressive. Use the calendar to answer the questions.

January

S	M	T	W	T	F	S
					1	2
3	4	5	6	7	8	9
10	11	12	13	14	15	16
17	18	19	20	21	22	23
24	25	26	27	28	29	30
31						

February

S	M	T	W	T	F	S
	1	2	3	4	5	6
7	8	9	10	11	12	13
14	15	16	17	18	19	20
21	22	23	24	25	26	27
28						

March

S	M	T	W	T	F	S
	1	2	3	4	5	6
7	8	9	10	11	12	13
14	15	16	17	18	19	20
21	22	23	24	25	26	27
28	29	30	31			

April

S	M	T	W	T	F	S
				1	2	3
4	5	6	7	8	9	10
11	12	13	14	15	16	17
18	19	20	21	22	23	24
25	26	27	28	29	30	

May

S	M	T	W	T	F	S
						1
2	3	4	5	6	7	8
9	10	11	12	13	14	15
16	17	18	19	20	21	22
23	24	25	26	27	28	29
30	31					

June

S	M	T	W	T	F	S
		1	2	3	4	5
6	7	8	9	10	11	12
13	14	15	16	17	18	19
20	21	22	23	24	25	26
27	28	29	30			

1. On January 1, Debbie Hart started saving $15 a week.

   QUESTION: (by February 19 / how long / save)

   By February 19, how long will Debbie have been saving?

   ANSWER: *By February 19, she'll have been saving for seven weeks.*

2. On March 1, Valerie Morgan started saving $5 a week.

   QUESTION: (by April 19 / how much / save)

   _____

   ANSWER: _____

3. On March 3, Sung Park began reading a book a week.

   QUESTION: (by June 16 / how many books / read)

   _____

   ANSWER: _____

4. On April 24, Don Caputo began running 2 miles a day.

   QUESTION: (how long / run / by May 29)

   _____

   ANSWER: _____

5. On April 24, Tania Zakov began running 2 miles a day.

QUESTION: (how many miles / run / by May 29)

_____

ANSWER: _____

6. On February 6, Rick Gregory began saving $10 a week.

QUESTION: (save $100 / by March 27)

_____

ANSWER: _____

7. On May 8, Tim Rigg began painting two apartments a week in his building.

QUESTION: (how many apartments / paint / by May 29)

_____

ANSWER: _____

8. Tim's building has 12 apartments.

QUESTION: (finish / by June 19)

_____

ANSWER: _____

9. Talia began a fitness program on January 1. She is losing one pound a week.

QUESTION: (lose 20 pounds / by May 21)

_____

ANSWER: _____

10. Erik enrolled in a Spanish class on February 22.

QUESTION: (how long / study / by April 26)

_____

ANSWER: _____

11. In March, Jeff Hassad began paying $10.00 a month interest on a loan.

QUESTION: (how much interest / pay / by the end of June)

_____

ANSWER: _____

EXERCISE 5: Editing

Read this blog entry. There are nine mistakes in the use of the future perfect and future perfect progressive. The first mistake is already corrected. Find and correct eight more.

To My Credit

Jonathon Daly   January 1

    I have five credit cards. If nothing changes, I *will* have doubled the credit card debt I had as a freshman by the time I graduate. According to statistics, that makes me a typical college student. But I've decided to change. By this time next year, I'll has gotten my debt under control. I won't had become debt-free, but I'll have made a good start. Here's my debt-free timeline so far:

- I just found a part-time job, and when I start working, I'll use that money to pay debts.

- By February, I'll have been recorded all my spending for a month. Then I'll be able to make a spending plan. Only essentials—food, basic clothes, tuition—will be on this budget.

- By March 1, I'll only have two credit cards left. By that time, I'll already have been transferring all of my balances to those two cards with the lowest interest rate. And I'll have closing six accounts by then too!

- When I graduate, I've been paying more than the minimum on my cards for three months, so I might be able to get a lower interest rate. I expect a lot of financial challenges after I graduate, but by then I had experience in managing debt. I'll add goals to the timeline and record my progress during the year.

    I'd love to hear stories and suggestions from readers about getting debt-free. If you're a college student in my situation, send in your timeline and let's change the statistics together. How much progress will we "typical" college students have been making by next January 1?

EXERCISE 6: Listening

A | *Don and Thea Caputo want to save for a summer vacation with their two children, Ned and Valerie. Read the list of things the family can do to cut back on spending. Then listen to their conversation. Listen again and check (✓) the correct boxes.*

By next summer, who will have . . . ?	Thea	Don	Ned	Valerie
1. been packing lunch	☑	☑	☐	☐
2. only bought new scarves and earrings	☐	☐	☐	☐
3. gotten some clothes at thrift shops	☐	☐	☐	☐
4. been taking the commuter van to work	☐	☐	☐	☐
5. been ordering pizza and watching DVDs at home	☐	☐	☐	☐

B | *Look at the chart. Listen again to the conversation and write the amount the family will have saved in each category by next summer.*

Amount They Will Have Saved by Next Summer	
Lunches	*$1,000*
Clothing	
Transportation	
Entertainment	
Total of all categories	

C | *With their savings, where can they go for a two-week vacation? Check (✓) the correct box(es).*

☐ **1.** A car trip to British Columbia, renting camping equipment $3,000

☐ **2.** A car trip to British Columbia, staying in motels $3,500

☐ **3.** A trip to Disneyland $4,000

☐ **4.** A trip by airplane to Mexico and two weeks in a hotel $5,000

EXERCISE 7: Pronunciation

A | *Read and listen to the Pronunciation Note.*

> **Pronunciation Note**
>
> In the **future perfect** and **future perfect progressive**, we often pronounce *have* like "of."
>
> **EXAMPLES:** Thea **will have** left already. → "Thea **will of** left already."
> I **won't have** spoken to her by then. → "I **won't of** spoken to her by then."
> She**'ll have** been driving for an hour. → "She**'ll of** been driving for an hour."

B | *Listen to people talking about accomplishments. Then listen again to their conversations and complete the sentences with the verb forms that you hear.*

1. **A:** We're doing really well with our savings plan.

   B: You're right. By next summer, we _____ enough for a great vacation.

2. **A:** How are the kids?

   B: Great. In May, my daughter _____ on her degree for almost a year.

3. **A:** Uh-oh. I think this is your credit card bill.

   B: No problem! As of this month, I _____ a late payment for two years.

4. **A:** Your English is so good! How long have you been living here?

   B: Let me think . . . On December 1, I _____ in this country for three years.

5. **A:** Do you think Ned's team will win again today?

   B: I hope so. If they do, they _____ a game all year.

6. **A:** In June, Don and Thea _____ married for fifteen years.

   B: Let's throw a party for them!

7. **A:** What's up? You're looking very pleased with yourself.

   B: And I should! By 6:00 this evening, I _____ a cigarette for six months.

8. **A:** As of this Saturday, my girlfriend and I _____ each other for three years.

   B: Congratulations! What will you do to celebrate?

C | *Practice the conversations with a partner.*

EXERCISE 8: Conversation

What will some of the people in your life (including you!) have achieved by the end of this year, this month, or this week? Talk about some of these accomplishments with a partner. (Remember, even small accomplishments are important!) Use some of the ideas in the list and your own.

- making a budget
- managing time
- exercising
- learning new things
- overcoming a bad habit
- starting a good habit
- spending time with friends and family
- _____
- _____
- _____

EXAMPLE: **A:** I'm really proud of my roommate. She's always had a problem oversleeping, but by the end of this month, she won't have missed any of her morning classes!
B: That's great. How did she solve her problem?

EXERCISE 9: What About You?

A | *Think of three goals you would like to achieve in the next five years and discuss them in a small group. They can be big goals, such as buying a house, or smaller goals, such as learning a new skill.*

EXAMPLES: **A:** I'd like to get fit and then run in a 10 km race. What about you?
B: I want to save enough money to buy a digital camera and learn how to use photo editing software.
C: I'd like to learn to skateboard.

B | *Arrange your goals on the timeline. Write the goals and the years you want to achieve them.*

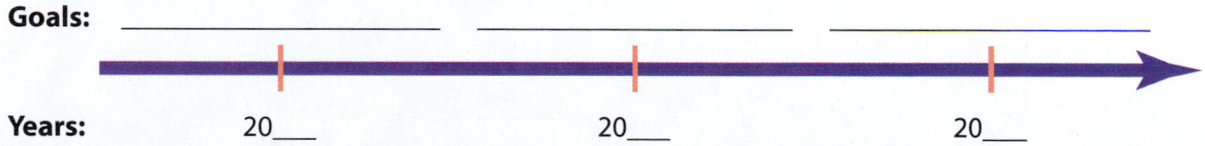

Goals: _____   _____   _____

Years: 20___   20___   20___

C | *Discuss your goals with a group. Talk about things you'll need to do before you achieve each goal. Use the future perfect and the future perfect progressive with time clauses.*

EXAMPLES: **A:** Before I run my first 10 km race, I'll have been training for three months.
B: By the holidays this year, I'll have bought a camera.

EXERCISE 10: Writing

A | *Write about the activities and goals of some of your classmates for a class website. Use information from Exercises 8 and 9, or work in small groups to exchange information. Find out the following:*

- What personal or school activities have your classmates been involved in?

- How long will they have been doing those activities by the end of the year or semester?

- What will they have achieved by the end of this year or this semester?

B | *Write three or four sentences about each student.*

EXAMPLE: Dannie Munca wants to buy an iPod®. He got a part-time job in the library to help him save money. By the end of the semester, he'll have been working there for two months. He'll have saved about $200 by then, and he'll be able to get his new electronic toy. Good planning, Dannie.

C | *Check your work. Use the Editing Checklist.*

Editing Checklist

Did you use . . . ?

☐ the future perfect for actions that will already be completed by a certain time in the future

☐ the future perfect progressive for actions that will still be in progress at a specific time in the future

☐ time clauses to show the relationship between two future events

---

A | *Circle the correct words to complete the sentences.*

1. Kareem will <u>have saved / have been saving</u> a total of almost $1,000 by next year.

2. When we <u>get / 'll get</u> to my parents' house, they'll already have eaten dinner.

3. By the end of this week, Mia will <u>exercise / have been exercising</u> for six months.

4. When I finish this story by Sue Grafton, I <u>'ll have read / have been reading</u> all of her mysteries.

5. <u>By / Since</u> 2015, he'll have been living here for 10 years.

B | *Complete the conversation with the simple present, future perfect, or future perfect progressive form of the verbs in parentheses. Use the future perfect progressive if possible.*

A: Do you realize that in September we _____ here for two years?
                                                    1. (live)

B: Amazing! And you _____ here for four years.
                          2. (study)

A: I know. Next year at this time I _____ already.
                                        3. (graduate)

B: I hope that by the time you _____, I _____ a good job.
                                    4. (graduate)   **5. (find)**

A: Well, one thing is certain. By that time we _____ a lot of friends here.
                                                    6. (make)

B: Yes. And we _____ almost $400 by walking and taking the bus everywhere.
                    7. (save)

C | *Find and correct eight mistakes.*

I'm so excited about your news! By the time you read this, you'll have already moving into your new house! And I have some good news too. By the end of this month, I will have been saving $3,000. That's enough for me to buy a used car! And that means that by this time next year, I drive to California to visit you! I have more news too. By the time I will graduate, I will have been started my new part-time job. I hope that by this time next year, I'll also had paid off some of my loans.

It's hard to believe that in June, we will have been being friends for 10 years. Time sure flies! And we'll have been stayed friends even though we live 3,000 miles apart. Isn't the Internet a great thing?

From Grammar to Writing
AVOIDING SENTENCE FRAGMENTS

Time clauses begin with **time words and phrases** such as *by the time*, *when*, *while*, *as soon as*, *before*, *after*, and *since*. A time clause by itself is not a complete sentence. When you write sentences with time clauses, avoid sentence fragments (incomplete sentences) by **connecting the time clause to a main clause**.

EXAMPLES:

Sentence Fragment	Complete Sentence
TIME CLAUSE	TIME CLAUSE + MAIN CLAUSE
~~As soon as I find a job.~~ →	*As soon as* I find a job, **I'll move**.
TIME CLAUSE	MAIN CLAUSE + TIME CLAUSE
~~Since I moved.~~ →	**I've been much happier** *since* I moved.

Notice that the time clause can come first or second. When it comes first, a **comma** separates the two clauses.

1 | *Read this letter. Correct the sentence fragments by connecting the time clause to a main clause. Use appropriate punctuation and capitalization.*

December 10, 2012

Hi Jamie,

As of today, I'm a working man! ~~By the time you get this letter.~~ *By the time you get this letter,* I'll have been taking tickets at Cine Moderne for more than a week. It's going to be hard to work and go to school full time, but you'll understand why I'm doing it. When you hear my plans.

As soon as school ends. My brother Alex and I are going to take a trip to Greece and Turkey. I plan to buy a used car, and we'll camp most of the way. By the end of January, I'll have been saving for more than a year for this trip—and I'll have enough to buy a car.

Why don't you come with us? Your exams are over on May 31, but mine don't end until June 10. That means you'll have already finished. While I'm still taking my finals. Maybe you can come early and do some sightseeing until I'm ready to leave.

Alex has some business to complete. Before he goes on vacation. He won't have finished until July 15, but he can join us then.

I'm leaving Paris on June 17. I'll drive through Italy and take the ferry from Brindisi to Greece. I'll stay in Greece. Until Alex joins me. Just think, while your friends are in summer school, you could be swimming in the Aegean! We'll be leaving Greece. As soon as Alex arrives so we'll have a month in Turkey. We'll start back around August 20. Your classes won't have started by then, will they?

I hope you'll be able to join us for this trip. Alex is looking forward to seeing you again too.

Your friend,

Philippe

---

2 | *Complete the timeline with information from the letter in Exercise 1.*

December 10   *Philippe starts his new job.*

January 31

May 31

June 10

June 17

July 15

August 20

---

3 | *Before you write . . .*

1. Think about some plans you are making for the future.

2. Make a timeline about your plans like the one in Exercise 2.

3. Work with a partner. Discuss each other's plans. Use time clauses.

---

4 | *Write a letter to a friend about some plans you are making. Use information from your timeline. Remember to connect some of the events with time clauses.*

5 | *Exchange letters with a different partner. Underline the time clauses. Write a question mark* (**?**) *above any time clauses that seem wrong. Then answer the questions.*

	Yes	No
1. Are the time clauses part of complete sentences?	☐	☐
2. Are the sentences with time clauses punctuated correctly?	☐	☐
3. Are the verb forms correct in the sentences with time clauses?	☐	☐
4. Is the sequence of events clear?	☐	☐

5. What are some details you would like information about? _____

_____

_____

6 | *Work with your partner. Discuss each other's editing questions from Exercise 5. Then rewrite your own letter and make any necessary corrections.*

PART III

NEGATIVE QUESTIONS, TAG QUESTIONS, ADDITIONS AND RESPONSES

UNIT	GRAMMAR FOCUS	THEME
7	Negative *Yes / No* Questions and Tag Questions	Places to Live
8	Additions and Responses: *So, Too, Neither, Not either,* and *But*	Similarities and Differences

Negative *Yes / No* Questions and Tag Questions

PLACES TO LIVE

STEP 1 GRAMMAR IN CONTEXT

Before You Read

Look at the photos. Discuss the questions.

1. How do these places look to you?
2. Which one of these places would you like to visit or live in? Why?
3. What do you like about the town or city where you live? What don't you like?

Read

Read the on-the-street interviews reported in a travel magazine.

● **Life Abroad Magazine**

IT'S A GREAT PLACE TO LIVE, **ISN'T IT?**

Our reporters around the world interviewed people living in foreign countries. Our question: How do you like living here? Here's what we learned from Lydia Sousa, Kinoro Okaya, Anton Kada, and Tessa Bradley.

Rio de Janeiro, Brazil

● ●

Reporter: Excuse me. Do you speak English?

Sousa: Yes, I do. Hey! I've seen you on TV. . . . **Aren't you** Paul Logan?

Reporter: That's right. I'm conducting a survey for *Life Abroad Magazine*. You're not from Rio, **are you**?

Sousa: No, I'm not. I'm originally from Portugal. You could tell by my accent, **couldn't you?**

Reporter: Uh-huh. You don't speak English like a Brazilian. So, how do you like living here?

Sousa: I love it. Just look around you—the beach, the bay, the mountains, the sky. It's fantastic looking! I walk along this beach every day on the way to my office.

Reporter: It's not a bad way to get to work, **is it?**

Sousa: It's not a bad place to play either! Besides this beautiful beach, there are so many restaurants and clubs. It's a great place to live, **isn't it?**

IT'S A GREAT PLACE TO LIVE, **ISN'T IT?**

Cairo, Egypt

Reporter: This is one of the oldest markets in Cairo, **isn't it?**

Okaya: Yes, and one of the most interesting. Hey, **didn't you** buy anything?

Reporter: Not today. So, what brought you from Nairobi to Cairo?

Okaya: My job. I work for a company that provides Internet services for a lot of businesses here.

Reporter: It gets awfully hot here in the summer, **doesn't it?**

Okaya: Yes, but the winters are mild. And it almost never rains. You can't beat that,[1] **can you?**

Seoul, South Korea

Reporter: You're a student, **aren't you?**

Kada: No, actually, I'm a teacher. I'm teaching a course in architecture at the Kaywon School of Art and Design this semester.

Reporter: So, how do you like living here? **Doesn't the cold weather** bother you?

Kada: Not really. I'm from Berlin, so I'm used to it. I love this city. You can see skyscrapers right next to ancient structures.

Reporter: That's true. That's the old city gate over there, **isn't it?**

Kada: Yes. And there are several beautiful palaces nearby.

Reporter: You're from England, **aren't you?**

Bradley: Yes. I moved here 10 years ago.

Reporter: Was it a difficult adjustment?

Bradley: No, not really. First of all, having the same language makes things easy, **doesn't it?** And people here are very friendly.

Reporter: Why Canada?

Bradley: England's a very small country. I was attracted by Canada's wide-open spaces. It seems to offer endless possibilities.

Vancouver, Canada

[1] **You can't beat that:** Nothing is better than that.

After You Read

A | Vocabulary: *Circle the letter of the word or phrase that best completes each sentence.*

1. A _____ is NOT an example of a **structure**.
   a. bridge
   b. building
   c. beach

2. Foreigners living abroad often have a difficult **adjustment** because of _____.
   a. friendly people
   b. good weather
   c. a different language

3. If you're **originally** from South Korea, you _____.
   a. were born there
   b. still live there
   c. have relatives there

4. If something **bothers** you, it makes you feel _____.
   a. good
   b. bad
   c. fantastic

5. If you are **attracted** to something, you want to _____ it.
   a. avoid
   b. change
   c. get to know

6. If someone **provides** you with information, he or she _____ information.
   a. wants
   b. gives you
   c. corrects

B | Comprehension: *Check (✓)* **True** *or* **False**. *Correct the false statements.*

	True	False
1. Lydia Sousa doesn't know the reporter.	☐	☐
2. The reporter thinks Sousa is from Rio.	☐	☐
3. The reporter bought a lot of things at the Cairo market.	☐	☐
4. The reporter doesn't think the cold weather bothers Kada.	☐	☐
5. The reporter thinks Tessa Bradley comes from Canada.	☐	☐
6. The move was not a difficult adjustment for Bradley.	☐	☐

NEGATIVE *YES / NO* QUESTIONS

With *Be* as the Main Verb

Questions	Short Answers	
Be + *Not* + Subject	**Affirmative**	**Negative**
Aren't you from Rio de Janeiro?	**Yes**, I **am**.	**No**, I'm **not**.

With All Auxiliary Verbs Except *Do*

Questions	Short Answers			
Auxiliary + *Not* + Subject + Verb	**Affirmative**		**Negative**	
Aren't you moving?	**Yes**,	I **am**.	**No**,	I'm **not**.
Hasn't he been here before?		he **has**.		he **hasn't**.
Can't they move tomorrow?		they **can**.		they **can't**.

With *Do* as the Auxiliary Verb

Questions	Short Answers			
Do + *Not* + Subject + Verb	**Affirmative**		**Negative**	
Doesn't he live here?	**Yes**,	he **does**.	**No**,	he **doesn't**.
Didn't they move last year?		they **did**.		they **didn't**.

TAG QUESTIONS

With *Be* as the Main Verb

Affirmative Statement	Negative Tag
Subject + *Be*	*Be* + *Not* + Subject
You're from Rio,	**aren't you?**

Negative Statement	Affirmative Tag
Subject + *Be* + *Not*	*Be* + Subject
You're not from Rio,	**are you?**

With All Auxiliary Verbs Except *Do*

Affirmative Statement	Negative Tag
Subject + Auxiliary	Auxiliary + *Not* + Subject
You're moving,	**aren't you?**
He's been here before,	**hasn't he?**
They can move tomorrow,	**can't they?**

Negative Statement	Affirmative Tag
Subject + Auxiliary + *Not*	Auxiliary + Subject
You're not moving,	**are you?**
He hasn't been here before,	**has he?**
They can't move tomorrow,	**can they?**

With *Do* as an Auxiliary Verb

Affirmative Statement	Negative Tag
Subject + Verb	*Do* + *Not* + Subject
He lives here,	**doesn't he?**
They moved last year,	**didn't they?**

Negative Statement	Affirmative Tag
Subject + *Do* + *Not* + Verb	*Do* + Subject
He doesn't live here,	**does he?**
They didn't move,	**did they?**

GRAMMAR NOTES

1 Use **negative *yes / no* questions** and **tag questions** to:

    a. check information you believe is true

- **Doesn't Anton** live in Seoul?
- Anton lives in Seoul, **doesn't he?**
  (The speaker believes that Anton lives in Seoul.)

    b. comment on a situation

- **Isn't it** a nice day?
- It's a nice day, **isn't it?**
  (The speaker is commenting on the weather.)

2 Like affirmative *yes / no* questions, **negative *yes / no* questions** begin with a form of *be* or an auxiliary verb, such as *have, do, will, can,* or *should.*

- **Aren't you** Paul Logan?
- **Haven't I** seen you on TV?
- **Don't you** like the weather here?
- **Won't you** be sorry to leave?
- **Can't you** stay longer?

We almost always use **contractions** in negative questions.

- **Shouldn't we** think about moving?
  Not: ~~Should we not~~ think about moving?

BE CAREFUL! Use *are* (not *am*) in negative questions with *I* and a contraction.

- **Aren't I** right?
  Not: ~~Am'nt~~ I right?

3 Form **tag questions** with **statement + tag**. The statement expresses an **assumption**. The tag means *Right?* or *Isn't that true?*

STATEMENT	TAG

- You're Paul Logan, **aren't you?**
  (You're Paul Logan, right?)
- You're not from Cairo, **are you?**
  (You're not from Cairo. Isn't that true?)

    a. If the statement verb is affirmative, the tag verb is negative.

AFFIRMATIVE	NEGATIVE

- You **work** on Thursdays, **don't** you?

    b. If the statement verb is negative, the tag verb is affirmative.

NEGATIVE	AFFIRMATIVE

- You **don't work** on Thursdays, **do** you?

Form **the tag** with a form of *be* or an auxiliary verb, such as *have, do, will, can,* or *should.* Use the **same auxiliary** that is in the statement.

- It's a nice day, **isn't** it?
- There **are** good schools here, **aren't** there?
- You**'ve** lived here a long time, **haven't** you?

If the statement does not use *be* or an auxiliary verb, use an appropriate form of *do* in the tag.

- You **come** from London, **don't** you?

We almost always use **contractions** in the tag.

- You **can** drive, **can't** you?
  Not: You can drive, ~~can you not~~?

BE CAREFUL! In the tag, only use **pronouns**.

When the subject of the statement is **this** or **that**, the subject of the tag is **it**.

- **Tom** works here, doesn't **he?**
  Not: Tom works here, doesn't ~~Tom~~?
- **That's** a good idea, isn't **it?**
  Not: That's a good idea, isn't ~~that~~?

(continued on next page)

4 Use **tag questions** in conversations when you **expect the other person to agree** with you. In this type of tag question, the <u>voice falls</u> on the tag.

Use this type of tag question to:

a. **check** information you believe is correct. You expect the other person to answer (and agree).

b. **comment** on a situation. This type of tag question is more like a statement than a question. The other person can just nod or say *uh-huh* to show that he or she is listening and agrees.

A: It's getting warmer, **isn't it?**
B: Uh-huh. Seems more like spring than winter.

A: It doesn't snow here, **does it?**
B: No, never. That's why I love it.

A: Beautiful day, **isn't it?**
B: Uh-huh. The weather here is great.

---

5 **Tag questions** can also be used when you want to **check information**. This type of tag question is more like a *yes / no* question. You want to confirm your information because you are not sure it is correct. Like a *yes / no* question, the <u>voice rises</u> on the tag, and you usually get an answer.

USAGE NOTE: Even though you expect an answer, these questions for information are <u>different from</u> <u>*yes / no* questions</u>.
a. In *yes / no* **questions**, you <u>have no idea of the</u> <u>answer</u>.
b. In **tag questions**, <u>you have an opinion</u> that you want to check.

A: You're not moving, **are you?**
    (Are you moving?)
B: Yes. I'm returning to Berlin. OR
    No. I'm staying here.

- **Do you** live in Vancouver?
  (I don't know if you live in Vancouver.)
- You live in Vancouver, **don't you?**
  (I think you live in Vancouver, but I'm not sure.)

---

6 **Answer negative *yes / no* questions** and **tag questions** the same way you answer affirmative *yes / no* questions. The answer is *yes* if the information is correct and *no* if the information is not correct.

A: **Don't you** work in Vancouver?
B: **Yes, I do.** I've worked there for years. OR
    That's right.

A: You work in Vancouver, **don't you?**
B: **No, I don't.** I work in Montreal.

EXERCISE 1: Discover the Grammar

Read this conversation between Anton Kada's mother, Petra, and a Canadian neighbor, Ken.
Underline all the negative **yes** / **no** *questions and circle all the tags.*

PETRA: Hi, Ken. Nice day, (isn't it)?

KEN: Sure is. What are you doing home today? <u>Don't you usually work on Thursdays?</u>

PETRA: I took the day off to help my son. He just got back to Berlin, and he's looking for an apartment. You don't know of any vacant apartments, do you?

KEN: Isn't he going to stay with you?

PETRA: Well, he just got a new job at an architecture firm downtown, and he wants a place of his own in a quiet neighborhood. Do you know of anything?

KEN: As a matter of fact, I do. The Edwards family lives in a nice residential neighborhood near the river. You know them, don't you?

PETRA: Yes, I think Anton went to school with their son. But they're not moving, are they?

KEN: Yes, they're moving back to Vancouver next month.

PETRA: Are they? What kind of apartment do they have?

KEN: A one-bedroom. It's very nice. The owner is Canadian too.

PETRA: It's not furnished, is it? Anton really doesn't have any furniture.

KEN: Can't he rent some? I did that in my first apartment.

PETRA: I don't know. Isn't it less expensive to buy?

A quiet residential neighborhood in Berlin

EXERCISE 2: Affirmative and Negative Tag Questions

(Grammar Note 3)

Mr. and Mrs. Edwards are talking about their move to Vancouver. Match the statements with
the tags.

	Statements		Tags
_f_	**1.** You've called the movers,	**a.**	do we?
_____	**2.** They're coming tomorrow,	**b.**	isn't it?
_____	**3.** This isn't going to be cheap,	**c.**	don't they?
_____	**4.** You haven't finished packing,	**d.**	have you?
_____	**5.** We don't need any more boxes,	**e.**	is it?
_____	**6.** We need to disconnect the phone,	**f.**	haven't you?
_____	**7.** The movers provide boxes for us,	**g.**	don't we?
_____	**8.** Moving is hard,	**h.**	aren't they?

EXERCISE 3: Affirmative and Negative Tags

(Grammar Note 3)

Complete this interview with Tessa Bradley. Use appropriate tags.

HOST: You're originally from England, _____*aren't you*_____?
1.

BRADLEY: Yes. I'm from London.

HOST: You've lived in Vancouver for many years, _____?
2.

BRADLEY: Since I came here to teach video arts. Seems like ages ago. Looking back now, I can't

believe I just packed one suitcase and got on a plane.

HOST: You didn't know anyone here either, _____?
3.

BRADLEY: No. And I didn't have a cent to my name. Just some ideas and a lot of hope. It sounds

crazy, _____?
4.

HOST: Not when you look at all the TV shows you've done. Things have sure worked out for you,

_____? You've already worked on two big TV series, and you've done some
5.

work for the movies as well. You're working on another show now, _____?
6.

BRADLEY: Yes. It's a comedy about some kids who become invisible.

HOST: Sounds like a good show for the whole family. I know I'll certainly take my kids to see it.

Speaking of kids, you have some of your own, _____?
7.

BRADLEY: Two boys and a girl—all very visible!

HOST: I know what you mean. Do you ever wish they were invisible?

BRADLEY: Hmm. That's an interesting thought, _____?
8.

EXERCISE 4: Negative *Yes / No* Questions and Short Answers

(Grammar Notes 2, 6)

Anton Kada is looking at the apartment the Edwardses just left. Complete the negative
yes / no *questions. Write short answers. Use the verbs that are in the sentences following*
the short answers.

1. **OWNER:** Hi, you look familiar. _____ *Isn't your name* _____ John Radcliffe?

    KADA: _____ *No, it isn't.* _____ My name is Anton Kada.

2. **OWNER:** Oh. _____ this apartment before?

    KADA: _____ I've never seen it before. This is the first time.

3. **KADA:** _____ the previous tenants from Vancouver?

    OWNER: _____ They just moved back there.

4. **KADA:** The apartment feels hot. _____ an air conditioner?

    OWNER: _____ I don't provide one. But there is a fan.

5. **KADA:** I notice that there are marks on the walls. _____ it?

    OWNER: _____ I'm going to paint it next week.

6. **OWNER:** _____ a nice apartment?

    KADA: _____ It's very nice. But I'm not sure I can take it.

7. **OWNER:** _____ big enough?

    KADA: _____ It's big enough, but I can't afford it.

EXERCISE 5: Negative *Yes / No* Questions and Tag Questions

(Grammar Notes 1–3)

Rewrite the sentences. Change the sentence in parentheses into a negative question or
a tag question.

ROLAND: Hi, Tessa. _____ *Isn't it a nice day?* OR *It's a nice day, isn't it?* _____

1. (I think it's a nice day.)

TESSA: It sure is. _____

2. (I think you have class today.)

ROLAND: I do. But not until 3:00. _____

3. (I think it's only 2:30 now.)

TESSA: You're right. You have plenty of time. _____

4. (I'm surprised you don't have your bike with you.)

ROLAND: I lost it. That's why I'm walking.

TESSA: Well, it's a nice day for a walk. _____

5. (I think Vancouver is a beautiful city.)

ROLAND: Yes. And a great city for video artists. _____

6. (I'm pretty sure you're coming to see my film tonight.)

TESSA: I wouldn't miss it. Hey, _____? We took the wrong path.

7. (I'm pretty sure your class is that way.)

EXERCISE 6: Negative *Yes / No* Questions and Tag Questions

(Grammar Notes 1–3)

Read this information about video artist Nam-June Paik. Imagine you are going to interview his agent, and you are not sure of the information in parentheses. Write negative **yes / no** questions or tag questions to check that information.

1. born July 1932 in Korea (in Seoul?)
2. at age 14, studied music (took piano lessons?)
3. family left Korea in 1950 (moved to Tokyo?)
4. moved to Germany in 1956 (originally studied music composition there?)
5. attracted to electronic music (wrote traditional music?)
6. during the 1960s created a new art form with TV screens and video (painted on paper?)
7. produced a huge art installation for 1988 Seoul Olympics (the structure used 1,003 TV monitors?)
8. after an illness in 1996 started painting on flat surfaces (did installations after that?)
9. lived in New York (became a U.S. citizen?)
10. died in January 2006 in Florida (was 75 years old?)

Nam-June Paik with his video art

1. <u>Wasn't he born in Seoul?</u> OR <u>He was born in Seoul, wasn't he?</u>
2. _____
3. _____
4. _____
5. _____
6. _____
7. _____
8. _____
9. _____
10. _____

EXERCISE 7: Editing

Tessa Bradley is working on a script for a movie that takes place in Vancouver. There are ten mistakes in the use of negative **yes** / **no** *questions, tag questions, and short answers. The first mistake is already corrected. Find and correct nine more.*

BEN: It's been a long time, Joe, ~~haven't~~ *hasn't* it?

JOE: That depends on what you mean by a long time, doesn't that?

BEN: Are not you afraid to show your face here in Vancouver?

JOE: I can take care of myself. I'm still alive, amn't I?

BEN: Until someone recognizes you. You're still wanted by the police, are you? Don't that bother you?

JOE: I'll be gone by morning. Look, I need a place to stay. Just for one night.

BEN: I have to think about my wife and kid. Don't you have any place else to go?

JOE: Yes, I do. There's no one to turn to but you. You have to help me.

BEN: I've already helped you plenty. I went to jail for you, haven't I? And didn't I kept my mouth shut the whole time?

JOE: Yeah, OK, Ben. Don't you remember what happened in Vegas, do you?

BEN: Don't ever think I'll forget that! OK, OK. I can make a call.

STEP 4 COMMUNICATION PRACTICE

EXERCISE 8: Pronunciation

A | *Read and listen to the Pronunciation Note.*

Pronunciation Note

In **tag questions**:

The **voice rises** at the end when the speaker **expects the other person to give information**.

Example: **A:** He's a student, **isn't he?**
B: Yes, he goes to my college.

The **voice falls** at the end when the speaker is making a comment and **expects the other person to agree**.

Example: **A:** Seoul's interesting, **isn't it?**
B: Uh-huh.

B | *Read the tag questions. Then listen to them and decide if the voice rises (↗) or falls (↘) at the end of the tag. Draw the correct arrow over the tag.*

1. You're originally from Vancouver, aren't you?
2. It's a beautiful city, isn't it?
3. It's been a big adjustment, hasn't it?
4. That building isn't new, is it?
5. It doesn't have any vacancies, does it?
6. You haven't lived there very long, have you?
7. You don't know Anne, do you?
8. She works around here, doesn't she?
9. It's near the river, isn't it?
10. It's a great place to live, isn't it?

C | *Listen again to the tag questions and repeat.*

EXERCISE 9: Listening

🎧 **A** | *Listen to the people ask questions. Notice if their voices rise or fall at the end of each question. Then listen again and decide if the speaker expects the other person to give information or just expects the other person to agree. Check (✓) the correct column.*

	Expects Information	Expects Agreement
1.	☑	☐
2.	☐	☐
3.	☐	☐
4.	☐	☐
5.	☐	☐
6.	☐	☐
7.	☐	☐
8.	☐	☐
9.	☐	☐
10.	☐	☐

🎧 **B** | *Read the statements. Listen again to the conversations and decide if the statements are* **True** *or* **False**. *Check (✓) the correct boxes.*

		True	False
1.	The man wants to know if Rio is the capital of Brazil.	☑	☐
2.	The man thinks Rio has an exciting night life.	☐	☐
3.	The woman wants to know if Anton was teaching a course in Korea.	☐	☐
4.	The woman wants to know if it is hard to find an apartment in Berlin.	☐	☐
5.	The first man wants to know if the second man speaks Arabic.	☐	☐
6.	The second man is asking about the traffic.	☐	☐
7.	The woman thinks Anne is from Vancouver.	☐	☐
8.	The woman wants to know if the man is from Vancouver.	☐	☐
9.	The man is commenting on the weather.	☐	☐
10.	The man is surprised that the woman was in Scotland.	☐	☐

EXERCISE 10: Information Gap: London and Vancouver

Work in pairs (A and B). **Student B,** *go to page 116 and follow the instructions there.* **Student A,** *look at the questions below. What do you know about London? Complete the questions by circling the correct words and writing the tags.*

1. London is / isn't the largest city in the United Kingdom, _____*isn't it*_____?

2. It is / isn't the capital of the United Kingdom, _____?

3. London lies on a river / the ocean, _____?

4. It consists of two / thirty-two "boroughs," or parts, _____?

5. It has / doesn't have a lot of theaters, _____?

6. Many / Not many tourists visit London, _____?

7. It is / isn't a very safe city, _____?

Ask Student B the questions. Student B will read a paragraph about London and tell you if your information is correct or not.

EXAMPLE: **A:** London is the largest city in the United Kingdom, isn't it?
            B: That's right.

Now read about Vancouver and answer Student B's questions.

VANCOUVER

Vancouver is the third largest city in Canada. Lying on the Pacific coast, it is surrounded on three sides by water and has the largest and busiest seaport in the country. It is also home to Stanley Park, one of the largest city parks in North America. Because of its great natural and architectural beauty and its moderate climate, Vancouver is a very popular place to live. It also attracts millions of tourists each year. It is a very international city, and more than 50 percent of its residents do not speak English as their first language. Today Vancouver is called the "Hollywood of the North" because of the number of films made in this exciting city.

EXAMPLE: **B:** Vancouver isn't the largest city in Canada, is it?
            A: No, it isn't. It's the third largest city.

EXERCISE 11: Conversation

How well do you know your classmates? Work with a partner. Complete the questions with information about your partner that you think is correct. Then ask the questions to check your information. Check (✓) each question that has the correct information. Which one of you knows the other one better?

EXAMPLES: **A:** You're from Venezuela, aren't you?
B: That's right. OR No, I'm from Colombia.

_____ 1. _____, aren't you?

_____ 2. Don't you _____?

_____ 3. _____, haven't you?

_____ 4. _____, did you?

_____ 5. _____, do you?

_____ 6. Aren't you _____?

_____ 7. _____, will you?

_____ 8. Didn't you _____?

EXERCISE 12: Writing

A | *You are going to interview a classmate about his or her city. Write eight questions. Use negative **yes** / **no** questions and tag questions. Ask your questions and take notes on your classmate's answers.*

EXAMPLE: You're originally from Venezuela, aren't you? *yes–Caracas*
Isn't that the capital? *yes*

B | *Write up the interview.*

EXAMPLE: INTERVIEWER: You're originally from Venezuela, aren't you?
MIGUEL: Yes, I am. I'm from Caracas.
INTERVIEWER: Isn't that the capital?
MIGUEL: Yes, it is.

C | *Check your work. Use the Editing Checklist.*

Editing Checklist

Did you use . . . ?
☐ contractions in negative *yes* / *no* questions
☐ contractions in tags
☐ negative tags with affirmative statements
☐ affirmative tags with negative statements
☐ the same auxiliary in the tag and in the statement
☐ *it* in the tag when the statement used **this** or **that**

Student B, read about London and answer Student A's questions.

LONDON

London is the capital and largest city of the United Kingdom. It is also one of the oldest and largest cities in the world. Located in southeastern England, the city lies on the River Thames, which links it to shipping routes throughout the world. Because of its size, the city is divided into 32 "boroughs" or parts. With its many museums, palaces, parks, and theaters, tourism is a major industry. In fact, millions of tourists visit the city every year to take advantage of its many cultural and historical offerings. Unfortunately, like many great urban centers, London has problems such as traffic congestion, crime, and homelessness.

> **EXAMPLE:** **A:** London is the largest city in the United Kingdom, isn't it?
> **B:** That's right.

Now look at the questions below. What do you know about Vancouver? Circle the correct words and complete the tag questions.

1. Vancouver is / isn't the largest city in Canada, _____ *is it* _____?

2. It lies / doesn't lie on the Atlantic Coast, _____?

3. It has / doesn't have a very large port, _____?

4. It is / isn't a very beautiful city, _____?

5. Many / Not many tourists visit the city, _____?

6. You can / can't hear many different languages there, _____?

7 Movie production is / isn't an important industry in Vancouver, _____?

Ask Student A the questions. Student A will read a paragraph about Vancouver and tell you if your information is correct or not.

> **EXAMPLE:** **B:** Vancouver isn't the largest city in Canada, is it?
> **A:** No, it isn't. It's the third largest city.

Check your answers on page UR-2.

Do you need to review anything?

A | *Circle the correct words to complete the sentences.*

1. It's a beautiful day, <u>isn't</u> / <u>is</u> it?

2. <u>Didn't</u> / <u>Aren't</u> you order coffee?

3. You<u>'ve</u> / <u>haven't</u> heard from Raoul recently, haven't you?

4. That was a great movie, wasn't <u>that</u> / <u>it</u>?

5. <u>Hasn't</u> / <u>Didn't</u> he lived in Vancouver for several years?

6. Lara can't move out of her apartment yet, can <u>Lara</u> / <u>she</u>?

7. <u>Shouldn't</u> / <u>Should not</u> we leave soon? It's getting late.

B | *Complete the conversation with negative* **yes** / **no** *questions and tag questions. Use the correct verbs and short answers.*

A: You _____ lived in Vancouver for very long, have you?
                1.

B: _____. Only for a month. _____ you tell by the way I'm dressed?
      2.   **3.**

A: I sure can. But it's warm today! You're not really *that* cold, _____ you?
                                       4.

B: _____! But I'm originally from Rio de Janeiro. I'll get used to this,
      5.

_____ I?
    6.

A: _____. It won't take long, and winter here isn't very cold. This is a great city.
      7.

C | *Find and correct six mistakes.*

A: Ken hasn't come back from Korea yet, has Ken?

B: No, he has. He got back last week. Didn't he call you when he got back?

A: No, he didn't. He's probably busy. There are a lot of things to do when you move, isn't it?

B: Definitely. And I guess his family wanted to spend a lot of time with him, won't they?

A: I'm sure they will. You know, I think I'll just call him. You have his phone number, have you?

B: Yes, I do. Could you wait while I get it off my computer? You're not in a hurry, aren't you?

STEP 1 GRAMMAR IN CONTEXT

Before You Read

Look at the photos of twins. Discuss these questions.

1. What is different about them? What is the same?
2. How are you similar to family members? How are you different?

Read

Read the article about identical twins.

The TWIN Question:
Nature or Nurture?

by Ruth Sanborn, *Family Life* Editor

MARK AND GERALD are identical twins. Mirror images of each other, they also share many similarities in lifestyle. Mark was a firefighter, and **so was Gerald**. Mark has never been married, and **neither has Gerald**. Mark likes hunting, fishing, and old movies. **Gerald does too**.

These similarities might not be unusual in identical twins, except that Mark and Gerald were separated when they were five days old. They grew up in different states with different families. Neither one knew that he had a twin until they found each other at age 31.

Average people are fascinated by twins, and **so are scientists**. Identical twins share the same genes. Therefore, they offer researchers the chance to study the effect of genetic heredity on health and personality.

However, when identical twins grow up together, they also experience the same social environment.[1] How can researchers separate these environmental factors from genetic factors? By looking at identical twins who were separated at birth!

MARK AND GERALD

[1] ***social environment:*** the social conditions in which people live, for example: family members, religion, education, financial situation, location

The TWIN Question

JIM AND JIM

Twins with completely different childhoods give researchers the chance to study the age-old question: Which has more effect on our lives—heredity (the genes we receive from our parents) or environment (the social influences on our childhood)? In other words: nature or nurture?

Some startling coincidences have turned up in these studies. One astonishing pair is the Springer and Lewis brothers, who were adopted by different families soon after birth. The Springer family named their adopted son Jim. **So did the Lewis family**. When the two Jims met for the first time as adults, they discovered more surprising similarities. Jim Lewis had worked as a gas station attendant and a police officer. **So had Jim Springer**. Both men had owned dogs. Lewis had named his Toy; **so had Springer**. And believe it or not, Lewis had married a woman named Linda, divorced her, and later married a woman named Betty. **So had Springer**.

Do our genes really determine our names, our spouses, our jobs, even our pets? The lives of other twins indicate that the question of nature or nurture is even more complicated.

Identical twins Tamara Rabi and Adriana Scott, for example, were born in Mexico and separated at birth. Each girl was adopted by a different family from New York. Tamara grew up in the city with a Jewish family, but Adriana was raised Catholic in the suburbs. It wasn't until the age of 20 that the two sisters learned about each other and met for the very first time. The similarities were amazing. Apart from a light birthmark over Tamara's right eyebrow and the fact that Adriana had colored her hair lighter, the girls looked exactly the same. They even talked the same and had had the same nightmare since childhood.

TAMARA AND ADRIANA

There were other differences beyond the small physical ones, however. Tamara loves Chinese food, **but Adriana doesn't**. More importantly, Tamara is a very outgoing person, **but Adriana isn't**. She's very shy, despite her identical heredity. And although both girls grew up as only children, Adriana was more eager to get to know her sister after they first met. (Now, however, they consider each other a gift.)

Clearly, our heredity doesn't completely control our lives. Our **environment doesn't either**. The lives of twins separated at birth suggest that we have a lot to learn about the complex[2] role these two powerful forces play in shaping human lives.

---

[2] **complex:** difficult to understand because of its many connected parts

A | **Vocabulary:** *Complete the sentences with the words from the box.*

| coincidence | despite | factor | identical | image | outgoing |

1. Some parents like to dress their twins in _____ clothes. Others prefer to focus

   on differences.

2. What an amazing _____! My twin and I bought the same kind of car in the

   same color, on the same day.

3. When Don saw the _____ of his twin in the photo, he thought at first that he

   was looking at himself.

4. Karyn's sister is friendly and _____, but Karyn is quite shy.

5. _____ their similarities, the twins have very different personalities.

6. Mia's education was an important _____ in her success.

B | **Comprehension:** *Check (✓) the boxes to complete the sentences. Check **all** the true information from the article.*

1. Mark and Gerald have had the same _____.

   □ marriage histories   □ types of jobs   □ hobbies

2. By studying separated twins, scientists hope to discover the _____ twins.

   □ best environment for   □ effects of nature and   □ similarities between
   nurture on

3. The Springer and Lewis brothers have the same _____.

   □ first names   □ marriage histories   □ job histories

4. The question of nature or nurture is _____ to answer.

   □ easy   □ difficult   □ impossible

5. Tamara and Adriana do NOT have the same _____.

   □ food preferences   □ hair color   □ language

6. Heredity _____ our lives.

   □ partly controls   □ completely controls   □ has a weak effect on

SIMILARITY: *SO* AND *NEITHER*

Affirmative

Statement	Addition	
Subject + Verb	*And so*	**Verb* + Subject**
Amy *is* a twin,		*am* I.
She *has* **traveled**,	**and so**	*have* we.
She *can* **ski**,		*can* they.
She *likes* dogs,		*does* Bill.

*The verb in the addition is a form of *be*, an auxiliary, or a modal.

Negative

Statement	Addition	
Subject + Verb + *Not*	***And neither***	**Verb + Subject**
Amy *isn't* a twin,		*am* I.
She *hasn't* **traveled**,	**and neither**	*have* we.
She *can't* **ski**,		*can* they.
She *doesn't* **like** dogs,		*does* Bill.

SIMILARITY: *TOO* AND *NOT EITHER*

Affirmative

Statement	Addition	
Subject + Verb	*And*	**Subject + Verb + *Too***
Amy *is* a twin,		I *am* **too**.
She *has* **traveled**,	**and**	we *have* **too**.
She *can* **ski**,		they *can* **too**.
She *likes* dogs,		Bill *does* **too**.

Negative

Statement	Addition	
Subject + Verb + *Not*	*And*	**Subject + Verb + *Not either***
Amy *isn't* a twin		I'*m not* **either**.
She *hasn't* **traveled**,	**and**	we *haven't* **either**.
She *can't* **ski**,		they *can't* **either**.
She *doesn't* **like** dogs,		Bill *doesn't* **either**.

DIFFERENCE: *BUT*

Affirmative + Negative

Statement		Addition
Subject + Verb	***But***	**Subject + Verb + *Not***
Amy *is* a twin,		I*'m not.*
She *has* traveled,	but	we *haven't.*
She *can* ski,		they *can't.*
She *likes* dogs,		Bill *doesn't.*

Negative + Affirmative

Statement		Addition
Subject + Verb + *Not*	***But***	**Subject + Verb**
Amy *isn't* a twin,		I *am.*
She *can't* ski,	but	we *can.*
She *hasn't* traveled,		they *have.*
She *doesn't* like dogs,		Bill *does.*

GRAMMAR NOTES

1   **Additions** are clauses or short sentences that follow a statement. They express **similarity** or **difference** with the information in the statement. We use additions to <u>avoid repeating</u> information.

SIMILARITY:
- Bill bites his fingernails, **and so does Ed**.
  (Bill bites his fingernails. Ed bites his fingernails.)

DIFFERENCE:
- Ana lived in the city, **but Eva didn't**.
  (Ana lived in the city. Eva didn't live there.)

---

2   Use *so*, *too*, *neither*, or *not either* to express **similarity**. Additions of similarity can be **clauses** starting with *and*.

Additions of similarity can also be separate **sentences**.

   a. Use *so* or *too* if the addition follows an <u>affirmative</u> statement.

   b. Use *neither* or *not either* if the addition follows a <u>negative</u> statement.

BE CAREFUL! Notice the **word order** after *so* and *neither*. The verb comes before the subject.

CLAUSE
- Mark is a firefighter, **and *so* is Gerald**. OR
- Mark is a firefighter, **and Gerald is *too***.
  (Mark is a firefighter. Gerald is a firefighter.)

SENTENCE
- Mark isn't married. ***Neither* is Gerald**. OR
- Mark isn't married. **Gerald *isn't either***.
  (Mark isn't married. Gerald isn't married.)

AFFIRMATIVE STATEMENT
- Mark **is** a firefighter, and **so is** Gerald.
- Mark **is** a firefighter, and Gerald **is too**.

NEGATIVE STATEMENT
- Mark **didn't** marry. ***Neither* did** Gerald.
- Mark **didn't** marry. Gerald **did*n't* either**.

- So **is Gerald**. NOT: So ~~Gerald is~~.
- Neither **did Gerald**. NOT: Neither ~~Gerald did~~.

---

3   Use *but* in additions that show **difference**.
   a. If the statement is <u>affirmative</u>, the addition is <u>negative</u>.

   b. If the statement is <u>negative</u>, the addition is <u>affirmative</u>.

AFFIRMATIVE   **NEGATIVE**
- Ana **has** a birthmark, ***but*** Eva **doesn't**.
- Ana **lived** in Mexico, ***but*** Eva **didn't**.

NEGATIVE   **AFFIRMATIVE**
- Ana **doesn't like** to read, ***but*** Eva **does**.
- Ana **didn't** speak English, ***but*** Eva **did**.

---

4   **Additions** always use a form of *be*, an auxiliary verb, or a modal.
   a. If the statement uses *be*, use *be* in the addition.
   b. If the statement uses an auxiliary verb (*be*, *have*, *do*, or *will*), or a modal (*can*, *could*, *should*, *would*) use the **same auxiliary verb or modal** in the addition.
   c. If the statement doesn't use *be* or an auxiliary verb, use an appropriate form of *do* in the addition.

BE CAREFUL! The verb in the addition agrees with the subject of the addition.

- I**'m** a twin, and so **is** my cousin.
- Jim Lewis **had** worked in a gas station, and so **had** Jim Springer.
- I **can't** drive, and neither **can** my twin.

- Bill **bought** a Chevrolet, and so **did** Ed.
- Bill **owns** a dog, and so **does** Ed.

- They**'ve learned** Spanish, and so ***has*** she.
  NOT: They've learned Spanish, and so ~~have~~ she.

(continued on next page)

5 In conversation, you can use **short responses** with *so*, *too*, *neither*, *not either*, and *but*.

a. Use *so*, *too*, *neither*, and *not either* to express **agreement** with another speaker.

A: I like sports.
B: *So do I*. OR **I do *too*.**

A: I don't like sports.
B: *Neither* do I. OR **I don't *either*.**

USAGE NOTE: In **informal speech**, people say ***Me too*** to express agreement with an affirmative statement and ***Me neither*** to express agreement with a negative statement.

A: I think twin studies are fascinating.
B: *Me too*.
A: I've never heard of the Jim twins.
B: *Me neither*.

b. Use *but* to express **disagreement** with another speaker. You can often leave out *but*.

A: I wouldn't like to have a twin.
B: Oh, *(but)* **I would**.

STEP 3 FOCUSED PRACTICE

EXERCISE 1: Discover the Grammar

Read these short conversations between reunited twins. Decide if the statement that follows is **True (T)** *or* **False (F).**

1. **MARK:** I like Chinese food.

   GERALD: So do I.

   __T__ Gerald likes Chinese food.

2. **ADRIANA:** I don't want to go out tonight.

   TAMARA: Neither do I.

   _____ Tamara wants to go out tonight.

3. **AMY:** I didn't understand that article.

   KERRIE: Oh, I did.

   _____ Kerrie understood the article.

4. **JEAN:** I'm not hungry.

   JOAN: Me neither.

   _____ Jean and Joan are hungry.

5. **TAMARA:** I was nervous about our meeting.

   ADRIANA: So was I.

   _____ Tamara and Adriana were both nervous about their meeting.

6. **AMY:** I've always felt lonely.

   KERRIE: So have I.

   _____ Kerrie has felt lonely.

7. **MARK:** I'm pretty outgoing.

   GERALD: I'm not.

   _____ Gerald is outgoing.

8. **DAVE:** I can meet at eight o'clock.

   PETE: I can too.

   _____ Pete can meet at eight o'clock.

9. **JIM:** I have a headache.

   JIM: So do I.

   _____ Both Jims have headaches.

10. **DAVE:** I'm not looking forward to the TV interview.

    PETE: Oh, I am.

    _____ Pete isn't looking forward to the TV interview.

EXERCISE 2: Additions

(Grammar Notes 1–4)

Circle the correct words to complete the paragraph about being a twin.

Sometimes being a twin can cause trouble. In high school, I was in Mr. Jacobs's history class.

Neither / (So) was Joe. One day we took a test. The results were identical. I got questions 18 and 20
   1.

wrong. Joe did so / too.
   2.

I didn't spell *Constantinople* correctly, and either / neither did Joe. The teacher was sure we had
   3.

cheated. As a result, I got an F on the test, and so did / got Joe. We tried to convince Mr. Jacobs
   4.

that it was just a coincidence. After all, I had sat on the left side of the room, but Joe didn't / hadn't.
   5.

As always, he sat on the right. But Mr. Jacobs just thought we had developed some complex

way of sharing answers across the room. Our parents believed we were honest, but Mr. Jacobs

didn't / weren't. The principal didn't either / too. We finally convinced them to give us another test.
   6.   **7.**

Despite the fact that we were in separate rooms so cheating *couldn't* be a factor, I got questions 3

and 10 wrong. Guess what? Neither / So did Joe. Our teacher was astounded, and / but we weren't.
   8.   **9.**

EXERCISE 3: Short Responses

(Grammar Note 5)

Two twins are talking. They agree on everything. Complete their conversation with short responses.

MARTA: I'm so happy we finally found each other.

CARLA: So _____*am I*_____. I always felt like something was missing from my life.
                      1.

MARTA: So _____. I always knew I had a double somewhere out there.
                      2.

CARLA: I can't believe how alike we look!

MARTA: Neither _____.
                      3.

CARLA: And we like and dislike all the same things.

MARTA: Right. I hate lettuce.

CARLA: I _____. And I detest liver.
                 4.

MARTA: So _____. I love pizza, though.
                      5.

CARLA: So _____. Especially with mushrooms. But I can't stand pepperoni.
                      6.

MARTA: Neither _____.
                      7.

CARLA: This is amazing! I'd like to find out if our husbands have a lot in common too.

MARTA: So _____! That would be quite a coincidence!
                      8.

EXERCISE 4: Additions: Similarity or Difference

(Grammar Notes 1–4)

Look at this chart about the twins' husbands. Then complete the sentences about them. Add statements with **so, too, neither, not either,** *and* **but.**

	Bob	**Randy**
AGE	32	32
HEIGHT	6'2"	6'
WEIGHT	160 lb	160 lb
HAIR COLOR	blond	blond
EYE COLOR	blue	brown
HOBBIES	tennis	tennis
FAVORITE FOOD	steak	steak
MILITARY SERVICE	yes	no
EDUCATION	graduate degree	graduate degree
LANGUAGES	English, Spanish	English, French
JOB	lawyer	engineer
BROTHERS OR SISTERS	none	none

1. Bob is 32, *and so is Randy*. OR *and Randy is too.* _____

2. Bob is 6'2", _____

3. Bob weighs 160 pounds, _____

4. Bob has blond hair, _____

5. Bob doesn't have green eyes, _____

6. Bob plays tennis, _____

7. Bob likes steak, _____

8. Bob served in the military, _____

9. Bob has attended graduate school, _____

10. Bob doesn't speak French, _____

11. Bob became a lawyer, _____

12. Bob doesn't have any brothers or sisters, _____

EXERCISE 5: Editing

Read Ryan's composition. There are five mistakes in the use of sentence additions. The first mistake is already corrected. Find and correct four more.

My Brother and I

My brother is just a year older than I am. (I'm 18.) We have a lot of things in common. We look alike. In fact, sometimes people ask us if we're twins. I am 5'10", and so ~~he is~~ *is he*. I have straight black hair and dark brown eyes. So does he. We share some of the same interests too. I love to play soccer, and he too. Both of us swim every day, but I can't dive, and either can he.

Although there are a lot of similarities between us, there are also many differences. For example, he likes eating all kinds of food, but I don't. Give me hamburgers and fries every day! My brother doesn't want to go to college, but I don't. I believe it's important to get as much education as possible, but he wants to get real-life experience. I think our personalities are an important factor in these choices. I am quiet and easygoing, but he doesn't. He's very outgoing and talks a lot. When I think about it, despite the many things we have in common, we really are more different than similar.

EXERCISE 6: Understanding Additions

(Grammar Notes 1–4)

Look at Exercise 5. Complete the chart by checking (✓) the correct column(s).

	Ryan	Ryan's Brother
1. is 18 years old	✓	☐
2. is 5'10" tall	☐	☐
3. has black hair	☐	☐
4. has dark brown eyes	☐	☐
5. loves soccer	☐	☐
6. swims	☐	☐
7. dives	☐	☐
8. prefers hamburgers and fries	☐	☐
9. wants to go to college	☐	☐
10. prefers real-life experience	☐	☐
11. is quiet and easygoing	☐	☐

EXERCISE 7: Listening

A | *A couple is on a date. Read the sentences. Then listen to their conversation. Listen again and circle the correct words to complete each statement.*

1. The man and woman know /don't know each other very well.

2. They're eating dinner at the woman's home / in a restaurant.

3. She likes to cook the same / new recipes.

4. Both people probably prefer to read mystery stories / history.

5. They probably won't play tennis / go on another date together.

6. They're going to watch a movie / TV show at eight o'clock.

B | *Look at the information. Listen again to the couple's conversation. Check (✓) the correct box(es).*

	Man	Woman			Man	Woman
1. loves Italian food	✓	✓	6. enjoys fiction		☐	☐
2. cooks	☐	☐	7. plays sports		☐	☐
3. eats out a lot	☐	☐	8. watches sports on TV		☐	☐
4. enjoys old movies	☐	☐	9. watches news programs		☐	☐
5. reads biographies	☐	☐	10. wants to see the documentary		☐	☐

EXERCISE 8: Pronunciation

A | *Read and listen to the Pronunciation Note.*

> **Pronunciation Note**
>
> In **additions** and **short responses** of **similarity**, we usually **stress** *so*, *neither*, *too*, *either* and the **subject** of the addition. We do NOT stress the verb.
>
> EXAMPLES: **A:** Maya is a student, **and so am I**.
>
> **B:** She doesn't spend much time studying.
>
> **A:** **I don't either**.
>
> In **additions** and **short responses** that show **difference**, we usually **stress** the **subject** and the **verb**. We do NOT stress *but*.
>
> EXAMPLES: **A:** My brother loves baseball, **but I don't**.
>
> **B:** And you love to swim.
>
> **A:** **But he doesn't**.

1. **A:** I really enjoyed the show.

   B: So did I.

2. **A:** My friends haven't seen it yet.

   B: Mine haven't either.

3. **A:** Did you go dancing with Sue and Kate last night?

   B: Just with Sue. Sue loves to dance, **but Kate doesn't**.

4. **A:** I don't like to watch TV for very long.

   B: Neither do I. Want to take a walk?

5. **A:** Your friend Bob's a twin, **and I am too**.

   B: You're a twin? I didn't know that.

6. **A:** My twin isn't identical.

   B: Oh, **Bob's is**. His name is Steve.

7. **A:** They both love music. Bob plays the piano.

   B: So does Steve.

8. **A:** It's getting late. I should go home pretty soon.

   B: I should too. Let's get together again sometime.

🎧 **C** | *Listen again and repeat the short responses and additions. Then practice the conversations with a partner.*

EXERCISE 9: Discussion

Work in small groups. Look at Exercise 7. Do you think that the man and woman are a good match? Is it important for couples to have a lot in common? What other factors are important in a good match?

EXAMPLE: **A:** The man and woman have a lot in common.
   B: He loves Italian food, and so does she. I think they're a good match.
   C: Oh, but I don't. The woman doesn't . . .

EXERCISE 10: Picture Discussion

Work with a partner. Look at the picture of reunited twins. Imagine their conversations. You can use these topics or your own.

- abilities
- appearance
- childhood
- clothes
- education
- food preferences
- health
- hobbies
- language
- marriage history
- occupation
- personality

EXAMPLE: **A:** I drink a lot of soda.
B: So do I.

EXERCISE 11: Find Someone Who . . .

A *Complete these statements. Then read your statements to a classmate. He or she will give you a short response. Check (✓) the items the two of you have in common. Then do the same with another classmate.*

EXAMPLE: **A:** I like to walk in the rain.
B: So do I. OR Oh, I don't. I like to stay home and watch TV.

I have these things in common with:

	(Classmate 1)	(Classmate 2)
1. I like to _____.	☐	☐
2. I never _____.	☐	☐
3. I love _____. (name of food)	☐	☐
4. I can't _____.	☐	☐
5. I would like to _____.	☐	☐
6. I've never _____.	☐	☐
7. When I was younger, I didn't _____.	☐	☐
8. I'll never _____.	☐	☐

B *Count the number of checkmarks for each of the two classmates. Which classmate do you have more in common with?*

EXERCISE 12: Compare and Contrast

Work with a partner. Look at the pictures of these twins. How many things do they have in common? How many differences can you find? You have eight minutes to write your answers. Then compare your answers with those of another pair.

Michael

Matthew

EXAMPLE: Michael has a mustache, and so does Matthew.

EXERCISE 13: What Do You Think?

Reread the article beginning on page 118. What do you think is more important, nature or nurture? Tell the class. Give examples to support your views.

EXAMPLE: In my opinion, nature is more important than nurture. For example, despite the fact that my brother and I grew up together, we're very different. He could throw a ball when he was only three, but I couldn't. I hate sports . . .

EXERCISE 14: Writing

A | *Write two paragraphs about two people who are close (twins or other siblings, cousins, friends, spouses, etc.). What do they have in common? What are their differences? Use* **so, too, neither, not either,** *and* **but.** *You can use Exercise 5 on page 127 as a model.*

EXAMPLE: My friends Marcia and Tricia are identical twins, but they work very hard to look different from each other. Marcia is 5'3", and so is Tricia. Marcia has black hair and brown eyes, and Tricia does too. However, Marcia wears her hair very short and loves lots of jewelry. Tricia doesn't. She . . .

B | *Check your work. Use the Editing Checklist.*

Editing Checklist
Did you use . . . ? ☐ *so*, *too*, *neither*, or *not either* to express similarity ☐ *so* or *too* after an affirmative statement ☐ *neither* or *not either* after a negative statement ☐ *but* to show difference ☐ the correct form of *be*, *have*, *do*, *will*, or a modal in the additions

A | *Circle the correct words to complete the sentences.*

1. Mary lives in Houston, and so <u>lives / does</u> Jan.

2. Doug moved to Florida. <u>So / Neither</u> did his brother.

3. Mia isn't married. Her sister <u>is too / isn't either</u>.

4. My friends play tennis, <u>but / so</u> I don't.

5. They speak French, but she <u>does / doesn't</u>.

6. Dan plays tennis, and I do <u>so / too</u>.

B | *Combine each pair of sentences. Use an addition with* **so, too, neither, not either,** *or* **but.**

1. I speak Spanish. My brother speaks Spanish.

   _____

2. Jaime lives in Chicago. His brother lives in New York.

   _____

3. Chicago is an exciting city. New York is an exciting city.

   _____

4. Chen doesn't play tennis. His sister plays tennis.

   _____

5. Diego doesn't eat meat. Lila doesn't eat meat.

   _____

C | *Find and correct nine mistakes.*

My friend Alicia and I have a lot in common. She comes from Los Angeles, and so I do.

She speaks Spanish. I speak too. Her parents are both teachers, but mine are too. (My mother

teaches math, and her father do too.) I don't have any brothers or sisters. Either does she. There

are some differences too. Alicia is very outgoing, and I'm not. I like to spend more time alone.

I don't enjoy sports, but she doesn't. She's on several school teams, but not I'm. I just think our

differences make things more interesting, and so my friend does!

From Grammar to Writing
AVOIDING REPETITION WITH SENTENCE ADDITIONS

When you write, one way to **avoid repetition** is to use **sentence additions**.

EXAMPLES: Brasília is a capital city. Washington, D.C. is a capital city. ➔
Brasília is a capital city, *and so* is Washington, D.C.

Brasília's shape is modern. Washington's shape isn't modern. ➔
Brasília's shape is modern, *but* Washington's isn't.

1 | *Read this student's essay comparing and contrasting Brasília and Washington, D.C. Underline once additions that express similarity. Underline twice additions that express contrast.*

BRASÍLIA AND WASHINGTON, D.C.

Citizens of Brasília and citizens of Washington, D.C. live on different continents, but their cities still have a lot in common. Brasília is its nation's capital, and so is Washington. Brasília did not exist before it was planned and built as the national capital. Neither did Washington. Both cities were designed by a single person, and both have a definite shape. However, 20th-century Brasília's shape is modern—that of an airplane—but the shape of 18th-century Washington isn't. Its streets form a wheel.

The cities reflect their differences in location and age. Brasília is located in a dry area in the highlands, while Washington was built on wet, swampy land. As a result, Brasília has moderate temperatures all year, but Washington doesn't. Washington is famous for its cold winters and hot, humid summers. Brasília was built 600 miles from the Atlantic coast in order to attract people to an unpopulated area. Washington, near the Atlantic coast, includes old towns that had already existed. Brasília is home to many famous theaters and museums, and so is the city of Washington. However, as a new city, Brasília has not yet become its nation's real cultural center. Washington hasn't either. Washington is its country's capital, but it is not its country's most popular city. Neither is Brasília. Many people still prefer the excitement of Rio and New York.

2 | *Before writing the essay in Exercise 1, the student made a Venn diagram showing the things that Brasília and Washington, D.C., have in common, and the things that are different. Complete the student's diagram.*

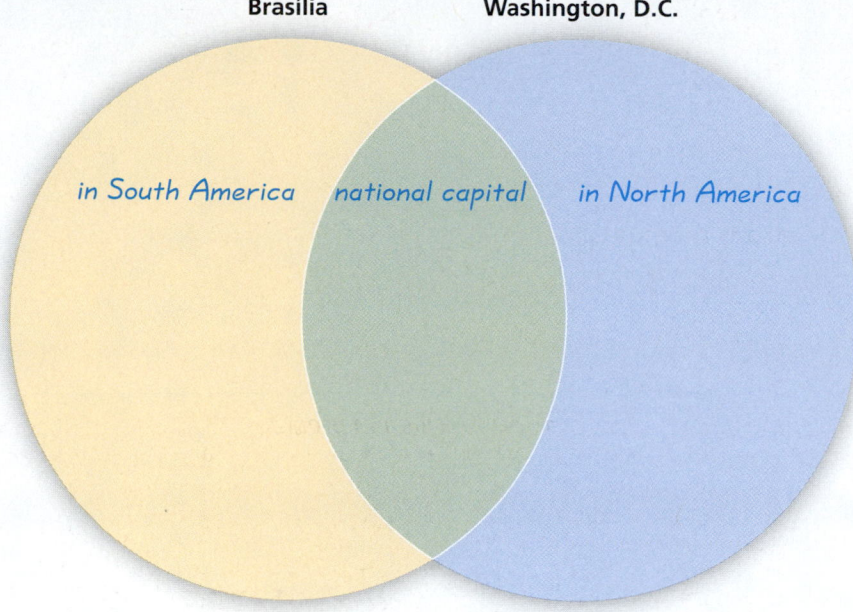

Brasília   Washington, D.C.

in South America   national capital   in North America

3 | *Before you write . . .*

1. Work with a partner. Agree on a topic for an essay of comparison and contrast. For example, you can compare two places, two people, two types of food, or two TV programs.

2. Brainstorm ideas and complete a Venn diagram like the one in Exercise 2.

4 | *Write an essay of comparison and contrast using your diagram in Exercise 3.*

5 | *Exchange essays with a different partner. Underline once additions that show similarity. Underline twice additions that show difference. Write a question mark (?) above the places where something seems wrong. Then answer the following questions.*

	Yes	No
1. Did the writer use the correct auxiliary verbs in the additions?	☐	☐
2. Did the writer use correct word order?	☐	☐
3. Do the examples show important similarities and differences?	☐	☐

4. What are some details you would like to know about the two things the writer compared?

_____

_____

6 | *Work with your partner. Discuss each other's editing questions from Exercise 5. Then rewrite your own paragraph and make any necessary corrections.*

PART IV

GERUNDS AND INFINITIVES

UNIT	GRAMMAR FOCUS	THEME
9	Gerunds and Infinitives: Review and Expansion	Fast Food
10	*Make*, *Have*, *Let*, *Help*, and *Get*	Zoos and Water Parks

Gerunds and Infinitives: Review and Expansion

FAST FOOD

Before You Read

Look at the title of the article and the photos. Discuss the questions.

1. Why do you think the title is *McWorld*? *picture*
2. What do you think of fast-food restaurants like McDonald's? *are not good*
3. Do you eat in fast-food restaurants? Why or why not? *Yes sometimes not when I don't have time to cook*

Read

Read the article about the largest fast-food restaurant chain in the world.

"**I**'ll have a Big Mac, a large fries, and a medium soda." The language may change, but you can **expect to hear** this order in more than 115 countries all over the world. Fast food has become almost synonymous[1] with McDonald's, the best known of all the multinational fast-food restaurant chains. At the moment, Antarctica is the only continent that doesn't (yet!) have one. And the numbers **keep growing**. In the United States, most McDonald's customers **need to travel** less than four minutes **to arrive** at the next pair of golden arches.

Dining on fast food has become a way of life for millions and millions of people from Illinois, U.S.A. (the very first McDonald's), to Colombo, Sri Lanka (a more recent one). What is it **about eating** on the run that so many people find appealing? Of course, the most obvious answer is that, true to its name, fast food is fast. In today's hectic society, people **don't want to waste** time. But apart from the speed **of ordering** and **getting** served, satisfied customers often talk about convenience, price, and, yes, even good taste.

Many people also like the reliability that fast-food chains provide. You can **count on getting** the same thing every time, every place. McDonald's **has started to introduce** some local variety, though. For example, in

[1]*synonymous:* having the same meaning

New Delhi, India

the New England region of the United States, you can get a lobster roll; in Japan, you can order a teriyaki McBurger; and in India, you can have a Maharaja Mac or a vegetable burger. And although most McDonald's restaurants resemble one another, some **try to adjust** to the surroundings. In Freiburg, Germany, one McDonald's is housed in an historic building more than 700 years old, and in Sweden, there's even a McSki lodge.

Not everyone is **in favor of** fast-food restaurants' **spreading** over the globe. In fact, a lot of people are **fed up with seeing** the same restaurants wherever they go. "**Walking** down the Champs Elysées just isn't as romantic as it once was. When I see McDonald's or KFC (Kentucky Fried Chicken) everywhere I go, I feel that the world is shrinking too much," complained one traveler. But there are more serious objections too.

Nutritionists[2] point to the health consequences **of eating** fast foods since they are generally high in calories, fat, and salt, but low in fiber and nutrients. They blame the world-wide problem of obesity,[3] in part, **on eating** fast food. Sociologists[4] complain that fast-food restaurants may prevent

families **from spending** quality time together around the dinner table. Social critics condemn fast-food chains **for introducing** these unhealthy foods to other countries and **for underpaying** their workers. Then there is the question of pollution. Those Big Macs and Quarter Pounders come wrapped in a lot of paper and plastic, which create waste that pollutes the air and water. It's a high **price to pay** for convenience.

But like it or not, it's **easy to see** that fast-food restaurants like McDonald's are **here to stay**. From Rovaniemi, Finland, in the north; Invercargill, New Zealand, in the south; Tokyo, Japan, in the east; and Vancouver, Canada, in the west, the sun never sets on the golden arches.

Tokyo, Japan

[2]*nutritionist:* an expert on what people should eat
[3]*obesity:* the condition of being extremely fat
[4]*sociologist:* an expert on how people behave in groups

Fast Facts

- The average adult in the United States visits a fast-food restaurant six times a month.
- Hamburgers are the most popular fast food in the United States.
- Tacos are the second most popular fast-food choice in the United States, followed by pizza and chicken.
- Men are more **likely** than women **to order** a hamburger.
- Lunch is the most popular meal at a fast-food restaurant.

After You Read

A | **Vocabulary:** *Complete the sentences with the words from the box.*

| appealing | consequence | globe | objection | region | reliability |

1. As a newspaper reporter, Ozawa travels all over the ___globe___. In fact, last year she was in 40 countries.

2. I have no ___objection___ to the report. It's excellent.

3. There are only two Japanese restaurants in the ___region___, but another one is opening up soon.

4. People like the newspaper's ___reliability___. They know that the information is correct.

5. One ___consequence___ of the nutrition report was that some people stopped eating fast food.

6. The idea of low-cost, healthy food choices is very ___appealing___.

B | **Comprehension:** *Circle the letter of the word or phrase that best completes each sentence.*

1. The number of McDonald's restaurants is ___.

   a. decreasing   **b.** remaining the same   **c.** increasing

2. The article does NOT mention ___ as a reason for McDonald's popularity.

   a. cost   **b.** attractiveness   **c.** quick service

3. All McDonald's serve ___.

   a. soda   **b.** vegetable burgers   **c.** teriyaki McBurgers

4. ___ happy to see fast-food chains all around the globe.

   a. Some people are   **b.** Everyone is   **c.** Nobody is

5. One big objection to fast food is that it is ___.

   a. cheap   **b.** unhealthy   **c.** bad-tasting

6. According to the article, workers at fast-food chains don't ___.

   a. eat well   **b.** make enough money   **c.** spend time with their families

GERUNDS AND INFINITIVES

Gerunds	Infinitives
Gerund as Subject	***It* + Infinitive**
Eating fast foods is convenient.	***It*'s** convenient **to eat** fast foods.
Verb + Gerund	**Verb + Infinitive**
They *recommend* **reducing** fats in the food.	They *plan* **to reduce** fats in the food.
Verb + Gerund or Infinitive	**Verb + Gerund or Infinitive**
She *started* **buying** McBreakfast every day.	She *started* **to buy** McBreakfast every day.
Preposition + Gerund	**Adjective + Infinitive**
We're tired *of* **reading** calorie counts.	We were *surprised* **to read** the number of calories.
Possessive + Gerund	**Object Pronoun + Infinitive**
I didn't like ***his* ordering** fries.	I urged ***him* to order** fries.

GRAMMAR NOTES

1 A **gerund** (base form + *-ing*) is a verb used as a noun. We often use a **gerund** as the **subject** of a sentence.

REMEMBER: A gerund can have a <u>negative</u> form (*not* + base form + *-ing*), and it is always <u>singular</u> (**gerund** + **third-person singular** form of verb).

A gerund is often part of a phrase. When a **gerund phrase** is the **subject** of a sentence, make sure the following verb is in the <u>singular</u>.

- **Cooking *is*** a lot of fun.

- **Not exercising *leads*** to health problems.

- **Eating too many fries *is*** unhealthy.
  NOT: Eating too many fries ~~are~~ unhealthy.
- **Not caring about calories *is*** a mistake.

2 A **gerund** often follows certain verbs as the **object** of the verb.

You can use a **possessive** (*Anne's, the boy's, my, your, his, her, its, our, their*) before a gerund.

USAGE NOTE: In informal spoken English, many people use **nouns** or **object pronouns** instead of possessives before a gerund.

- I *dislike* **eating** fast food every day.
- Julio *considered* **not eating** fast foods.

- I dislike ***Julio's* eating** fast foods.
- I dislike ***his* eating** fast foods.

- I dislike ***Julio* eating** fast foods.
- I dislike ***him* eating** fast foods.

(continued on next page)

Gerunds and Infinitives: Review and Expansion   **141**

3	Some verbs can be followed by an **infinitive** (**to** + base form). These verbs fall into three groups:	
	• **verb** + **infinitive**	• They **hope to open** a new McDonald's. • She **chose not to give up** meat.
	• **verb** + **object** + **infinitive**	• I **urge you to try** that new restaurant. • She **convinced him not to order** fries.
	• **verb** + **infinitive** OR **verb** + **object** + **infinitive**	• I **want to try** that new restaurant. • I **want her to try** it too.
4	Some verbs can be followed by either a **gerund or an infinitive**. The <u>meanings are the same</u>.	• I **started** bringing my own lunch. OR • I **started** to bring my own lunch.
	BE CAREFUL! A few verbs (for example, **stop**, **remember**, and **forget**) can be followed by either a gerund or an infinitive, but the <u>meanings are very different</u>.	• She **stopped** eating pizza. *(She doesn't eat pizza anymore.)* • She **stopped** to eat pizza. *(She stopped another activity in order to eat pizza.)*
		• He **remembered** meeting her. *(He remembered that he had already met her in the past.)* • He **remembered** to meet her. *(First he arranged a meeting with her. Then he remembered to go to the meeting.)*
		• I never **forgot** eating lunch at McDonald's. *(I ate lunch at McDonald's, and I didn't forget the experience.)* • I never **forgot** to eat lunch. *(I always ate lunch.)*
5	A **gerund** is the only verb form that can follow a **preposition**.	• I read an article **about** counting calories.
	There are many common **verb** + **preposition** and **adjective** + **preposition** combinations that must be followed by a gerund and not an infinitive.	• I don't **approve of** eating fast food. • We're very **interested in** trying different types of food.
	BE CAREFUL! **To** can be part of an infinitive or it can be a preposition. Use a <u>gerund after the preposition **to**</u>.	• We look forward **to having** dinner with you. NOT: We look forward ~~to have~~ dinner with you.

6	An **infinitive** often follows:	
	a. an **adjective** Many of these adjectives express feelings or attitudes about the action in the infinitive.	• They were *eager* **to try** the new taco. • She was *glad* **to hear** that it was low in calories. • We're *ready* **to have** something different.
	b. an **adverb**	• It's too *soon* **to eat**. • The restaurant is *here* **to stay**.
	c. certain **nouns**	• It's *time* **to take** a break. • I have the *right* **to eat** what I want. • They made a *decision* **to lose** weight. • It's a high *price* **to pay**. • He has *permission* **to stay** out late.

why?

7	Use an **infinitive** to explain the **purpose** of an action.	• Doug eats fast food **to save** time.

8	To make **general statements** you can use:	
	gerund as subject OR ***It*** + **infinitive**	• **Cooking** is fun. OR • ***It***'s fun **to cook**.

REFERENCE NOTES

For a list of **verbs that can be followed by gerunds**, see Appendix 3 on page A-2.

For lists of **verbs that can be followed by infinitives**, see Appendices 4 and 5 on page A-3.

For a list of **verbs that can be followed by either gerunds or infinitives**, see Appendix 6 on page A-3.

For a list of **verb + preposition combinations**, see Appendix 7 on page A-3.

For a list of **adjective + preposition expressions**, see Appendix 8 on page A-3.

For a list of **adjectives that can be followed by infinitives**, see Appendix 9 on page A-4.

For a list of **nouns that can be followed by infinitives**, see Appendix 10 on page A-4.

urge = strong advice

EXERCISE 1: Discover the Grammar

Read this questionnaire about fast-food restaurants. Underline the gerunds and circle the infinitives.

FAST-FOOD QUESTIONNAIRE

Please take a few minutes (to complete) this questionnaire about fast-food restaurants. Check (✓) all the answers that are appropriate for you.

1. In your opinion, eating fast food is _____.
  ☐ convenient   ☑ fast   ☐ healthy   ☐ cheap   ☐ fun

2. Which meals are you used to eating at a fast-food restaurant?
  ☐ breakfast   ☐ lunch   ☐ dinner   ☐ snacks   ☐ None

3. Which types of fast food do you like to eat?
  ☐ hamburgers   ☑ pizza   ☐ fried chicken   ☐ tacos   ☐ sushi
  ☐ Other: _____   ☐ None

4. What is the most important issue to you in selecting a fast-food restaurant?
  ☐ choice of food   ☑ quality of food
  ☐ fast service   ☐ low prices
  ☐ reliability   ☐ Other: _____

5. How often are you likely to eat at a fast-food restaurant?
  ☐ 1–3 times a week   ☐ more than 6 times a week
  ☐ 4–6 times a week   ☐ Never

6. How much do you enjoy going to fast-food restaurants?
  ☐ I like it very much.   ☐ I don't enjoy it.
  ☑ It's just OK.   ☐ I never go.

7. How do you feel about seeing the same fast-food restaurants all over the world?
  ☐ I like it.   ☐ I have no objections.   ☐ I don't like it.

8. Do you think the government should require fast-food restaurants to include healthy choices?
  ☐ Yes   ☐ No

EXERCISE 2: Gerund or Infinitive

(Grammar Notes 1–6, 8)

Complete the statements with the correct form—gerund or infinitive—of the verbs in parentheses. Use the bar graph to find the number of calories.

People are starting ____*to think*____ about the consequences of ____*eating*____ in
1. (think) **2 (eat)**

fast-food restaurants. Here are some facts ____*to consider*____ before you order.
3. (consider)

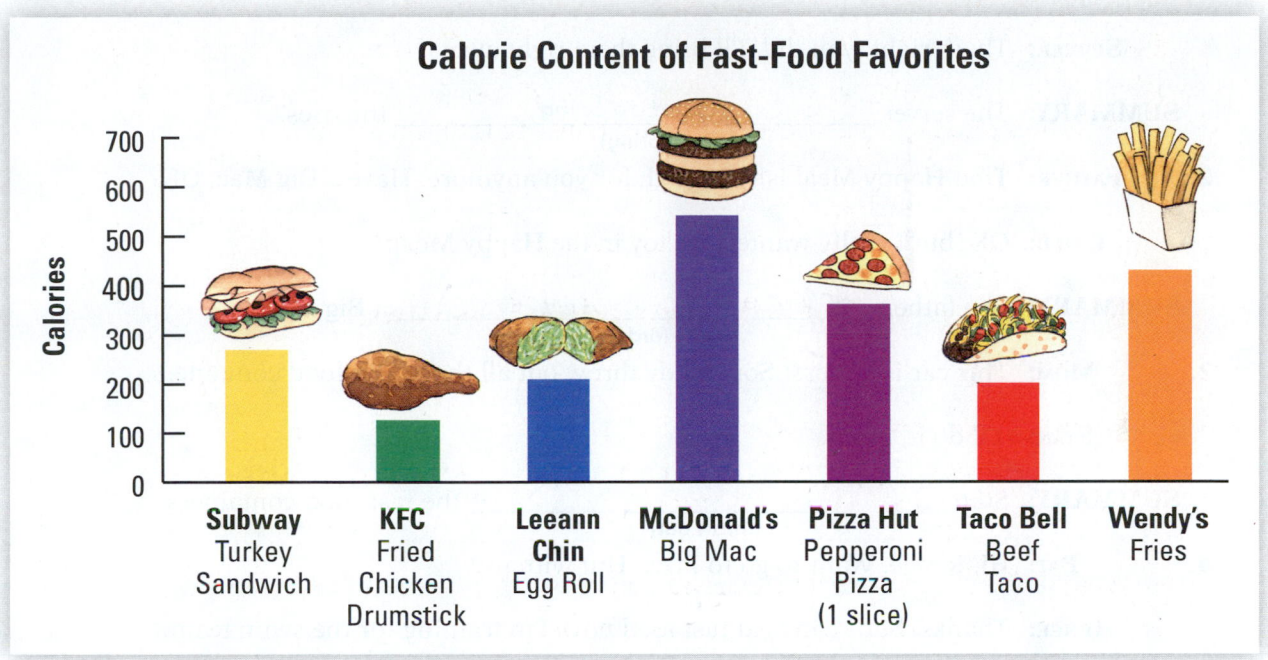

Source: www.calorieking.com

- ____*ordering*____ a Big Mac will "cost" you about _____550_____ calories.
  4. (order)

- ____*having*____ a Taco Bell taco is much less fattening. One taco has only about
  5. (have)

  ____*200*____ calories.

- If you want ____*to lose*____ weight, you should also consider ____*eating*____ a
  6. (lose) **7. (eat)**

  Subway turkey sandwich. It contains around ____*300*____ calories.

- You're likely ____*to gain*____ weight if you eat half of a medium pepperoni pizza. A single
  8. (gain)

  slice at Pizza Hut has about ____*350*____ calories.

- Stop ____*eating*____ so many French fries! An order at Wendy's contains about
  9. (eat)

  ____*400*____ calories.

- Think about ____*choosing*____ an egg roll instead of fries. Leeann Chin's has just a little over
  10. (choose)

  ____*200*____ calories.

- Nutritionists advise people ____*to stay away*____ from fried chicken. A drumstick at KFC
  11. (stay away)

  contains about ____*100*____ calories—but people usually eat much more!

EXERCISE 3: Verb + Gerund or Infinitive

(Grammar Notes 2–4)

Complete each summary with the appropriate form of a verb from the box plus the gerund or infinitive form of the verb in parentheses. Go to Appendices 3 and 4 on pages A-2 and A-3 for help.

admit	deserve	~~forget~~ *gerund*	recommend	remember	stop	try	volunteer

1. **CUSTOMER:** Uh, didn't I order a large fries too?

   SERVER: That's right, you did. I'll bring them right away.

   SUMMARY: The server _____ *forgot to bring* _____ the fries.
   (bring)

2. **FATHER:** That Happy Meal isn't enough for you anymore. Have a Big Mac, OK?

   CHILD: OK, but I really wanted the toy in the Happy Meal.

   SUMMARY: The father _____ *recommended ordering* _____ a Big Mac.
   (order)

3. **MOM:** This car is a mess! Somebody throw out all those fast-food containers!

   STAN: I'll do it, Mom.

   SUMMARY: Stan _____ *volunteered to throw out* _____ the fast-food containers.
   (throw out)

4. **PAT:** Hi, Renee. Want to go to Pizza Hut with us?

   RENEE: Thanks, but I can't eat fast food now. I'm training for the swim team.

   SUMMARY: Renee _____ *stoped eating* _____ fast food.
   (eat)

5. **EMPLOYEE:** Thanks for the raise. I can really use it.

   MANAGER: You've earned it. You're our best drive-through server.

   SUMMARY: The employee _____ *deserve to receive* _____ a raise.
   (receive)

6. **MOTHER:** I think you should quit that fast-food job. Your grades are suffering.

   CAROL: It's hard to decide. I need to save for college, but if my grades are bad . . .

   SUMMARY: Carol _____ *try to decide* _____ whether to keep her job.
   (decide)

7. **MOM:** You're not eating dinner. You had some fast food on the way home, didn't you?

   CHRIS: Well . . . Actually, I stopped at Arby's, but I only had a large fries.

   SUMMARY: Chris _____ *admited stopping* _____ at Arby's after school.
   (stop)

8. **TIM:** I used to stay in the McDonald's playground for hours when I was little.

   WANG: Yeah, me too. My mother couldn't get me to leave.

   SUMMARY: The boys _____ *remember playing* _____ in the McDonald's playground.
   (play)

EXERCISE 4: Gerund or Infinitive with and without Object

(Grammar Notes 2–4)

Use the correct forms of the words in parentheses to complete the letters to the editor of a school newspaper. Go to Appendices 3–10 on pages A-2—A-4 for help.

To the Editor,

Yesterday, my roommate Andre ___*wanted me to have*___ lunch with him in the dining hall.
1. (want / I / have)

I was surprised about __Andre's choosing to go__ there because last year he'd completely
2. (Andre / choose / go)

__stopped using__ the dining hall. It just wasn't appealing to him. But when we went
3. (stop / use)

in yesterday, instead of __finding__ the usual greasy fries and mystery meat,
4. (find)

I was happy __to see__ the colorful Taco Bell sign. In my opinion,
5. (see)

__changing__ to fast foods is the thing __to do__ . The
6. (change) ____ **7. (do)**

administration made a great choice. I __support their selling__ fast food, and I really
8. (support / they / sell)

__appreciate my friend encouraging__ me to give campus food another try.
9. (appreciate / my friend / encourage)

M. Rodriguez

To the Editor,

I'm writing this letter __to express__ my anger and great disappointment at
10. (express)

__having__ fast-food chains in the dining halls. When a classmate and I went
11. (have)

to eat yesterday, I __expected to find__ the usual healthy choices of vegetables and
12. (expect / find)

salads. I __did not expect to see__ a fast-food court. In my opinion, it's simply wrong
13. (not expect / see)

__to bring__ fast food into the college dining hall. The consequence of
14. (bring)

__eating__ fast food is bad health. As a commuter, I absolutely
15. (eat)

__need to have__ a healthy meal every evening before class, so I usually
16. (need / have)

__try to stay away__ from fast foods. I __urge the administration to set up__ a salad bar so
17. (try / stay away) ____ **18. (urge / the administration / set up)**

that students like me can __keep on buying__ meals on campus. I'm sure other
19. (keep on / buy)

commuters will agree with my objections.

B. Chen

EXERCISE 5: Editing

Read these posts to an international online discussion group. There are fifteen mistakes in the use of gerunds and infinitives. The first mistake is already corrected. Find and correct fourteen more.

Re: love those tacos

eating OR *to eat*

I love ~~eat~~ tacos for my lunch. I think they are delicious, convenient, nutritious, and inexpensive. I

having

don't mind to have the same thing every day! And I'm not worried about any health consequences.

What do you think?

Re: vegetarian travel

eating

I'm a vegetarian. I stopped to eat meat two years ago. I feel a little nervous about traveling to other

Finding

countries. I'm going to Ghana in September. Is to find meatless dishes there easy?

Re: takoyaki

Hi! I am Paulo, and I come from Brazil. I travel a lot, and I enjoy trying different foods from all

to try

over the globe. I hope I have a chance trying takoyaki (fish balls made with octopus) when I go to

hearing

Japan. Is there a takoyaki shop you can recommend my going to? I look forward to hear from you.

Re: recipe exchange

ing

My name is Natasha. I'm interested in exchange recipes with people from other countries. If you

want to know about Russian food, I'd be glad sending you some information.

to send

Re: calamari

Hi! I was in Italy last month. The region I was visiting is famous for seafood. I don't usually like

to try

eating seafood, so I was not eager trying calamari (squid). I was surprised finding that I liked it! I

to be   *to find*

expected it being tough, but it's actually quite tender if prepared well.

Re: cheap and delicious in Taiwan

trying

Are you going to Taiwan? If so, I suggest to try the appealing little restaurants around the National

eating   *to find*

University in Taipei. Eat there is cheap, and it's easy find the neighborhood. The dumpling shops

are great—once you eat at one, you won't want stopping.

to stop

EXERCISE 6: Listening

A | *Read the statements. Then listen to two college students discuss their responses to a food service survey. Listen again and circle the correct answers.*

1. Lily and Victor are in <u>class</u> / <u>a fast-food restaurant</u> / <u>the school dining hall</u>.

2. Lily thinks the meatloaf is <u>disgusting</u> / <u>appealing</u> / <u>unhealthy</u>.

3. Victor asks to borrow a <u>pen</u> / <u>pencil</u> / <u>survey</u>.

4. Victor thinks you can't prevent students from eating <u>fast food</u> / <u>quickly</u> / <u>fat</u>.

5. Victor and Lily both think the school food is pretty <u>good</u> / <u>cheap</u> / <u>healthy</u>.

6. Lily wants the cafeteria to hire someone to <u>plan menus</u> / <u>clean tables</u> / <u>cook Chinese food</u>.

7. Victor says he doesn't want to <u>get up earlier</u> / <u>miss breakfast</u> / <u>go for a run</u> in the morning.

B | *Listen again to the conversation. Check (✓) the suggestions that each student agrees with.*

School Food Service Survey

We're changing and you can help! Please complete the survey by checking (✓) the changes you want to see.

		Lily	Victor
1. Introducing Burger Queen fast foods	☐	☐	☑
2. Showing fat and calorie contents of each serving	☐	☐	☐
3. Providing more healthy choices	☐	☐	☐
4. Lowering prices	☐	☐	☐
5. Improving food quality	☐	☐	☐
6. Offering Chinese food	☐	☐	☐
7. Starting breakfast at 6:30 A.M.	☐	☐	☐

EXERCISE 7: Pronunciation

A | *Read and listen to the Pronunciation Note.*

B | *Listen to the short conversations. Notice how the speaker says the last sentence in each conversation. Decide if the speaker is being **sincere** or **sarcastic**. Check (✓) the correct box.*

	The speaker is being . . .	Sincere	Sarcastic
1.	**A:** What's for dinner tonight?		
	B: Liver.		
	A: **That's great!**	☐	☐
2.	**A:** Another fast-food restaurant is opening on Main Street.		
	B: Really?		
	A: Yeah. **Great, huh?**	☐	☐
3.	**A:** What's that thing on your plate?		
	B: Meatloaf!		
	A: Oh. **That looks appealing.**	☐	☐
4.	**A:** The cafeteria is going to start opening at 6:30 A.M.		
	B: 6:30 A.M. **Great idea!**	☐	☐
5.	**A:** What did you think of Ana's suggestion?		
	B: **Another great idea!**	☐	☐
6.	**A:** Bye. I'm leaving now. How's the weather?		
	B: Take a look outside.		
	A: **Nice day!**	☐	☐

C | *Listen again and repeat the last sentence in each conversation. Then practice the conversations with a partner.*

EXERCISE 8: Information Gap: The Right Job?

Work in pairs (A and B). **Student B**, go to page 154 and follow the instructions there.
Student A, ask Student B questions to complete the quiz. Answer Student B's questions.

> **EXAMPLE:** **A:** What does Jennifer enjoy doing?
> **B:** She enjoys working with others. What does Jennifer expect to do?
> **A:** She expects to make a lot of money.

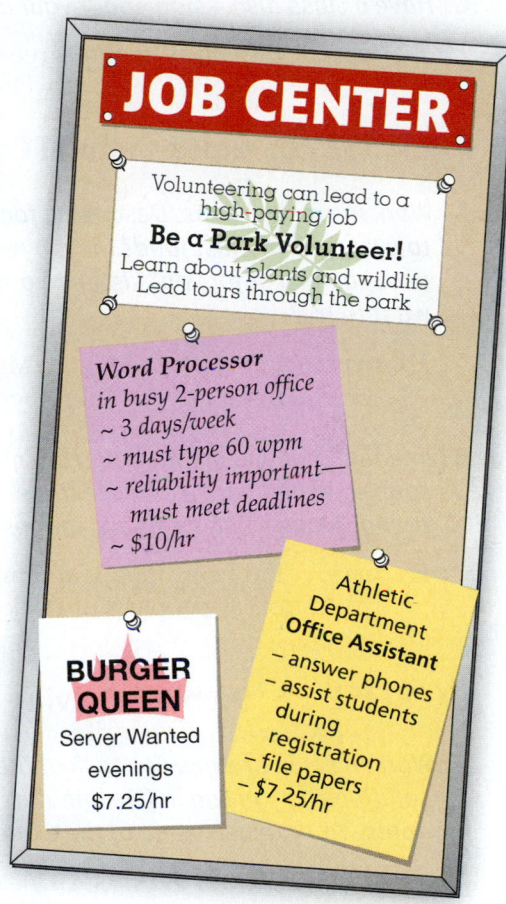

JOB / PERSONALITY QUIZ

Before you start looking at job ads, take this quiz to find out about your job preferences. Complete the statements with information about yourself.

Name: _Jennifer Johnson_

1. I enjoy _working with others_.
2. I expect _to make a lot of money_.
3. I'm good at _____.
4. I dislike _working inside_.
5. I don't mind _____.
6. I'm willing _to learn new skills_.
7. I never complain about _____.
8. I'm eager _to meet new people_.
9. I plan _____ next year.
10. I dream about _owning my own business_ one day.
11. I can't stand _____.
12. I expect people _to be friendly_.

JOB CENTER

Volunteering can lead to a high-paying job
Be a Park Volunteer!
Learn about plants and wildlife
Lead tours through the park

Word Processor
in busy 2-person office
~ 3 days/week
~ must type 60 wpm
~ reliability important—
   must meet deadlines
~ $10/hr

BURGER QUEEN
Server Wanted
evenings
$7.25/hr

Athletic Department **Office Assistant**
– answer phones
– assist students during registration
– file papers
– $7.25/hr

When you are finished, compare quizzes. Are they the same?

Now look at the job notices to the right of the quiz. Which jobs do you think would be good for Jennifer? Which jobs wouldn't be good for her? Explain your choices.

EXERCISE 9: Questionnaire

A | *Complete the fast-food questionnaire on page 144.*

B | *Work with a partner. Compare your answers on the questionnaire with your partner's.*

> **EXAMPLE:** **A:** What's your answer to number 1?
> **B:** In my opinion, eating fast food is convenient, fast, and cheap. What do you think?
> **A:** I agree. And, it's not healthy, but it is fun!

C | *Have a class discussion about your answers. Tally the results.*

> **EXAMPLE:** Fifteen students agree that eating fast food is convenient and fast.

EXERCISE 10: Cross-Cultural Comparison

A | *Work in small groups. Describe a food from your culture that you would like to introduce to others. Is it a fast food? Do you remember eating it at special times? If so, when? Who used to make it for you? Listen to other students' favorite foods. Which ones do you want to try?*

> **EXAMPLE:** I'm from Colombia. My favorite food is *ajiaco*, a kind of potato soup. It is definitely not a fast food! I remember eating it . . .

B | *Imagine that you are planning an international food festival. Which foods from your country would you like to see there? Which foods from other countries would you enjoy trying? Make a list. Compare your list with other groups' lists.*

> **EXAMPLE:** I'm from Japan, and my favorite food is *takoyaki*. I'd like to introduce this food to other people. For myself, I'm interested in trying Turkish food, such as . . .

EXERCISE 11: Problem Solving

A | *Work in small groups. For each of the social problems below, brainstorm as many solutions as you can in five minutes. (You can also add a problem not listed.) Take notes. You can use some of the expressions from the list.*

I'm in favor of . . .	**I'm opposed to . . .**
I support . . .	**I'm against . . .**
I suggest . . .	**What about . . .**
I go along with . . .	**We need . . .**
I advise . . .	**I recommend . . .**
We should start / stop . . .	**I urge . . .**

1. In many countries, a lot of people are overweight. What can people do about this problem?

> **EXAMPLE:** **A:** What about improving physical education programs in schools?
> **B:** I'm in favor of offering healthier meals in schools.
> **C:** We need to educate people about the role of exercise.

2. Heavy traffic is a big problem in both cities and suburbs. What can we do about it?

3. Many adults can't read or write well enough to function in society. What can be done about this problem?

4. There are millions of homeless people living in the streets and parks. How can we help solve this problem?

5. Another social problem: _____

B | *Compare your answers with those of another group.*

EXERCISE 12: Writing

A | *Write a short editorial in response to one of the statements below or another issue involving food. Express your opinions and give reasons for your ideas. Use gerunds and infinitives and some of the expressions from the list in Exercise 11.*

- There ought to be a law requiring restaurants to list the number of calories for each dish.
- Schools and hospitals shouldn't be allowed to sell fast food.
- There should be a tax on soft drinks, candy, and other foods that contain a lot of sugar.
- Schools should expand their physical education programs to help prevent obesity.
- Candy and soft drink advertising on children's TV programs should be banned or limited.

EXAMPLE: I'm in favor of requiring restaurants to list the calorie content of the foods on their menu. If diners have that information they can consider . . .

B | *Exchange editorials with a classmate. After you read your classmate's editorial, write a letter to the editor explaining why you agree or disagree with your classmate's opinions.*

EXAMPLE: To the Editor:
I go along with requiring restaurants to list the number of calories in each dish, but I don't think that is enough. To make good decisions, diners also need to know . . .

C | *Check your work. Use the Editing Checklist.*

Editing Checklist

Did you use . . . ?
☐ gerunds as subjects
☐ correct **verbs** + **gerunds**
☐ correct **verbs** + **infinitives**
☐ **prepositions** + **gerunds**
☐ infinitives after adjectives, adverbs, and certain nouns
☐ *it* + **infinitive** for general statements

Student B, answer Student A's questions. Then ask Student A questions to complete the quiz.

EXAMPLE: **A:** What does Jennifer enjoy doing?
B: She enjoys working with others. What does Jennifer expect to do?
A: She expects to make a lot of money.

JOB / PERSONALITY QUIZ

Before you start looking at job ads, take this quiz to find out about your job preferences. Complete the statements with information about yourself.

Name: _____ Jennifer Johnson _____

1. I enjoy _____ working with others _____.
2. I expect _____ to make a lot of money _____.
3. I'm good at _____ talking to people _____.
4. I dislike _____.
5. I don't mind _____ working nights _____.
6. I'm willing _____.
7. I never complain about _____ following orders _____.
8. I'm eager _____.
9. I plan _____ to major in business _____ next year.
10. I dream about _____ one day.
11. I can't stand _____ rushing _____.
12. I expect people _____.

JOB CENTER

Volunteering can lead to a high-paying job
Be a Park Volunteer!
Learn about plants and wildlife
Lead tours through the park

Word Processor
in busy 2-person office
~ 3 days/week
~ must type 60 wpm
~ reliability important
  must meet deadlines
~ $10/hr

BURGER QUEEN
Server Wanted
evenings
$7.25/hr

Athletic Department
Office Assistant
– answer phones
– assist students during registration
– file papers
– $7.25/hr

When you are finished, compare quizzes. Are they the same?

Now look at the job notices to the right of the quiz. Which jobs do you think would be good for Jennifer? Which jobs wouldn't be good for her? Explain your choices.

A | Complete the paragraph with the gerund or infinitive form of the verbs in parentheses.

Cost and convenience often persuade people ___to use___ fast-food restaurants. If
1. (use)

you're eating a fast-food lunch ___to save___ money, think about ___ordering___
2. (save) **3. (order)**

from the dollar menu. A fast-food dinner can leave you free ___to relax___ or
4. (relax)

___to study___ instead of ___preparing___ food. ___stopping___ for fast food is a
5. (study) **6. (prepare)** **7. (stop)**

cheap and convenient way ___to eat___. But you should avoid ___having___ fast
8. (eat) **9. (have)**

food too often. ___Cooking___ at home provides better quality food for less money.
10. (cook)

B | Read the conversations. Complete each summary (**S**) with the correct form of the words
in parentheses.

1. **DAD:** You used to love Taco Bell as a kid.

   LYDIA: I *did*? Did you take me there a lot?

   S: Lydia ___didn't remember eating___
   (remember / eat)
   at Taco Bell.

2. **IVAN:** I'm sick of eating fast food.

   NIKA: You should take a cooking class.

   S: Nika ___wants Ivan to take___
   (want / Ivan / take)
   a cooking class.

3. **CHU:** I ate in the cafeteria today.

   ANYA: That's strange. You hate that food.

   S: Anya ___wonders about chu eating___
   (wonder about / Chu / eat)
   in the cafeteria.

4. **DINA:** I made lasagna. Would you like some?

   ERIKA: Sure! I haven't eaten since breakfast.

   S: Erika ___stopped having___
   (stop / have)
   some lunch.

5. **PAULO:** Did you mail that letter I gave you?

   TANYA: Oops. Sorry. I'll mail it tomorrow.

   S: Tanya ___forgot to mail___
   (forget / mail)
   Paulo's letter.

C | Find and correct five mistakes.

A: I was happy to hear that the cafeteria is serving salads now. I'm eager ~~trying~~ to try them.

B: Me too. Someone recommended eating more salads in order for ~~losing~~ to lose weight.

A: It was that TV doctor, right? He's always urging ~~we~~ us to exercise more too.

B: That's the one. He's actually convinced me to stop ~~to eat~~ eating meat.

A: Interesting! It would be a hard decision for us ~~making~~ make, though. We love to barbecue.

Make, Have, Let, Help, and *Get*
ZOOS AND WATER PARKS

STEP 1 GRAMMAR IN CONTEXT

Before You Read

Look at the photos. Discuss the questions.

1. How do you think these animals learned to perform like this?
2. Do you think people should use animals for entertainment?

Read

Read the article about performance animals.

That's Entertainment?

"Ooooh!" cries the audience as the orcas leap from the water in perfect formation. "Aaaah!" they shout as the trainer rides across the pool on the nose of one of the graceful giants.

For years, dolphins, orcas, and other sea mammals have been **making** *audiences* **say** *ooooh* and *aaaah* at water parks like Sea World. But how do trainers **get** *nine-ton whales* **to do** acrobatic tricks[1] or **make** *them* "dance"?

It's not easy. Traditional animal trainers controlled animals with collars and leashes and **made** *them* **perform** by using cruel[2] punishments. Then, in the 1940s, water parks wanted to

have *dolphins* **do** tricks. The first trainers faced big problems. You can't **get** *a dolphin* **to wear** a collar. And you can't punish a dolphin—it will just swim away from you! This challenge **made** *the trainers* **develop** a kinder, more humane method to teach animals.

"Ooooh!"

[1]*acrobatic trick:* the kind of act that animals and people do at the circus (example: walking on a wire)
[2]*cruel:* causing pain

That's Entertainment?

This method, positive reinforcement, uses rewards rather than punishments for training. To begin teaching, a trainer **lets an animal act** freely. When the trainer sees the "correct" behavior, he or she rewards the animal immediately, usually with food. The animal quickly learns that a reward follows the behavior.

Elephant performing in circus

For complicated acts, the trainer breaks the act into many smaller parts and **has the animal learn** each part separately.

Positive reinforcement has completely changed our treatment of animals in zoos. Elephants, for example, need a lot of physical care. However, traditional trainers used force to **make elephants "behave."** Elephants sometimes rebelled[3] and hurt or even killed their keepers. Through positive reinforcement, elephants at modern zoos have learned to stand at the bars of their cage and **let keepers draw** blood for tests and **take care of** their feet. Trainers even **get primates** (monkeys and apes) **to bring** their own bedding to the keepers for washing. Gary Priest, a former orca trainer, **helped the keepers train** the elephants at the San Diego Zoo. Do the elephants like the new system? "They love it! They'll do anything we ask. They'd fly for us if they could," Priest said.

Unfortunately, not all trainers use positive reinforcement. Animal rights organizations have found abuses[4] of animal actors by circuses and other entertainment companies. And the question remains: Even with kind treatment, should we keep these animals captive[5] and **have them perform** just for our entertainment? In the wild, orcas may travel 100 miles a day. Is it really kind to **make them live** in small pools of chemically treated water? Today, more and more people say the only real kindness is to **let these captive animals** live natural lives.

---

[3]**rebel:** to fight against someone in authority (for example a trainer, a parent, the president of a country)
[4]**abuse:** cruel or violent treatment
[5]**captive:** kept in a place that you are not allowed to leave

After You Read

A | Vocabulary: *Circle the letter of the word or phrase that best completes each sentence.*

1. _____ is NOT an example of a **reward**.

    a. Money

    b. Homework

    c. Ice cream

2. As a **punishment**, the child couldn't _____.

    a. go to school

    b. clean her room

    c. watch TV

3. The opposite of **complicated** is _____.

    a. easy

    b. cheap

    c. small

4. A **physical** problem is a problem with your _____.

    a. job

    b. body

    c. home

5. **Humane** treatment of animals _____.

    a. shows kindness

    b. uses power

    c. is full of mistakes

6. If someone is a **former** teacher, he or she _____.

    a. is famous

    b. teaches art

    c. used to teach

B | Comprehension: *Check (✓)* **True** *or* **False**. *Correct the false statements.*

	True	False
1. It's easy to train orcas and dolphins.	☐	☐
2. Many dolphins wear collars.	☐	☐
3. Methods of animal training have changed a lot since the 1940s.	☐	☐
4. Today most elephants and their trainers have a better relationship than in the past.	☐	☐
5. Many people think it is wrong to keep animals in zoos and water parks.	☐	☐

MAKE, HAVE, LET, HELP, AND GET

Make, Have, Let, Help					
Subject	**Make / Have / Let / Help**		**Object**	**Base Form**	
They	(don't)	**make** **have** **let** **help***	animals them	**learn**	tricks.

* *Help* can also be followed by an infinitive.

Get, Help				
Subject	**Get / Help**		**Object**	**Infinitive**	
They	(don't)	**get** **help**	animals them	**to learn**	tricks.

GRAMMAR NOTES

1 Use **make**, **have**, and **get** to talk about things that someone causes another person (or an animal) to do. These verbs show how much choice the other person or animal has about doing the action.

  a. *make* + **object** + **base form of the verb** means to force a person or animal to do something. There is no choice.

  b. *have* + **object** + **base form of the verb** often means to cause a person or animal to do a task. There is some choice.

  c. *get* + **object** + **infinitive** often means to persuade a person or animal to do something by giving rewards or reasons. There is a choice.

BE CAREFUL! *Get* is always followed by **object** + **infinitive**, NOT base form of the verb.

Make can also mean to have an effect on someone or something.

- The trainer **made *the elephant* do** tricks for the audience.

- On one TV show, pet owners **have *their pets* perform** tricks.

- Jan **got *her parents* to take** her to the zoo for a school assignment.

LESS CHOICE

MORE CHOICE

Not: Jan got her parents ~~take~~ her . . .

- The monkeys always **make *me* laugh.** (*They have this effect on me.*)

2 *Let* + **object** + **base form of the verb** means to allow a person or animal to do something.

- Our teacher **let *us* leave** early after the test.
- Some zoos **let *animals* interact** with humans.

3 *Help* means to make something easier for a person or an animal. *Help* can be followed by: **object** + **base form of the verb** OR **object** + **infinitive** The meaning is the same.

- She **helped *me* do** the homework. OR
- She **helped *me* to do** the homework. (*She made it easier for me to do the homework.*)

EXERCISE 1: Discover the Grammar

Read each numbered statement. Circle the letter of the sentence that is similar in meaning.

1. Ms. Bates got the principal to arrange a class trip to the zoo.

    a. Ms. Bates arranged the class trip.

    b. The principal arranged the class trip.

2. Mr. Goldberg had us do research about animals.

    a. Mr. Goldberg did the research for us.

    b. We did the research.

3. My teacher made me rewrite the report.

    a. I wrote the report again.

    b. I didn't write the report again.

4. She got me to do research on sea mammals.

    a. I agreed to do the research.

    b. I didn't agree to do the research.

5. The zoo lets small birds and animals wander freely inside the habitat.[1]

    a. They can choose where they go.

    b. They have to stay in cages.

6. I was sick, so my mother didn't let me go on the trip to the zoo.

    a. I stayed home.

    b. I went on the trip.

7. The homework was complicated, but Paulo helped Maria finish it.

    a. Paulo did Maria's homework for her.

    b. Both Paulo and Maria worked on her homework.

8. Their trip to the zoo made the students really appreciate animals.

    a. The trip forced the students to appreciate animals.

    b. The trip changed the students' opinions of animals.

---

[1] **habitat:** in a zoo, a place outdoors or in a building that is like the natural environment of the animals

EXERCISE 2: Meaning: *Make, Have, Let, Help,* and *Get*

(Grammar Notes 1–3)

Students in a conversation class are talking about their experiences with authority figures. Complete the sentences by circling the correct verb. Then match each situation with the person in authority.

	Situation	Person in Authority

Situation   **Person in Authority**

___c___ **1.** The elephant was tired, so she didn't <u>help</u> /(have) it perform.

a. my teacher

_____ **2.** I didn't really want to work overtime this week, but she <u>made / let</u> me work late because some of my co-workers were sick.

b. my doctor

c. the trainer

_____ **3.** I forgot to turn on my headlights before I left the parking lot a few nights ago. She <u>made / let</u> me pull over to the side of the road and asked to see my license.

d. my father

e. a police officer

f. the judge

_____ **4.** At first, we didn't really want to write in our journals. He explained that it would help us. Finally, he <u>had / got</u> us to try it.

g. my landlord

h. my boss

_____ **5.** My check was delayed in the mail. I told him what had happened, and he <u>had / let</u> me pay the rent two weeks late.

i. my mother

_____ **6.** I needed to get a blood test for my physical exam. He <u>got / had</u> me roll up my sleeve and make a fist.

_____ **7.** We're a big family, and we all have our own chores. While she washed the dishes, she <u>helped / had</u> me dry. My brother, a former high school wrestling star, swept the floor!

_____ **8.** I'm an only child, and when I was young I felt lonely. He <u>let / got</u> me sleep over at my friend's house.

_____ **9.** I wasn't paying attention, and I hit a parked car. He <u>let / made</u> me tell the court what happened.

EXERCISE 3: Affirmative and Negative Statements

(Grammar Notes 1, 3)

Complete each summary. Use the correct form of the verbs in parentheses. Choose between affirmative and negative.

1.   **PABLO:** Ms. Allen, do I have to rewrite this paper on elephants?

     MS. ALLEN: Only if you want to.

     SUMMARY: Ms. Allen <u>*didn't make Pablo rewrite*</u> OR <u>*didn't make him rewrite*</u> his paper.
                                            (make / rewrite)

2.   **ANA:** Could I work alone? I really don't like to work in a group.

     MS. ALLEN: You need to work in a group today. Don't look so sad. It's not a punishment!

     SUMMARY: She _____ in a group.
                         (make / work)

(continued on next page)

3.   **Ms. Allen:** Fernando, could you do me a favor and clean the board before you leave?

     Fernando: Sure.

     SUMMARY: She _____ the board.
                                    (have / clean)

4.   **Ms. Allen:** Uri, I know you're busy, but I'd like you and Greta to research orcas. You're

            both so good at Internet research.

            Uri: Oh, OK!

     SUMMARY: She _____ orcas on the Internet.
                                    (get / research)

5.   **Uri:** We need some really great orca photos, and I can't find any.

         Greta: Try the *National Geographic* site. They have fantastic nature photographs.

     SUMMARY: Greta _____ photographs of orcas.
                                    (help / find)

6.   **Hector:** What does *positive reinforcement* mean?

     Ms. Allen: Why don't you see if one of your classmates can explain it to you?

     SUMMARY: Ms. Allen _____ his classmates for help.
                                    (have / ask)

EXERCISE 4: Affirmative and Negative Statements   *(Grammar Notes 1–3)*

Complete each summary. Use **make, have, let, help,** *or* **get** *plus the correct form of the verbs
in parentheses. Choose between affirmative and negative.*

1.   **Masami:** Can we use our dictionaries during the test?

     Ms. Allen: No. You should be able to guess the meaning of the words from the context.

     SUMMARY: She _____ *didn't let them use* _____ their dictionaries.
                                    (use)

2.   **María:** Mom, can I borrow the car?

            Mom: Only if you drive your sister to soccer.

     SUMMARY: María's mother _____ her sister to soccer.
                                    (drive)

3.   **John:** Can I borrow your camera for our class trip to the zoo?

            Dad: Sure. I know you'll take good care of it.

     SUMMARY: John's father _____ his camera.
                                    (borrow)

4.   **John:** Excuse me, could I take pictures in here?

         Worker: Yes, but don't use the flash. Light bothers these animals.

     SUMMARY: The zoo worker _____ the flash on his camera.
                                    (use)

5.   **PAUL:**   Ms. Allen, which movie on this list do you think we should watch?

     MS. ALLEN: You might like *Free Willy*. It's about a captive orca.

     SUMMARY: Ms. Allen _____ a movie to watch.
                                                (choose)

6.   **MARÍA:**   John, the group wants you to read your report to the class.

     JOHN: No way! Sorry, but speaking in front of the class makes me nervous.

     SUMMARY: María _____ the report to the class.
                                             (read)

EXERCISE 5: Editing

Read this email petition about orcas. There are eight mistakes in the use of **make, have, let, help,** *and* **get***. The first mistake is already corrected. Find and correct seven more.*

LET THEM GO!

                                                 to buy

Orcas are beautiful and intelligent, so aquariums easily get audiences ~~buy~~ tickets for orca shows. What does this mean for the orcas? In the wild, an orca may swim up to 100 miles a day and dive hundreds of feet below the surface of the ocean. In captivity, an orca can't have normal physical or emotional health. We make this animal lives in a small, chemically-treated pool where it may get sick and die of an infection. Is that humane? Some people argue that captive orcas have helped us learned about these animals. However, orcas cannot behave naturally in an aquarium. In captivity, trainers make them to perform embarrassing tricks for a "reward." In the wild, these animals have rich and complicated social lives in families. How can watching tricks help we learn about their lives? Orcas don't belong in aquariums!

Don't let these beautiful animals suffering in order to entertain us! First, help us stop aquarium shows. Stop going to these shows, and get your friends and family stop also. Next, we must make aquariums stop buying orcas. Write to your mayor and tell him or her how you feel. Can former captives live in the wild? It's a difficult question, but aquariums must let others retrained these animals and try to release them to a normal life.

Help us help the orcas! It's the humane thing to do. Sign this e-letter and send it to your friends.

EXERCISE 6: Listening

A | *Read the statements. Then listen to a student talk to his teacher about a writing assignment. Listen again and circle the correct words to complete the statements.*

1. Simon wrote an essay about his uncle / *(animals in zoos)*.

2. Simon and his uncle used to go to the wildlife park / zoo together to look at animals.

3. Ms. Jacobson gets Simon to answer some *yes / no* questions / *wh-* questions to make his essay more interesting.

4. Simon is having trouble using the gerund / simple past.

5. Simon would like to make an appointment for a physical exam / another conference on Wednesday.

B | *Read the statements. Then listen again and check (✓)* **True** *or* **False**. *Correct the false statements.*

	True	False
1. Ms. Jacobson ~~made~~ *let* Simon write about animals in zoos.	☐	☑
2. She let him change the topic of his essay.	☐	☐
3. She had him remove some details from his second paragraph.	☐	☐
4. She got him to talk about his uncle.	☐	☐
5. She helped him correct a grammar mistake.	☐	☐
6. Simon got Ms. Jacobson to correct the gerunds in his essay.	☐	☐
7. Ms. Jacobson made Simon look for the gerunds in his essay.	☐	☐
8. She let Simon make an appointment for another conference.	☐	☐

EXERCISE 7: Pronunciation

A | *Read and listen to the Pronunciation Note.*

Pronunciation Note
In conversation, we often **don't pronounce the first sound** of the pronouns *him*, *her*, and *them* and we **connect the pronoun to the word** that comes before it.
EXAMPLES: let **her** go → "let'**er** go"   made **him** work → "made'**im** work"   got **them** to come → "got'**em** to come"
Notice that '**im** and '**em** sound the same: /**əm**/.
You can **understand** if /**əm**/ means *him* or *them* **from the context** (other words the speaker says). For example, if you hear "Bob's mother made'im do his homework," you know that "im" is "him" because of *Bob* and *his*.

B | *Listen to the short conversations. Complete the sentences. Use the full forms.*

1. **A:** Was she happy with the essay topic?

   B: Yes, her teacher _____ _____ write about pets.

2. **A:** Where did they go for their class trip?

   B: The teacher _____ _____ to the children's zoo.

3. **A:** Did he enjoy the trip?

   B: Yes. They _____ _____ feed the rabbits.

4. **A:** What are the elephants doing?

   B: The trainer _____ _____ to stand on one foot!

5. **A:** Is Ellie walking the dog?

   B: Yes, we finally _____ _____ to do it.

6. **A:** Why does Jack look so angry?

   B: They _____ _____ stop taking pictures of the monkey.

C | *Listen again to the conversations and repeat the responses. Then practice the conversations with a partner. Use the short forms.*

EXERCISE 8: Discussion

Work with a partner. Talk about someone who helped you learn something (for example, a parent, other relative, teacher, friend). Answer the following questions. You can also choose to write about how you learned something from taking care of or observing an animal. Use **make, have, let, help,** *and* **get.**

- What did the person get you to do that you never did before?
- How did this person help you?
- Did he or she let you make mistakes in order to learn?

EXAMPLE: **A:** My older brother was a big help to me when I was a teenager.
B: Oh? What did he do?
A: Well, he got me to try a lot of new things. He even taught me to dance. And he never laughed at my mistakes or made me feel stupid.

EXERCISE 9: For or Against

Is it humane to keep animals captive for human entertainment and research? What are some reasons for and against keeping animals in zoos and water parks? You can check the Internet for ideas (search **zoos good or bad.**) *Discuss your ideas in small groups. Use* **make, have, let, help,** *and* **get.**

EXAMPLE: **A:** I think it's cruel to make wild animals live in small habitats.
B: I'm not sure. But having them perform . . .
C: I think zoos can help us . . .

EXERCISE 10: Writing

A | *Write a three-paragraph essay for and against keeping animals in zoos and water parks. Give the arguments* **for** *in your first paragraph. Give the arguments* **against** *in your second. Give your own opinion in the third paragraph. You can use information from Exercise 9.*

EXAMPLE: Many people believe that it is good to keep animals in zoos and water parks. They say that people can . . .
Others argue that it is bad. Animals in zoos and water parks cannot . . .
I believe that . . . .

B | *Check your work. Use the Editing Checklist.*

Editing Checklist

Did you use . . . ?
☐ **object** + **base form** of the verb after *make*, *have*, and *let*
☐ **object** + **base form or infinitive** after *help*
☐ **object** + **infinitive** after *get*
☐ the correct verb to express your meaning

A | *Circle the correct words to complete the sentences.*

1. I didn't know what to write about, so my teacher <u>helped / made</u> me choose a topic by suggesting ideas.

2. Before we began to write, she <u>had / got</u> us research the topic online.

3. At first I was annoyed when my teacher <u>let / made</u> me rewrite the report.

4. She was very helpful. She always <u>let / helped</u> me ask her questions.

5. It was a good assignment. It really <u>made / got</u> me to think a lot.

B | *Complete the sentences with the correct form of the verbs in parentheses. Choose between affirmative and negative and use pronoun objects.*

1. When I was little, my parents _____ a pet. They said I was too young.
   (let / have)

2. When I was 10, I finally _____ me a dog. His name was Buttons.
   (get / give)

3. It was a lot of responsibility. My parents _____ him every day.
   (make / walk)

4. They _____ him too. He ate a lot!
   (have / feed)

5. I was annoyed at my older brother. He _____ care of Buttons very much.
   (help / take)

6. Sometimes I _____ Buttons a bath. Both my brother and Buttons enjoyed it.
   (get / give)

7. When I have children, I plan to _____ a pet. It's a great learning experience.
   (let / have)

C | *Find and correct eight mistakes.*

Lately I've been thinking a lot about all the people who helped me adjusting to moving here when I was a kid. My parents got me join some school clubs so that I met other kids. Then my dad helped me improves my soccer game so I could join the team. And my mom never let me to stay home. She made me to get out and do things. My parents also spoke to my new teacher, and they had her called on me a lot so the other kids got to know me quickly. The neighbors helped too. They got I to walk their dog Red, and Red introduced me to all her human friends! The fact that so many people wanted to help me made me to realize that I was not alone. Before long I felt part of my new school, my new neighborhood, and my new life.

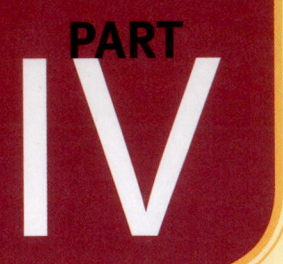

From Grammar to Writing
USING PARALLEL FORMS: GERUNDS AND INFINITIVES

When you write a **list using gerunds or infinitives**, make sure the items are in **parallel form**. If a list starts with a gerund, all items in that list should be gerunds. If it starts with an infinitive, all items in the list should be infinitives.

EXAMPLE: Homer loved hunting, fishing, and ~~to hike~~. ➜
Homer loved **hunting**, **fishing**, and **hiking**.
OR
Homer loved **to hunt**, **fish**, and **hike**.

Notice that in a list of infinitives it is not necessary to repeat *to*.

1 | *Read this movie summary. Correct any gerunds or infinitives that are not parallel.*

OCTOBER SKY
Directed by Joe Johnston

It's October 1957, and the Soviet Union has just launched *Sputnik*. Homer, a teenage boy (played by Jake Gyllenhaal), watches the satellite fly over his poor coal-mining town in West Virginia and dreams of building and ~~to launch~~ *launching* his own rocket. He teams up with three friends, and "The Rocket Boys" start to put together and firing their homemade missiles. The boys' goal is to win the regional science fair. First prize will bring college scholarships and a way out of Coalwood. The school science teacher, Miss Riley, encourages him, but Homer's father (played by Chris Cooper) is angry about the boys' project. He wants Homer to follow in his footsteps and working at the mine. Nevertheless, the boys continue launching rockets, failing in different ways, and to learn with each failure. People begin changing their minds and to admire the Rocket Boys. Some even help them.

However, success does not come easily in Coalwood. When a forest fire starts nearby, a rocket is blamed, and the boys must give up their project. Then Homer's father is injured, and Homer quits school to support his family as a miner. His father is proud of him, but Homer can't stand giving up his dream and to work in the mine.

He uses mathematics to prove a rocket did not start the fire. Then he tells his father he plans to leave the mine and returning to school.

The Rocket Boys win first prize at the science fair, and all four of them receive scholarships. The whole town celebrates, and Homer wins another very valuable prize—his father attends the science fair and launches the rocket. It's clear that father and son will try to make peace and respecting each other.

2 | *Complete the story map with information from Exercise 1.*

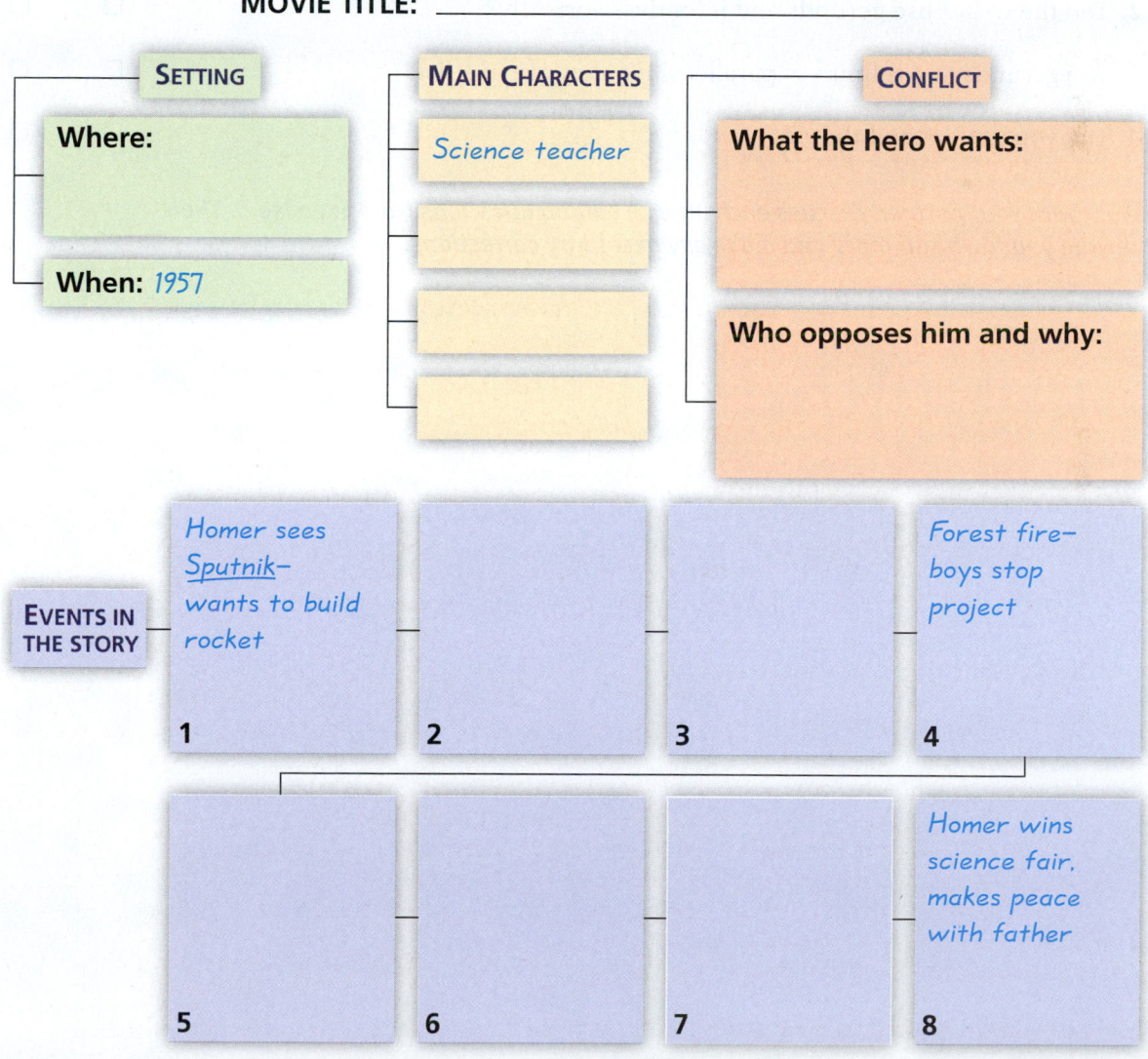

MOVIE TITLE: _____

SETTING

Where:

When: *1957*

MAIN CHARACTERS

Science teacher

CONFLICT

What the hero wants:

Who opposes him and why:

EVENTS IN THE STORY

1. *Homer sees Sputnik— wants to build rocket*
2.
3.
4. *Forest fire— boys stop project*
5.
6.
7.
8. *Homer wins science fair, makes peace with father*

3 | *Before you write . . .*

    1. Work with a partner. Choose a movie or TV show that you have both seen or a story that you have both read.

    2. Create a story map like the one in Exercise 2.

4 | *Write a summary about the movie, TV show, or story you chose in Exercise 3. Use your story map for information. Remember to use gerunds and infinitives.*

5 | *Exchange your writing with a different partner. Underline gerunds once. Underline infinitives twice. Write a question mark (**?**) over anything that seems wrong in your partner's summary. Answer the following questions.*

	Yes	No
1. Did the writer use gerunds and infinitives?	☐	☐
2. Did the writer use gerunds and infinitives correctly?	☐	☐
3. Are gerunds and infinitives parallel when they are in a list?	☐	☐
4. Did you understand the story?	☐	☐

6 | *Work with your partner. Discuss each other's editing questions from Exercise 5. Then rewrite your own summary and make any necessary corrections.*

PHRASAL VERBS

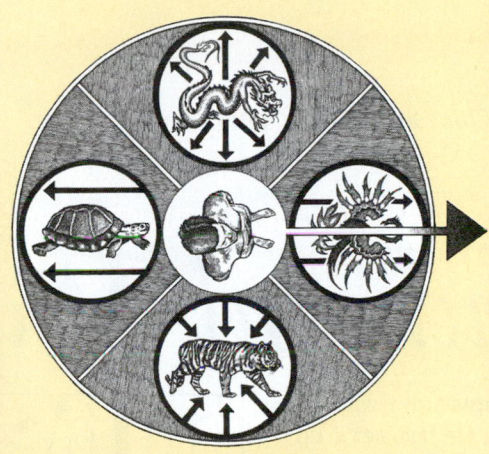

UNIT	GRAMMAR FOCUS	THEME
11	Phrasal Verbs: Review	Feng Shui
12	Phrasal Verbs: Separable and Inseparable	Telemarketing

Phrasal Verbs: Review
FENG SHUI

Before You Read

Look at the photo and read the caption. Discuss the questions.

1. What kind of advice do you think a feng shui consultant gives about people's homes?
2. Do you think the furniture and colors in your home affect your life? If yes, how?

Read

Read the article about the ancient Chinese art of feng shui.

Wind and Water

A feng shui consultant on the job with his *loupan*

Ho Da-ming couldn't **figure out** why his restaurant was failing. He had **set it up** on a busy street. His chef was famous. He had paid a fortune for interior design.[1] But customers rarely **came back**. Why? Mr. Ho **called in** a feng shui consultant to **find out**. Feng shui (meaning "wind and water" and pronounced FUNG SHWAY) is the ancient Chinese art of placing things in the environment. According to this art, the arrangement of furniture, doors, and windows affects our health, wealth, and happiness.

The consultant used a *loupan* (a feng shui compass) to **look into** the patterns of energy in the restaurant. He told Mr. Ho that the entrance was **letting** prosperity[2] **out**. The desperate owner quickly **tore down** the old entrance and **put up** a new one. His action **paid off**. Soon business **picked up**, and Mr. Ho became rich.

---

[1] *interior design:* the selection and arrangement of furniture and other objects in a room
[2] *prosperity:* having money and other things needed for a good life

Wind and Water

Feng shui has **caught on** with modern architects and homeowners everywhere. Although the complex charts of feng shui are hard to **work out**, the theory is simple: We are part of nature, and we must adjust to its natural energies. To be healthy and prosperous, we must **lay out** our homes and workplaces to allow *chi* (good energy) to circulate gently and to **cut off** *sha* (harmful energy).

Try this activity **out** in your home, dorm room, or office. First **sit down** and think about how you feel in this room. Now look around. Try to **pick out** the things that make you feel good or bad. To **find out** more, **look up** the topic online or go to your library or bookstore and **pick up** a book on basic feng shui. You'll be surprised at what you learn.

After You Read

A | Vocabulary: *Complete the sentences with the words from the box.*

complex	consultant	environment	harmful	theory

1. If you need advice, you can hire a(n) _____.

2. What is the _____ behind feng shui?

3. It's not an easy question. In fact, it's very _____.

4. It's very important to have a nice _____ to live and work in.

5. What's wrong with having a window there? Why is that _____?

B | Comprehension: *Check (✓)* **True** *or* **False**. *Correct the false statements.*

	True	False
1. Mr. Ho called in a consultant because his chef needed help.	☐	☐
2. Mr. Ho hadn't spent much on the restaurant's appearance.	☐	☐
3. The restaurant's customers usually didn't return.	☐	☐
4. Feng shui has been used for a very long time.	☐	☐
5. Mr. Ho changed the location of his restaurant.	☐	☐
6. Today, many architects use the ideas of feng shui.	☐	☐
7. To find out more about feng shui, you need to hire a consultant.	☐	☐

PHRASAL VERBS: REVIEW

Transitive Phrasal Verbs

Not Separated			
Subject	**Verb**	**Particle**	**Direct Object**
She He	**called**	**in**	a consultant.
	figured	**out**	the problem.

Separated			
Subject	**Verb**	**Direct Object**	**Particle**
She He	**called**	a consultant him	**in**.
	figured	the problem it	**out**.

Intransitive Phrasal Verbs

Not Separated			
Subject	**Verb**	**Particle**	
They It	**came**	**back**	quickly.
	caught	**on**	everywhere.

GRAMMAR NOTES

1 A **phrasal verb** (also called a *two-word verb*) has two parts: a verb and a particle.

verb + particle = phrasal verb

Particles look like prepositions, but they act differently.

a. Prepositions <u>do not change the meaning</u> of the verb.

b. Particles often <u>change the meaning</u> of the verb.

VERB + PARTICLE
- Let's **figure out** this problem now.

VERB + PARTICLE
- Ho **called in** a consultant.

VERB + PREPOSITION
- He **looked into** the room.
  *(He was outside the room and **looked** in.)*

VERB + PARTICLE
- He **looked into** the problem.
  *(He **researched** the problem.)*

2 A **phrasal verb** has a **special meaning**, often very different from the meanings of its parts.

PHRASAL VERB	MEANING
call in	hire
figure out	understand
find out	discover
look into	research
pick up	improve

- Let's **call in** an expert to help.
- We had to **figure out** the problem.
- Did you **find out** what was wrong?
- We **looked into** feng shui.
- Business has **picked up**.

USAGE NOTE: Phrasal verbs are more **informal** than one-word verbs with similar meaning. They are very **common in everyday speech**. You have to learn the meaning of phrasal verbs to understand spoken English.

- We're **putting up** signs for our business.
  (We're erecting signs for our business.)

BE CAREFUL! Like other verbs, phrasal verbs often have **more than one meaning**.

- Please **turn down** the radio. It's too loud.
  (Please lower the volume.)
- Bill didn't get the job. They **turned down** his application.
  (They rejected his application.)

(continued on next page)

3 Many phrasal verbs are **transitive**. They have **objects**.

Phrasal Verb	Meaning
call off something	cancel
pick out something	choose
take away something	remove
think up something	invent
work out something	solve

PHRASAL VERB + OBJECT
- Let's **call off** *the meeting*.
- **Pick out** *the chair* you like best.
- **Take away** *the dishes*.
- He **thought up** *good answers*.
- He **worked out** *the problem*.

Most transitive phrasal verbs are **separable**. This means that **noun objects** can go:
- **after** the particle OR

- **between** the verb and the particle

VERB + PARTICLE + OBJECT
- They **tore down** *the entrance*. OR

VERB + OBJECT + PARTICLE
- They **tore** *the entrance* **down**.

BE CAREFUL! If the direct object is a **pronoun**, it must go <u>between</u> the verb and the particle.

- I didn't understand the word, so I **looked** *it* **up** in the dictionary.
  Not: I ~~looked up it~~

USAGE NOTE: When the noun object is part of a **long phrase**, we usually <u>do not separate</u> the verb and particle of a phrasal verb.

- Ho **tried out** *the many complex theories of feng shui*.
  Not: Ho ~~tried the many complex theories of feng shui out.~~

4 Some phrasal verbs are **intransitive**. They do **NOT** have an object. They are always **inseparable**.

Phrasal Verb	Meaning
catch on	become popular
get ahead	make progress
show up	appear
sit down	take a seat

- Feng shui has **caught on** all over.
- Tina is **getting ahead** in her career.
- The consultant **showed up** early.
- **Sit down** over there.

BE CAREFUL! Do **NOT separate** an intransitive phrasal verb.

Not: Sit ~~over there down~~.

REFERENCE NOTES

For a list of **transitive phrasal verbs**, see Appendix 18 on page A-6.
For information about **transitive verbs that are inseparable**, see Unit 12.
For a list of **intransitive phrasal verbs**, see Appendix 19 on page A-8.

EXERCISE 1: Discover the Grammar

A | *Read the article about feng shui. Underline all the phrasal verbs and circle the direct objects of the transitive phrasal verbs. Go to Appendices 18 and 19 on pages A-6 and A-8 for help.*

Everyday Feng Shui

Have you noticed that some spaces cheer you up and give you energy, while others bring you down? This feng shui diagram uses mythological animals[1] to explain why. Look it over, and then imagine yourself in the center. According to feng shui theory, a phoenix takes off in front of you and gives you inspiration.[2] Behind you, a tortoise guards you from harmful things you cannot see. On your left and right, a dragon and a tiger balance each other. The dragon floats above the floor and helps you take in the big picture, not just small details. The tiger's energy gives you courage.

These symbols can be important in setting up a work environment. Dana, for example, needed ideas and energy in order to get ahead. Unfortunately, her undecorated, windowless cubicle[3] took away most of her powers. After she hung up a scenic poster in the phoenix area in front of her desk, she began to feel more inspired. She gave her tiger some power by picking out plants to put on the file cabinet to her right. For her dragon, she hung a cheerful mobile from the top of the left wall of her cubicle. Try these ideas out in your own work area and see what happens!

_____

[1] **mythological animals:** animals in ancient stories about natural or historical events
[2] **inspiration:** something that causes you to produce good or beautiful things
[3] **cubicle:** a small part of a room, especially in an office, that is separated from the rest of the room by low walls

B | Read the statements and check (✓) True or False. Correct the false statements.

	True	False
1. Your environment ~~can't~~ *can* bring about changes in your mood.	☐	✓
2. The phoenix remains sitting in the space ahead of you.	☐	☐
3. The dragon's energy helps you understand an overall plan.	☐	☐
4. Dana wanted a promotion.	☐	☐
5. From the beginning, Dana's work area inspired her.	☐	☐
6. She removed a poster from the area in front of her desk.	☐	☐
7. There were no plants in her cubicle at first.	☐	☐

EXERCISE 2: Particles

(Grammar Note 1)

Circle the correct particles to complete these questions and answers from an online feng shui message board. Go to Appendix 18 on page A-6 for help.

Q: I've been having a lot of trouble sleeping. My bed faces north. Is that *really* harmful?

A: Yes. Turn it (around) / up so that your head is to the north and your feet to the south.
           1.

Q: Our building owner has cut down / up all the trees in our garden. Now he's going to put on / up
                          2.   **3.**

a tall building there! This will block away / out all our light. What can we do?
                            4.

A: I don't know if you can work this problem off / out. You may need to think about moving.
                                      5.

Q: I am opening a new restaurant in Los Angeles. I would like to have a feng shui consultant look it

over / up to see if the energy is positive. Could you recommend someone?
   6.

A: We don't give out / up names online. Email me, and I will put together / off a list for you.
             7.   **8.**

Q: I hung up / out a beautiful mirror on my bedroom wall. Then I read that mirrors bring too much
         9.

energy into a bedroom. I don't want to take it out / down! What can I do?
                                   10.

A: Before you go to sleep, put a scarf over the mirror. That will keep on / out the "bad energy."
                                                11.

Q: I don't know much about feng shui. How can I find after / out more about the theory behind it?
                                 12.

A: There are hundreds of books about feng shui. Go to your local library and take some out / up.
                                                  13.

Or look after / up feng shui on an online bookstore website to get a list of titles.
   14.

EXERCISE 3: Meaning of Phrasal Verbs

(Grammar Notes 2–3)

Read about one of the most famous modern architects. Complete the information with the correct forms of the phrasal verbs from the boxes. Go to Appendices 18 and 19 on pages A-6 and A-8 for help.

~~grow up~~	put up	settle on	turn out

Born in 1917, Ieoh Ming Pei (better known as I. M. Pei) _____*grew up*_____ in Canton, China. As a child,
1.

Pei watched workers _____ large new
2.

buildings. When he was 17, he went to the United States to learn about building. He considered becoming an engineer or an architect. However, he didn't finally

_____ his career until after he enrolled in
3.

I. M. Pei in front of the Louvre pyramid

college. As it _____, Pei became one of the most famous modern architects in
4.

the world.

figure out	go up	let in	put on	tear down

Pei is famous for his strong geometric forms made of steel, glass, concrete, and stone. One of his most controversial projects was his glass pyramid at the Louvre in Paris. The old museum was dark, confusing, and crowded, but no one wanted to _____ the
5.

old structure. Pei had to _____ a solution to the Louvre's complex problems
6.

and still be sensitive to the famous old building and its surroundings. When he proposed his 71-foot-high glass pyramid as a new entrance to the museum, many Parisians were shocked,

and they _____ buttons asking "Why the pyramid?" However, the glass
7.

pyramid _____ anyway, blending with the environment, reflecting the sky,
8.

and _____ the sunlight. Today, many people say that it is a good example of
9.

the principles of feng shui.

(continued on next page)

| give up | go back | keep on | set up |

In spite of harsh criticism, Pei _____
10.
building structures that reflected their environment—
from the 70-story Bank of China skyscraper in Hong
Kong to the Rock 'n' Roll Hall of Fame in Cleveland,
Ohio. He has received many prizes and has become very
prosperous. He has used some of the prize money to
_____ a scholarship fund for Chinese
11.
students to study architecture in the United States and then to _____ to China
12.
to work as architects.

Inside the Louvre pyramid

Pei is both creative and persistent. Throughout his career, many people have criticized

his work, but Pei strongly believes that "you have to identify the important things and press

for them and not _____."
13.

EXERCISE 4: Pronoun Objects

(Grammar Note 2)

Complete the conversations. Use the correct form of the phrasal verb in the first line of the conversation. Include a pronoun object.

1. **A:** Could I borrow your truck? I need to pick up some chairs this week.

   B: Sure. When are you _____*going to pick them up*_____?

2. **A:** Hey! Who took down my feng shui posters?

   B: Sorry. I _____. I thought you didn't like them anymore.

3. **A:** I need to cheer up my roommate. He just flunked a big test.

   B: Why don't you straighten up the room? That will _____.

4. **A:** This room is depressing. Let's try out some of these feng shui ideas.

   B: I agree. Let's _____ this weekend.

5. **A:** We need something to light up that corner. It's awfully dark.

   B: I have an extra lamp. This will _____ nicely.

6. **A:** Can someone touch up the paint in my dorm room? It's cracked in several places.

   B: Sure. We'll send someone to _____ next week.

EXERCISE 5: Editing

Read this student's journal entry. There are ten mistakes in the use of phrasal verbs. The first mistake is already corrected. Find and correct nine more. Go to Appendices 18 and 19 on pages A-6 and A-8 for help.

>   I just read an article about feng shui. The author suggests sitting ~~up~~ ^{down} in your home and thinking about how your environment makes you feel. I tried out it.
>
>   My apartment is bright and sunny. This cheers me out. At night, it's very dark, but I've figured up what to do. I'm going to buy another lamp to light the apartment at night up. I'll leave it on when I go out at night so I can see light as soon as I come in. I also like the light green walls in my bedroom, but the chipped paint has been bringing down me. I'm going to touch it over soon.
>
>   My apartment is too small, but I can't tear up the walls. I think it'll look more spacious if I just straighten it up. I'll try to put books back after I take them off the shelves and hang away my clothes at night. With just a few small changes, I'll end up feeling happier in my home. It's worth trying on. And I won't even need a consultant!

STEP 4 COMMUNICATION PRACTICE

EXERCISE 6: Listening

A | *Read the statements. Then listen to the short conversations. Listen again and check (✓) True or False. Correct the false statements.*

	True	False
1. Amy and Ben are talking about the ~~noise~~ *temperature* in their apartment.	☐	☑
2. Amy is interested in trying out feng shui.	☐	☐
3. Ben has finished redecorating his office.	☐	☐
4. Ben is a student.	☐	☐
5. Amy and Ben agree about the curtains.	☐	☐
6. The mattress is very comfortable.	☐	☐
7. Amy and Ben are going to paint the kitchen.	☐	☐

1. It's a little too cold for me. Do you mind if I turn the air conditioner _____*down*_____?

2. I haven't had the chance to look it _____ yet.

3. I'm going to the furniture store today to pick _____ a new couch.

4. I'll put them _____ as soon as I'm done with my homework.

5. I'm going to take them _____ tomorrow.

6. I think we need to turn it _____.

7. Let's look _____ some colors online.

EXERCISE 7: Pronunciation

🎧 **A** | *Read and listen to the Pronunciation Note.*

Pronunciation Note
For many **phrasal verbs**, the verb ends in a consonant sound and the particle begins with a vowel sound. In conversation, we often **link** the **final consonant** sound to the **beginning vowel** sound. **EXAMPLES:** Could you **pick up** a book about feng shui? I'm going to **turn on** the heat.

🎧 **B** | *Listen to the short conversations. Draw linking lines (‿) from the final consonant in the verb to the beginning vowel in the particle.*

1. **A:** Did you **find out** anything more about feng shui?

   B: No. I'm going to **look over** some information now.

2. **A:** Have you **made up** your mind about the paint color?

   B: Not yet. But I'm sure I'll **come up** with something.

3. **A:** So, do you think we should **hang up** some paintings on that wall?

   B: Maybe we can just **pick up** a few posters from the store.

4. **A:** We need a better lamp to **light up** this room.

   B: I know. Maybe we can **pick out** one from this website.

5. A: This room is a mess. Can you **put away** some of your stuff?

B: No problem. As soon as I **clean out** this closet.

6. A: Hey, it's dark in here. Let's **turn on** some lights.

B: OK. And I'll **turn off** the heat too. It's hot in here.

C | *Listen again to the conversations. Then practice them with a partner.*

EXERCISE 8: Problem Solving

Work in small groups. How would you like to change your classroom or your school? What would you like to remain the same? Use some of these phrasal verbs in your discussion.

cover up	light up	put away	throw away
do over	make up	put up	touch up
hang up	move around	straighten up	turn around
leave on	pick out	tear down	turn on / off

EXAMPLE: **A:** I think we should hang up some posters.
B: It would be nice to hang some photographs up too.
C: We could hang some paintings up too.

EXERCISE 9: Compare and Contrast

*Work with a partner. Look at the **Before** and **After** pictures of Amy's room for two minutes. Write down all the differences you can find. Then compare your list with another pair's list.*

Before

After

EXAMPLE: **A:** She took the curtains down.
B: Right. And she also . . .

EXERCISE 10: Writing

A | *Write two paragraphs about how you feel in your home, office, dorm, or classroom. What makes you feel good? What makes you feel bad? What would you like to change? Use phrasal verbs. You can use the journal entry in Exercise 5 on page 181 as a model.*

EXAMPLE: My dorm room is bright and sunny. The room always cheers me up when I get back from a hard day at school. My roommate and I picked out the curtains together. We also put up some new posters on the walls . . .

B | *Check your work. Use the Editing Checklist.*

Editing Checklist
Did you . . . ? ☐ use phrasal verbs ☐ use the correct particles ☐ put pronoun objects between the verb and the particle of separable phrasal verbs

A | *Circle the correct words to complete the sentences.*

1. We called <u>up / off</u> the meeting because so many people were on vacation.

2. The house was badly damaged by the storm. They're planning to tear <u>down it /it down</u>.

3. Ina is really getting <u>ahead / away</u> in her career. She's just gotten another promotion.

4. I hadn't heard of I. M. Pei, so I looked him <u>out / up</u> online.

5. Let's straighten this room up. I'll start by putting <u>away / over</u> my books.

6. I really don't like the new lamp. Let's take it <u>over / back</u> to the store and get another one.

7. I just bought a new couch. I'm going to pick <u>it up / up it</u> tomorrow.

B | *Complete the conversations with the correct form of the phrasal verbs from the box.*

figure out	leave on	show up	touch up
find out	settle on	take down	turn off

- **A:** Why did you _____ my poster?

1.

  B: I needed to _____ the paint on that wall.

2.

- **A:** Will Ana ever _____ a career? She changes her mind every month.

3.

  B: It's a problem, but I think she'll _____ it _____ herself.

4.

- **A:** The plumber was supposed to come today, but he didn't _____.

5.

  B: Why don't you call and _____ what happened?

6.

- **A:** We _____ the light _____ in the car. I can see it from here.

7.

  B: You're right. I'll go _____ it _____.

8.

C | *Find and correct five mistakes.*

A: This apartment is bringing me down. Let's do over it.

B: It *is* depressing. Let's put around a list and figure out what to do first.

A: OK. Write this down: Pick on new paint colors. We can look at some online.

B: The new streetlight shines into the bedroom. We need to block up the light somehow.

A: We could put on some dark curtains in that room. That should take care of the problem.

STEP 1 GRAMMAR IN CONTEXT

Before You Read

Look at the cartoon. Discuss the questions.

1. Who do you think is calling the man? How does the man feel about the call?
2. Do you receive unwanted calls? How do you feel about them?

Read

Read the magazine article about telemarketers.

WELCOME HOME!

You just **got back** from a long, hard day at the office. You're exhausted. All you want to do is **take off** your jacket, **put down** your briefcase, and relax over a great dinner. Then, just as you're about to **sit down** at the table, the phone rings. You hesitate to **pick** it **up**. It's probably just another telemarketer trying to **talk** you **into** buying something you really don't need. But, what if it's not? It could be important. Maybe there's a family emergency. You have to **find out**!

"Hello?" you answer nervously.

"Hello, is this Mr. Groaner?" a strange voice asks. You know right away that it's a telemarketer. Your last name is Groden.

"I just got home. Can you call back tomorrow when I'm still at work?"

"We have great news for you! You've been chosen to receive an all-expense-paid trip to the Bahamas! It's an offer you can't afford to **turn down**!"

Telemarketing—the practice of selling products and services by phone—is rapidly spreading throughout the world as the number of household phones **goes up** and phone rates **come down**. To most people, these annoying calls are about as welcome as a bad case of the flu.

What can be done about this invasion of privacy?[1] Look at the next page for several tactics you can **try out**.

[1]*invasion of privacy:* interrupting or getting involved in another's personal life in an unwelcome way

WELCOME HOME!

☎ **Sign up** to have your phone number placed on "Do Not Call" lists. Many countries are **setting up** lists of people who do not want to be called by telemarketers. These lists actually make it against the law for telemarketers to call you. If you still receive these calls, **write down** the date and time of the call. **Find out** the name of the organization calling you. You can then report the illegal call to the proper authorities.

☎ Use Caller ID to help identify telemarketers. If an unfamiliar number **shows up** on your ID screen, don't **pick up** the phone.

☎ If you *have* answered the phone, say (firmly but politely!): "I'm **hanging up** now," and **get off** the phone.

☎ Ask the telemarketing company to **take** you **off** their list. But don't **count on** this happening immediately. You may have to ask several times before it takes effect.

None of these measures will eliminate all unwanted telephone solicitations,[2] but they should help **cut down** the number of calls that you receive.

Telemarketing, however, is just part of the larger problem. We are constantly being flooded with unwanted offers and requests. "Junk mail" **fills up** our mailboxes (and later our trash cans when we **throw** it **out**).

And the invasion is, of course, not limited to paper. When you **turn on** your computer to check your email, you are greeted by dozens of commercial messages. Known as *spam*, it's the electronic equivalent of junk mail.

What's the solution? Leave home? Move to a desert island? Maybe not. They'll probably **get to** you there too!

---

[2]*solicitation:* asking someone for something such as money or help

After You Read

A | Vocabulary: *Circle the word or phrase that best completes each sentence.*

1. If Jason **constantly** calls you, he <u>always / sometimes / never</u> calls you.

2. The **authorities** are people that <u>buy / control / write</u> about things.

3. If you **eliminate** a problem, the problem <u>disappears / gets better / gets worse</u>.

4. If two things are **equivalent**, they are <u>the same / different / expensive</u>.

5. Telemarketers' **tactics** are their <u>products / sales methods / prices</u>.

6. If you can **identify** someone, you <u>ask / know / like</u> the person's name.

B | Comprehension: *Check (✓)* **True** *or* **False**. *Correct the false statements.*

	True	False
1. Mr. Groden got a call from a telemarketer in the morning.	☐	☐
2. The telemarketer didn't pronounce his name correctly.	☐	☐
3. Most people welcome these calls.	☐	☐
4. If your name is on a Do Not Call list, it is illegal for a telemarketer to call you.	☐	☐
5. You can do something to stop *all* of these unwanted calls.	☐	☐
6. Telemarketing is just one example of an invasion of privacy.	☐	☐

STEP 2 GRAMMAR PRESENTATION

PHRASAL VERBS: SEPARABLE AND INSEPARABLE

Separable Transitive			
Subject	**Verb**	**Particle**	**Direct Object**
She	**picked**	**up**	the phone.

Separable Transitive			
Subject	**Verb**	**Direct Object**	**Particle**
She	**picked**	the phone it	**up**.

Inseparable Transitive			
Subject	**Verb**	**Particle**	**Direct Object**
He	**counts**	**on**	your calls. them.

Intransitive		
Subject	**Verb**	**Particle**
They	**sat**	**down**.

GRAMMAR NOTES

1

As you learned in Unit 11, **phrasal verbs** have two parts: a verb and a particle.

verb + particle = **phrasal verb**

Particles look like prepositions, but they act differently.

Particles often **change the meaning** of the verb, but prepositions do not.

VERB + PARTICLE
- I **got off** the phone quickly.

VERB + PREPOSITION
- I **looked up** and saw a large bird.
  (*I looked toward the sky.*)

VERB + PARTICLE
- I **looked up** his number online.
  (*I tried to find his number.*)

2

Many phrasal verbs are **transitive**: they take an **object**. And most transitive phrasal verbs are **separable**. This means that **noun objects** can go <u>after</u> the particle <u>or between</u> the verb and the particle.

BE CAREFUL! If the direct object is a **pronoun**, it must go <u>between</u> the verb and the particle.

USAGE NOTE: When the noun object is part of a **long phrase**, we usually <u>do not separate</u> the verb and particle of a phrasal verb.

A small group of transitive phrasal verbs **must be separated**.

PHRASAL VERB	MEANING
keep something **on**	not remove
ask someone **over**	invite to one's home

VERB + PARTICLE + OBJECT
- I just **took off** *my coat*. OR

VERB + OBJECT + PARTICLE
- I just **took** *my coat* **off**.

- I **wrote** *it* **down**.
  NOT: I wrote ~~down it~~.

- I **filled out** *the form from the Do Not Call service*.
  NOT: ~~I filled the form from the Do Not Call service out.~~

- **Keep** *your coat* **on**. NOT: Keep ~~on your coat~~.
- **Ask** *Ian* **over**. NOT: Ask ~~over Ian~~.

3

Some **transitive** phrasal verbs are **inseparable**. This means that both noun and pronoun objects always go <u>after</u> the particle. You cannot separate the verb from its particle.

REMEMBER: Some phrasal verbs are **intransitive**: They do not take an object.

Like other verbs, some phrasal verbs can be **both transitive and intransitive**. The meaning is often the same.

BE CAREFUL! Some phrasal verbs have a completely **different meaning** when they are transitive or intransitive.

- I **ran into** *Karim* at work.
  NOT: I ~~ran Karim into~~ at work.
- I **ran into** *him* at work.
  NOT: I ~~ran him into~~.

- He's been away and just **got back**.
- They don't **give up**. They keep calling.

- He **called** *me* **back**.
- He **called back**.

- We **made up** a story. (*=invented*)
- We **made up**. (*=ended a disagreement*)

(continued on next page)

4 Some **transitive phrasal verbs** are used in combination with **prepositions** such as *of*, *to*, *with*, *at*, and *for*.

A **phrasal verb + preposition** combination (also called a *three-word verb*) is usually **inseparable**.

PHRASAL VERB	MEANING
come up *with* something	invent
drop out *of* something	quit
keep up *with* something/someone	go as fast as

- She **came up** *with* a way to stop junk mail.
- I **dropped out** *of* school and got a job.
- He couldn't **keep up** *with* his email. There was too much to read.

REFERENCE NOTES

For a list of **separable phrasal verbs**, see Appendix 18 on page A-6.
For a list of **inseparable transitive phrasal verbs**, see Appendix 18 on page A-6.
For a list of **phrasal verbs that must be separated**, see Appendix 18 on page A-6.
For a list of **phrasal verb + preposition combinations**, see Appendix 18 on page A-6.
For a list of **intransitive phrasal verbs**, see Appendix 19 on page A-8.

STEP 3 FOCUSED PRACTICE

EXERCISE 1: Discover the Grammar

A *Read this article about ways of dealing with telemarketers. Underline the phrasal verbs.*

HOLD ON, PLEASE! Your phone number is on the Do Not Call list, but you keep on receiving telemarketing calls. Constantly. Why not have some fun with them? We came up with these amusing tactics:

- When the telemarketer asks, "How are you today?"—tell her! Don't leave anything out. Say, "I have a headache you wouldn't believe, and my back is acting up again. Now I can't figure out the instructions for my DVD player . . ."

- When a telemarketer calls during dinner, request his home telephone number so you can call him back. When he refuses, ask him to hold on. Put the phone down and continue eating until you hear the dial tone.

- Ask the telemarketer to spell her first and last name and the name of the company. Tell her to speak slowly—you're taking notes. Ask questions until she hangs up.

- To credit card offers, say, "Thanks a lot! My company just laid me off, and I really need the money!"

B | *Write down each phrasal verb from the article next to its meaning.*

1. _____ causing problems   6. ___*hold on*___ not end a phone call

2. _____ continue   7. _____ omit

3. _____ ends a phone call   8. _____ return a call

4. _____ fired from a job   9. _____ stop holding something

5. _____ invented   10. _____ understand

EXERCISE 2: Meaning

(Grammar Note 1)

A scam is a dishonest plan, usually to get money. Read about how to avoid some common scams. Complete the information with the correct forms of the phrasal verbs from the boxes. Go to Appendices 18 and 19 on pages A-6 and A-8 for help.

| end up with | hang up | let down | ~~throw out~~ |

I just _____*threw out*_____ my first issue of *Motorcycle Mama*. I'm nobody's mama, and I
       1.
don't own a motorcycle, so how did I _____ this subscription? Well, my neighbor's
                2.
son was raising money for his soccer team, and I didn't want to _____ him

_____. It's easy to _____ on telemarketers, but it's hard to say *no* to
  3.   **4.**
your friends and neighbors.

| fall for | get to | help out | watch out for |

The magazine company _____ me through a friendship. It's one of the ways
         5.
"persuasion professionals" get us to say *yes*. Of course it's OK to _____ the local soccer
                6.
team. But a lot of people _____ scams because of similar techniques. Learn to identify
       7.
and _____ these common scams.
  8.

| find out | give back | go along with | turn down |

When someone gives you something, you want to _____ something

_____. This desire to return a favor can cost you money when a telemarketer
  9.
announces you've won a vacation or a new car. These offers aren't free. When people

_____ them, they always _____ that there's a tax or a fee to
  10.   **11.**
collect the "free" prize. Since they've accepted the offer, they feel obligated to pay. You should

_____ these offers _____. These are scams and they are illegal.
      12.

(continued on next page)

Phrasal Verbs: Separable and Inseparable   **191**

count on	fill out	pick out	put on	turn up

A TV actor will _____ a doctor's white jacket and talk about cough medicine. In
13.

a magazine ad, a woman in a business suit will help you _____ the best investment
14.

firm. Ads with fake "authority figures" are quite easy to identify, but there's an Internet scam called

phishing that's harder to recognize. The scammer sends emails that seem to be from well-known

banks. They tell you that a problem with your account has _____. Then they send you
15.

to an Internet site to _____ forms with your account information and password. The
16.

site looks like the real thing, but a real bank will NEVER ask for your information over the Internet.

You can _____ that! Tell the authorities right away about any phishing scams.
17.

EXERCISE 3: Separable Phrasal Verbs and Pronoun Objects   *(Grammar Note 2)*

Complete the conversations. Use phrasal verbs and pronouns.

1. **A:** Tell Ana not to pick up the phone. It's probably a telemarketer. They call constantly.

   B: Too late. She's already _____*picked it up*_____.

2. **A:** You can't turn down this great offer for cat food!

   B: I'm afraid I have to _____. I don't *have* a cat.

3. **A:** Did you fill out the online Do Not Call form?

   B: I _____ yesterday. I hope this will take care of the

   problem. I'm tired of these calls.

4. **A:** I left out my office phone and fax numbers on that form.

   B: Why did you _____?

5. **A:** Remember to call your mother back.

   B: I _____ last night.

6. **A:** Did you write down the dates of the calls?

   B: I _____, but then I lost the piece of paper.

7. **A:** Can you take my mother's name off your calling list?

   B: Sure. We'll _____ right away.

8. **A:** Let's turn the phone off and have dinner.

   B: I can't _____. I'm expecting an important call.

EXERCISE 4: Separable and Inseparable Phrasal Verbs

(Grammar Notes 2–4)

Complete the ads from spam emails. Use the correct forms of the phrasal verbs and objects in parentheses. Place the object between the verb and the particle when possible. Go to Appendices 18 and 19 on pages A-6 and A-8 for help.

Lose Weight!

Take those extra pounds off fast! Love bread and cake? Don't _____.
1. (take off / those extra pounds)   **2. (give up / them)**

No diet! No pills! No exercise! Our delicious drinks will _____ while you
                                                                                 3. (fill up / you)

lose weight. _____ at no cost. It's FREE for one month!
                 4. (try out / our plan)

Our weight loss secrets can be yours today. _____ as soon as you
                                                                      5. (find out / them)

_____. Want to know more? Click here for our information request form.
    6. (sign up for / our plan)

_____ to get our brochure. Just _____ and watch
    7. (fill out / it)   **8. (stick to / our plan)**

those pounds come off! If you do not want to receive email from us, we will be more than happy to

_____ our list.
    9. (take off / you)

Make $$$$$ working from home!

_____ cash and increase your savings without leaving your home!
    1. (turn into / your hobby)

My home-based business constantly _____ a day. That's right—and I
                                                             2. (take in / $2,000)

_____ every week. Sure, I could _____, but I'd
    3. (turn down / work)   **4. (take on / employees)**

rather teach **you** how to _____. This is an easy business, and you can
                                   5. (go after / those jobs)

_____ in a few days. Click on the $, and I'll _____
    6. (set up / it)   **7. (send out / the materials)**

right away. _____. If you don't like them, _____.
                 8. (check out / them)   **9. (send back / them)**

It's as simple as that! Don't _____! This offer is a money machine, so
                                          10. (put off / it)

don't _____. Start to _____ by next week!
         11. (pass up / it)   **12. (cash in on / this great opportunity)**

EXERCISE 5: Editing

*Read the transcript of a phone call between a telemarketer (**TM**) and Janis Linder (**JL**). There are fourteen mistakes in the use of phrasal verbs. The first mistake is already corrected. Find and correct thirteen more.*

TM: Hello, Ms. Linder?

JL: Yes. Who's this?

TM: This is Bob Watson from *Motorcycle Mama*. I'm calling to offer you a 12-month subscription for the low price of just $15 a year. Can I sign ~~up you~~? *you up*

JL: No thanks. I'm trying to eliminate clutter, so I'm not interested in signing in for any more magazine subscriptions. Besides, I just sat up for dinner.

TM: Why don't you at least try out it for six months? Don't pass this great opportunity down! It's a once in a lifetime chance.

JL: Sorry, I'm really not interested. I don't even have a motorcycle.

TM: Well then, this is a great opportunity to find all about them out! We'll send you a free copy, and you can look over it.

JL: You're not going to talk me in it! In fact, I'm going to hang the phone down right now. And please take my name out your list. If you keep calling, I'll notify the authorities.

TM: No, hold out! Don't go away! Don't turn this great offer down! You'll be sorry if you do. Chances like this don't come around every day! Don't miss it out on!

JL: OK. I have an idea. Why don't you give me your phone number, and I'll call back you during YOUR dinner?

[The telemarketer hangs the phone.]

JL: Hello? Hello?

EXERCISE 6: Listening

A | *Look at Mr. Chen's notes from a telemarketing call. Then listen to the call. Listen again and complete the notes.*

Get Together Program

- Just _____five cents_____ a minute on all long-distance calls
  1.
- Cell phone service included
- $ _____ monthly fee
  2.
- $20 fee to _____ new plan
  3.
- (Fee will _____ on first bill.)
  4.
- _____ activation fee (to _____ the phone service _____)
  5.   **6.**   **7.**
- New cell phone usually costs _____ .
  8.
- If I _____ right now, they'll _____ me _____ $20.
  9.   **10.**   **11.**
- Offer good for only _____
  12.

B | *Listen again to the call. Check (✓) True or False. Correct the false statements.*

	True	False
Mr. 1. ~~Mrs.~~ Chen picks up the phone.	☐	☑
2. The telemarketer says she wants to help Mr. Chen out with his phone rates.	☐	☐
3. With the new program, Mr. Chen will run out of cell phone minutes after 20 hours a month.	☐	☐
4. There's a charge for setting up the new plan.	☐	☐
5. The cell phone is free.	☐	☐
6. The telemarketer is going to give Mr. Chen some time to think over the plan.	☐	☐
7. Mr. Chen is going to sign up for the service.	☐	☐

EXERCISE 7: Pronunciation

A | *Read and listen to the Pronunciation Note.*

> ### Pronunciation Note
>
> When a phrasal verb is **not separated**, the **verb and particle** usually have **equal stress**.
>
> But, when the **object** of a phrasal verb is a **pronoun** that comes between the verb and its **particle**, the **particle** usually receives **stronger stress** than the verb.
>
> EXAMPLES: Don't **pick up** the phone.   BUT   Don't **pick** it **up**.

B | *Listen to the short conversations. Put a small dot (•) or a large dot (●) over each part of the phrasal verbs to show stress.*

1. **A:** Don't pick up the phone. It's probably a telemarketer.

   B: Don't worry. I won't pick it up.

2. **A:** Did the phone wake up the baby?

   B: No. It didn't wake her up.

3. **A:** Can you write down the information?

   B: Sure. I'll write it down on the pad.

4. **A:** Did you fill out the form?

   B: I filled it out yesterday.

5. **A:** I think you left out your phone number.

   B: I didn't leave it out. Here it is.

6. **A:** Did you turn down the offer?

   B: Yes. I turned it down.

7. **A:** Let's turn off the phone and have dinner.

   B: I already turned it off.

C | *Listen again to the conversations and repeat each sentence. Then practice the conversations with a partner.*

EXERCISE 8: For or Against

A | *Work in a small group. Talk about these questions.*

- What do you think of telemarketing? Does it offer consumers anything positive? Or is it equivalent to junk mail?

- Should telemarketing be illegal? Do you go along with the idea of Do Not Call lists? Should some organizations be allowed to keep on calling you? If yes, what kind?

- Do you get a lot of calls from telemarketers? How do you handle them? Do you think people should just hang up? Or should they put them off with a polite excuse, such as, "Thanks. I'll think it over."?

    EXAMPLE: **A:** I think telemarketing is a terrible idea.
                        B: Me too. I've never gotten anything useful out of a telemarketing call.
                        C: I just politely say I have to hang up, and then I get off the phone.

B | *Compare your answers with those of the rest of the class.*

EXERCISE 9: Discussion

Bring in an ad from a magazine, a piece of junk mail, spam, or an offer from the Internet. Discuss these ads in a group. Talk about these questions. Try to use some of the phrasal verbs in the list in your discussion. Go to Appendices 18 and 19 on pages A-6 and A-8 for help.

- What group of people might want this product or service (children, teenagers, older people, men, women)?

- What tactics does the ad use to get people to want this product or service?

- Is this an honest offer or a scam? What makes you think so?

cash in on s.t.	fall for s.t.	get to s.o.	miss out
catch on	fill s.t. out	go after s.o.	miss out on s.t.
count on s.t.	find s.t. out	help s.o. out	pay off
end up	get ahead	leave s.t. out	send s.t. back
end up with s.t.	get s.t. out of s.t.	make s.t. up	turn s.t. down

    EXAMPLE: **A:** I think this ad is trying to get to teenagers.
                        B: I agree. It shows a group of teens fooling around and having a good time while they're drinking soda.
                        C: Right, but I don't think many teens will fall for this.

EXERCISE 10: Writing

A | *Write a paragraph about an experience you have had on the phone. It could be a conversation with a friend, a wrong number, or a telemarketing call. Use some of these phrasal verbs:*

call back	fall for	go on	keep on	think over
check out	figure out	go over	pick up	turn down
come up	find out	hang up	sign up	turn out
end up	give up	hold on	talk into	wake up

EXAMPLE: When I first got to this country, I had difficulty understanding English speakers on the phone. I often couldn't figure out what people were saying to me. I kept on asking the person to repeat. Sometimes I had to give up, say "Sorry," and hang up.

B | *Check your work. Use the Editing Checklist.*

Editing Checklist
Did you . . . ? ☐ use phrasal verbs ☐ use the correct particles ☐ put pronoun objects between the verb and the particle of separable phrasal verbs

Check your answers on page UR-3.

Do you need to review anything?

A | *Match each phrasal verb with its meaning.*

_____ **1.** pick up   **a.** remove

_____ **2.** look up   **b.** meet by accident

_____ **3.** take off   **c.** complete

_____ **4.** fill out   **d.** return

_____ **5.** run into   **e.** find in a dictionary

_____ **6.** get back   **f.** lift

_____ **7.** give up   **g.** quit

B | *Complete each sentence with the correct form of the phrasal verb and object in parentheses. Place the object between the verb and particle when possible.*

1. The phone rang at 11:00 P.M. It _____.
            (wake up / Jason)

2. I didn't want to _____, but I did.
            (pick up / it)

3. It was Ada. I can always _____ to call too late!
            (count on / her)

4. I asked her to _____ in the morning.
            (call back / me)

5. Then I _____.
            (get off / the phone)

6. I _____ and went to bed.
            (put on / my nightshirt)

7. Then I _____ and fell asleep.
            (turn off / the lights)

C | *Find and correct six mistakes.*

I'm so tired of telemarketers calling me up as soon as I get from work back or just when I sit up for a relaxing dinner! It's gotten to the point that I've stopped picking the phone when it rings between 6:00 to 8:00 P.M. up. I know I can count on it being a telemarketer who will try to talk me into spending money on something I don't want. But it's still annoying to hear the phone ring, so sometimes I turn off it. Then, of course, I worry that it may be someone important. So I end up checking caller ID to find out. I think the Do Not Call list is a great idea. Who thought up it? I'm going to sign for it up tomorrow!

From Grammar to Writing
USING THE APPROPRIATE LEVEL OF FORMALITY

Phrasal verbs are very common in **informal writing**. In more **formal writing**, however, we often use **one-word verbs or phrases** with similar meanings in place of some phrasal verbs.

> **EXAMPLES:** I **threw away** your address by mistake. Can you resend it? (*less formal*)
> I **discarded** your address by mistake. Could you resend it please? (*more formal*)

1 | *Match the phrasal verbs on the left with the more formal verbs and phrases on the right.*

Less Informal	More Formal
_f_ **1.** check out	**a.** appear
____ **2.** fix up	**b.** awaken
____ **3.** get on	**c.** assemble
____ **4.** get together with	**d.** board
____ **5.** give up	**e.** discard
____ **6.** go along with	**f.** examine
____ **7.** light up	**g.** illuminate
____ **8.** look into	**h.** indicate
____ **9.** pick up	**i.** meet
____ **10.** point out	**j.** purchase
____ **11.** put together	**k.** quit
____ **12.** show up	**l.** redecorate
____ **13.** sign up	**m.** register
____ **14.** throw away	**n.** research
____ **15.** wake up	**o.** support

2 | *Read the two notes. Complete them with the correct form of the verbs and phrases from Exercise 1. Use the appropriate level of formality.*

Hi Van,

I just moved into my new apartment, and I'm only half an hour from school! This morning I

___*woke up*___ at 6:30 and jogged 2 miles before breakfast. I looked at my watch as I
　　 1.

_____ the bus, and it was just 8:15—plenty of time to get to my 9:00 English class.
　　 2.

In addition to English, I've also _____ for statistics this semester. It's hard, but I'm
　　　　　　　　　　　　　　　 3.

not going to _____. I'll need it for business school. The apartment has some
　　　　　 4.

problems, but I've been using your feng shui tips to _____ the living room. I just
　　　　　　　　　　　　　　　　　　　　　　 5.

_____ a new computer workstation on sale, which I'm going to _____
　　 6.　　　　　　　　　　　　　　　　　　　　　　　　　　　　　　　 **7.**

this weekend. I'll need it for business school, which I _____ now. I also bought a
　　　　　　　　　　　　　　　　　　　　　 8.

desk lamp to help _____ my work area. More later . . .
　　　　　　　　　 9.

Marta

Dear Mr. Livingston:

I've just moved into apartment 4B, and I need to report some problems.

- The previous tenant _____ some furniture in front of the apartment house.
　　　　　　　　　　　　 1.

  It looks awful. Please have someone remove it.

- Before I moved in, I _____ that there was a problem with the lock on the back
　　　　　　　　　　 2.

  door. This is an important safety issue. A locksmith needs to _____ the lock
　　　　　　　　　　　　　　　　　　　　　　　　　　　　　　　 3.

  and replace it if necessary.

- The tenant in 5B is very noisy. Some of the tenants would like to talk to her about this.

We hope you will _____ this plan and _____ at our next tenant's
　　　　　　　　 4.　　　　　　　　　　　　　 **5.**

meeting. If you would like to _____ to discuss these issues, please let me know.
　　　　　　　　　　　　　 6.

Sincerely,

Marta Nosko
Marta Nosko

3 | *Imagine that you have just moved into a new apartment building. Look at the picture of the lobby of the building. Work with a partner. Discuss the problems and make a list of the things that you want the landlord to do. Go to Appendices 18 and 19 on pages A-6 and A-8 for help.*

EXAMPLES: **A:** They really need to clean this place up. It's a mess.
B: The first thing they could do is throw out the trash. It looks terrible.
A: And they need to touch up the paint. It's peeling in several places.

1. *throw out the trash*

2. *touch up the paint*

3. _____

4. _____

5. _____

6. _____

7. _____

8. _____

9. _____

10. _____

4 | *Work with your partner. Together, write a letter to the landlord of the building in Exercise 3. Describe the problems and ask the landlord to fix them. Try to use some more formal verbs when possible. Go to Appendices 18 and 19 on pages A-6 and A-8 for help.*

EXAMPLE: Dear Ms. Bryce:

We'd like to make you aware of several problems in the lobby. Here are some things that would improve its appearance and safety:

• Discard the trash. It looks terrible.

• Touch up the paint. It's peeling in several places.

We hope you can take care of these issues as soon as possible. Thank you for your attention.

Sincerely,

5 | *Exchange notes with another pair. Underline the verbs that suggest what the landlord should do. Then answer the following questions.*

	Yes	No
1. Are there places where the writers could use more formal verbs instead of phrasal verbs?	☐	☐
2. If there are phrasal verbs with pronouns, are the pronouns in the right place?	☐	☐

6 | *Discuss your editing suggestions with the other pair. Then rewrite your own letter. Make any necessary corrections.*

ADJECTIVE CLAUSES

Adjective Clauses with Subject Relative Pronouns

FRIENDS AND PERSONALITY TYPES

Before You Read

Look at the cartoon and the caption. Discuss the questions.

1. What is the personality of an extrovert? An introvert?
2. Can people with very different personalities get along?

Read

Read the article about introverts and extroverts.

Section 5 • October 2012

Health & Wellness • Page 15

EXTROVERTS
AND
INTROVERTS

By Kurt Chattery

My friend Nadia, **who needs to spend several hours alone each day**, avoids large social gatherings whenever possible. She hates small talk, and at office holiday parties, **which are "must-attend" events**, she's always the first one to leave.

You probably know someone like Nadia. Maybe you're even one of those people **that nag[1] a friend like her to get out more**. If so, stop! Nadia is an introvert, and there's really nothing wrong with that. Introverts are people **that get their energy by spending time alone**. Their opposites are extroverts, people **whose energy comes from being around others**. Neither type is better than the other. However, because there are so many more extroverts than introverts, there is a lot of misunderstanding about the introverts among us.

Extrovert: someone **who loves being in a group of people**
Introvert: someone **who avoids extroverts**

First, most people think that all introverts are shy. Not so. Shy people fear social situations, but many introverts just try to avoid the ones **that drain[2] their energy**. Nadia, **who is great at leading big, noisy business meetings**, isn't afraid of those meetings. But she needs a lot of recovery time afterwards. Unlike extroverts, **who love the small talk at those meetings**, she prefers private conversations **that focus on feelings and ideas**.

[1] **nag:** to keep telling someone to do something in a way that is very annoying
[2] **drain:** to use too much of something so that there is not enough left

EXTROVERTS AND INTROVERTS

Secondly, people also assume that you have to be an extrovert (or act like one) in order to succeed. However, every day the news is full of examples **that contradict that belief**. Microsoft's Bill Gates is one famous introvert **who comes to mind**. Another is Avon's very successful CEO Andrea Jung. Jung, **who grew up in a traditional Chinese family**, considers herself "reserved,[3]" but not shy. A writer **who has studied the personality traits[4] of business leaders** points out that the one trait **that absolutely defines successful leaders** is creativity. Introverts are known for being creative, so it shouldn't be a surprise to find many of them at the top of their professions.

What happens when an extrovert and an introvert become friends or fall in love? Opposites attract, but can first attraction survive really big personality differences? Yes, but only if both can accept the other person's needs—and it's not always easy. Extroverts like me, **who have to talk through everything before we even know what we think**, can drive an introvert crazy. Nadia, **who always thinks before she speaks**, doesn't always understand my need to talk. On the other hand, many extroverts, **who reach for their cell phones after two minutes alone**, can't see why an introvert like Nadia requires so much time by herself. (Is that really *normal*? they wonder.) However, if both people take the time to understand the other's personality type, the results can pay off. The introvert, **who has a rich inner life**, can help the extrovert become more sensitive to feelings. And the risk-loving[5] extrovert can help the introvert develop a sense of adventure **that he or she might miss** on his or her own. As a result, each friend's personality becomes more complete.

It's important to remember that no one is a pure introvert or extrovert. In fact, we are probably all ambiverts, **people who act like introverts in some situations and extroverts in others**. Like everyone else, you have a unique personality—your own special combination of traits **that makes you *you!***

---
[3] ***reserved:*** not talkative
[4] ***trait:*** a quality in someone's character such as honesty or cruelty
[5] ***risk-loving:*** attracted to situations that might fail or be dangerous

After You Read

A | **Vocabulary:** *Complete the sentences with the words from the box.*

contradict	define	personality	require	sensitive	unique

1. Megan's _____ is very outgoing. She loves to be with other people.

2. Rahul is so _____. He knows when I'm upset even when I hide my feelings.

3. Nadia hates to _____ people, even when they're obviously wrong.

4. Introverts _____ time alone. They get very unhappy without it.

5. No two people are exactly alike. Everyone is _____.

6. It's hard to _____ creativity. It's such a complicated personality trait.

B | Comprehension: *Check (✓)* **Introvert** *or* **Extrovert** *for each description.*

Who . . . ?	Introvert	Extrovert
1. gets energy from being alone	☐	☐
2. gets energy from other people	☐	☐
3. enjoys small talk	☐	☐
4. likes to talk about ideas and feelings	☐	☐
5. talks while thinking	☐	☐
6. thinks before talking	☐	☐
7. is sensitive to feelings	☐	☐
8. likes to take risks	☐	☐

STEP 2 GRAMMAR PRESENTATION

ADJECTIVE CLAUSES WITH SUBJECT RELATIVE PRONOUNS

Adjective Clauses After the Main Clause

Main Clause			Adjective Clause		
Subject	**Verb**	**Predicate Noun/Pronoun**	**Subject Relative Pronoun**	**Verb**	
I	read	a book	*that* / *which*	discusses	personality.
An introvert	is	someone	*that* / *who*	needs	time alone.
			Whose + Noun		
I	have	a friend	*whose* personality	is	like mine.

Adjective Clauses Inside the Main Clause

Main Clause	Adjective Clause			Main Clause (cont.)	
Subject Noun / Pronoun	**Subject Relative Pronoun**	**Verb**		**Verb**	
The book	*that* / *which*	discusses	personality	is	by Ruben.
Someone	*that* / *who*	needs	time alone	may be	an introvert.
	Whose + Noun				
My friend,	*whose* personality	is	like mine,	loves	parties.

GRAMMAR NOTES

1 Use **adjective clauses** to **identify** or give **additional information** about **nouns** (people, places, or things).

- I have a *friend* **who avoids parties**.
  (*The clause* who avoids parties *identifies the friend.*)
- She lives in *Miami*, **which is my hometown**.
  (*The clause* which is my hometown *gives additional information about* Miami.*)

Adjective clauses can also identify or describe **indefinite pronouns** such as *one*, *someone*, *somebody*, *something*, *another*, and *other(s)*.

- I'd like to meet *someone* **who is outgoing**.

2 You can think of **sentences with adjective clauses** as a <u>combination of two sentences</u>.

Notice that the **adjective clause**:
- **directly follows** the noun or pronoun it is identifying or describing
- comes **after** the main clause or **inside** the main clause

I have a friend. + She is an extrovert. =
- I have a friend **who is an extrovert**.

Lea calls often. + She lives in Rome. =
- Lea, **who lives in Rome**, calls often.

She has a son. + His name is Max. =
- She has a son **whose name is Max**.

3 Adjective clauses begin with **relative pronouns**. Relative pronouns that can be the **subject** of the clause are *who*, *that*, *which*, and *whose*.

a. Use *who* or *that* for **people**.

SUBJECT
- I have a **friend** *who* lives in Mexico. OR

SUBJECT
- I have a **friend** *that* lives in Mexico.

b. Use *which* or *that* for **places** or **things**.

SUBJECT
- The **book** *which* I bought is about friends. OR

SUBJECT
- The **book** *that* I bought is about friends.

USAGE NOTE: In conversation, we use *that* more often than *who* and *which*. It's less formal.

c. Use *whose* + **noun** to show **possession** or **relationship**.

SUBJECT
- She's the **neighbor** *whose* **house** is for sale.

BE CAREFUL! Do **NOT use a subject pronoun** (*I, you, he, she, it, we, they*) and a subject relative pronoun in the same adjective clause.

- Scott is someone *who* **avoids** parties.
  NOT: Scott is someone who ~~he~~ avoids parties.

(continued on next page)

4	Relative pronouns always have the same form. They do not change for singular and plural nouns or pronouns, or for males and females.	• That's the **person** *that* gives great parties. • Those are the **people** *that* give great parties. • That's the **man** *who* gives great parties. • That's the **woman** *who* gives great parties.
5	The **verb in the adjective clause** is singular if the subject relative pronoun refers to a singular noun or pronoun. It is plural if it refers to a plural noun or pronoun. **BE CAREFUL!** When *whose* + **noun** is the subject of an adjective clause, the verb agrees with the subject of the adjective clause.	• Ben is my **friend** *who* **lives** in Boston. • Al and Ed are my **friends** *who* **live** in Boston. • Ed is a man *whose* **friends are** like family. Not: Ed is a man whose friends ~~is~~ like family.

6	There are two kinds of adjective clauses, **identifying** and **nonidentifying**:
	
	a. An **identifying** adjective clause is **necessary to identify** the noun it refers to.
	
	b. A **nonidentifying** adjective clause gives additional information about the noun it refers to. It is **NOT necessary to identify** the noun. The noun is often **already identified** with an adjective such as *first*, *last*, *best*, or *most*, or is the name of a person or place.
	
	BE CAREFUL! Do **NOT use** *that* to introduce nonidentifying adjective clauses. Use *who* for people and *which* for places and things.
		• I have a lot of good friends. My friend **who lives in Chicago** visits me often.
		(The adjective clause is necessary to identify which friend.)
		
		• I have a lot of good friends. My ***best*** friend, **who lives in Chicago,** visits me often.
		(The friend has already been identified as the speaker's best friend. The adjective clause gives additional information, but it isn't needed to identify the friend.)
		
		• **Marielle**, *who* introduced us at the party, called me last night.
		  Not: Marielle, ~~that~~ introduced us at the party, called me last night.
		• **Miami**, *which* reminds me of home, is my favorite vacation spot.
		  Not: Miami, ~~that~~ reminds me of home, is my favorite vacation spot.

7	In **writing**, use **commas** to separate a nonidentifying adjective clause from the rest of the sentence. In **speaking**, use short **pauses** to separate the nonidentifying adjective clause. **Without commas or pauses**, an adjective clause has a very different meaning.	**NONIDENTIFYING ADJECTIVE CLAUSE** • My sister, **who lives in Seattle,** is an introvert. **NONIDENTIFYING ADJECTIVE CLAUSE** • My sister *(pause)* **who lives in Seattle** *(pause)* is an introvert. *(I have only one sister. She's an introvert.)* **IDENTIFYING ADJECTIVE CLAUSE** • My sister **who lives in Seattle** is an introvert. *(I have several sisters. This one is an introvert.)*

EXERCISE 1: Discover the Grammar

Read this article about two other personality types. Circle the relative pronouns and underline the adjective clauses. Then draw an arrow from the relative pronoun to the noun or pronoun that it refers to.

Wellness Today   September–October 2012   **47**

It's All How You Look at It

"It's half full!"   "It's half empty!"

Look at the photo. Do you see a glass (which) is half full or a glass which is half empty? For optimists, people who believe that things in the future will work out fine, the glass is half full. On the other hand, for pessimists, people who expect things to go badly, the glass is half empty.

Most of us know people who have a strong tendency[1] to be either optimistic or pessimistic. I have a friend whose life motto is "Things have a way of working out." Even when something bad happens, Cindi remains optimistic. Last year, she lost a job that was extremely important to her. She didn't get depressed; she just thought "Well, maybe I'll find a new job that's even better than this one!" But then there is the example of Monica, who always sees the dark side of every situation, even when something good happens. She recently won a lot of money in a contest. Is she happy about this windfall? Not really. She worries that she won't know how to spend the money wisely. And now she's also worried that her friend Dan, a talented web designer who is struggling to start a business, will be jealous of her.

Cindi and Monica are women whose outlooks on life are as different as day and night. But the two women are best friends! Is it true what they say?

Do opposites attract? Cindi says that their very different ways of seeing things help balance each other. Sometimes Monica has views that are more realistic than her friend's. Right after Cindi was laid off, for example, Monica persuaded her to take a temporary job. "Just until you find that dream job," she said. On the other hand, Monica admits that she's sometimes too negative, and that Cindi, whose nickname is "Miss Sunshine," often gets her to see opportunities in a difficult situation. "Why not invest in Dan's business?" Cindi suggested the other day.

Former U.S. president Harry Truman defined the two personalities well: "A pessimist is one who makes difficulties of his opportunities, and an optimist is one who makes opportunities of his difficulties." However, as Cindi and Monica are learning, we can learn to make these tendencies less extreme. Today's experts agree: Half full or half empty, you may not be able to change how much water is in your glass, but you can often change how you view the situation and how you respond to it. Optimists and pessimists may be able to help each other do this more appropriately.

---

[1] *tendency:* the way that someone usually thinks or behaves

EXERCISE 2: Relative Pronouns and Verbs

(Grammar Notes 5–7)

Complete each sentence with an appropriate relative pronoun and the correct form of the verbs in parentheses.

Personality Quiz

Do you agree with the following statements? Check (✔) **True** or **False**.

	True	False
1. People _____who_____ _____talk_____ a lot tire me. **(talk)**	☐	☐
2. On a plane, I like to speak to the stranger _____ . _____ the seat next to me. **(take)**	☐	☐
3. At a social event, I am often the first one _____ _____ . **(leave)**	☐	☐
4. My best friend, _____ _____ a lot, is just like me. **(talk)**	☐	☐
5. I prefer to have conversations _____ _____ on feelings and ideas. **(focus)**	☐	☐
6. I am someone _____ idea of a great time _____ reading a good book. **(be)**	☐	☐
7. People can have close friends _____ personalities _____ different from theirs. **(be)**	☐	☐
8. I'm someone _____ always _____ the glass as half full, not half empty. **(see)**	☐	☐
9. Difficult situations are often the ones _____ _____ the best opportunities. **(provide)**	☐	☐
10. I like people _____ _____ sensitive to others' feelings. **(be)**	☐	☐

EXERCISE 3: Identifying Adjective Clauses

(Grammar Notes 2–7)

A | *We often use identifying adjective clauses to define words. First, match the words on the left with the descriptions on the right.*

__h__	**1.** difficulty	**a.**	This situation gives you a chance to experience something good.
_____	**2.** extrovert	**b.**	This attitude shows your ideas about your future.
_____	**3.** introvert	**c.**	This ability makes you able to produce new ideas.
_____	**4.** opportunity	**d.**	This person usually sees the bright side of situations.
_____	**5.** opposites	**e.**	This person requires a lot of time alone.
_____	**6.** optimist	**f.**	This money was unexpected.
_____	**7.** outlook	**g.**	This person usually sees the dark side of situations.
_____	**8.** pessimist	**h.**	This problem is hard to solve.
_____	**9.** creativity	**i.**	These people have completely different personalities.
_____	**10.** windfall	**j.**	This person requires a lot of time with others.

B | *Now write definitions with adjective clauses for the words on the left. Use the correct description on the right and an appropriate relative pronoun.*

1. *A difficulty is a problem that is hard to solve.* OR *A difficulty is a problem which is hard to solve.*
2. _____
3. _____
4. _____
5. _____
6. _____
7. _____
8. _____
9. _____
10. _____

EXERCISE 4: Nonidentifying Adjective Clauses

(Grammar Notes 2–7)

Combine the pairs of sentences. Make the second sentence in each pair an adjective clause. Use the correct punctuation. Make any other necessary changes.

1. I'm attending English 101. It meets three days a week.

   I'm attending English 101, which meets three days a week .

2. Sami is an optimist. He's in my English class.

   Sami, who is in my English class, is an optimist.

3. He drives to school with his sister Jena. She wants to go to law school.

   _____ .

4. Jena is always contradicting him. She loves to argue.

   _____ .

5. That never annoys cheerful Sami. He just laughs.

   _____ .

6. Jena is going to have a great career. Her personality is perfect for a lawyer.

   _____ .

7. I always look forward to the class. The class meets three days a week.

   _____ .

8. San Antonio has a lot of community colleges. San Antonio is in Texas.

   _____ .

9. My school has students from all over the world. It's one of the largest colleges in the country.

   _____ .

EXERCISE 5: Identifying or Nonidentifying Adjective Clauses (Grammar Notes 2–7)

Read the conversations. Then use the first and last sentences in each conversation to help you write a summary. Use adjective clauses. Remember to use commas where necessary.

1. **A:** This article is really interesting.

    B: What's it about?

    A: It discusses the different types of personalities.

    SUMMARY: *This article, which discusses the different types of personalities, is really interesting.*

2. **A:** The office party is going to be at the restaurant.

    B: Which restaurant?

    A: You know the one. It's across the street from the library.

    SUMMARY: _____

3. **A:** I liked that speaker.

    B: Which one? We heard several!

    A: I forget his name. He talked about optimists.

    SUMMARY: _____

4. **A:** Bill and Sue aren't close friends with the Swabodas.

    B: No. The Swabodas' interests are very different from theirs.

    SUMMARY: _____

5. **A:** I lent some chairs to the new neighbors.

    B: Why did they need chairs?

    A: They're having a party tonight.

    SUMMARY: _____

6. **A:** I'm watching an old video of Jason.

    B: Look at that! He was telling jokes when he was five!

    A: I know. This totally defines his personality.

    SUMMARY: _____

7. **A:** My boyfriend left me a lot of plants to water.

    B: How come?

    A: He's visiting Venezuela with some friends.

    SUMMARY: _____

Read this student's essay about a friend. There are eleven mistakes in the use of adjective clauses and their punctuation. Each incorrectly punctuated clause counts as one mistake. (For example, "My mother who is my best friend just turned 50" needs two commas, but it counts as one mistake.) The first mistake is already corrected. Find and correct ten more.

Good Friends

A writer once said that friends are born, not made. I think he meant that friendship is like love at first sight—we become friends immediately with people who ~~they~~ are compatible with us. I have to contradict this writer. Last summer I made friends with some people who's completely different from me.

In July, I went to Mexico City to study Spanish for a month. In our group, there were five adults, which were all language teachers from our school. Two teachers stayed with friends in Mexico City, and we only saw those teachers during the day. But we saw the teachers, who stayed with us in the dormitory, both day and night. They were the ones who they helped us when we had problems. Bob Taylor who is much older than I am became a really good friend. After my first two weeks, I had a problem that was getting me down. Mexico City, that is a very exciting place, was too distracting. I'm a real extrovert—someone who wants to go out all the time—and I stopped going to my classes. But my classes required a lot of work, and my grades suffered as a result. When they got really bad, I wanted to leave. Bob, who have studied abroad a lot, was very sensitive to those feelings. But he was also a lot more optimistic about my situation. He helped me get back into my courses which were actually pretty interesting. I managed to do well after all! After the trip I kept writing to Bob, who's letters are always friendly and encouraging. Next summer, he's leading another trip what sounds great. It's a three-week trip to Spain, which is a place he knows a lot about. I hope I can go.

EXERCISE 7: Listening

A | *Some friends are at a high school reunion. They haven't seen one another for 25 years. Read the statements. Then listen to the conversation. Listen again and circle the correct words to complete the statements.*

1. People at the reunion (have) / haven't changed a lot.

2. Ann is wearing <u>a lot of jewelry / a scarf</u>.

3. It's the <u>man / woman</u> who first recognizes Kado.

4. Bob and Pat are the students who <u>worked on the school paper / ran for class president</u>.

5. Asha is looking at <u>a photo / Bob</u>.

6. Asha is the woman who married <u>Pete Rizzo / Raza Gupta</u>.

7. The man and woman <u>know / don't know</u> who is sitting between Asha and Pat.

B | *Look at the picture. Then listen again to the conversation and write the correct name next to each person.*

| Ann | Asha | ~~Bob~~ | Kado | Pat | Pete |

EXERCISE 8: Pronunciation

🎧 **A** | *Read and listen to the Pronunciation Note.*

> **Pronunciation Note**
>
> In **writing**, we use **commas** around **nonidentifying adjective clauses**.
>
> In **speaking**, we **pause** briefly **before and after** nonidentifying adjective clauses.
>
> **EXAMPLE:**   Marta**,** who lives across from me**,** has become a good friend. ➔
>
> "Marta [PAUSE] who lives across from me [PAUSE] has become a good friend."

🎧 **B** | *Listen to the sentences. Add commas if you hear pauses around the adjective clauses.*

1. My neighbor who is an introvert called me today.

2. My neighbor who is an introvert called me today.

3. My brother who is one year older than me is an extrovert.

4. My sister who lives in Toronto visits us every summer.

5. My friend who is in the same class as me lent me a book.

6. The book which is about personality types is really interesting.

7. The article that won a prize is in today's newspaper.

8. My boyfriend who hates parties actually agreed to go to one with me.

🎧 **C** | *Listen again and repeat the sentences.*

EXERCISE 9: Discussion

A | *Take the quiz in Exercise 2.*

B | *Work with a partner. Discuss your answers to the quiz. What do you think your answers show about your personality?*

> **EXAMPLE:**   **A:** Question 1. People who talk a lot tire me. That's true.
> **B:** I think that means you're probably an introvert. It wasn't true for me. I myself talk a lot, and I enjoy people who talk a lot too.

EXERCISE 10: Questionnaire

A | Complete the questionnaire. Check (✓) all the items that you believe are true. Then add your own idea.

A friend is someone who . . .

☐ 1. always tells you the truth

☐ 2. has known you for a very long time

☐ 3. cries with you

☐ 4. lends you money

☐ 5. talks to you every day

☐ 6. helps you when you are in trouble

☐ 7. listens to your problems

☐ 8. does things with you

☐ 9. respects you

☐ 10. accepts you the way you are

☐ 11. is sensitive to your feelings

☐ 12. gives you advice

☐ 13. keeps your secrets

☐ 14. never contradicts you

Other: _____

B | Now compare questionnaires with a partner. Discuss the reasons for your choices.

EXAMPLE: **A:** I think a friend is someone who always tells you the truth.
B: I don't agree. Sometimes the truth can hurt you.

C | After your discussion, tally the results of the whole class. Discuss the results.

EXERCISE 11: Quotable Quotes

Work in small groups. Choose three of these quotations and talk about what they mean. Give examples from your own experience to support your ideas.

1. Show me a friend who will weep[1] with me; those who will laugh with me I can find myself.
   —*Slavic proverb*

   EXAMPLE: **A:** I think this means that it's easier to find friends for good times than for bad times.
   B: I agree. A true friend is someone who is there for you during good *and* bad times.
   C: My best friend in high school was like that. She was someone who . . .

2. An optimist is a guy that has never had much experience.
   —*Don Marquis (U.S. writer, 1878–1937)*

3. A pessimist is one who has been compelled[2] to live with an optimist.
   —*Elbert Hubbard (U.S. writer, 1856–1915)*

4. He is wise who can make a friend of a foe.[3]
   —*Scottish proverb*

5. Very few people can congratulate without envy a friend who has succeeded.
   —*Aeschylus (Greek playwright, 525–456 B.C.E)*

---

[1] **weep:** to cry

[2] **compelled:** forced

[3] **foe:** an enemy

6. A pessimist is one who makes difficulties of his opportunities and an optimist is one who makes opportunities of his difficulties.
—*Harry Truman (33rd U.S. president, 1884–1972)*

7. Wherever you are it is your own friends who make your world.
—*Ralph Barton Perry (U.S. philosopher, 1876–1957)*

8. Blessed[4] is the person who is too busy to worry in the daytime and too sleepy to worry at night.
—*Author Unknown*

9. A true friend is somebody who can make us do what we can.
—*Ralph Waldo Emerson (U.S. writer, 1803–1882)*

10. How much pain they have cost us, the evils[5] which have never happened.
—*Thomas Jefferson (3rd U.S. president, 1743–1826)*

---

[4] ***blessed:*** lucky

[5] ***evil:*** a bad thing

EXERCISE 12: Writing

A | *Write a two-paragraph essay about a friend. You may want to begin your essay with one of the quotations from Exercise 11. Use adjective clauses with subject relative pronouns. You can use the essay in Exercise 6 as a model.*

EXAMPLE: Do friends have to be people who have the same interests or personality? I don't think so. My friend Richie and I are best friends who are complete opposites. He's an extrovert who can walk into a room that is full of strangers with no problem. In an hour, they'll all be new friends. I'm an introvert who . . .

B | *Check your work. Use the Editing Checklist.*

Editing Checklist

Did you use . . . ?
☐ ***who*** or ***that*** for people
☐ ***which*** or ***that*** for places and things
☐ ***whose*** to show possession or relationship
☐ the correct verb form in adjective clauses
☐ identifying adjective clauses to identify a noun
☐ nonidentifying adjective clauses to give more information about a noun
☐ commas to separate nonidentifying adjective clauses

A | *Circle the correct words to complete the sentences.*

1. I have a lot of friends who <u>is / are</u> introverts.

2. Maria is someone <u>whose / who</u> idea of a good time is staying home.

3. Ben, who always <u>think / thinks</u> carefully before he speaks, is very sensitive to people's feelings.

4. He lives in Los Angeles, <u>which / where</u> is a city I'd love to visit.

5. He wrote this book, <u>that / which</u> is very interesting, about personality types.

6. My friend <u>who / which</u> read it liked it a lot.

B | *Complete each sentence with a relative pronoun and the correct form of the verb in parentheses.*

1. Thinkers and Feelers are types of people _____ _____ very differently.
   (behave)

2. A Thinker, _____ _____ decisions based on facts, is a very logical person.
   (make)

3. Emotions, _____ usually _____ a Feeler, are more important than facts to
   (convince)
   this personality type.

4. A Thinker is someone _____ always _____ fairly and honestly.
   (speak)

5. A Feeler avoids saying things _____ _____ another person's feelings.
   (hurt)

6. I dislike arguments, _____ usually _____ me. I guess I'm a Feeler.
   (upset)

7. Ed, _____ personality _____ different from mine, loves to argue.
   (be)

C | *Find and correct seven mistakes. Remember to check punctuation.*

It's true that we are often attracted to people whose are very different from ourselves. An extrovert, which personality is very outgoing, will often connect with a romantic partner who are an introvert. They are both attracted to someone that have different strengths. My cousin Valerie who is an extreme extrovert, recently married Bill, whose idea of a party is a Scrabble game on the Internet. Can this marriage succeed? Will Bill learn the salsa, that is Valerie's favorite dance? Will Valerie start collecting unusual words? Their friends, what care about both of them, are hoping for the best.

Before You Read

Look at the book reviews and photos. Discuss the questions.

1. Where do you think the two cities in the photographs are located? Describe them.
2. Do the cities look different from where you live now? If yes, how?
3. What do you think the title means?

Read

 Read the book reviews.

TORN¹ BETWEEN TWO WORLDS

"I'm filled to the brim² with what I'm about to lose—images of Cracow, **which I loved as one loves a person**, of the sun-baked villages **where we had taken summer vacations**, of the hours **I spent poring over passages of music with my music teacher**, of conversations and escapades³ with friends."

These sad words were written by Eva Hoffman, author of *Lost in Translation: A Life in a New Language* (New York: Penguin, 1989). Hoffman, an award-winning journalist⁴ and author, spent her early childhood in Cracow, Poland. She moved with her family to Vancouver, Canada, when she was 13. Her autobiography⁵ describes her experiences as she leaves her beloved Cracow and struggles to find herself in a new place and a new language.

In spite of her family's poverty and small, crowded apartment, Ewa Wydra (Hoffman's Polish name) loved her native Cracow.

(continued on next page)

---

¹**torn:** not able to decide between two people, places, or things because you want both
²**filled to the brim:** completely filled (like a glass with water that goes to the top)
³**escapade:** an adventure
⁴**journalist:** a person who writes professionally for newspapers or magazines
⁵**autobiography:** a book a person writes about his or her own life

Hoffman remembers Cracow as a place **where life was lived intensely**. She remembers visiting the city's cafés with her father, **who she watched in lively conversations with his friends**. She also remembers neighbors, "People **between whose apartments there's constant movement with kids, sugar, eggs, and teatime visits**." As she grew up, her friendship with Marek, **whose apartment she visited almost daily**, deepened, and the two always believed that they would one day be married.

Madame Witeszczak, Hoffman's piano teacher, was the last person **she said goodbye to** before she left Poland.

"What do you think you'll miss most?" her teacher asked. "Everything. Cracow. The school … you. Everything …"

At her new school in Vancouver, Hoffman is given her English name, Eva, **which her teachers find easier to pronounce**. Hoffman, however, feels no connection to the name. In fact, she feels no real connection to the English name of anything **that she feels is important**. All her memories and feelings are still in her first language, Polish. The story of Hoffman as she grows up and comes to terms with[6] her new identity and language is fascinating and moving.[7]

---

[6]**come to terms with:** to learn to accept
[7]**moving:** causing strong feelings

Also recommended is *The Rice Room*, by Ben Fong-Torres (New York: Hyperion, 1994). Unlike Hoffman, Fong-Torres was born in the United States. However, his parents had emigrated from China, and many of the problems **that he describes** are, like Hoffman's, connected to language. Fong-Torres struggles to bring together his family's culture and his new culture. He doesn't have the language **he needs to do this** because he only knows the Chinese **that he had learned as a child**. A successful radio announcer and journalist in English, Fong-Torres cannot really talk to his parents, **for whom English is still a foreign language**.

"When we talk, it sounds like baby talk—at least my half of it. … I don't know half the words **I need**; I either never learned them, or I heard but forgot them." The language barrier[8] separated Fong-Torres and his parents "… through countless moments **when we needed to talk with each other**, about the things **parents and children usually discuss**: jobs and careers; marriage and divorce; health and finances; history, the present, and the future. This is one of the great sadnesses of my life. … I'm a journalist

and a broadcaster[9]—my job is to communicate—and I can't with the two people **with whom I want to most**."

Whether first- or second-generation immigrant, the issues are the same. These two books describe the lives of people trying to connect the worlds **that they left behind** and the worlds **that they now call home**.

---

[8]**language barrier:** problem caused by not being able to speak another person's language
[9]**broadcaster:** someone who talks professionally on radio or TV

A | Vocabulary: *Complete the sentences with the words from the box.*

connection	generation	immigrant	issue	poverty	translation

1. The author wrote in Spanish, but I'm reading an English _____.

2. It's always interesting to hear the older _____ talk about how life used to be.

3. My grandfather's parents were very poor. They left their country to escape from a life of

   _____.

4. What's your _____ to Poland? Is your family from there?

5. At my first job, the language barrier with my boss was the biggest _____.

6. Life can be very difficult for a(n) _____, who often has to learn a lot of new

   things in a very short time.

B | Comprehension: *Check (✓) the correct boxes. For some items, you will check both boxes.*

Who . . . ?	Hoffman	Fong-Torres
1. studied music	☐	☐
2. was a first-generation American	☐	☐
3. went to cafés with a parent	☐	☐
4. had to learn English	☐	☐
5. had a name change	☐	☐
6. had immigrant parents	☐	☐
7. has difficulty communicating with family	☐	☐
8. is a professional writer	☐	☐

ADJECTIVE CLAUSES WITH OBJECT RELATIVE PRONOUNS OR *WHEN* AND *WHERE*

Adjective Clauses After the Main Clause

Main Clause			Adjective Clause		
Subject	**Verb**	**Predicate Noun / Pronoun**	**(Object Relative Pronoun)**	**Subject**	**Verb**
He	read	the book	*(that)* *(which)*	she	wrote.
She	is	someone	*(who[m])*	I	respect.
			Whose + Noun		
That	is	the author	*whose* book	I	read.
			***Where* / (When)**		
She	loves	the city	*where*	she	grew up.
They	cried	the day	*(when)*	they	left.

Adjective Clauses Inside the Main Clause

Main Clause	Adjective Clause			Main Clause *(cont.)*	
Subject	**(Object Relative Pronoun)**	**Subject**	**Verb**	**Verb**	
The book	*(that)* *(which)*	I	read	is	great.
Someone	*(who[m])*	you	know	was	there.
	Whose + Noun				
The man	*whose* sister	you	know	writes	books.

Main Clause	Adjective Clause			Main Clause *(cont.)*	
Subject	***Where* / (When)**	**Subject**	**Verb**	**Verb**	
The library	*where*	I	work	has	videos.
The summer	*(when)*	she	left	passed	slowly.

GRAMMAR NOTES

1

In Unit 13, you learned about adjective clauses in which the **relative pronoun** was the **subject** of the clause.

SUBJ.
Eva is a writer. + ***She** was born in Poland.* =
SUBJ.
- Eva, ***who** was born in Poland*, is a writer.

A **relative pronoun** can also be the **object** of an adjective clause.

OBJ.
Eva is a writer. + *I saw **her** on TV.* =
OBJ.
- Eva, ***who** I saw on TV*, is a writer.

Notice that:

a. relative pronouns (subject or object) come at the **beginning** of the adjective clause.

SUBJ.
- Ben, ***who** lives in California*, is a journalist.
OBJ.
- Ben, ***who** we just met*, reports on music.

b. relative pronouns (subject or object) always have the **same form**. They do not change for singular and plural nouns, or for males and females.

- That's the **man *who*** I met.
- That's the **woman *who*** I met.
- Those are the **people *who*** I met.

c. the **object relative pronoun** is followed by the subject and verb of the adjective clause. The **verb in the adjective clause** is singular if the subject of the clause is singular. It is plural if the subject of the clause is plural.

SUBJ. **VERB**
- I like the **columns which *he writes***.
- I like the **column which *they write***.

BE CAREFUL! Do **NOT use an object pronoun** (*me, you, him, her, it, us, them*) and an object relative pronoun in the same adjective clause.

- She is the writer *who* **I saw on TV**.
- Not: She is the writer who I saw ~~her~~ on TV.

2

REMEMBER: There are two kinds of adjective clauses, **identifying** and **nonidentifying**.

IDENTIFYING:
- I read a lot of books. The book **which I just finished** was very moving.
  (*The adjective clause is necessary to identify which book I mean.*)

NONIDENTIFYING:
- I read a lot of books. This book**, which I just finished,** was very moving.
  (*I'm pointing to the book, so the adjective clause isn't necessary to identify it. The clause gives additional information.*)

In **writing**, use **commas** to separate a nonidentifying adjective clause from the rest of the sentence.
In **speaking**, use short **pauses** to separate the nonidentifying adjective clause.

You can often **leave out an object** relative pronoun in an **identifying** adjective clause.

- The book *which* **I just finished** is great. OR
- The book **I just finished** is great.

But do **NOT leave out the object** relative pronoun in a **nonidentifying** adjective clause.

Not: ~~The book, I just finished, is great.~~

(continued on next page)

3 **Relative pronouns** that can be the **object** of the adjective clause are **who(m)**, **that**, **which**, and **whose**.

a. Use **whom**, **who**, or **that** for **people**. You can also <u>leave out</u> the relative pronoun.

USAGE NOTE: **Whom** is very formal. Most people do not use **whom** in everyday speech. **That** is less formal than **who**. In everyday speech, most people use no relative pronoun.

Formality
MORE

- She's the writer **whom** I met.
  OR
- She's the writer **who** I met.
  OR
- She's the writer **that** I met.
  OR
- She's the writer **I met**.

LESS

MORE

b. Use **which** or **that** for **things**. You can also leave out the relative pronoun.

USAGE NOTE: **That** is less formal than **which**. In everyday speech, most people use no relative pronoun.

- I read a book **which** she wrote.
  OR
- I read a book **that** she wrote.
  OR
- I read a book **she wrote**.

LESS

c. Use **whose** + **noun** to show **possession** or **relationship**. You cannot leave out **whose**.

- That's the author **whose** book I read.
  NOT: That's the author ~~book I read~~.

REMEMBER: Don't leave out relative pronouns in nonidentifying adjective clauses.

- She remembers Marek, **who she visited often**.
  NOT: She remembers Marek, ~~she visited often~~.

4 The relative pronouns **who(m)**, **that**, **which**, and **whose** can be the **object of a preposition**.

Formality
MORE

He's the writer. + I work for him. =
- He's the writer **for whom** I work.
  OR
- He's the writer **whom** I work **for**.
  OR
- He's the writer **who** I work **for**.
  OR
- He's the writer **that** I work **for**.
  OR
- He's the writer I work **for**.

LESS

You can <u>leave out</u> who(m), that, and which, but not **whose**.

He's the writer. + I work for his wife. =
- He's the writer **whose wife** I work **for**.

USAGE NOTES:
a. In **formal English**, we put the preposition <u>at the beginning</u> of the clause. When the preposition is at the beginning, we use only **whom** (not *who* or *that*) for <u>people</u>, and **which** (not *that*) for <u>things</u>.

- He's the writer **for whom** I work.
- That's the book **about which** he spoke.

b. In **everyday spoken English** and in **informal writing**, we put the preposition <u>at the end</u> of the clause.

- He's the writer **who** I work **for**.
- That's the book **that** he spoke **about**.

5   *When* and *where* can also begin adjective clauses.

a. Use *where* for a **place**.

* That's the library *where* **she works**.

b. Use *when* or *that* for a **time**.

* I remember the day *when* **I met him**.

OR

* I remember the day *that* **I met him**.

OR

You can <u>leave out</u> *when* and *that* in identifying adjective clauses.

* I remember the day **I met him**.

REFERENCE NOTE

For additional information about **identifying and nonidentifying adjective clauses**, see Unit 13, page 210.

STEP 3   FOCUSED PRACTICE

EXERCISE 1:   Discover the Grammar

A | *This excerpt from* Lost in Translation *describes Eva Hoffman's home in Cracow. Underline the adjective clauses and circle the relative pronouns,* **when,** *and* **where.** *Then draw an arrow from each relative pronoun to the noun or pronoun that it refers to. There are both subject and object relative pronouns.*

The kitchen is usually steamy with large pots of soup cooking on the wood stove for hours, or laundry being boiled in vats[1] for greater whiteness; behind the kitchen, there's a tiny balcony, barely big enough to hold two people, on which we sometimes go out to exchange neighborly gossip[2] with people peeling vegetables, beating carpets, or just standing around on adjoining[3] balconies. Looking down, you see a paved courtyard, in which I spend many hours bouncing a ball against the wall with other kids, and a bit of garden, where I go to smell the few violets that come up each spring and climb the apple tree, and where my sister gathers the snails that live under the boysenberry bushes, to bring them proudly into the house by the bucketful. . . .

Across the hall from us are the Twardowskis, who come to our apartment regularly . . . I particularly like the Twardowskis' daughter, Basia, who is several years older than I and who has the prettiest long braids,[4] which she sometimes coils around her head. . . .

---

[1]*vat:* a large container for liquid
[2]*gossip:* conversations or comments about other people's actions or their private lives
[3]*adjoining:* next to
[4]*braid:* a hair style where three pieces of hair are twisted like a rope

B | *Read another excerpt from the same book about Hoffman's music school. There are four adjective clauses in which the relative pronouns have been left out. The first one is already underlined. Find and underline three more. Then add appropriate relative pronouns.*

Pani Konek teaches at the Cracow Music School, which I've been attending for two years—ever since it has been decided that I should be trained as a professional pianist. I've always liked going to school. At the beginning of the year, I like buying smooth navy blue fabric from which our dressmaker will make my school uniform—an anonymous[1] *that* OR *which* overdress we are required to wear over our regular clothes in order to erase economic and class distinctions; I like the feel of the crisp, untouched notebook . . . and dipping my pen into the deep inkwell in my desk, and learning how to make oblique[2] letters. It's fun to make up stories about the eccentric characters[3] I know, or about the shapes icicles make on the winter windows, and try to outwit the teacher when I don't know something, and to give dramatic recitations of poems we've memorized. . . .

[1]*anonymous:* not showing a person's identity or personality
[2]*oblique:* slanted, not straight (for example, *italicized* letters are oblique)
[3]*eccentric characters:* strange or unusual people

EXERCISE 2: Relative Pronouns and Verbs

(Grammar Notes 1–5)

Complete the interview from a school newspaper. Use **who, that, which, when** *or* **where,** *and the correct forms of the verbs in parentheses.*

The Grover   September 19, 2012   page 3

Meet Your Classmates

Maniya, _____ *who* _____ a lot of our readers already _____ *know* _____,
1. (know)
has been at Grover High for three years now. We interviewed Maniya, who is from the Philippines, about her experiences as a new immigrant in the United States.

INTERVIEWER: How did your family choose Atlanta, Maniya?

MANIYA: My cousin, _____ we _____ with at
2. (stay)
first, lives here.

INTERVIEWER: What were your first impressions?

MANIYA: At first it was fun. We got here at the beginning of the summer, _____ there
_____ no school, so I didn't feel much pressure to speak English.
3. (be)

INTERVIEWER: What was the most difficult thing about going to school?

MANIYA: Of course, the class in _____ I _____ the biggest problems at
4. (have)
first was English. It was so hard for me to write compositions or to say the things
_____ I _____ to say. It was really a big issue for me. Now it's
5. (want)
much easier. I have a much stronger connection to English now.

INTERVIEWER: What was the biggest change for you when you got here?

MANIYA: We used to live in a big house, _____ there _____ always a lot
6. (be)
of people. We were several generations under one roof. Here I live with just my parents and
sister, _____ I _____ after school.
7. (take care of)

INTERVIEWER: How did you learn English so quickly?

MANIYA: At night, I write words and idioms on a small piece of paper _____ I
_____ in my shirt pocket. Then I study them at school whenever I have a
8. (put)
chance between classes.

INTERVIEWER: Is there anything _____ you still _____ trouble with?
9. (have)

MANIYA: One thing _____ I still _____ hard to do is to make jokes in
10. (find)
English. Some things are funny in Tagalog but not in English.

EXERCISE 3: Identifying Adjective Clauses

(Grammar Notes 2–5)

Complete the story. Use the sentences from the box. Change them to identifying adjective
clauses and use relatives pronouns, **when**, or **where**.

I drank coffee there every day.	**I knew her sister from school.**
I had to leave Cracow then.	~~**I loved it very much.**~~
I hoped it would continue to grow.	**Many students attended it.**

Cracow is a city in Poland _____ *that I loved very much* _____. My parents
1.
owned a café _____. One day I met a woman
2.
there _____. Her sister and I were in a class
3.
together _____. The woman and I felt a strong
4.
connection _____. For me it was a sad day
5.
_____.
6.

Adjective Clauses with Object Relative Pronouns or *When* and *Where*   **229**

EXERCISE 4: Nonidentifying Adjective Clauses

(Grammar Notes 2–5)

Complete the information about Ben Fong-Torres. Use the sentences in parentheses to write nonidentifying adjective clauses with relative pronouns, **when**, or **where**. Add commas where necessary.

Ben Fong-Torres was born in Alameda, California, in 1945. He was the son of first-generation Chinese parents. To escape a life of poverty, his father immigrated to the Philippines and then to the United States *, where he settled down* .

1. (He settled down there.)

His mother came to the United States 10 years later _____ .

2. (Their marriage was arranged by relatives then.)

Fong-Torres, along with his brother and sister, grew up in Oakland, California, _____ . His family owned a Chinese restaurant

3. (There was a large Chinese community there.)

_____ when they were not in school. Young

4. (All the children worked there.)

Ben was always an enthusiastic reader of cartoons and a huge fan of popular music

_____ . At the age of 12, Ben went with his

5. (He heard it on the radio.)

father to Texas _____ . It was a difficult time

6. (They opened another Chinese restaurant there.)

for Ben because he was among people who had had no previous contact with Asians.

Back in Oakland, after the failure of the Texas restaurant, Ben got jobs writing for various magazines and newspapers. His interviews with hundreds of famous musicians included the Beatles, the Rolling Stones, Grace Slick, and an interview with Ray Charles

_____ . Fong-Torres was also a DJ for San

7. (He won an award for it.)

Francisco radio station KSAN, which plays rock music, and in 1976 he won an award for broadcasting excellence.

Fong-Torres and Diane Sweet _____ still

8. (He married her in 1976.)

live in San Francisco. He hosts many events for the Chinese community in that city, and continues to write about music for publications such as the e-zine (Internet magazine) www.AsianConnections.com.

EXERCISE 5: Identifying and Nonidentifying Adjective Clauses

(Grammar Notes 1–5)

Combine the pairs of sentences. Make the second sentence in each pair an adjective clause. Make any other necessary changes. Use relative pronouns only when necessary.

1. That's the house. I grew up in the house.

   <u>That's the house I grew up in.</u>

2. I lived with my parents and my siblings. You've met them.

   _____

3. I had two sisters and an older brother. I felt a close connection to my sisters.

   _____

4. My sisters and I shared a room. We spent nights talking there.

   _____

5. My brother slept on the living room couch. I hardly ever saw him.

   _____

6. It was a large old couch. My father had made the couch himself.

   _____

7. My best friend lived across the hall. I loved her family.

   _____

8. We went to the same school. We both studied English there.

   _____

9. Mr. Robinson was our English teacher. Everyone was a little afraid of Mr. Robinson.

   _____

10. After school I worked in a bakery. My aunt and uncle owned it.

    _____

11. They sold delicious bread and cake. People stood in line for hours to buy the bread and cake.

    _____

12. My brother and sisters live far away now. I miss them.

    _____

13. When we get together we like to talk about the old days. We all lived at home then.

    _____

EXERCISE 6: Editing

*Read this student's essay. There are nine mistakes in the use of adjective clauses and their punctuation. The first **two** mistakes are already corrected. Find and correct seven more.*

Tai Dong, where I grew up, is a small city on the southeast coast of Taiwan. My family moved

there from Taipei the summer where I was born. I don't remember our first house, we rented from a

relative, but when I was two, we moved to the house that I grew up in. I have a very clear image of

it. The house, which my parents still live, is on a main street in Tai Dong. To me, this was the best

place in the world. My mother had a food stand in our front courtyard whom she sold omelets early

in the morning. All her customers, which I always chatted with, were very friendly to me. On the

first floor, my father conducted his tea business in the front room. After school, I always went

straight to the corner where he sat drinking tea with his customers. In the back was our huge

kitchen with its stone floor and brick oven. I loved dinnertime because the kitchen was always full

of relatives and the customers, that my father had invited to dinner. It was a fun and noisy place to

be. Next to the kitchen, there was one small bedroom. My oldest cousin, whose father wanted him

to learn the tea business, slept there. Our living room and bedrooms were upstairs. My two older

sisters slept in one bedroom, and my older brother and I slept in the other. My younger sister

shared a room with my grandmother, whose took care of her a lot of the time.

STEP 4 COMMUNICATION PRACTICE

EXERCISE 7: Listening

A | *Read the statements. Then listen to this description of an author's childhood room. Listen again and check (✓) **True** or **False**. Correct the false statements.*

	True	False
1. Maria originally wrote her book in ~~English~~. *Spanish*	☐	☑
2. Maria has a clear image of her childhood bedroom.	☐	☐
3. She shared a room with her sister.	☐	☐
4. There was a rug under Maria's bed.	☐	☐
5. The sisters liked looking at themselves in the mirror.	☐	☐

	True	False
6. They did their homework in the kitchen.	☐	☐
7. Maria played the guitar.	☐	☐
8. Maria has happy memories about her childhood.	☐	☐

B | *Look at the pictures. Then listen again to the description of the room and choose the correct picture.*

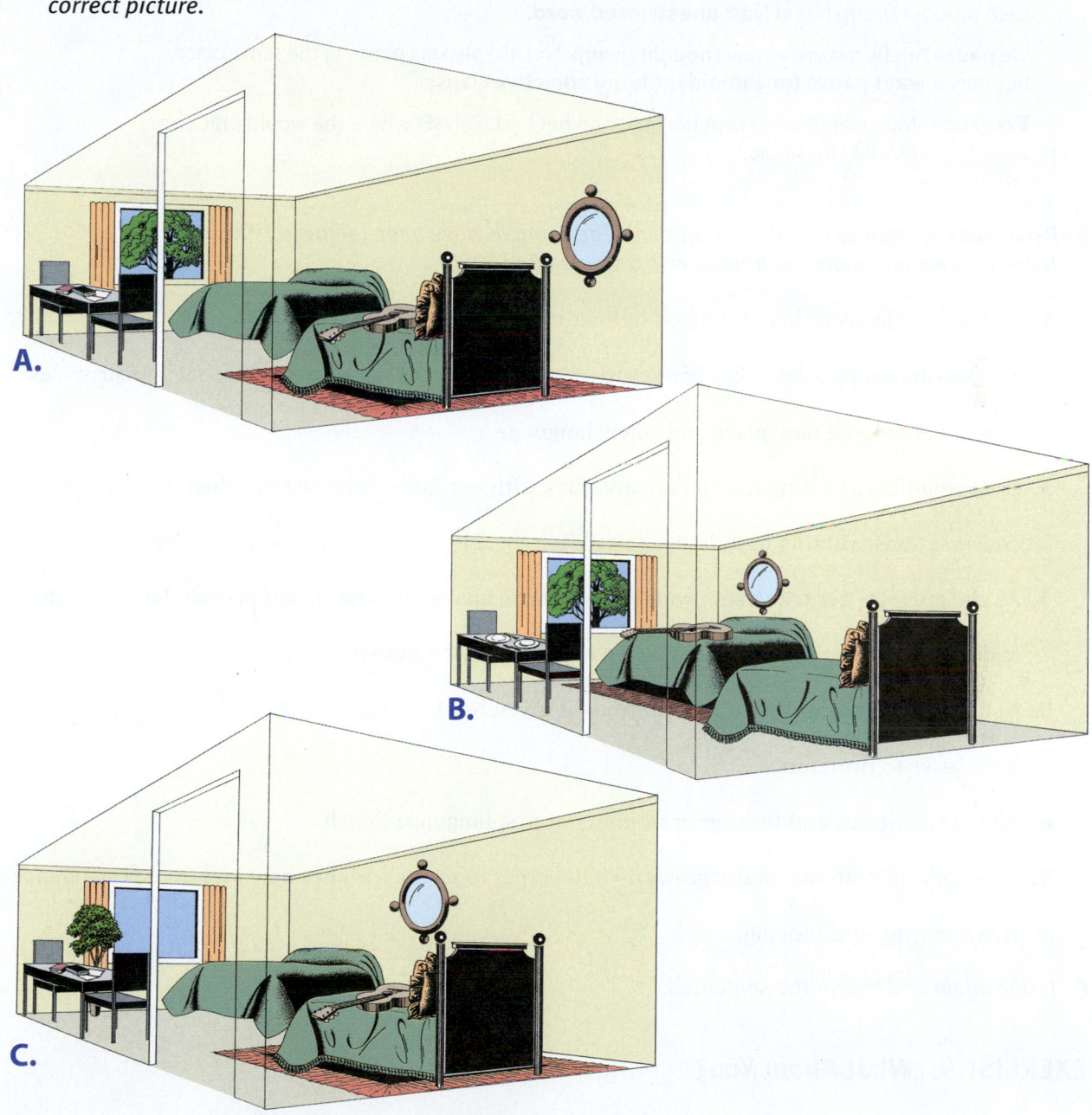

C | *Listen again to the description and check (✓) the correct box.*

This description is in _____ English.

☐ formal

☐ informal

EXERCISE 8: Pronunciation

A | *Read and listen to the Pronunciation Note.*

> **Pronunciation Note**
>
> When we speak, we **break long sentences** into parts called **thought groups**. This makes sentences easier to say and easier to understand.
>
> Each thought group has at least **one stressed word**.
>
> We **pause** briefly **before a new thought group**. Not all speakers pause in the same place, but they **always pause for a nonidentifying adjective clause**.
>
> **EXAMPLE:** My sister [PAUSE] kept her guitar on her bed [PAUSE] where she would practice [PAUSE] for hours.

B | *Read these sentences about Eva Hoffman. (The commas have been removed.) Then listen to them and mark the pauses with a slanted line (/).*

1. Hoffman who spent her childhood in Poland moved to Canada when she was 13.

2. Her autobiography describes her experiences as she leaves her beloved Cracow and struggles to find herself in a new place and a new language.

3. She remembers visiting the city's many cafés with her father who she watched in lively conversations with his friends.

4. As she grew up her friendship with Marek whose apartment she visited almost daily deepened and the two always believed that they would one day be married.

5. At her new school in Vancouver Hoffman is given her English name Eva which her teachers find easier to pronounce.

6. All her memories and feelings are still in her first language Polish.

7. The story of Hoffman as she grows up and comes to terms with her new identity and language is fascinating and moving.

C | *Listen again and repeat the sentences.*

EXERCISE 9: What About You?

Bring in some photos to share with your classmates. Work in small groups. Describe the people and places in your photos.

> **EXAMPLE:** **A:** This is the street where we lived before we moved here.
> **B:** Is that the house you grew up in?
> **A:** Yes, it is. I lived there until I was 10.

EXERCISE 10: Quotable Quotes

Work in small groups. Choose three of these quotations and talk about what they mean. Give examples from your own experience to support your ideas.

1. Home is where the heart is.
   —*Pliny the Elder (Roman soldier and encyclopedist, 23–79)*

   EXAMPLE: **A:** I think this means that home is not necessarily a place.
   B: I agree. It's a feeling that you have.
   C: I think it can be a place or person that you love.

2. Home is where one starts from.
   —*T. S. Eliot (British poet, 1885–1905)*

3. Home is the place where you feel happy.
   —*Salman Rushdie (Indian author, 1947–)*

4. Home is a place you grow up wanting to leave, and grow old wanting to get back to.
   —*John Ed Pearce (U.S. journalist, 1917–2006)*

5. Home is not where you live but where they understand you.
   —*Christian Morgenstern (German poet, 1871–1914)*

6. Home is the place where, when you have to go there, they have to take you in.
   —*Robert Frost (U.S. poet, 1874–1963)*

EXERCISE 11: Writing

A | *Write one or two paragraphs about a place you remember from your childhood. Use adjective clauses with object relative pronouns, **when**, or **where** to help you explain where things were and why they were important. You can use the essay in Exercise 6 as a model.*

EXAMPLE: The town where I grew up was a small farming village. Living there was like living in an earlier century. We didn't lock our doors, and my friends, who lived across the street, could visit whenever they wanted to . . .

B | *Check your work. Use the Editing Checklist.*

Editing Checklist

Did you use the correct . . . ?
☐ adjective clause (identifying or nonidentifying)
☐ relative pronoun, ***where***, or ***when***
☐ verb form in the adjective clause
☐ punctuation for nonidentifying adjective clauses

Check your answers on page UR-4.

Do you need to review anything?

A | *Circle the correct words to complete the sentences.*

1. Mrs. Johnson, <u>whom / whose</u> dog I walk, lives next door.

2. She lives in an old house <u>that / who</u> her father built.

3. It's right next to the park <u>where / when</u> I run every morning.

4. She has a daughter <u>which / who</u> I went to school with.

5. We became best friends in 2000 <u>where / when</u> we were in the same class.

6. Ann, <u>that / who</u> I still call every week, moved to Canada last year.

B | *Complete each sentence with a relative pronoun, **when,** or **where**.*

1. Today I took a trip back to Brooklyn, _____ I grew up.

2. I saw the house _____ my family lived in for more than 10 years.

3. I walked to the high school _____ I attended.

4. I saw some old neighbors _____ I remembered well.

5. Mrs. Gutkin, _____ son I used to help with his homework, still lives next door.

6. She's a very nice woman _____ I always liked.

7. Today brought back a lot of good memories _____ I had forgotten.

C | *Find and correct seven mistakes. Remember to check punctuation.*

I grew up in an apartment building who my grandparents owned. There was a small dining room when we had family meals and a kitchen in that I ate my breakfast. My aunt, uncle, and cousin, in who home I spent a lot of my time lived in an identical apartment on the fourth floor. I remember the time my parents gave me a toy phone set that we set up so I could talk to my cousin. There weren't many children in the building, but I often visited the building manager, who's son I liked. I enjoyed living in the apartment, but for me it was a happy day where we moved into our own house.

PART VI

From Grammar to Writing
ADDING DETAILS WITH ADJECTIVE CLAUSES

Details help to explain what you are writing about. One way to add details is with **adjective clauses** that give more **information about** *who*, *what*, *which*, *whose*, *where*, and *when*.

EXAMPLE: She was born in Chile. ➔
She was born in Chile, ***where* her parents had emigrated after the war**.

1 | *Read this student's essay about a famous person. Underline the adjective clauses.*

Writer, Poet, Diplomat

Octavio Paz is considered one of the greatest writers <u>that the Spanish-speaking world has produced</u>. He was born in Mexico in 1914. As a child, he was exposed to writing by his grandfather and father. His childhood was hard because of his father's political activities, which forced his family into exile and poverty.

Paz began writing when he was very young. He published his first poem at age 16. He attended law school in Mexico City, where he joined a Marxist student group. Around the same time, he married his first wife, Elena Garro. Paz's literary career received a boost in his early 20s when he sent a manuscript to the Chilean poet Pablo Neruda. Neruda was impressed, and he encouraged Paz to go to Spain to attend a writing conference. Paz remained there and joined the forces that were fighting against General Franco in the Spanish Civil War. Later, he went on to become a diplomat, representing his country in France, Japan, the United States, and India.

Paz wrote both poetry and prose. He is most famous for *The Labyrinth of Solitude*, a collection of essays that deal with the character of the Mexican people. He also founded *Vuelta*. In 1990 he received the Nobel Prize for Literature. He died eight years later.

2 | *The student added details in a second draft. Read the student's notes below. Then find places in the essay to add the information. Rewrite the sentences with adjective clauses. Remember to use commas when necessary.*

> **Additional Information**
> • Both his grandfather and father were political journalists.
> • Elena Garro was also a writer.
> • Pablo Neruda was already famous in Spain and Latin America.
> • <u>Vuelta</u> was one of Latin America's most famous literary magazines.

1. *As a child, he was exposed to writing by his grandfather and father, who were both political journalists.*

2. _____

3. _____

4. _____

3 | *Before you write . . .*

1. Choose a famous person to write about. Do some research in the library or on the Internet. Take notes about the main events in this person's life.

2. Exchange notes with a partner. Write a question mark **(?)** next to items you would like your partner to add more details about.

4 | *Write your essay. Answer your partner's questions using adjective clauses to add details.*

5 | *Exchange essays with a different partner. Underline the adjective clauses. Write a question mark **(?)** where you would like more information. Then answer the following questions.*

	Yes	No
1. Did the writer use adjective clauses?	☐	☐
2. Did the writer use the correct relative pronoun for each adjective clause?	☐	☐
3. Did the writer punctuate the adjective clauses correctly?	☐	☐
4. Did the writer give enough details?	☐	☐

6 | *Work with your partner. Discuss each other's editing questions from Exercise 5. Then rewrite your essay and make any necessary corrections.*

MODALS: REVIEW AND EXPANSION

"Why can't you use Facebook, like everyone else?"

I **should've used** a longer piece of paper...

"Here comes another one."

Modals and Similar Expressions: Review
SOCIAL NETWORKING

Before You Read

Look at the cartoon and the title of the article. Discuss the questions.

1. What is the man doing? What does the woman think he should do?
2. What do you think the title means?
3. Do you use social networking sites? Which ones?
4. Do you use them for connecting with friends or for school or business?

Read

Read the article about social networking.

facebook or face time[1]?

The Pros and Cons of Social Networking

By Netta Seiborg

"Why can't you use Facebook, like everyone else?"

Blaire Thomas's school friends **can find out** what she is doing almost every minute by checking Facebook. Vince Stevenson stays in touch with his family through MySpace. Vince says, "**I had to join**. My grandkids all use MySpace." Magda Tilia, an English teacher in Romania, uses Ning for her class. Her students **are able to discuss** lessons and **chat** with other students in France, Turkey, and Greece. She says, "Students **don't have to use** the Ning site. Class is just more fun for the ones who do."

The growth of social networking all over the world is exciting, but networking **may not** always **be** a good thing. Both children and adults **have to remember** that real-life relationships are more important than virtual[2] ones. Also, safety and privacy are big issues for everyone, but especially for teenagers and pre-teens[3] who are just learning to use the Internet.

[1]*face time:* time spent with someone in the same place, face-to-face
[2]*virtual:* on the Internet
[3]*pre-teen:* someone between the ages of 10 and 12

facebook or face time?

Parents **must teach** children about keeping personal information private. However, used with care, social networking **can be** a great tool for staying connected and improving your personal and professional life. Here are some ways to get the most out of social networking while avoiding some of the problems.

Making friends on Facebook or MySpace isn't that different from making friends at work or school. You **have to make** the effort to "meet" people with similar interests. Are you a tennis fan? Is *Survivor* a reality TV show you **could** never **miss**? If so, why don't you join those interest groups and begin conversations with people there? Once you've made some friends, you **should keep** posting new content on your own page: comments, photos, and videos that people **can respond** to.

However, while you're having fun getting to know people, you **should** never **forget** that what you post on the Internet is public information. Employers and schools often look at the social networking sites of applicants. Even if your page is only available to friends, embarrassing stuff **can** still **become** public. So maybe you**'d better think** twice before posting those party photos. Once they're out there, you **can't take** them back!

When you're networking for jobs, you **might need** a separate site. On your job-seeking site, you **must stay** absolutely professional. For example, you **should** never **use** abbreviations—remember, ur talking 2 other professionals! And you probably **shouldn't post** all your activities on this professional page, either—your colleagues **don't have to know** that you're eating chicken nuggets at 2:14 A.M.

Social networking is a great resource for students. When you're applying to school, your profile **should show** activities that will interest college admissions officers. You **can** also **network** by chatting with current students. They **could give** you an inside view of the school you're interested in. Once in school, you **can form** study groups, **organize** your schedule, and much more. But be careful: You **might** also **find** yourself wasting valuable study time.

Recently, Blaire has decided she**'s got to cut back** on her Facebook use. "I'm always chatting, and not doing homework," she said. Is she sorry she got so involved? "Not really. Everyone **ought to learn** how to use social networking. It's a big world out there, and you **can learn** a lot. You just **have to know** when to say 'enough is enough,' sign off, and get back to your *real* life."

After You Read

A | Vocabulary: *Match the words with their definitions.*

_____ 1. **comment**   a. something valuable or useful

_____ 2. **content**   b. taking part in something

_____ 3. **involved**   c. a statement of an opinion

_____ 4. **network**   d. the protection of personal information

_____ 5. **privacy**   e. the ideas, information, and pictures in a book or on a website

_____ 6. **resource**   f. to connect with people who also know each other

B | Comprehension: *Check (✓)* **True** *or* **False***. Correct the false statements.*

	True	False
1. Vince joined MySpace because he wanted to stay in touch with his friends.	☐	☐
2. It's very important for parents to teach children about Internet privacy.	☐	☐
3. It's not a good idea to post certain photos because private posts sometimes become public.	☐	☐
4. On a site you use for job seeking, it's a good idea to post messages with abbreviations.	☐	☐
5. Social networking doesn't have much to offer college students.	☐	☐
6. Blaire thinks it's not important for everyone to learn how to use social networking.	☐	☐

STEP 2 GRAMMAR PRESENTATION

MODALS AND SIMILAR EXPRESSIONS: REVIEW

Ability: *Can* and *Could*

Subject	Modal	Base Form of Verb	
She	can (not)	join	now.
	could (not)		last year.

Ability: *Be able to**

Subject	*Be able to*		Base Form of Verb	
She	is (not)	able to	join	now.
	was (not)			last year.

Advice: *Should, Ought to, Had better*

Subject	Modal	Base Form of Verb	
You	should (not) ought to had better (not)	use	Ning.

Necessity: *Must* and *Can't*

Subject	Modal	Base Form of Verb	
You	must (not) can't	post	photos.

Necessity: *Have (got) to**

Subject	*Have to Have (got) to*	Base Form of Verb	
They	(don't) have to have got to	post	photos.
He	has to has got to		

*Unlike modals, which have one form, *be* in *be able to* and *have* in *have (got) to* change for different subjects.

Conclusions: *May, Might, Could, Must, Can't*			
Subject	**Modal**	**Base Form of Verb**	
They	may (not) might (not) could (not) must (not) can't	know	him.

Conclusions: *Have (got) to**			
Subject	***Have to Have got to***	**Base Form of Verb**	
They	have to have got to	know	him.
He	has to has got to		

*Unlike modals, which have one form, *have* in *have (got) to* changes for different subjects.

Future Possibility: *May, Might, Could*			
Subject	**Modal**	**Base Form of Verb**	
It	may (not) might (not) could	happen	soon.

GRAMMAR NOTES

1

Modals are auxiliary ("helping") verbs. Use modals and similar expressions to express:

a. **social functions** such as describing **ability**, giving **advice**, and expressing **necessity**

- We **can learn** to use it. (*ability*)
- She **should join** Facebook. (*advice*)
- You **must respond** to him. (*necessity*)

b. **logical possibilities** such as coming to **conclusions** and talking about **future possibilities**

- It **could be** the best site. (*conclusion*)
- I **might join**. (*future possibility*)

REMEMBER: Modals have **only one form**. They do not have *-s* in the third person singular. Always use **modal + base form** of the verb.

- She **might post** photos.
  NOT: She ~~mights~~ post photos.
  NOT: She might ~~to post photos~~.

2

Use the following **modals** for **ability**:

a. *can* or *be able to* for **present ability** (*can* is much more common)

- She **can speak** French.
- We **aren't able to view** his site.

b. *could* or *was / were able to* for **past ability**

- Before she took lessons, she **could speak** French, but she **wasn't able to speak** English.

c. *can*, *will be able to*, or *be going to be able to* for **future ability**

- She **can register** for class soon.
- She**'ll be able to register** for class soon.
- She**'s going to be able to attend** class soon.

REMEMBER: Use the correct form of *be able to* for <u>all other verb forms</u>.

- Since her lessons, she **has been able to chat** online in English.

(*continued on next page*)

3 Use the following **modals** for **advice**:

a. *should* and *ought to*
(*should* is much more common)

b. *had better* for **urgent advice**—when you believe that something bad will happen if the person does not follow the advice

c. *should* to **ask for advice**

d. *shouldn't* and *had better not* for **negative advice**

- You **should watch** *Survivor* tonight.
- Terri **ought to watch** it too.

- You**'d better stop** watching so much TV or your grades will suffer.

- **Should** I **join** Facebook?

- You **shouldn't spend** so much time online.
- You**'d better not stay up** too late.

4 Use the following **modals** for **necessity**:

a. *have to* and *have got to*
(in conversation and informal writing)

USAGE NOTE: We often use *have got to* to express strong feelings.

b. *must*
(in writing, such as forms, signs, manuals)

USAGE NOTE: When we use *must* in **spoken** English, the speaker is usually:

- in a position of power

- expressing urgent necessity

c. *must not* or *can't* for **prohibition**

USAGE NOTE: We often use *can't* for prohibition in **spoken** English.

BE CAREFUL! The meanings of *must not* and *don't have to* are very different.

- Use *must not* to express **prohibition**.

- Use *don't have to* to say that something is **not necessary**.

Use *have to*, *have got to*, and *must* for the present or future. Use the correct form of *have to* for all other verb forms.

- I **have to get** an email address to join.
  (email message to a friend)

- You**'ve got to see** this! It's really funny!
  (friend talking to another friend)

- You **must be** at least 13 years old to join.
  (instructions for joining a networking site)
- Students **must post** their homework assignments by next Friday.
  (teacher to students on an online course site)

- You **must go** to bed right now, Tommy!
  (mother talking to her young son)
- You **must see** a doctor about that cough.
  (friend talking to a friend)

- Students **must not leave** before the test ends.
  (written instructions on a test form)
- You **can't leave** yet, Jeff. The test isn't over.
  (teacher speaking to a student)

- They **must not stay up** past 10:00.
  (They are not allowed to stay up past 10:00.)
- They **don't have to stay up** past 10:00.
  (It isn't necessary for them to stay up past 10:00.)

- Bob **had to get** an email address to join.
  (simple past)
- He **has had to change** his password twice.
  (present perfect)

5 Use the following **modals and similar expressions** for **conclusions** ("best guesses"). They show how certain we are about our conclusions.

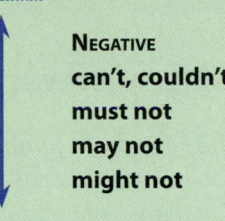

AFFIRMATIVE	NEGATIVE
must	can't, couldn't
have (got) to	must not
may	may not
might, could	might not

VERY CERTAIN

LESS CERTAIN

Use:

a. *must*, *have to*, and *have got to* when you are **very certain** that something is true

- That **must be** Blaire in that photo. It looks just like her.
- It **has to be** her. She used the same photo on her Facebook profile.

b. *may*, *might*, and *could* when you are **less certain**

- She **may want** her picture on Bob's page.
- They **could be** friends.

c. *can't* and *couldn't* when you are almost 100% certain that something is **impossible**

- Vince **can't be** a member of the *Survivor* fan group. He doesn't watch TV.
- It **couldn't be** that hard to do social networking. Millions of people do it.

d. *must not* when you are **slightly less certain**

- He **must not belong** to MySpace. I couldn't find his name.

e. *may not* and *might not* when you are **even less certain**

- He **may not use** his real name. A lot of people don't.

For **questions** about conclusions, use *can*, *could*, or expressions such as *Do you think . . . ?* or *Is it possible that . . . ?*
In **answers**, you can use *must (not)*, *have (got) to*, *may(not)*, *might (not)*, *could(n't)*, and *can't*.

A: Could Magda's students **be** online now?
B: No, they **can't be**. The lab is closed.
A: *Do you think she knows* how to set up an online study group?
B: She **must**. She set up a group for her class.

6 Use the following **modals** for **future possibility**:

a. *may*, *might*, and *could* to express the possibility that something **will happen** (The three modals have very similar meanings.)

- Terry **may get** online later. I'm not sure.
- He **might go** to the library tonight.
- Or he **could decide** to go to sleep early.

b. *may not* and *might not* to express the possibility that something **will not happen**

- I **may not** join Facebook.
- It **might not be** a good site for me.

BE CAREFUL! *Couldn't* means that something is **impossible**.

- Terry **couldn't go** to the library tonight. It's closed on Sunday.

We usually do not begin **questions** about possibility with *may*, *might*, or *could*. Instead we use *will* or *be going to* and phrases such as *Do you think . . . ?* or *Is it possible that . . . ?* However, we often use *may*, *might*, or *could* in **short answers** to these questions.

A: *Will* Josh *join* our Facebook study group?
B: He **might not**. He's very involved with his job right now.
A: *Do you think it'll help* us pass chemistry?
B: It **could**. People say study groups help.

EXERCISE 1: Discover the Grammar

A | *Read the FAQ about joining Facebook. Underline the modals and similar expressions. Also underline the verbs that follow.*

FAQs about facebook

How do I join Facebook?

It's easy. You just <u>have to complete</u> an online form with some basic information—your name, birthday, relationship status, etc. Oh, and you must have an email address.

Are there any age restrictions?

Yes. You must be 13 or older to join.

I'm worried about privacy. Do I really have to provide personal information such as my date of birth?

Yes you do. But you will be able to hide personal information if you'd like.

Do I have to post a photo of myself?

It's not required, but most people do. To get the full benefit of making connections, you ought to give as much information as you feel comfortable with. Remember: Facebook is a great resource, so get involved!

Can someone post a photo of me without my permission?

Yes. As long as it doesn't break any of Facebook's rules, people don't have to ask. However, if the photo is embarrassing, a lot of users feel the poster *really* ought to get permission.

What if I don't like a photo that someone has posted of me?

Unfortunately, Facebook cannot remove a photo if it hasn't broken any rules. If you're unhappy, however, you can choose to remove your name from it.

There must be some dangers in social networking. What should I do to protect myself?

The number 1 rule is this: You must not give your password to anyone. Ever.

Also, you should never give out information that strangers could use to contact you in the real world.

And remember: Facebook tries to make the environment as safe as possible, but one day you may encounter objectionable content.[1]

---

[1]*objectionable content:* information and pictures that may upset people

B | *Write the underlined verbs in the correct column.*

MEANING	VERBS		
Ability	1. _____	3. _____	
	2. _____	4. _____	
Advice	1. _____	3. _____	
	2. _____	4. _____	
Necessity	1. *have to complete*	3. _____	5. _____
	2. _____	4. _____	6. _____
Prohibition	1. _____		
Future Possibility	1. _____		
	2. _____		
Conclusions	1. _____		

EXERCISE 2: Affirmative and Negative Modals

(Grammar Notes 1–5)

Circle the correct words to complete these posts on a social networking site.

1. Blaire Thomas wrote at 6:30 am

I (can't) / shouldn't believe I slept this late again! This might / has got to stop—or I'm going
   a.   **b.**
to flunk my early class.

Aneesh Hussain wrote at 6:35 am

LOL! You'd better / may stop posting and get going, girl! We have tests today.
      c.

Adam Hall wrote at 6:55 am

Hey, maybe you should / must get off Facebook a little earlier every night.
        d.

2. Vince Stevenson wrote at 7:00 am

I just saw the weather forecast. Looks like we couldn't / 'll be able to do that fishing trip
                                                  a.
this weekend. Tell the kids to get their stuff ready Friday night—they must / can't sleep late
                                                                   b.
on Saturday!

(continued on next page)

Ellie Stevenson wrote at 7:30 am

Good Morning, Dad. Macy says we <u>ought to / must not</u> bring the video camera—she's sure
              c.
she'll catch the biggest fish. Ben's bringing some friends, so we<u>'ll have to / won't have to</u>
                                                       d.
find the big cooler. Do you have it?

Ben Stevenson wrote at 4:00 pm

Grandpa, I think our boat <u>may not / can't</u> be big enough. Dylan wants to come with us too.
                                 e.
What do you think? <u>Should / May</u> we rent a bigger one?
                      f.

3. Magda Tilia wrote at 9:00 pm

Hi, Class. Great work today! I <u>can / ought to</u> see your English improving every week. Next
                     a.
week <u>couldn't / could</u> be the last time you <u>can / should</u> chat with your Eukliedis High School
      b.   **c.**
friends in Greece—they're going on summer break. So please show up online for them.

See you Friday—and remember, I <u>must / 'd better not</u> get your journals by then. I'll make
                                   d.
comments and send them back right away.

Lucian Banika wrote at 9:30 pm

Ms. Tilia, I won't <u>have to / be able to</u> come to class on Friday because of a family problem.
                      e.
I <u>could / must</u> leave my journal in your mailbox on Thursday. Is that OK?
      f.

4. Blaire Thomas wrote at 8:01 pm

It's 8:00—time for *Survivor*! I guess all you fans <u>must / must not</u> be in front of your TVs
                                      a.
right now. Who's your favorite contestant so far? Who <u>should / may</u> they kick off the island
                                                  b.
tonight? Any comments?

Ben Sutter wrote at 8:15 pm

My favorite is Christine. She <u>may not / must</u> be the best contestant, but she's pretty good,
                              c.
and she works hard. Mel <u>has to / could</u> be the one they kick off. I'm sure of it—there's no
                   d.
excuse for keeping him.

Sara Fry wrote at 9:00 pm

Hi Everybody. I'm posting from my Smart Phone. I'm on a camping trip so I <u>can / couldn't</u>
                                                          e.
watch *Survivor* tonight. Let me know what happened, please. And Blaire—you

<u>must / shouldn't</u> go to sleep now!
     f.

EXERCISE 3: Affirmative and Negative

(Grammar Notes 1–5)

Complete these posts to a reality TV message board. Rewrite the phrases in parentheses.
Use modals and similar expressions.

REALITY TV MESSAGE BOARD

[Follow-Ups] [Post a Reply] [Message Board Index]

bigfan: Any comments about *Pop Idols* last night? I _____*couldn't believe*_____ Jennifer
1. (didn't have the ability to believe)
Tasco didn't win!

aisha: I watched it, and you _____ more wrong. Jason deserved the prize.
2. (it's impossible for you to be)
He's a star. Jennifer isn't.

Kitsdad: Tonight on *Get a Job*, Ronald Trunk interviewed Lateesha and Sam. Too bad Trunk

_____ only one of them. I think he _____
3. (has the ability to keep)   **4. (will possibly get rid of)**
Lateesha, but I really think Sam _____ the one.
5. (it's a good idea for Sam to be)

winz1: Everybody knows that Sam was really sick last week. He _____
6. (it was necessary for him to go)
to the doctor! If you don't know that, then you _____ very much
7. (it's very certain that you don't know)
about the show.

Elly: *Survivor* is starting again soon! I love that show, and now that I'm not in school anymore, I

_____ missing classes to watch. They _____
8. (it won't be necessary to worry about)   **9. (will possibly go)**
to Palau this year, but it's not certain yet. I wish *I* were going to Palau!

bigfan: Elly, you _____ the show. You _____
10. (it would be a good idea to get on)   **11. (it's possible for you to win)**
a million dollars!

EXERCISE 4: Editing

Read the article about Wikipedia. There are ten mistakes in the use of modals. The first mistake is already corrected. Find and correct nine more.

Wikipedia (pronounced WIK-i-PEE-dee-a) It's fast (*wiki* means *quick* in Hawaiian), it's convenient (you ~~must not~~ *don't have to* go to the library), and, best of all, it's free. It's the world's most popular online encyclopedia, and you don't even have to register to use it. It's called "the free encyclopedia that anyone can edits." Volunteers around the world contribute to the millions of articles on its website, which are usually more up-to-date than what you may find in a book. You can't also click on hyperlinks to get more information. But, critics say, users ought be aware that the content may not always be 100 percent accurate. A "paper" encyclopedia has professional editors who fact check every article. Not so with Wikipedia. As a result, many teachers say their students should rely on it when they write reports. It's wrong to think that just because an article is on a famous website, it must be reliable. It mights be a good starting point when researching a topic, but writers should then check the facts with other sources. Then there is always the issue of plagiarism.[1] Remember: Wikipedia information is free to use and edit, but you don't have to copy other people's writing without giving them credit. It's against the law!

Along with the freedom of Wikipedia come some dangers. People can "vandalize" articles. This means that they maliciously[2] insert wrong information into a text or remove important facts. Wikipedia says it deals quickly with these attacks, but, again, users has to be aware that information could be wrong.

Online encyclopedias have changed the way we get information. May they one day replace paper encyclopedias? It's possible. But for now, it might be a good idea to hold on to that library card. In the meantime, it's safe to say that despite some disadvantages, an online encyclopedia can't be a very useful resource if you are careful and use common sense.

---

[1] **plagiarism:** using someone else's words in your own work without giving that person credit
[2] **maliciously:** doing something to deliberately hurt someone

EXERCISE 5: Listening

A | *Read the statements. Then listen to the conversation. Listen again and check (✓)* **True** *or* **False**. *Correct the false statements.*

	True	False

doesn't use

1. The woman ~~uses~~ Facebook. ☐ ☑

2. The woman is very busy. ☐ ☐

3. The man thinks Facebook is dangerous. ☐ ☐

4. The woman would like to make new friends online. ☐ ☐

5. The man thinks the woman should join Facebook. ☐ ☐

6. The man and woman can chat online on Facebook. ☐ ☐

7. The woman promises to consider joining. ☐ ☐

B | *Complete the conversation with modals that you think are possible. Then listen again and check your work. If the conversation uses a different modal, write the modal that you hear.*

A: Lea, you really _____*must*_____ join Facebook. You're my only friend who isn't on it.
1.

B: I just don't have time for it. There are too many other things that I _____ do.
2.

A: You _____ have *some* free time.
3.

B: Sure I do. But I _____ afford to spend it online. Besides, isn't it a little dangerous?
4.

A: Not really. Of course, you _____ be careful and use common sense. Just like
5.

with other things.

B: Well, I guess you _____ be right.
6.

A: Trust me. It's a lot of fun. And you _____ meet a lot of interesting people that
7.

way. Like me, for example!

B: I _____ join Facebook to meet interesting people. But on second thought,
8.

I suppose it _____ be fun to reconnect with old friends.
9.

A: Exactly. You really _____ give it some thought. Will you think about it?
10.

B: _____ we _____ chat online if I join?
11.

A: Sure.

B: In that case, I _____ !
12.

EXERCISE 6: Pronunciation

A | *Read and listen to the Pronunciation Note.*

B | *Listen to the short conversations and write the words you hear. Use full forms.*

1. A: You _____ join Facebook. It's a lot of fun.

   B: I know. But first I _____ get a new email address.

2. A: Do you _____ post a photo of yourself?

   B: No. But you _____ give information about yourself.

3. A: You _____ see Jason's new photos. They're great.

   B: I've heard about them, but I _____ sign on last night.

4. A: Will you _____ email me the photos?

   B: No problem. I just _____ find them on my computer.

5. A: I _____ write a report about social networking.

   B: You _____ look it up on Wikipedia first.

C | *Listen again to the conversations and repeat each question and statement. Then practice the conversations with a partner.*

EXERCISE 7: Discussion

Look at Blaire Thomas's profile on a social networking site. Work with a partner and discuss the site. Use modals. Answer these questions:

- What information shouldn't Blaire have on her profile? What should she keep?
- Does she have too many social networking friends? Why or why not?
- What skills and talents do you think Blaire has?
- What can you guess about her interests?

Blaire shares other profile information with her friends. Click here to make friends.

Blaire Thomas
Female, Age 17
Orlando, Florida, USA

Networks: Waterfront High School
Disney Resorts
Interests: My guitar class, part-time job at Disney Resorts, working out with friends
Danny and Mica
Music: Anything on the guitar, High School Musical, Taylor Swift, Jonas Brothers
Movies: *The Social Network, Avatar, Date Night, La Gloire de Mon Père, Amelie*
TV: *Survivor!* I must be this show's biggest fan!
Books: Books? What are they?

Blaire's bumper stickers

My friends are
pretty awesome.

Hang up and drive!

It's never too late to
have a happy childhood.

Blaire has 840 Friends (top 3)

Ben   Sara   Jesse

Blaire's quizzes and games:
Desert Island
Know-it-All

EXAMPLE: **A:** She should protect her privacy better. For example, she shouldn't give so much
personal information.
B: That's true. It could be dangerous to give your full name and . . .
A: I think Blaire might . . .

EXERCISE 8: Reaching Agreement

Work in small groups. Imagine you are designing a class website. What will you include?
What issues will you have to consider? For example:

- information that you should and shouldn't include about students and your class

- people who can and can't post on the site (for example, classmates, teacher, friends, and family)

- content and features that students might or might not want (for example, photos, videos, chat, discussion forums, fun quizzes and games)

- links to other Internet sites that could be helpful resources (for example, online dictionaries and information about other countries)

- ways that you can get your classmates involved in the website

EXAMPLE: **A:** We should post photos of class members.
B: But we'd better not give too much personal information.
C: Students might like to post recipes from their countries.

EXERCISE 9: Problem Solving

A *Many social networking sites have fun quizzes that people link to their pages. Take this quiz about surviving on a desert island.*

IMAGINE YOU ARE IN A GROUP ON A REALITY TV SHOW CALLED DESERT ISLAND. WHAT SHOULD YOU DO? TAKE THE QUIZ.

1. You only have time to grab one thing. What *must* you have to survive?
○ We've got to bring a knife.   ○ We should take a mirror.
○ We'll need a fishing rod.   ○ Other

2. You've just arrived on the island. What should you do first?
○ We'd better take a nap.   ○ We should build a campfire.
○ We ought to find fresh water.   ○ Other

3. There are no fast-food places on the island. What's for dinner?
○ Maybe we can catch some fish.   ○ We could eat insects.
○ Yuck. There must be a village nearby. ○ Other

4. The island is getting boring. How can you pass the time?
○ We could explore the island.   ○ We've got to build a shelter.
○ We should practice swimming.   ○ Other

5. There are other people on the island! You hear their voices. What should you do?
○ We should say hello.   ○ Avoid them. They may not be friendly.
○ Watch first. They may be friendly.   ○ Other

6. Planes and ships sometimes pass by. How can you attract their attention?
○ We've got to build a big fire on the beach. ○ We could use a mirror to signal them.
○ We should scream loudly.   ○ Other

B | *Work in small groups. Compare your choices and decide what your group should do.*

> EXAMPLE: **A:** We have to bring a mirror. With a mirror, we can start a fire . . .
> **B:** We'd better not take a nap. We've got to . . .
> **C:** For dinner, we ought to . .

EXERCISE 10: For or Against

A | *In a group, discuss the advantages and the disadvantages of online social networking. You can use these ideas and your own knowledge and experience.*

- How can social networking help people?

- What should you do to get the most benefit from networking?

- What are some of the problems?

- What are some of the things you must do to be safe and protect your privacy?

- Do the advantages outweigh the disadvantages?

B | *Share your ideas in a discussion with the whole class.*

> EXAMPLE: **A:** You can find out other students' opinions about schools.
> **B:** You could also learn about jobs.
> **C:** You might even . . .

EXERCISE 11: Writing

A | *Write a post for a personal blog about your plans for the week. Write about things that you are **going to do**, **might do**, **should do**, and **have to do**.*

> EXAMPLE: Next week is going to be a busy week. I have exams on Monday and Wednesday, so I really should study this weekend. I've got to bring that math grade up. I've finally chosen some colors, so on Saturday I'm going to paint the living room. I can't do it myself in one weekend, so I posted my plan on Facebook. Some friends might help me paint . . .

B | *Check your work. Use the Editing Checklist.*

> ### Editing Checklist
>
> Did you use . . . ?
> ☐ modals for ability
> ☐ modals for advice
> ☐ modals for necessity
> ☐ modals for possibility
> ☐ the base form of verbs after modals

Check your answers on page UR-4.

Do you need to review anything?

A | *Circle the correct words to complete the conversations.*

- **A:** Were you able to <u>get / got</u> in touch with Carla?
  1.

  B: No, but I left her a message on Facebook. She <u>couldn't / may</u> see it there.
  2.

- **A:** You <u>'ve got / must</u> to see my photos of our class trip. They're really funny.
  3.

  B: I <u>can't / not able to</u> log on right now. I'll check them out later.
  4.

- **A:** Could my MySpace page <u>helps / help</u> me get into college?
  5.

  B: It <u>might be / might</u>. You ought to <u>post / posted</u> information about your school activities.
  6. **7.**

- **A:** The rules say that to join this site you <u>must not / don't have to</u> be under 13.
  8.

  B: So you're still too young. But you'll <u>can / be able to</u> join next month.
  9.

B | *Rewrite the phrases in parentheses using modals and similar expressions.*

1. You _____ personal information on the Internet.
   (it's a very bad idea to give)

2. We _____ today or we won't be able to attend classes.
   (it's urgent that we register)

3. Sasha _____ online. I'm sure she's studying for her test.
   (it's almost certain that Sasha isn't)

4. Takumi _____ more sleep. He fell asleep in class again today.
   (it's absolutely necessary that Takumi get)

5. Sorry, you _____ here. See the sign?
   (it's against the rules to eat)

6. Paulo _____ to the party tonight, but he hasn't decided yet.
   (will possibly come)

C | *Find and correct five mistakes.*

1. Could that being Amelie in this photograph?

2. No, that's impossible. It doesn't look anything like Amelie. It doesn't have to be her.

3. I don't know this person. I guess I'd not better accept him as a friend on my Facebook page.

4. With MySpace, I must not call to keep in touch with friends. It's just not necessary.

5. May hi5 be as popular as Facebook someday?

Advisability in the Past
REGRETS

Before You Read

Look at the photo. Discuss the questions.

1. How do you think the woman feels?
2. What is she thinking about?
3. What are some typical things that people have regrets about?

Read

Read the article from a popular psychology magazine.

Useless Regrets

"It **might have been**." These are not only the saddest words, but perhaps the most destructive. According to recent ideas in psychology, our feelings are mainly the result of the way we *think* about reality, not reality itself.

According to Nathan S. Kline, M.D., it's not unusual to feel deep regret about things in the past that you think you **should have done** and did not do—or the opposite, about things you did and feel you **should not have done**. In fact, we learn by thinking about past mistakes. For example, a student who fails a test learns that he or she **should have studied** more and can improve on the next test.

However, thinking too much about past mistakes and missed opportunities can create such bad feelings that people become paralyzed[1] and can't move on with their lives. Arthur Freeman, Ph.D., and Rose DeWolf have labeled this process "woulda/coulda/shoulda thinking," and they have written an entire book about this type of disorder.

*For all sad words of tongue or pen The saddest are these: "It **might have been**."*
—John Greenleaf Whittier

I **should've been** rich and famous by now.

I **ought to have applied** to college.

I **could've become** a doctor.

My parents **shouldn't have discouraged** me.

(continued on next page)

_____
[1]*paralyzed:* not able to think clearly and make decisions or act

Useless Regrets

In *Woulda/Coulda/Shoulda: Overcoming Regrets, Mistakes, and Missed Opportunities,* Freeman and DeWolf suggest challenging regrets with specifics. "Instead of saying, 'I **should've done** better,'" they suggest, "Write down an example of a way in which you **might have done** better. Exactly what **should** you **have done** to produce the results you were hoping for? Did you have the skills, money, experience, etc., at the time?" Perhaps the student who **should have studied** more was exhausted from job and family responsibilities and really couldn't spend more time studying.

When people examine their feelings of regret about the past, they often find that many of them are frequently based on simple misunderstandings of a situation. A mother regrets missing a football game in which her son's leg was injured. She blames herself and the officials. "I **should've gone**," she keeps telling herself. "I **could've prevented** the injury.

They **might** at least **have telephoned** me as soon as it happened." Did she *really* have the power to prevent her son's injury? **Should** the officials **have called** her *before* looking at the injury? Probably not.

Once people realize how unrealistic their feelings of regret are, they are more ready to let go of them. Psychologist David Burns, M.D., suggests specific strategies for dealing with useless feelings of regret and getting on with the present. One amusing technique is to spend 10 minutes a day writing down all the things you regret. Then say them all aloud (better yet, record them), and listen to yourself.

After you recognize how foolish most feelings of regret sound, the next step is to let go of them and to start dealing with the problems you face right now.

I **shouldn't have told** that joke in the office. My career is ruined.

I **ought to have cleaned** the house instead of going out this weekend. My mother's right. I'm just lazy.

My boyfriend **could have told** me he was going out of town this weekend. He's an inconsiderate[2] jerk.[3] I **should** never **have started** going out with him.

I **should've used** a longer piece of paper...

REGRETS

---

[2]*inconsiderate:* not caring about other people's needs or feelings
[3]*jerk:* (informal) a stupid or very annoying person

After You Read

A | Vocabulary: *Circle the letter of the word or phrase closest in meaning to the words in* blue.

1. Rosa has a new **strategy** for finding a new job.

    a. plan of action

    b. suit

    c. Internet site

2. Sarah wants to help people, so she has decided to major in **psychology**.

    a. the science of how to eat in a healthy way

    b. the study of exercise and movement

    c. the study of how people think and feel

3. Jeb's career wasn't **ruined** because he told that joke. He's still got the same job.

    a. improved

    b. destroyed

    c. changed

4. Petros's goal to learn English in two months is **unrealistic**.

    a. impossible

    b. not popular

    c. really smart

5. The teacher mentioned several good **techniques** for learning vocabulary.

    a. DVDs

    b. methods

    c. schools

6. When I was applying to school, the **process** seemed long and difficult.

    a. series of steps

    b. application form

    c. school catalog

B | Comprehension: *Circle the correct word or phrase to complete each statement.*

1. Some psychologists say that it is our thoughts / real situations that cause our feelings.

2. Thoughts like "I should have studied more" can get a student to give up / improve.

3. "Woulda/Shoulda/Coulda" thinking often paralyzes / helps people.

4. Arthur Freeman and Rose DeWolf suggest ignoring / questioning regrets.

5. The thought "I could have prevented the injury" was realistic / unrealistic.

6. Dr. David Burns suggests a strategy for dealing with regrets that might make you cry / laugh.

7. Saying regrets aloud can make them sound silly / intelligent.

ADVISABILITY IN THE PAST:
Should Have, Ought to Have, Could Have, Might Have

Statements				
Subject	**Modal***	***Have***	**Past Participle**	
He	should (not) ought (not) to could might	**have**	**told**	her.

Contractions		
should have	=	**should've**
could have	=	**could've**
might have	=	**might've**
should not have	=	**shouldn't have**

**Should, ought to, could,* and *might* are modals. Modals have only one form. They do not have *-s* in the third person singular.

Yes / No Questions				
Should	**Subject**	***Have***	**Past Participle**	
Should	he	**have**	**told**	her?

Short Answers							
Affirmative				**Negative**			
Yes,	he	**should**	**have.**	**No,**	he	**shouldn't**	**have.**

Wh- Questions					
***Wh-* Word**	***Should***	**Subject**	***Have***	**Past Participle**	
When	**should**	he	**have**	**told**	her?

GRAMMAR NOTES

1 Use the modals **should have**, **ought to have**, **could have**, and **might have** to talk about **past advisability**.

   a. These past modals often express **regret** about something that happened, especially when we use them with **I** or **we**.

- **I should've applied** to college.
  (I didn't apply, and now I'm sorry.)
- **We could've gone** to a much better school.
  (We didn't go to a better school. Now we regret our choice.)

   b. These past modals often **express blame** or **criticism** about something that happened, especially when we use them with **you**, **she**, **he**, or **they**.

- **You shouldn't have sent** that letter. It hurt her.
  (You sent the letter. That was wrong.)
- **They could have called** us. We waited for hours.
  (They didn't call. That was inconsiderate.)

USAGE NOTE: We use **should have**, **ought to have**, and **could have** for **regret** or **blame**. **Might have** (with *you*, *she*, *he*, or *they*) usually expresses **blame**.

- **I ought to have studied** more.
  (I didn't study. I regret it.)
- **He might've told** me. I needed to know.
  (He didn't tell me. That was wrong.)

2 In **affirmative statements**, use **should have**, **ought to have**, **could have**, and **might have**. *Should have* is the most common form.

- He **should have taken** the math exam.
- He **could've left** home earlier.

In **negative statements**, use **shouldn't have** and **ought not to have**. *Shouldn't have* is more common.
Do NOT use *couldn't have* or *might not have* for past advisability.

- He **shouldn't have missed** the exam.
- He **ought not to have left** so late.

Noт: He ~~could'nt have~~ left so late. That was a mistake.

In **questions** (both *yes / no* and *wh-* questions), use **should have**. Notice that **short answers** include **modal** + **have**.

A: **Should** he **have** called the teacher?
B: Yes, he **should've**.
   Noт: Yes, he ~~should~~.
A: When **should** he **have** called?
B: Before the test started.

3 We use the **contractions should've**, **could've**, and **might've** in speech, emails, and informal notes.

- I **should've** answered sooner.
  (*informal note*)

We sometimes use "**shoulda**," "**coulda**," "**mighta**," and "**oughta**" in **very informal** notes, emails, and text messages.

- I **shoulda** answered sooner.
  (*email to friend*)

BE CAREFUL! Do NOT use these forms in **formal** writing.

- I **should have** answered sooner.
  (*business letter*)

REFERENCE NOTE

Could have and **might have** are also used for **speculations about the past** (see Unit 17).

EXERCISE 1: Discover the Grammar

Read each numbered statement. Circle the letter of the sentence that is similar in meaning.

1. I shouldn't have called him.
   - **a.** I called him.
   - **b.** I didn't call him.

2. My parents ought to have moved away from that neighborhood.
   - **a.** They're going to move, but they're not sure when.
   - **b.** Moving was a good idea, but they didn't do it.

3. I should have studied psychology.
   - **a.** I didn't study psychology, and now I regret it.
   - **b.** I studied psychology, and it was a big mistake.

4. He might have warned us about the traffic.
   - **a.** He didn't know, so he couldn't tell us.
   - **b.** He knew, but he didn't tell us.

5. Felicia could have been a vice president by now.
   - **a.** Felicia didn't become a vice president.
   - **b.** Felicia is a vice president.

6. They shouldn't have lent him their car.
   - **a.** They refused to lend him their car.
   - **b.** They lent him their car.

7. I ought not to have bought that sweater.
   - **a.** I bought the sweater.
   - **b.** I didn't buy the sweater.

EXERCISE 2: Statements, Questions, and Short Answers   (Grammar Note 2)

A class is discussing an ethical problem. Read the problem. Complete the discussion with the correct form of the verbs in parentheses or with short answers. Choose between affirmative and negative.

PROBLEM: Greg, a college student, worked successfully for a clothing store for a year. He spent most of his salary on books and tuition. One week he wanted some extra money to buy a sweater to wear to a party. He asked for a raise, but his boss, Mr. Thompson, refused. The same week, Greg discovered an extra sweater in a shipment he was unpacking. It was very stylish and just his size. Greg "borrowed" it for the weekend and then brought it back. Mr. Thompson found out and fired him.

TEACHER: _____Should_____ Mr. Thompson _____have given_____ Greg a raise?
                                          1. (should / give)

STUDENT A: Yes, he _____should have_____. After all, Greg had worked there for a whole
                          2.

year. Mr. Thompson _____shouldn't have refused_____ at that point.
                          3. (should / refuse)

STUDENT B: But maybe Mr. Thompson couldn't afford to give Greg a raise. Anyway, Greg still

_____ the sweater. It wasn't his.
       4. (should / take)

TEACHER: What strategy _____ Greg _____ instead?
                                                    5. (should / use)

STUDENT C: He _____ Mr. Thompson to sell him the sweater. Then
                   6. (might / ask)

he _____ for it slowly, out of his salary.
        7. (could / pay)

STUDENT A: He _____ his old clothes to the party. His behavior was
                   8. (ought to / wear)

destructive. He just hurt himself by taking the sweater.

TEACHER: Well, _____ Mr. Thompson _____ Greg?
                                                    9. (should / fire)

STUDENT B: No, he _____. Greg had been a good employee for a
                          10.

year, and he brought the sweater back. Now Greg's reputation might be ruined.

TEACHER: How _____ Mr. Thompson _____ the situation?
                                                    11. (should / handle)

STUDENT C: He _____ Greg. He _____ just
                   12. (ought to / warn)

_____ Greg without any warning.
       13. (should / fire)

EXERCISE 3: Affirmative and Negative Statements   (Grammar Note 2)

Complete Greta's regrets or complaints about the past using the modals in parentheses.
Choose between affirmative and negative.

1. I didn't go to college. Now I'm depressed about my job.

   (should) *I should have gone to college.* _____

2. My brother quit his job. He thought he could find another job right away. I knew that was
   unrealistic, but I didn't warn him. How inconsiderate of me.

   (might) _____

3. I feel sick. I ate all the chocolate.

   (should) _____

(continued on next page)

4. Christina didn't come over. She didn't even call. My entire evening was ruined.

(might) _____

5. I tried to tell Christina how I felt, but it was useless. She just didn't listen to me.

(could) _____

6. I jogged 5 miles yesterday, and now I'm exhausted.

(should) _____

7. I didn't apply for a good job because the application process was so long. I gave up.

(should) _____

8. I didn't do the laundry yesterday, so I don't have any clean socks. Everyone else gets their laundry done on time. Why can't I?

(ought to) _____

9. I didn't invite Cynthia to the party. Now she's angry at me.

(should) _____

10. Yesterday was my birthday, and my brother didn't send me a card. I'm hurt.

(might) _____

EXERCISE 4: Editing

(Grammar Notes 1–3)

Read this journal entry. There are six mistakes in the use of modals. The first mistake is already corrected. Find and correct five more.

> December 15
>
> About a week ago, Jennifer was late for work again, and Doug, our boss, told me he
> wanted to fire her. I was really upset. Of course, Jennifer shouldn't ~~had~~ *have* been late so
> often, but he might has talked to her about the problem before he decided to let her
> go. Then he laughed and told me to make her job difficult for her so that she would
> quit. He thought it was amusing! I just pretended I didn't hear him. What a mistake!
> It was unrealistic to think the problem would just go away. I ought confronted him
> right away. Or I could at least have warned Jennifer. Anyway, Jennifer is still here, but
> now I'm worried about my own job. Should I have telling Doug's boss? I wonder. Maybe
> I should handle things differently last week. The company should never has hired this
> guy. I'd better figure out some techniques for handling these situations.

264   UNIT 16

EXERCISE 5: Listening

A | *Jennifer is taking Dr. David Burns's advice by recording all the things she regrets at the end of the day. Look at Jennifer's list. Then listen to her recording. Listen again and check (✓) the things she did.*

TO DO

☐ Do homework ☐ Call Aunt Rose
☑ Walk to work ☐ Call Ron
☐ Make $100 bank deposit ☐ Go to supermarket
☐ Buy coat ☐ Finish David Burns's book

B | *Read these statements from Jennifer's recording. Then listen and complete the statements.*

1. I _____*could've done*_____ my homework.

2. I _____ to work today.

3. I really _____ that $100 deposit today.

4. I _____ that new coat.

5. I _____ at least _____ to wish her a happy birthday.

6. I _____ to the supermarket.

7. I _____ that David Burns book.

EXERCISE 6: Pronunciation

A | *Read and listen to the Pronunciation Note.*

Pronunciation Note

In **past modals**, we sometimes pronounce **have** or its contraction **'ve** like the word "a." We only do this in fast, informal conversation.

EXAMPLES:
I **should have** called you. → "I **shoulda** called you."
They **could have** helped more. → "They **coulda** helped more."
He **might have** told me sooner. → "He **mighta** told me sooner."

We sometimes pronounce **ought to have** like "oughta of."

EXAMPLE: They **ought to have** come on time. → "They **oughta of** come on time."

1. **A:** Doug _____ sent that email.

   B: I know. But you _____ told him that yesterday.

2. **A:** We _____ taken the train.

   B: You're right. We _____ been home by now.

3. **A:** I guess I _____ accepted that job.

   B: Well, maybe you _____ waited a few days before deciding.

4. **A:** You _____ washed that T-shirt in cold water.

   B: I guess I _____ read the label before I washed it.

5. **A:** I _____ asked my sister to lend me some money

   B: She's your *sister*! She _____ *offered* to help.

C | *Practice the conversations with a partner.*

EXERCISE 7: Game: Find the Problems

Work with a partner. Look at the picture of Jennifer's apartment. What should she have done? What shouldn't she have done? Write as many sentences as you can in five minutes. When you are done, compare your answers with those of your classmates.

EXAMPLE: **A:** She should have paid the electric bill.
   B: She shouldn't have left the window open.

EXERCISE 8: Survey

A | *A sense of obligation is a feeling that you (or someone else) should have done or shouldn't have done something. How strong is your sense of obligation? Take this test and find out.*

Sense of Obligation Survey (S.O.S.)

INSTRUCTIONS: Read each situation. Circle the letter of your most likely response.

1. You want to lose 10 pounds, but you just ate a large dish of ice cream.
   - **a.** I shouldn't have eaten the ice cream. I have no willpower.
   - **b.** I deserve to enjoy things once in a while. I'll do better tomorrow.

2. Your friend quit her job. Now she's unemployed.
   - **a.** Maybe she was really depressed at work. It's better that she left.
   - **b.** She shouldn't have quit until she found another job.

3. You had an appointment with your doctor. You arrived on time but had to wait more than an hour.
   - **a.** My doctor should have scheduled better. My time is valuable too.
   - **b.** Maybe there was an emergency. I'm sure it's not my doctor's fault.

4. You bought a coat for $140. A day later you saw it at another store for $100.
   - **a.** That was really bad luck.
   - **b.** I should have looked around before I bought the coat.

5. Your brother didn't send you a birthday card.
   - **a.** He could have at least called. He's so inconsiderate.
   - **b.** Maybe he forgot. He's really been busy lately.

6. You just got back an English test. Your grade was 60 percent.
   - **a.** That was a really difficult test.
   - **b.** I should have studied harder.

7. You just found out that an electrician overcharged you.
   - **a.** I should have known that was too much money.
   - **b.** How could I have known? I'm not an expert.

8. You forgot to do some household chores that you had promised to do. Now the person you live with is angry.
   - **a.** I shouldn't have forgotten. I'm irresponsible.
   - **b.** I'm only human. I make mistakes.

9. You got a ticket for driving 5 miles per hour above the speed limit.
   - **a.** I ought to have obeyed the speed limit.
   - **b.** The police officer could've overlooked it and not given me the ticket. It was only 5 miles over the speed limit.

10. You went to the movies but couldn't get a ticket because it was sold out.
    - **a.** I should've gone earlier.
    - **b.** Wow! This movie is really popular!

SCORING
Give yourself one point for each of these answers:

1. **a**	6. **b**
2. **b**	7. **a**
3. **a**	8. **a**
4. **b**	9. **a**
5. **a**	10. **a**

The higher your score, the stronger your sense of obligation.

B | *Now interview a classmate and compare your survey results.*

EXAMPLE: **A:** What was your answer to Question 1?
            B: I said I shouldn't have eaten the ice cream. What about you?

EXERCISE 9: Problem Solving

Work in small groups. Read and discuss each case. Did the people act properly or should they have done things differently?

Case 1: Sheila was in her last year of college when she decided to run for student council president. During her campaign, a school newspaper reporter asked her about something he had discovered about her past. In high school, Sheila had once been caught cheating on a test. She had admitted her mistake and repeated the course. She never cheated again. Sheila felt that the incident was over, and she refused to answer the reporter's questions. The reporter wrote the story without telling Sheila's side, and Sheila lost the election.

> **EXAMPLE:**
> **A:** Should Sheila have refused to answer questions about her past?
> **B:** I don't think so. It's useless to refuse to answer reporters' questions. They always report about it anyway.
> **C:** I agree. She should've . . .

Case 2: Mustafa is a social worker who cares deeply about his clients. Recently, there was a fire in his office building. After the fire, the fire department declared the building unsafe and wouldn't allow anyone to go back in. Mustafa became worried and depressed because all his clients' records were in the building. He needed their names, telephone numbers, and other information in order to help them. He decided to take the risk, and he entered the building to get the records. His supervisor found out and fired him.

Case 3: Pierre's wife has been sick for a long time. One day, the doctor told Pierre about a new medicine that might save her life. He warned Pierre that the medicine was still experimental, so Pierre's insurance would not pay for it. At the pharmacy, Pierre discovered that the medicine was so expensive that he didn't have enough money to pay for it. The pharmacist refused to let Pierre pay for it later. At first, Pierre was paralyzed by fear and hopelessness. Then he took extra work on nights and weekends to pay for the medicine. Now he's too exhausted to take care of his wife as well as he had before.

EXERCISE 10: Writing

A | *Write three paragraphs about a dilemma that you have faced.*

- **Paragraph 1:** Describe the problem and what you did.
- **Paragraph 2:** Evaluate what you should or should not have done.
- **Paragraph 3:** Write about what you learned.

B | *Check your work. Use the Editing Checklist.*

Editing Checklist

Did you use . . . ?

☐ *should have*, *ought to have*, *could have*, *might have* + **past participle** for affirmative statements

☐ *should not have* and *ought not to have* + **past participle** for negative statements

A | *Circle the correct words to complete the sentences.*

1. I got a C on my test. I should <u>had / have</u> studied more.

2. I <u>ought / should</u> to have asked for help.

3. Dara <u>could / couldn't</u> have offered to help me. She's very good at math.

4. The teacher might have <u>gave / given</u> me a little more time.

5. I was tired. I <u>couldn't / shouldn't</u> have stayed up so late the night before.

6. What <u>should I / I should</u> have done differently?

B | *Rewrite the sentences with the correct form of the modals in parentheses. Choose between affirmative and negative.*

1. I regret that I didn't study for the math test.

   (should) _____

2. It was wrong of you not to show me your class notes.

   (could) _____

3. I regret that I stayed up so late the night before the test.

   (should) _____

4. It was wrong of John not to call you.

   (ought to) _____

5. I blame you for not inviting me to join the study group.

   (might) _____

C | *Find and correct nine mistakes.*

I shouldn't have stay up so late. I overslept and missed my bus. I ought have asked Erik for a
ride. I got to the office late, and my boss said, "You might had called." She was right. I shouldn't
have called. At lunch my co-workers went out together. They really could of invited me to join
them. Should have I said something to them? Then, after lunch, my mother called. She said,
"Yesterday was Aunt Em's birthday. You could've sending her a card!" I really think my mother
might has reminded me. Not a good day! I shouldn't have just stayed in bed.

UNIT 17 Speculations and Conclusions About the Past

UNSOLVED MYSTERIES

STEP 1 GRAMMAR IN CONTEXT

Before You Read

Look at the photo. Discuss the questions.

1. What do you think the design represents?
2. Who do you think made it? When?

Read

Read about one writer's theories on ancient cultures.

CLOSE ENCOUNTERS

In 1927, Toribio Mexta Xesspe of Peru **must have been** very surprised to see lines in the shapes of huge animals and geometric[1] forms on the ground below his airplane. Created by the ancient Nazca culture, these beautiful forms (over 13,000 of them) are too big to recognize from the ground. However, from about 600 feet in the air, the giant forms take shape. Xesspe **may have been** the first human in almost a thousand years to recognize the designs.

Since their discovery, many people have speculated about the Nazca lines. Without airplanes, how **could** an ancient culture **have made** these amazing pictures? What purpose **could** they **have had**?

Nazca lines

---

[1] **geometric:** using lines or shapes from geometry, such as circles, rectangles, and squares

One writer, Erich von Däniken, has a theory as amazing as the Nazca lines themselves. According to von Däniken, visitors from other planets brought their civilization to the Earth thousands of years ago. When these astronauts[2] visited ancient cultures here on Earth, the people of those cultures **must have believed** that the visitors were gods. Since the Nazcans **could have built** the lines according to instructions from an aircraft, von Däniken concludes that the drawings **might have marked** a landing strip for the spacecraft of the ancient astronauts. Von Däniken writes, "The builders of the geometrical figures **may have had** no idea what they were doing. But perhaps they knew perfectly well what the 'gods' needed in order to land."

In his book *Chariots[3] of the Gods?* von Däniken offers many other "proofs" that ancient cultures had contact with visitors from other planets. Giant statues on Easter Island provide von Däniken with strong evidence of the astronauts' presence. Von Däniken estimates that the island **could** only **have supported** a very small population. After examining the simple tools that the islanders probably used, he concludes that even 2,000 men working day and night **could not have been** enough to carve the figures out of hard stone. In addition, he says that at least part of the population **must have worked** in the fields, **gone** fishing, and **woven** cloth. "Two thousand men alone **could not have made** the gigantic statues." Von Däniken's conclusion: Space visitors **had to have built** them.

Archeologists,[4] among others, are skeptical[5] and prefer to look for answers closer to home. However, von Däniken's theories continue to fascinate people, both believers and nonbelievers. And even nonbelievers must admit that visitors from space **might have contributed** to human culture. After all, no one can prove that they didn't.

Easter Island: Statues of space visitors?

[2]**astronaut:** someone who travels and works in a spacecraft

[3]**chariot:** a vehicle with two wheels, pulled by a horse, used in ancient times in battles and races

[4]**archeologist:** someone who studies ancient societies by examining the remains of their buildings, tools, and other objects

[5]**skeptical:** having doubts whether something is true; not believing something

A | Vocabulary: *Complete the sentences with the words from the box.*

conclusion	contribute	encounter	estimate	evidence	speculate

1. Dr. Shane has good _____ to support her theory about the Nazca lines.

2. Please _____ ideas for the class project. We need to hear everyone's thoughts.

3. I _____ that there were about 50 people at the party. I don't know the exact

   number, but the restaurant was very crowded.

4. It's fun to _____ about space aliens, but there are almost no facts to support

   their existence.

5. After looking at the facts, we came to the _____ that space visitors didn't build

   the statues.

6. Rob had an interesting _____ with his old roommate at the concert. He didn't

   expect to see him, and they had a great time talking.

B | Comprehension: *How certain was Erich von Däniken about his ideas? Check (✓) the correct column for each statement.*

	Certain	Possible	Impossible
1. The Nazca people believed that the visitors were gods.	☐	☐	☐
2. The Nazca lines marked a landing strip for ancient astronauts.	☐	☐	☐
3. There were enough people on Easter Island to carve the huge statues.	☐	☐	☐
4. Space visitors built the statues.	☐	☐	☐

SPECULATIONS AND CONCLUSIONS ABOUT THE PAST:
May have, Might have, Could have, Must have, Had to have

Statements				
Subject	**Modal* / *Had to***	***Have***	**Past Participle**	
They	**may (not)** **might (not)** **could (not)** **must (not)** **had to**	**have**	**seen**	the statues.

* *May, might, could,* and *must* are modals. Modals have only one form. They do not have -s in the third person singular.

Contractions
may have = **may've**
might have = **might've**
could have = **could've**
must have = **must've**
could not = **couldn't**

NOTE: We usually do not contract *may not have, might not have,* or *must not have.*

Questions			
Do / Be	**Subject**	**Verb**	
Did	they	**carve**	these statues?
Were			aliens?

Short Answers			
Subject	**Modal / *Had to***	***Have***	***Been***
They	**may (not)** **might (not)** **could (not)**	**have.**	
	must (not) **had to**	**have**	**been.**

Yes / No Questions: *Could*				
Could	**Subject**	***Have***	**Past Participle**	
Could	he	**have**	**seen**	aliens?
			been	an alien?

Short Answers			
Subject	**Modal / *Had to***	***Have***	***Been***
He	**may (not)** **might (not)** **could (not)**	**have.**	
	must (not) **had to**	**have**	**been.**

Wh- Questions			
***Wh-* Word**	***Could***	***Have***	**Past Participle**
Who			**built**	the statues?
What	**could**	**have**	**happened**	to these people?

1 Use *may have*, *might have*, and *could have* to talk about **past possibilities**. These **speculations** about past situations are usually based on only a few facts.

FACT:
Archeologists found many pictures of creatures with wings.

SPECULATIONS:
- Space beings **may have visited** that civilization.
- The pictures **might have marked** a landing strip for a spacecraft.
- The pictures **could have shown** mythological creatures.

2 Use *must have* and *had to have* when you are almost certain about your **conclusions**.

FACT:
The Easter Island statues are made of stone.

CONCLUSIONS:
- The islanders **must have had** very sharp tools.
- They **had to have been** skilled stoneworkers.

In **negative conclusions**, do NOT use *didn't have to have*. Use *must not have* instead.

- The stones **must not have been** easy to move.
NOT: The stones ~~didn't have to have been~~ . . .

3 *Couldn't have* often expresses a feeling of disbelief or **impossibility**.

- He **couldn't have believed** space visitors helped them! It doesn't make any sense.

4 **Questions** about past possibility usually use *could have*. They do not usually use *may have* or *might have*.

- **Could** the Nazcans **have drawn** those lines?
NOT COMMON: ~~Might~~ the Nazcans have drawn . . . ?

5 In **short answers** to questions about past possibility use:

a. *been* when the questions include a form of *be*

A: *Was* Mexta Xesspe surprised when he saw the Nazca lines?
B: He **must have** *been*. No one knew about them at that time.

b. modal + *have* when the questions do NOT include forms of *be*

A: **Did** archeologists **measure** the drawings?
B: They **must have**. They studied them.

6 We sometimes use "**coulda**" in **very informal** notes, emails, and text messages.

- I think you **coulda** been right about my research topic. (*informal email*)

BE CAREFUL! Do NOT use "*coulda*" in **formal** writing.

NOT: Dear Professor Johnson, I think you ~~coulda~~ been right . . . (*formal note*)

REFERENCE NOTE
Could have and *might have* are also used for **past advisability** (see Unit 16).

EXERCISE 1: Discover the Grammar

Match the facts with the speculations and conclusions.

Facts

_e_ **1.** The original title of *Chariots of the Gods?* was *Erinnerungen an die Zukunft*.

____ **2.** Erich von Däniken visited every place he described in his book.

____ **3.** In 1973, he wrote *In Search of Ancient Gods*.

____ **4.** He doesn't have a degree in archeology.

____ **5.** *Chariots of the Gods?* was published the same year as the Apollo moon landing.

____ **6.** In the 1900s, writer Annie Besant said beings from Venus helped develop culture on Earth.

____ **7.** Von Däniken's books sold millions of copies.

____ **8.** As soon as von Däniken published his book, scientists attacked his theories.

Speculations and Conclusions

a. He must have made a lot of money.

b. He may have known about her unusual ideas.

c. He could have learned about the subject on his own.

d. He must have traveled a lot.

e. He must have written his book in German.

f. This great event had to have increased sales of the book.

g. He must not have had scientific evidence for his beliefs.

h. He might have written some other books too.

EXERCISE 2: Questions and Statements

(Grammar Notes 1–4)

Circle the correct words to complete the review of Erich von Däniken's book, Chariots of the Gods?

Who could have <u>make</u> / (<u>made</u>) the Nazca lines? Who
1.
could have <u>carve / carved</u> the Easter Island statues?
2.
According to Erich von Däniken, ancient achievements

like these are mysteries because our ancestors could not

<u>have / had</u> created these things on their own. His
3.
conclusion: They <u>must / couldn't</u> have gotten help from
4.
space visitors.

"Here comes another one."

Von Däniken's readers may not realize that experiments

have contributed to our understanding of some of these

"mysteries." Von Däniken asks: How <u>may / could</u> the Nazcans have planned the lines from
5.
the ground? Archeologists now speculate that this civilization might <u>have / has</u> developed flight.
6.
They think ancient Nazcans may <u>draw / have drawn</u> pictures of hot-air balloons on pottery. To test
7.

(continued on next page)

the theory, archeologists built a similar balloon with Nazca materials. The balloon soared[1] high

enough to view the Nazca lines, showing that Nazcans themselves <u>could / couldn't</u> have designed the

        8.

pictures from the air.

    But what about the Easter Island statues? <u>Did / Could</u> islanders have carved the huge statues

        9.

from hard rock with primitive tools? And how could only 2,000 people <u>had / have</u> moved them?

        10.

---

[1] *soar:* to fly very fast or very high up in the sky

EXERCISE 3: Affirmative and Negative Statements   *(Grammar Notes 1–4)*

Complete the rest of the review of Chariots of the Gods? *Use the verbs in parentheses.*

    Explorers thought that Easter Island's ancient culture _____*must have been*_____

        1. (must / be)

simple. They assumed that the island _____ many natural

        2. (must not / have)

resources, so it _____ a civilization. They were wrong. Studies

        3. (couldn't / support)

have shown that a large population and a complex culture _____

        4. (could / develop)

on the island. Large palm trees once grew there. Islanders _____

        5. (must / make)

large boats from the trees. They _____ in deep water from the

        6. (must / fish)

boats because ancient garbage dumps are full of the bones of deep sea fish. Ancient islanders

_____ very well, and archeologists have estimated that as many

        7. (must / eat)

as 15,000 people _____ on the island. From the trees, they also

        8. (may / live)

_____ ropes to pull their statues. In 1994, DNA tests proved that

        9. (could / make)

the islanders _____ from Polynesia, where there is a tradition of

        10. (had to / come)

ancestor worship. Doubts still remained—in the language of Rapa Nui (Easter Island), the giant

statues are called *the living faces of our ancestors*. But how _____ the Rapa Nui

people _____ these lifeless images "living faces"? Then Sergio Rapu, a Rapa Nui

        11. (could / call)

archeologist, realized that the statues _____ coral[1] eyes. Pieces of

        12. (must / have)

coral that he had found fit one of the statues perfectly, and its face seemed to come to life. Scientists

are still experimenting with ways islanders _____ the huge images.

        13. (might / move)

However, now no one says, "The people of Rapa Nui _____ these

        14. (couldn't / create)

amazing statues."

---

[1] *coral:* a hard red, white, or pink substance formed from the shells of very small ocean creatures that live in warm water—often
   used to make jewelry

EXERCISE 4: Meaning

(Grammar Notes 1–3)

Read about these puzzling events. Then rewrite the answers to the questions about their causes. Substitute a modal phrase for the underlined words. Use the modals in parentheses.

Dinosaurs existed on the Earth for about 135 million years. Then, about 65 million years ago, these giant reptiles all died in a short period of time. What could have caused the dinosaurs to become extinct?

1. It's likely that the Earth became colder. (must)

   The Earth must have become colder.

2. Probably, dinosaurs didn't survive the cold. (must not)

   _____

3. It's been suggested that a huge meteor hit the Earth. (might)

   _____

In 1924, Albert Ostman went camping alone in Canada. Later, he reported that he had an encounter with a Bigfoot (a large, hairy creature that looks human). He said the Bigfoot had kidnapped him and taken him home, where the Bigfoot family treated him like a pet. Ostman escaped after several days. What do you think happened? Could a Bigfoot really have kidnapped Ostman?

4. A Bigfoot didn't kidnap Albert Ostman— that's impossible. (couldn't)

   _____

5. Ostman probably saw a bear. (must)

   _____

6. It's possible that Ostman dreamed about a Bigfoot. (could)

   _____

7. Some people think that he made up the story. (might)

   _____

8. Most likely the man changed the photo. (have to)

   _____

In 1932, a man was taking a walk around Scotland's beautiful Loch Ness. Suddenly, a couple hundred feet from shore, the water bubbled up and a huge monster appeared. The man took a photo. When it was developed, the picture showed something with a long neck and a small head. Since then, many people have reported similar sightings. What do you think? Did the man really see the Loch Ness monster?

9. Perhaps the man saw a large fish. (might)

   _____

10. It's possible that the man saw a dead tree trunk. (may)

   _____

11. It's very unlikely that a dinosaur was in the lake. (couldn't)

   _____

Speculations and Conclusions About the Past   **277**

EXERCISE 5: Short Answers

*Some archeology students are asking questions in class. Use the modals in parentheses to
write short answers.*

1. **A:** Were the Nazcans really able to fly?

   B: _____*They might have been*_____. There's some evidence that they had hot-air
                 (might)
   balloons made of cloth.

2. **A:** Is it possible that the Nazca lines were ancient streets?

   B: _____. Some of them just lead to the tops of mountains
           (could not)
   and then end suddenly.

3. **A:** Do you think the Nazcans used them during

   religious ceremonies?

   B: _____. But we
          (might)
   have no proof.

4. **A:** Do you think the people on Rapa Nui built the

   giant statues themselves?

   B: _____. They
          (could)
   had the knowledge and the tools.

5. **A:** Did the original settlers of Rapa Nui come from Polynesia?

   B: _____. There's a lot of scientific evidence to support this.
          (must)

6. **A:** Erich von Däniken says that many ancient artifacts show pictures of astronauts. Could

   these pictures have illustrated anything closer to Earth?

   B: _____. It's possible that the pictures show people dressed
          (may)
   in local costumes.

7. **A:** Did von Däniken believe his own theories?

   B: _____. Many of his ideas came from science fiction.
          (may not)

8. **A:** Was von Däniken upset by all the criticism he received?

   B: _____. After all, it created more interest in his books.
          (might not)

9. **A:** Do you think von Däniken helped increase general interest in archeology?

   B: _____. Just look at how many of you are taking this class!
          (must)

EXERCISE 6: Editing

Read this student's essay about Easter Island. There are ten mistakes in the use of modals.
The first mistake is already corrected. Find and correct nine more.

Rapa Nui (Easter Island) is a tiny island in the middle of the Pacific. To get there, the first

settlers had to ~~had~~ *have* traveled more than 1,000 miles in open boats. Some scientists

believed only the Polynesians of the Pacific Islands could have make the journey. Others

thought that Polynesians couldn't have carved the huge stone statues on Rapa Nui. They

speculated that Mayans or Egyptians maybe have traveled there. (Some people even

said that space aliens might helped!) Finally, a University of Oslo scientist was able to

study the DNA from ancient skeletons. Professor Erika Halberg announced, "These

people has to have been the descendants[1] of Polynesians."

   We now know that the islanders built the statues, but we have also learned that they

must had solved even more difficult problems. The first settlers came sometime between

the years 400 and 700. At first, Rapa Nui must be a paradise with its fishing, forests, and

good soil. Their society may have grown too fast for the small island, however. Botanical

studies show that by the 1600s they had cut down the last tree. The soil must not have

washed away, so they couldn't farm. And with no wood to build boats, they couldn't

have able to fish. For a period of time, people starved and fought violently, but when the

Dutch discovered Rapa Nui in 1722, they found a peaceful, healthy population growing

fields of vegetables. How the islanders could have learned in this short period of time to

live peacefully with so few resources? For our troubled world today, this might be the

most important "mystery of Easter Island."

_____

[1]*descendant:* someone related to people who lived a long time ago

EXERCISE 7: Listening

A | *Some archeology students are speculating about objects they have found at various sites. Read the statements. Then listen to the conversations. Listen again and check (✓)* **True** *or* **False** *for each statement. Correct the false statements.*

	True	False
1. The woman thinks that people might have used the tool for ~~building~~ *cutting* things.	☐	☑
2. The man thinks people could have worn this object around their necks.	☐	☐
3. The woman thinks this object might have been a hole for shoelaces.	☐	☐
4. The man thinks this piece came from the bottom of an object.	☐	☐
5. The woman thinks that the people who made this object were very smart.	☐	☐
6. The man thinks this object is a rock.	☐	☐

B | *Look at the pictures. Listen again to the conversations and match the pictures with the correct conversation.*

a. _____

b. _____

c. _____

d. _____

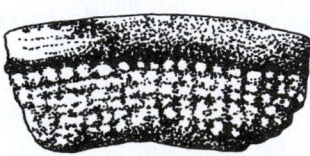

e. _____

f. ___1___

EXERCISE 8: Pronunciation

🎧 **A** | *Read and listen to the Pronunciation Note.*

> ### Pronunciation Note
>
> In **past modals**, we usually pronounce **have** or its contraction **'ve** like "**of**."
>
> **EXAMPLES:** This **could have** been a tool.   → "This **could of** been a tool."
>
> It **may have** happened a long time ago. → "It **may of** happened a long time ago."
>
> They **couldn't have** lived here long.   → "They **couldn't of** lived here long."
>
> You can also pronounce **could have** "coulda" and **might have** "mighta."
>
> In **writing**, we use **could have**, **couldn't have**, **may have**, and **might have**,
> NOT could ~~of~~, couldn't ~~of~~, may ~~of~~, or might ~~of~~.

🎧 **B** | *Listen to the short conversations. Write the contracted forms of the past modals.*

1. **A:** What was that used for?

   B: I'm not sure. It _____ been a spoon.

2. **A:** I called Rahul yesterday afternoon, but there was no answer.

   B: Oh. He _____ gone to the museum.

3. **A:** Is Sara still on Easter Island?

   B: I'm not sure. She _____ left already.

4. **A:** I think I saw John yesterday.

   B: You _____ seen him. He's in Peru.

5. **A:** Do you agree with the author's conclusion?

   B: I don't know. He _____ been wrong.

6. **A:** Alice got an A on her archeology test.

   B: She _____ been happy.

7. **A:** Could they have sailed that far in small boats?

   B: Sure they _____. They were expert sailors.

🎧 **C** | *Listen again to each conversation and repeat the response. Then practice the conversations with a partner. Use short forms.*

EXERCISE 9: Picture Discussion

Work in small groups. Look at the objects that archeologists have found in different places. Speculate on what they are and how people might have used them. After your discussion, share your ideas with the rest of the class.

1. Archeologists found this object in the sleeping area of an ancient Chinese house. It's about the size of a basketball.

   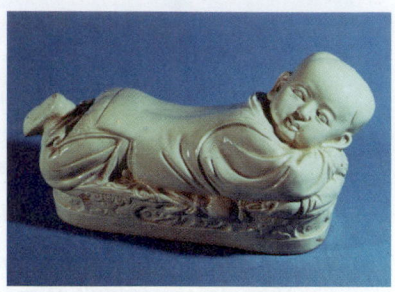

   EXAMPLE: **A:** I think people might have used this as a footstool. It's the right size.
   B: You're right. The floor must have gotten very cold at night.
   C: People could have rested their feet on this.

2. Archeologists found this in Turkey. People in many places have used objects like this on their clothing for thousands of years. This one is about 3,000 years old. It's the size of a small cell phone.

3. These objects were used by ancient Egyptians. The handles are each about the length of a toothbrush.

4. People in the Arctic started using these around 2,000 years ago. They used them when they were hunting or traveling. They are small enough to put in your pocket.

   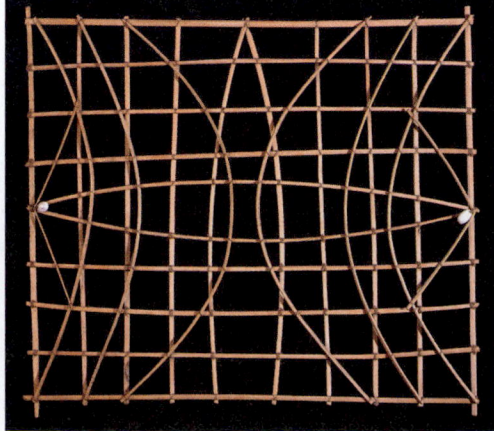

5. Polynesian people used these when they traveled. They made them with sticks, coconut fiber, and seashells. This one is about 30 centimeters (1 foot) wide and 30 centimeters long.

Answers: 1. a pillow; **2.** a large pin used to hold clothing together; **3.** a razor and a mirror for shaving; **4.** eye protection against bright light reflected from snow and ice; **5.** a chart showing islands and wave patterns in the ocean

EXERCISE 10: For or Against

A | *Reread the article that begins on page 270. Do you agree or disagree with Erich von Däniken's theory? Discuss your opinion with a partner.*

B | *Have a class discussion. How many students think space creatures might have visited the Earth? How many think space creatures couldn't have affected human culture?*

EXERCISE 11: Writing

A | *Read the paragraph about an unsolved mystery. Then complete the next paragraph. Use modals to speculate about the event. In your conclusion, state which explanation is most likely and why.*

> In 1991, hikers in the Italian Alps discovered a body in some melting ice. The body, which had been in the ice for more than 5,000 years, was in almost perfect condition. The "Ice Man" had several broken ribs. He had been wearing warm winter clothing, and had been carrying a knife, an ax, dried meat, and medicines. He had been making a bow and arrows, but he had not finished them.
>
> What could have happened to the Ice Man? There have been many speculations. The Ice Man might have . . .

EXAMPLE: The Ice Man might have brought his animals into the mountains to feed. . . .

B | *Check your work. Use the Editing Checklist.*

Editing Checklist

Did you use . . . ?
- ☐ *may have*, *might have*, and *could have* for past possibilities
- ☐ *must have* and *had to have* for things in the past you are almost certain about
- ☐ *couldn't have* to show disbelief or impossibility
- ☐ *could have* for questions about past possibility

A | *Circle the correct words to complete the sentences.*

1. Mayans built large cities. They <u>must / must not</u> have had an advanced civilization.

2. Their civilization disappeared. It <u>might not / might not have</u> rained enough to grow crops.

3. Look at this bowl. They could <u>of / have</u> used this to serve food.

4. You must have <u>taken / took</u> a hundred photos today.

5. Trish didn't come on the tour. She <u>may / couldn't</u> have been sick. She wasn't feeling well.

6. I can't find my wallet. I could <u>had / have</u> dropped it in the hotel gift shop.

7. Carla <u>must / couldn't</u> have gotten our postcard. We just mailed it yesterday.

B | *Rewrite the sentences in parentheses using past modals.*

1. Dan didn't call me back yesterday. He _____.
   (Maybe he didn't get my message.)

2. Selina got a C on the test. She _____.
   (It's almost certain that she didn't study.)

3. Why didn't Fahad come to dinner? He _____.
   (It's not possible that he forgot our date.)

4. Myra _____. I saw a woman there who looked like her.
   (It's possible that Myra was at the movies.)

5. The server didn't bring our dessert. She _____.
   (She probably forgot.)

6. Jan didn't say hello to me today. He _____.
   (It's almost certain that he didn't see me.)

C | *Find and correct seven mistakes.*

Why did the Aztecs build their capital city in the middle of a lake? Could they had wanted the protection of the water? They might have been. Or the location may has helped them to control nearby societies. At first it must have being an awful place, full of mosquitoes and fog. But it must no have been a bad idea—the island city became the center of a very powerful empire. To succeed, the Aztecs had to have became fantastic engineers quite quickly. When the Spanish arrived, they couldn't have expect the amazing palaces, floating gardens, and well-built canals. Unfortunately, they destroyed the city anyway.

Freewriting is a **way to develop ideas** about a topic. To freewrite, write for a specified length of time without stopping. Don't worry about mistakes. Then organize the ideas in your freewriting.

EXAMPLE: **Can't** stop thinking about **M's** wedding in Quito last year. *(freewriting)* ➔
I can't stop thinking about **Miguel's** wedding in Quito last year. *(formal writing)*

1 | *Read Clara's freewriting about a problem she had with her cousin Miguel. Underline her ideas about Miguel's reasons for what he did. Bracket ([ ]) her ideas about the appropriateness of Miguel's and her own behavior.*

> Can't stop thinking about Miguel's wedding in Quito last year. Still feeling hurt and confused. Why didn't he invite me? Or even tell me about it? [This was a family reunion, and he should have sent everyone an invitation.] He knows I'm a student, and <u>he must have thought I couldn't afford the airfare to Ecuador.</u> He could've sent me an invitation and let me decide for myself. On the other hand, I should have called him to discuss it. He might have even decided that I couldn't afford to send a gift. He shouldn't have decided for me. He couldn't have been angry with me! I've got to let him know how I feel. I should write a letter.

2 | *Clara decided to write a letter to Miguel. Read her outline in Exercise 3. Write the paragraph number where Clara decides to do each of the following:*

__3__   **1.** discuss the appropriateness of Miguel's behavior .

_____   **2.** introduce the problem

_____   **3.** suggest resolving the problem

_____   **4.** speculate on reasons for Miguel's behavior

3 | Complete Clara's letter with ideas from Exercise 1.

Dear Miguel,

   I'm sorry that I haven't written for some time, but I'm still feeling hurt and confused. Miguel, why didn't you invite me to your wedding last year? You didn't even tell me about it!

   Maybe your reasons for not inviting me were actually thoughtful. You know I'm a student, and ___you must have thought I couldn't afford the airfare.___

   _____

   _____

   _____

   However, I believe you should have handled the situation in a different way. This was a family reunion, and you should have sent everyone an invitation.

   _____

   _____

   _____

   We ought to solve this as soon as possible. I miss you. Please write as soon as you get this letter.
   Love,
   Clara

4 | Before you write . . .

1. Think of a problem you had with someone (for example, a friend, relative, neighbor). Freewrite about the problem: the reasons it might have happened and what you and other people could have done differently.

2. Choose ideas and organize them.

5 | Write a letter to the person you had the problem with. Include ideas from your freewriting in Exercise 4. Use past modals to speculate about reasons for your problem and to express regrets and obligations.

6 | *Exchange letters with a partner. Write a question mark (?) over anything in the letter that seems wrong. Then answer the following questions.*

	Yes	No
1. Did the writer correctly use past modals to speculate about reasons?	☐	☐
2. Did the writer correctly use past modals to express appropriateness?	☐	☐
3. Did the writer express his or her feelings and ideas clearly?	☐	☐

7 | *Work with your partner. Discuss each other's editing questions from Exercise 6. Then rewrite your letter and make any necessary corrections.*

PART VIII

THE PASSIVE

The Passive: Overview
GEOGRAPHY

Before You Read

Look at the title of the article and the photo. Discuss the questions.

1. What is geography?
2. Have you ever studied geography in school? If yes, did you enjoy it?
3. Is geography an important subject? Why or why not?

Read

Read the article about National Geographic, *a famous magazine.*

GEOGRAPHY
The Best Subject on Earth

Geography is the study of the Earth and its people. It sounds exciting, doesn't it? Yet for decades, students yawned just hearing the word. They **were forced** to memorize the names of capital cities, important rivers and mountains, and natural resources.[1] They **were taught** where places were and what **was produced** there. But they **weren't shown** how our world looks and feels.

And then came *National Geographic.* From the Amazon rain forests to the Sahara Desert, and from Baalbek to Great Zimbabwe, the natural and human-made wonders[2] of our world **have** now **been brought** to life **by** its fascinating reporting and beautiful photographs, such as this one, which **was taken by** photojournalist[3] Reza Deghati of a man planting a palm tree in Saudi Arabia.

---

[1]*natural resources:* a country's land, minerals, and energy
[2]*wonder:* something that makes you feel surprise and admiration
[3]*photojournalist:* someone who takes photos and writes reports for newspapers and magazines

GEOGRAPHY
The Best Subject on Earth

The National Geographic Society **was formed** in Washington, D.C., in 1888 **by** a group of professionals including geographers, explorers, teachers, and mapmakers. Nine months later, the first *National Geographic* magazine **was published** so that the Society could fulfill its mission: to spread knowledge of and respect for the world, its resources, and its inhabitants.

In 1995, the first foreign-language edition of *National Geographic* **was published** in Japan. Today, the magazine **is printed** in more than 30 languages and **sold** all over the world. *National Geographic* also puts out a number of special publications. *National Geographic Explorer*, for example, **has been created** for classrooms. Other publications feature travel and adventure. *National Geographic* TV programs **are watched** in over 160 million homes in more than 140 countries.

The study of geography has come a very long way since 1888. The Society's mission **has been fulfilled**. In fact, it **has** even **been extended** to include worlds beyond Earth. From the deep seas to deep space, geography has never been more exciting!

After You Read

A | Vocabulary: *Match the words with their definitions.*

_____ 1. **mission**

_____ 2. **decade**

_____ 3. **publication**

_____ 4. **inhabitant**

_____ 5. **explorer**

_____ 6. **edition**

a. 10 years

b. a book or magazine sold to the public

c. someone who travels for the purpose of discovery

d. an important purpose

e. the total number of copies of a magazine or book printed at the same time

f. one of the people living in a particular place

B | Comprehension: *Answer the questions.*

1. Who memorized names of capital cities?_____

2. What brought the wonders of our world to life?_____

3. Who took the photo of the Saudi man planting a palm tree?_____

4. Who formed the National Geographic Society?_____

5. Who watches *National Geographic* TV? _____

6. How has the Society's mission changed?_____

THE PASSIVE

Active	Passive
Millions of people **buy** it.	It **is bought** by millions of people.
Someone **published** it in 1888.	It **was published** in 1888.
They **have reached** their goal.	Their goal **has been reached**.

Passive Statements

Subject	Be (not)	Past Participle	(By + Object)	
It	**is (not)**	**bought**	**by** millions of people.	
It	**was (not)**	**published**		in 1888.
Their goal	**has (not) been**	**reached**.		

Yes / No Questions

Be / Have	Subject	(Been +) Past Participle	
Is		**sold**	
Was	it		in Japan?
Has		**been sold**	

Short Answers

Affirmative			Negative		
Yes,	it	is.	**No,**	it	isn't.
		was.			wasn't.
		has (been).			hasn't (been).

Wh- Questions

Wh-Word	Be / Have	Subject	(Been +) Past Participle
Where	**is**	it	**sold**?
	was		
	has		**been sold**?

GRAMMAR NOTES

1 **Active** and **passive** sentences often have similar meanings, but a **different focus**.

  a. **Active** sentences focus on the **agent** (the person or thing <u>doing</u> the action).

  b. **Passive** sentences focus on the **object** (the person or thing <u>receiving</u> the action).

ACTIVE:
• Millions of *people* **read** the magazine.
  (The focus is on people.)

PASSIVE:
• The *magazine* **is read** by millions of people.
  (The focus is on the magazine.)

2	Form the **passive** with a form of: *be* + past participle.	• It *is* **printed** in more than 30 languages. • It *was* first **published** in 1888. • It *has been* **sold** all over the world.
		TRANSITIVE VERB + OBJECT
	BE CAREFUL! Only **transitive verbs** (verbs that have objects) have passive forms.	• Ed Bly **wrote** *that article*. • That article **was written** by Ed Bly. *(passive form)*
		INTRANSITIVE VERB
	Intransitive verbs do NOT have passive forms.	• It **seemed** interesting. Not: It ~~was~~ seemed interesting. *(no passive form)*

3	Use the **passive** in the following situations:	
	a. When the **agent** (the person or thing doing the action) is <u>unknown or not important</u>.	• The magazine **was started** in 1888. *(I don't know who started it.)* • The magazine **is sold** at newsstands. *(It is not important who sells it.)*
	b. When you want to <u>avoid mentioning</u> the agent.	• Some mistakes **were made** in that article. *(I know who made the mistakes, but I don't want to blame the person.)*

| 4 | Use the passive with *by* if you mention the **agent**. Only mention the agent when it is <u>important to know who it is</u>. | • The photographs in this article are wonderful. They **were taken** *by a famous photographer*.
• One of the first cameras **was invented** *by Alexander Wolcott.* |
| | **BE CAREFUL!** In most cases, you do **NOT need to mention an agent** in passive sentences. Do NOT include an agent unnecessarily. | • Ed Bly took a really great photo. It **was taken** last February, but it won't appear until May.
   Not: It was taken last February ~~by him~~ . . . |

STEP 3 FOCUSED PRACTICE

EXERCISE 1: Discover the Grammar

Read the statements. Check (✓) Active or Passive.

	Active	Passive
1. The first *National Geographic* magazine was published in October 1888.	☐	☑
2. Today, millions of people read it.	☐	☐
3. The magazine is translated from English into 32 other languages.	☐	☐
4. My cousin reads the Russian edition.	☐	☐

(continued on next page)

	Active	Passive
5. Some of the articles are written by famous writers.	☐	☐
6. *Young Explorer*, another publication, is written for kids.	☐	☐
7. It is known for its wonderful photography.	☐	☐
8. A *National Geographic* photographer took the first underwater color photos.	☐	☐
9. Photographers are sent all over the world.	☐	☐
10. They take pictures of people and nature.	☐	☐
11. *National Geographic* is sold at newsstands.	☐	☐

EXERCISE 2: Active or Passive

(Grammar Notes 1–3)

The chart shows some of the 33 language editions that National Geographic *publishes. Use the chart to complete the sentences. Some sentences will be active; some will be passive.*

Language	Number of Speakers*
Chinese (all varieties)	1,231
English	460
Indonesian	23.2
Japanese	122
Korean	66.3
Russian	144
Spanish	329
Turkish	50.8

*first language speakers in millions

1. Spanish _is spoken by 329 million people_____.

2. Around 144 million people _____.

3. Indonesian _____.

4. _____ Chinese.

5. _____ by more than 66 million people.

6. _____ 122 million people.

7. 460 million people _____.

8. _____ more than 50 million people.

EXERCISE 3: *Wh-* Questions and Statements

(Grammar Note 2)

A | *Jill Jones, a magazine journalist, is preparing for a trip to Bolivia. Look at the online travel quiz she is going to take. Complete the questions with the correct form of the verbs in parentheses. Then take the quiz. Guess the answers!*

Travel Quiz
Destination: La Paz, Bolivia

The capital of Bolivia, La Paz, with Illimani mountain in the background

Map of Bolivia

1. In which part of the country _____ *is* _____ the capital _____ *located* _____?
(locate)

- ○ the north
- ○ the center
- ● the west

2. When _____ La Paz _____?
(establish)

- ○ 1448
- ○ 1548
- ○ 1648

3. Which of these items _____ in La Paz?
(produce)

- ○ agricultural tools
- ○ cars
- ○ electric appliances

4. What _____ the main street in La Paz _____?
(call)

- ○ La Rambla
- ○ El Prado
- ○ El Alto

5. Which sport _____ the most in La Paz?
(play)

- ○ baseball
- ○ soccer
- ○ basketball

B | Complete the answers with the correct form of the verbs in parentheses. Did you guess correctly?

Answers

1. The highest capital in the world, La Paz _____was built_____ in a canyon in the
   (build)

   west of the country. It _____ by mountains, such as the beautiful
   (surround)

   Illimani mountain, which _____ by snow all year.
   (cover)

2. The city _____ in 1548 by Spanish settlers.
   (establish)

3. Agricultural tools along with food products, clothing, and building materials

   _____ in the capital.
   (make)

4. The main street's name changes in different parts of the city, but the tree-lined

   section in downtown La Paz _____ as El Prado.
   (know)

5. Soccer is the favorite sport. The city has several teams. The Strongest, which

   _____ in 1908, has won many tournaments.
   (form)

EXERCISE 4: Questions, Statements, and Short Answers   *(Grammar Note 2)*

*Jill Jones is interviewing a Bolivian cultural attaché for an article she's writing. Complete her
interview with the passive form of the correct verbs from the boxes and with short answers.*

> create   grow   ~~inhabit~~   spell

JONES: Thanks for giving me some time today. Here is my first question: _____Was_____ the

area first _____inhabited_____ by the Inca?
                    1.

ATTACHÉ: _____No, it wasn't_____. Long before the Inca, a great civilization _____
                    2.   **3.**

around Lake Titicaca by the Aymara. The Aymara still live in Bolivia.

JONES: Fascinating. Let's talk about farming. I know potatoes are an important food crop[1] in the

mountains of the Andes. _____ corn _____ there as well?
                                                                              4.

ATTACHÉ: _____. The climate is too cold. But quinoa grows well there.
                    5.

JONES: Quinoa? How _____ that _____? With a *k*?
                                                              6.

---

[1] ***crop:*** a plant such as corn or wheat that is grown by a farmer

eat   mine²   raise   use

ATTACHÉ: No. With a *q*—q-u-i-n-o-a. It's a traditional grain, like corn and wheat in other places.

It _____ by the inhabitants of the Andes for 5,000 years.
7.

JONES: Everyone connects llamas with Bolivia. What _____ these animals

_____ for?
8.

ATTACHÉ: For many things—clothing, meat, transportation. But they only do well in the Andes. They

_____ in the lowlands of the Oriente, the eastern part of the country.
9. (negative)

JONES: I see. Now, about other resources. I know that tin is extremely important. Where

_____ it _____?
10.

find   produce   see   speak

ATTACHÉ: The richest sources of tin _____ in the Andes.
11.

JONES: How about the Oriente? What _____ there?
12.

ATTACHÉ: Oil, petroleum, and natural gas. Rice is important, and cattle, for meat and milk.

JONES: What other languages _____ besides Spanish?
13.

ATTACHÉ: Actually, more people speak Native American languages than Spanish.

JONES: Scientists love Bolivia. _____ jaguars still _____ there?
14.

ATTACHÉ: _____. And so are river dolphins and birds like the condor—many, many
15.

species. In the last decade, our government's mission has been to protect these rare and

beautiful animals.

JONES: Thank you for your time. I'll send you a copy of our publication as soon as the article

comes out.

---

² *mine:* to dig into the ground to get gold, coal, tin, and other natural resources

Jaguar

A | *Read Jill Jones's article. Her editor found and circled eight factual mistakes.*

A Land of Contrasts
by Jill Jones

Visitors to Bolivia are amazed by the contrasts and charmed by the beauty of this South American country's landscapes—from the breathtaking Andes in the west to the tropical lowlands in the east.

Two-thirds of Bolivia's 10 million people are concentrated in the cool western highlands, or *altiplano*. Today, as in centuries past, corn and kuinoa *(spelling?)* are grown in the mountains. Llamas are raised only for transportation. And tin, Bolivia's richest natural resource, is mined in the high Andes.

The Oriente, another name for the eastern lowlands, is mostly tropical. Rice is the major food crop, and llamas are raised for meat in the lowlands. Rubber is also found in this region.

Bolivia is home to many fascinating forms of wildlife. The colorful parrot can be seen flying above the highest mountains. Boa constrictors, jaguars, and many other animals are found in the rain forests.

Hundreds of years before the Inca flourished, a great civilization was created on the shores of the Pacific, probably by ancestors of Bolivia's Aymara people. Their descendants still speak the Aymara language. Today, Native American languages are still widely spoken in Bolivia. Although Portuguese is spoken in the government, Quechua and Aymara are used more widely by the people. Traditional textiles are woven by hand. Music is played on reed pipes whose tone resembles the sound of the wind blowing over high plains in the Andes.

Lake Titicaca

B | *Rewrite the incorrect sentences with information from Exercise 4.*

1. _Corn isn't grown in the mountains. Potatoes are grown in the mountains._

2. _____

3. _____

4. _____

5. _____

6. _____

7. _____

8. _____

EXERCISE 6: Including or Deleting the Agent

(Grammar Notes 3–4)

Read Ed Bly's soccer trivia column. Complete the information with the correct form of the verbs in the first set of parentheses. If the agent (in the second set of parentheses) is necessary, include it in your answer. If not, cross it out.

⚽ Soccer is the most popular sport in the world. It _____*is played by more than 20 million people*_____.

                           1. (play) (more than 20 million people)

⚽ It _____*is called*_____ football _____ in 144 countries.

        2. (call)   ~~(people)~~

⚽ Except for the goalie, players _____ to use their hands. Instead, the

                                  3. (not allow) (the rules)

   ball _____.

              4. (control) (the feet, the head, and the body)

⚽ Soccer _____ in the United States very much until 20 years

            5. (not play) (people)

   ago. Since then, the game _____.

               6. (make popular) (Pelé, Beckham, and other international stars)

⚽ Forms of soccer _____ for thousands of years. A form of

            7. (play) (different cultures)

   soccer _____ in China 2,000 years ago.

        8. (enjoy) (Chinese people)

⚽ It _____ in 1365—his archers spent

            9. (ban) (King Edward III of England)

   too much time playing and too little time practicing archery.

⚽ Medieval games _____ for entire days, over miles of territory.

            10. (play) (players)

⚽ Today, the World Cup games _____ every four years. The best

            11. (hold) (the World Cup Association)

   teams in the world compete.

EXERCISE 7: Editing

Read this short biography of an internationally famous photojournalist whose photos have appeared in National Geographic. *(He took the photo on page 290.) There are eight mistakes in the use of the passive. The first mistake is already corrected. Find and correct seven more.*

Seeing the World
by Diana Brodylo

    Reza Deghati ~~is~~ *was* born in Tabriz, Iran, in 1952. When he was only 14 years old, he began teaching himself photography. At first, he took pictures of his own country—its people and its architecture. When he was 25, he was decided to become a professional photographer. During a demonstration he was asked by a French news agency to take photos. He only shot one and a half rolls of film (instead of the usual 20 to 40), but his photos was published in *Paris Match* (France), *Stern* (Germany), and *Newsweek* (U.S.A.).

    Reza, as he is knew professionally, has covered several wars, and he has be wounded on assignment.[1] Among all his assignments, the project dearest to his heart is photographing children, who he calls "the real victims of war." He has donated these photos to humanitarian organizations. Always concerned with the welfare of children, Reza has made it his life's mission to help them receive an education. His organization AINA created, in part, to achieve this goal.

    When he was interviewed by an interviewer, Reza was asked to give advice to wannabe[2] photojournalists. He replied, "There is a curtain between the photographer and the subject unless the photographer is able to break through it. . . . Open your heart to them so they know you care."

    Today Reza Deghati lives in Paris. His photos is widely distributed in more than 50 countries around the world, and his work is published in *National Geographic* as well as many other internationally famous publications.

---

[1]*wounded on assignment:* injured on the job
[2]*wannabe:* (informal for *want-to-be*) a person who wants to become a member of a specific profession

EXERCISE 8: Listening

A | *Read the statements. Then listen to the conversations. Listen again and check (✓)* **True,** **False,** *or* **?** *(the information isn't in the conversation).*

	True	False	?
1. Ana took the photo of the desert.	☐	☑	☐
2. The hat was made by children.	☐	☐	☐
3. Jill's boss sent her to Morocco.	☐	☐	☐
4. Corn is grown in the mountains.	☐	☐	☐
5. The man's friend wrote an article about Bolivia.	☐	☐	☐
6. You can get *National Geographic* in Korea.	☐	☐	☐

B | *Listen again to the conversations and complete the sentences with the words you hear.*

1. It _____*wasn't taken*_____ by Ana.

2. It _____ there.

3. She _____ to Morocco to cover a story.

4. Potatoes _____ there.

5. It _____ by a friend of mine.

6. _____ *National Geographic* _____ in Korea?

EXERCISE 9: Pronunciation

A | *Read and listen to the Pronunciation Note.*

> ### Pronunciation Note
>
> When we **correct information**, we usually **stress**:
> - the **words we are correcting** (the wrong information)
> - the **correction** (the correct information)
>
> **EXAMPLES:** Corn isn't grown in the **mountains**. It's grown in the **valleys**.
>
> **Rice** isn't grown in the mountains. **Corn** is grown there.

🎧 **B** | *Listen to the short conversations. Put a dot (•) over the words that are stressed in the responses.*

1. **A:** Where is rice grown. In the north?

    B: No. It isn't grown in the north. It's grown in the south.

2. **A:** That's a great photo. Was it taken in Bolivia?

    B: It wasn't taken in Bolivia. It was taken in Peru.

3. **A:** This article was written by Omar, wasn't it?

    B: No. It wasn't written by him. It was edited by him.

4. **A:** The book I'm reading was written in 1950.

    B: It wasn't written in 1950, it was published then.

5. **A:** It was translated into French.

    B: It wasn't translated into French. It was translated into Spanish.

6. **A:** I heard that John's story was published last month.

    B: No, John's story wasn't published, Tom's was.

🎧 **C** | *Listen again and check your work. Then practice the conversations with a partner.*

EXERCISE 10: Quotable Quotes

Work in small groups. Choose three of these proverbs from around the world and discuss them. What do you think they mean? Are there proverbs from other cultures that mean the same thing?

1. Rome wasn't built in a day. (*English*)

    EXAMPLE: **A:** I think this means that big projects aren't finished quickly.
    B: Yes. They take a lot of time and you have to be patient.
    C: There's a proverb in French that means the same thing:
    "Paris wasn't built in a day."

2. He who was bitten by a snake avoids tall grass. (*Chinese*)

3. He ran away from the rain and was caught in a hailstorm. (*Turkish*)

4. Never promise a fish until it's caught. (*Irish*)

5. Write the bad things that are done to you in sand, but write the good things that happen to you on a piece of marble. (*Arab*)

6. Skillful sailors weren't made by smooth seas. (*Ethiopian*)

7. From one thing, ten things are known. (*Korean*)

8. What is brought by the wind will be carried away by the wind. (*Iranian*)

EXERCISE 11: Information Gap: The Philippines

The Philippines consist of many islands. The two largest are Luzon in the north and Mindanao in the south. Both islands have many natural resources.

Work in pairs (A and B). **Student B,** *go to page 306 and follow the instructions there.* **Student A,** *follow the instructions on this page.*

1. Look at the map of Luzon. Complete the chart for Luzon. Write *Y* for yes and *N* for no.

2. Student B has the map of Mindanao. Ask Student B questions about Mindanao and complete the chart for Mindanao.

   EXAMPLE: **A:** Is tobacco grown in Mindanao?
   B: No, it isn't.

3. Student B doesn't have the map of Luzon. Answer Student B's questions about Luzon.

   EXAMPLE: **B:** Is tobacco grown in Luzon?
   A: Yes, it is. It's grown in the northern and central part of the island.

		Mindanao	Luzon
GROW	tobacco	N	Y
	corn		
	bananas		
	coffee		
	pineapples		
	sugar		
RAISE	cattle		
	pigs		
MINE	gold		
	manganese		
PRODUCE	cotton		
	rubber		
	lumber		

When you are done, compare charts. Are they the same?

EXERCISE 12: Game: Trivia Quiz

A | National Geographic Explorer *often has games and puzzles. Work in pairs. Complete this quiz. Then compare answers with your classmates. The answers are on page 306.*

Do you know . . . ?

1. Urdu is spoken in _____.

   a. Ethiopia   **b.** Pakistan   **c.** Uruguay

2. Air-conditioning was invented in _____.

   a. 1902   **b.** 1950   **c.** 1980

3. The X-ray was invented by _____.

   a. Thomas Edison   **b.** Wilhelm Roentgen   **c.** Marie Curie

4. The Petronas Towers in Kuala Lumpur were designed by _____.

   a. Minoru Yamasaki   **b.** César Pelli   **c.** I. M. Pei

5. The 2010 Olympics were held in _____.

   a. Canada   **b.** Japan   **c.** Norway

6. An ocean route from Portugal to the East was discovered by Portuguese explorer _____.

   a. Hernán Cortés   **b.** Louis Jolliet   **c.** Vasco da Gama

7. A baby _____ is called a cub.

   a. cat   **b.** dog   **c.** jaguar

B | *Now, with your partner, make up your own questions with the words in parentheses. For item 11, add your own question. Ask another pair to answer your questions.*

EXAMPLE:

__*Guernica*__ __*was painted*__ by __*b*__ .
            (paint)

  a. __*Monet*__   **b.** __*Picasso*__   **c.** __*El Greco*__

8. _____ _____ _____ by ____.
          (invent)

  a. _____   **b.** _____   **c.** _____

9. _____ _____ _____ by ____.
          (compose)

  a. _____   **b.** _____   **c.** _____

10. _____ _____ _____ by ____.
          (write)

  a. _____   **b.** _____   **c.** _____

11. _____ _____ _____ by ____.

  a. _____   **b.** _____   **c.** _____

EXERCISE 13: Writing

A | *Before you write, complete the chart with information about a country you know well.*

Name of country	
Geographical areas	
Crops grown in each area	
Animals raised in each area	
Natural resources found in each area	
Wildlife found in each area	
Languages spoken	
Art, handicrafts, or music created	

B | *Write an essay about the country with the information you have gathered. Use the passive. You can use the article in Exercise 5 as a model (make sure your facts are correct).*

EXAMPLE: Turkey is both a European and an Asian country. European Turkey is separated from Asian Turkey by the Sea of Marmara, the Bosphorus, and the Dardanelles. Citrus fruits and tobacco are grown in . . .

C | *Check your work. Use the Editing Checklist.*

Editing Checklist

Did you . . . ?
- ☐ use passive sentences to focus on the object
- ☐ form the passive with a form of **be** + **past participle**
- ☐ use **by** if you mentioned the agent
- ☐ only mention the agent when it was important to know who it is

INFORMATION GAP FOR STUDENT B

Student B, follow the instructions on this page.

1. Look at the map of Mindanao below. Complete the chart for Mindanao. Write *Y* for yes and *N* for no.

2. Student A doesn't have the map of Mindanao. Answer Student A's questions about Mindanao.

   EXAMPLE: **A:** Is tobacco grown in Mindanao?
   B: No, it isn't.

3. Student A has the map of Luzon. Ask Student A questions about Luzon and complete the chart for Luzon.

   EXAMPLE: **B:** Is tobacco grown in Luzon?
   A: Yes, it is. It's grown in the northern and central part of the island.

		Mindanao	Luzon
GROW	tobacco	N	Y
	corn		
	bananas		
	coffee		
	pineapples		
	sugar		
RAISE	cattle		
	pigs		
MINE	gold		
	manganese		
PRODUCE	cotton		
	rubber		
	lumber		

Mindanao

When you are done, compare charts. Are they the same?

Answers to Trivia Quiz "Do you know . . . ?" on page 304: **1.** b **2.** a **3.** b **4.** b **5.** a **6.** c **7.** c

Check your answers on page UR-5.

Do you need to review anything?

A | Complete with active and passive sentences.

Active	**Passive**
1. They speak Spanish in Bolivia.	_____
2. _____	Soccer is played in Bolivia.
3. _____	The photo was taken by Reza Deghati.
4. They translated the articles into Spanish.	_____
5. They grow quinoa in the mountains.	_____
6. _____	The main street was named El Prado.

B | Complete the sentences with the correct passive form of the verbs in parentheses.

1. Jamaica _____ by Europeans in the 16th century.
        (discover)

2. Today, Creole, a mixture of languages, _____ by many Jamaicans.
                               (speak)

3. Some of the best coffee in the world _____ on the island.
                         (grow)

4. Sugar _____ to many countries.
        (export)

5. Many people _____ by the sugar industry.
               (employ)

6. Reggae music originated in Jamaica. It _____ popular by Bob Marley.
                               (make)

7. Since the summer of 1992, it _____ at the Sumfest festival on the island.
                       (perform)

8. Every year the festival _____ by music lovers from around the world.
        (attend)

C | Find and correct six mistakes.

    Photojournalist Alexandra Avakian was born and raise in New York. Since she began her career, she has covered many of the world's most important stories. Her work have been published in many newspapers and magazines including *National Geographic*, and her photographs have being exhibited around the world. Avakian has also written a book, *Window of the Soul: My Journey in the Muslim World*, which was been published in 2008. It has not yet been translated by translators into other languages, but the chapter titles appear in both English and Arabic. Avakian's book have be discussed on international TV, radio, and numerous websites.

STEP 1 GRAMMAR IN CONTEXT

Before You Read

Look at the article and the photos. Discuss the questions.

1. What does the title of the article mean?
2. What are some problems that can occur when people from different cultures must live and work together?

Read

Read the article about an international space project.

CLOSE QUARTERS

"**Will** decisions **be made** too fast?" the Japanese astronauts wondered. "**Can** they **be made** quickly enough?" the Americans wanted to know. "**Will** dinner **be taken** seriously?" was the question worrying the French and the Dutch, while the Italians were nervous about their personal space: "How **can** privacy **be maintained** in such very close quarters?"

The year was 2000. It was the beginning of the new millennium, and the focus of all these concerns was the International Space Station (ISS), the largest and most complex international project ever. It looked like the ISS **was** finally **going to be launched**[1] that year. But amid the hopes and excitement, many were asking themselves: "**Can** this huge undertaking

Crew members share a meal aboard the ISS.

really **be accomplished** by a multicultural group living in close quarters?" In addition to their other concerns, all the astronauts were worrying about language. English is

[1] **launch:** to send into the sky or space, usually with a rocket

CLOSE QUARTERS

the official language on the ISS, and a great number of technical terms **must be learned** by everyone on board. Some members of the first ISS teams also feared that they **might be treated** like outsiders because they didn't know American slang. Another major concern was food. What time **should** meals **be served**? How **should** preparation and cleanup **be handled**? **Can** religious dietary rules **be followed** on board?

Those worries **had to be tested** in space before anyone would know for sure. But by now the answer is clear. For over a decade, ISS astronauts have been proving that great achievements in technology and science **can be made** by an international group working together. Since November 2000, when the first crew boarded the ISS, the station has been operated by astronauts from 16 countries, including Brazil, Canada, Japan, Russia, the United States, and members of the European Union.

Perhaps their greatest challenge so far has been the ISS itself, which **had to be assembled** in space by astronauts floating outside the station. Despite delays, the last major sections of the ISS were attached in February 2010. Now, with the station completed, more focus **can be placed** on scientific goals. Important experiments **will be carried out** in the station's laboratories, and it's possible that more scientists will join the crew.

How has this international group of astronauts managed to cooperate and achieve these goals during long periods in a "trapped environment"? All astronauts receive cross-cultural training, but often sensitivity and tolerance **can't be taught** from a textbook. They**'ve got to be observed** and **experienced** personally.

Two researchers suggested that a model for space station harmony[2] **might be found** in the popular TV series *Star Trek*, in which a multicultural crew has been getting along for eons. However, real-life astronauts have found a more down-to-earth solution: the family dinner. Astronaut Nicolle Stott reports, ". . . we always spend mealtimes together . . . it's a lot like bringing your family together." The dinner table is where the world's (and each other's) problems **can be solved**, and where the astronauts "listen to good music, eat good food, improve our vocabulary in other languages, and laugh a lot."

The International Space Station and Earth seen from space

Astronauts also benefit from their unique perspective of Earth. They like to point out that national borders **can't be seen** from space. As Indian-American astronaut Sunita Williams says, "I consider myself a citizen of the universe. When we go up in space, all we can see is a beautiful Earth where there are no borders of nations and religions." This spirit of cooperation may turn out to be the project's greatest achievement.

---

[2]**harmony:** a situation in which people are friendly and peaceful together

The Passive with Modals and Similar Expressions **309**

After You Read

A | **Vocabulary:** *Complete the sentences with the words from the box.*

assemble	benefit	cooperate	period	perspective	undertaking

1. It took years to _____ the many parts of the Space Station.

2. Astronauts stay on the ISS for a(n) _____ of about three to five months.

3. The ISS is a big _____ and has required a lot of planning.

4. It hasn't been difficult for them to _____ on their missions. Everyone works together very well.

5. We all _____ from the scientific discoveries made in ISS laboratories.

6. Seeing Earth from space changed their _____. They see the world's problems in a different way now.

B | **Comprehension:** *Check (✓)* **True, False** *or* **?** *(the information isn't in the article).*

	True	False	?
1. Japanese and Italian astronauts worried about decision making.	☐	☐	☐
2. All ISS astronauts have to learn technical language in English.	☐	☐	☐
3. Astronauts from seven countries have been operating the ISS.	☐	☐	☐
4. The ISS was completely assembled in less than 10 years.	☐	☐	☐
5. Scientists do medical experiments in ISS laboratories.	☐	☐	☐
6. Astronauts rarely eat meals together.	☐	☐	☐

THE PASSIVE WITH MODALS AND SIMILAR EXPRESSIONS

Statements				
Subject	**Modal***	***Be***	**Past Participle**	
The decision	will (not) should (not) ought (not) to must (not) can (not) had better (not)	be	made	quickly.

*Modals have only one form. They do not have -s in the third person singular.

Statements				
Subject	***Have (got) to / Be going to****	***Be***	**Past Participle**	
The problem	has (got) to doesn't have to is (not) going to	be	solved	quickly.

**Unlike modals, *have* in *have (got) to* and *be* in *be going to* change for different subjects. Questions and negatives with *have (got) to* need a form of *do*.

Yes / No Questions				
Modal	**Subject**	***Be***	**Past Participle**	
Will				
Should	it	be	made	quickly?
Must				
Can				

Short Answers				
Affirmative			**Negative**	
Yes,	it	will. should. must. can.	No,	it	won't. shouldn't. doesn't have to be. can't.

Yes / No Questions				
Auxiliary Verb	**Subject**	***Have to / Going to***	***Be***	**Past Participle**
Does	it	have to	be	solved?
Is		going to		

Short Answers				
Affirmative			**Negative**	
Yes,	it	does. is.	No,	it	doesn't. isn't.

GRAMMAR NOTES

1	After a modal, form the passive with: *be* + past participle.	• The labs *will be used* for experiments. • The crew *won't be replaced* this month. • Crew members *must be trained* very carefully. • Decisions *shouldn't be made* too quickly.
2	Use *will* or *be going to* with the passive for the **future**.	• The ISS *will be used* for several years. OR • The ISS *is going to be used* for several years.
3	Use *can* with the passive for **present ability**. Use *could* with the passive for **past ability**.	• The space station *can be seen* from Earth. • It *could be seen* very clearly last year too.
4	Use *could*, *may*, *might*, and *can't* with the passive for **future possibility** or **impossibility**.	• The equipment *could be repaired* very soon. • Some anxiety *may be experienced* on takeoff. • New discoveries *might be made*. • The job *can't be handled* by just one person.
5	Use *should*, *ought to*, *had better*, *must*, and *have (got) to* with the passive for: a. advisability b. necessity	 • The crew *should be told* to leave now. • They *ought to be given* training. • Privacy *had better be taken* seriously. • Everyone *must be treated* with respect. • Technical language *has (got) to be learned*.

REFERENCE NOTES

For a review of **modals and similar expressions**, see Unit 15.

For information about **modals and their functions**, see Appendix 20 on page A-9.

EXERCISE 1: Discover the Grammar

Read the interview with scientist Dr. Bernard Kay (BK) by Comet Magazine (CM). *Underline the passive with modals and similar expressions.*

CM: Some parts of the ISS <u>had to be cancelled</u>, and some parts were delayed. But the whole station has finally been assembled. What an undertaking this has been! When was it completed?

BK: It was finished at the end of 2010. In February of that year, the last major sections—Tranquility[1] and the Cupola[2]—were attached. In Tranquility, oxygen can be produced and waste water can be recycled.[3] Tranquility's equipment will support life on the ISS if communication with Earth can't be maintained for a period of time.

CM: And the Cupola? I understand it was built by the European Space Agency.

BK: Yes, it was. It's amazing. It should be considered one of the most important parts of the station. It's got seven huge windows, and the views of Earth and space are spectacular.

CM: Why the big windows?

BK: Because robots have to be used for maintenance outside the space station. Astronauts can observe and control them more easily from these windows. But I think that the perspective of Earth and space that we gain from these views might be just as important.

---

[1] *tranquility:* a feeling of calm, peace, and freedom from worry
[2] *cupola:* a small round part on the roof of a building that has the shape of an upside down cup
[3] *recycle:* to clean or treat something such as water or paper so that it can be used again

(continued on next page)

CM: Why is that?

BK: Observing the Earth and space keeps the astronauts in touch with the importance of their mission. Originally the station was going to include sleeping cabins with windows, but that part of the project couldn't be accomplished for a number of reasons. Now the sleeping cabins are windowless, and the Cupola is everyone's favorite hangout.[4]

CM: Now that the station is complete, will more scientific work be done on the ISS?

BK: Yes, it will. The ISS is the first step to further exploration of our solar system. On the ISS, ways to grow food in space can be developed, and new materials can be tested, for example. But most important of all, human interactions have got to be understood better. An international crew from 16 different countries makes the ISS a wonderful laboratory for cross-cultural understanding. This could be one of the great benefits of the ISS.

CM: I guess we don't know what might be discovered, right?

BK: Right. That's what makes it so exciting.

---

[4] *hangout:* a place where people like to spend free time, especially with friends

EXERCISE 2: Affirmative and Negative Statements

(Grammar Notes 1–5)

Complete this article about zero-G (zero gravity or weightlessness) with the correct form of the words in parentheses.

Juggling oranges—it's easy in zero-G

Some tasks _____can be accomplished_____ more easily in zero-G. Inside the station,
        1. (can / accomplish)

astronauts _____ from the deadly conditions of space—but life in
            2. (can / protect)

almost zero-G still _____ normal. What's it like to live on the ISS?
                3. (can't / consider)

Getting Rest: Sleeping _____ to floating in water. It's
4. (can / compare)

relaxing, but sleeping bags _____ to the walls of the cabins.
5. (must / attach)

Otherwise, astronauts will drift around as they sleep.

Keeping Clean: Showers _____ because in zero-G water from
6. (can't / use)

a shower flies in all directions and sensitive equipment _____.
7. (might / damage)

Instead, astronauts take sponge baths. Used bath water _____ into
8. (have to / suck)

a container by a vacuum machine. Clothes _____ by putting them into a
9. (could / wash)

bag with water and soap, but astronauts really _____ with laundry. They
10. (not have to / concern)

usually put dirty clothes into a trash container which _____ back toward
11. (can / send)

Earth and _____ in Earth's atmosphere.
12. (burn up)

Dining: From the beginning, ISS planners have known that food _____
13. (should / take)

very seriously. Unlike meals on early space missions, food on the ISS _____
14. (not have to / squeeze)

out of tubes. Frozen, dried, canned, and fresh food _____ and
15. (can / heat)

_____ at a table. Regular utensils are used, but meals are packed
16. (eat)

into containers that _____ to a tray so they don't float away.
17. (must / attach)

Taking It Easy: Not surprisingly, a stressed astronaut is a grouchy astronaut. Free time

_____ for relaxing and enjoying views from the Cupola. All crew
18. (have got to / provide)

members have laptops that _____ for listening to music, reading
19. (can / use)

e-books, and accessing the Internet. In the past, the Internet _____
20. (could / access)

only for work, but now a direct Internet connection is available for astronauts' personal use.

Email _____ easily with friends and family. And blogs, tweets,
21. (can / exchange)

and videos from the astronauts _____ by millions of earthlings.
22. (be going to / enjoy)

Staying Fit: Time also _____ for exercise. In low-gravity
23. (must / allow)

environments, muscle and bone _____ quickly without exercise.
24. (will / lose)

EXERCISE 3: Affirmative and Negative Statements

(Grammar Notes 1–5)

Some scientists who are going to join the space station have just completed a simulation[1] of life on the station. Complete their conversations using the modals in parentheses and correct verbs from the boxes.

accept	do	~~keep~~	reject	send	train

CESAR: This simulation was great, but it was too warm in there. I think the temperature on the ISS

_____*should be kept*_____ at 68 degrees—no warmer than that.
   1. (should)

GINA: Shorts and T-shirts _____ to the station for you. That's what most
   2. (can)

astronauts ask for.

CESAR: That new space visitor _____ on our mission. They're considering
   3. (might not)

her application now. Her company wants her to do a space walk, and so far only astronauts

have done that.

GINA: Her application _____ just for that. But she ought to complete a
   4. (shouldn't)

simulation first.

LYLE: Of course she'll have to do a simulation. She _____ to work while
   5. (have got to)

wearing a space suit. That _____ except underwater in one of the
   6. (can't)

space labs.

approve	do	send	share	surprise

HANS: Did you fill in your food preference forms? They _____ to the Food
   7. (should)

Systems Lab today.

HISA: I did. I'm glad the new dishes _____ by everyone. We all benefit
   8. (have to)

from the variety. I really liked some of the Japanese and Russian meals.

HANS: You'll find that the food _____ by everyone too. Everyone enjoys
   9. (will)

trying different things.

LUIS: Shaving in zero-G is weird. The whisker dust from my beard and mustache kept flying back

into my face. I wonder if something _____ about that.
   10. (could)

HANS: I have a feeling we _____ by a lot of unexpected problems.
   11. (be going to)

---

[1] **simulation:** something you do in order to practice what you would do in a real situation

EXERCISE 4: Editing

Read an astronaut's journal notes. There are eight mistakes in the use of the passive with modals and similar expressions. The first mistake is already corrected. Find and correct seven more.

October 4

6:15 A.M. I used the sleeping restraints last night, so my feet and hands didn't float around as much. I slept a lot better. I'm going to suggest some changes in the restraints, though—I think they ought to be <del>make</del> *made* more comfortable. I felt really trapped. And maybe these sleeping quarters could designed differently. They're too small.

10:45 A.M. My face is puffy, and my eyes are red. Exercise helps a little—I'd better be gotten on the exercise bike right away. I can be misunderstanding very easily when I look like this. Sometimes people think I've been crying. And yesterday Max thought I was angry when he turned on *Star Trek*. Actually, I love that show.

1:00 P.M. Lunch was pretty good. Chicken teriyaki. It's nice and spicy, and the sauce can actually been tasted, even at zero gravity. They'd better fly in some more of it for us pretty soon. It's the most popular dish in the freezer.

4:40 P.M. I'm worried about my daughter. Just before I left on this mission, she said she was planning to quit school at the end of the semester. That's only a month away. I want to call her and discuss it. But I worry that I might get angry and yell. I might overheard by the others. They really should figure out some way to give us a little more privacy.

10:30 P.M. The view of Earth is unbelievably breathtaking! Tonight I spent a long time just looking out the window and watching Earth pass below. At night a halo of light surrounds the horizon. It's so bright that the tops of the clouds can see. It can't be described. It simply have to be experienced. I think it's even given me a better perspective on my problems with my daughter.

EXERCISE 5: Listening

A | *Some crew members aboard the ISS are watching a science fiction movie. Listen to the conversations from the movie. Listen again and check (✓)* **True** *or* **False** *about each statement. Correct the false statements.*

	True	False

1. A meteorite hit ~~Earth~~. *the spaceship* ☐ ☑

2. Picarra wants the people on CX5 to understand *Endeavor*'s messages. ☐ ☐

3. Picarra thinks both Lon and Torsha should be sent to CX5. ☐ ☐

4. Lon thinks that oxygen may be necessary on the planet. ☐ ☐

5. Picarra thinks that Lon and Torsha's equipment might not work. ☐ ☐

6. The plants will grow well in space. ☐ ☐

7. The spaceship crew can't fix the spaceship alone. ☐ ☐

B | *Listen again to the conversations. Circle the underlined words that you hear.*

1. It <u>can</u> / (<u>can't</u>) be repaired out here.

2. Our messages <u>could</u> / <u>should</u> be misunderstood.

3. We know that Lon <u>will</u> / <u>won't</u> be taken seriously down there.

4. Oxygen <u>must</u> / <u>mustn't</u> be used in this situation.

5. They'll <u>pick up</u> / <u>be picked up by</u> the radar.

6. They <u>can</u> / <u>can't</u> be grown in space.

7. As you know, we have to <u>help</u> / <u>be helped</u> with the repairs.

EXERCISE 6: Pronunciation

A | *Read and listen to the Pronunciation Note.*

Pronunciation Note

In conversation, we often **drop the final "t"** in *must be*, *mustn't be*, *couldn't be*, and *shouldn't be*.

EXAMPLES: The project **must be** finished soon. → "The **project mus' be** finished soon."
Oxygen **couldn't be** used. → "Oxygen **couldn' be** used."
The captain **shouldn't be** told. → "The captain **shouldn' be** told."

B | *Listen to the short conversations. Complete the sentences with the words that you hear.*

1. **A:** Could you see Tokyo or was it too cloudy?

   B: Too cloudy. Tokyo _____ seen at all.

2. **A:** Should I tell Commander Kotov about the problem?

   B: No. He _____ disturbed right now.

3. **A:** Did they decide on the new crew yesterday?

   B: No. It _____ decided then.

4. **A:** They haven't fixed our Internet connection yet.

   B: I know. But it _____ fixed by tomorrow.

5. **A:** When should we eat dinner?

   B: It probably _____ served before 6:00.

6. **A:** Mikel's working late on that experiment.

   B: Yeah. He says it _____ finished by next week.

C | *Listen again to the conversations and repeat the responses. Then practice the conversations with a partner. Use the short forms.*

EXERCISE 7: Reaching Agreement

A | *Work in small groups. Imagine that in preparation for a space mission, your group is going to spend a week together in a one-room apartment. Discuss the rules that should be made for living in close quarters.*

Some issues to consider:

- food
- clothes
- room temperature
- noise
- neatness

- cleanliness
- privacy
- language
- entertainment
- *Other:* _____

EXAMPLE: **A:** I think dinner should be served at 6:00 every night.
  B: Do meals have to be eaten together? Some people might not want to eat that early.
  C: Neatness has to be taken seriously. We'd better . . .

B | *Make a list of rules that you've agreed on. Use the passive with modals and similar expressions. Compare your list with another group's list.*

EXAMPLE: Dinner will be served at 6:00 P.M.
  The dishes must be washed after each meal.
  Noise has to be . . .

EXERCISE 8: Problem Solving

Work in groups. Look at the picture of a student lounge. You are responsible for getting it in order, but you have limited time and money. Agree on five things that should be done.

EXAMPLE: **A:** The window has to be replaced.
B: No. That'll cost too much. It can just be taped.
C: That'll look terrible. It's really got to be replaced.
D: OK. What else should be done?

EXERCISE 9: For or Against

Sending people to the International Space Station costs millions of dollars. Should money be spent for these space projects, or could it be spent better on Earth? If so, how should it be spent? Discuss these questions with your classmates.

EXAMPLE: **A:** I think space projects are useful. A lot of new products are going to be developed in space.
B: I don't agree. Some of that money should be spent on public housing.

EXERCISE 10: Writing

A | *Write two paragraphs about your neighborhood, your school, or your workplace. In your first paragraph, write about what might be done to improve it. In your second paragraph, write about what shouldn't be changed. Use the passive with modals and similar expressions.*

EXAMPLE: I enjoy attending this school, but I believe some things could be improved. First, I think that more software ought to be purchased for the language lab . . .

B | *Check your work. Use the Editing Checklist.*

Editing Checklist

Did you use . . . ?
- ☐ *be* + **past participle** to form the passive after modals
- ☐ *will* or *be going to* for the future
- ☐ *can* for present ability
- ☐ *could* for past ability and future possibility
- ☐ *may*, *might*, and *can't* for future possibility or impossibility
- ☐ *should*, *ought to*, and *had better* for advisability
- ☐ *must* and *have (got) to* for necessity

A | *Circle the correct words to complete the sentences.*

1. What should be <u>did / done</u> about the student lounge?

2. I think the furniture should <u>be replaced / replace</u>.

3. Maybe some computer workstations <u>could / have</u> be provided.

4. The air conditioning <u>has / had</u> better be repaired.

5. It might not <u>be / being</u> fixed by the summer.

6. The lounge <u>don't / won't</u> be used by students while it's being painted.

7. The school office <u>has / had</u> got to be told about these problems.

8. In the future, problems <u>will / are</u> going to be handled faster.

B | *Complete the sentences with the correct form of the verbs in parentheses.*

1. Astronauts _____ in zero gravity.
   (should / train)

2. They _____ the chance to work in those conditions.
   (have to / give)

3. Equipment _____ also _____ in conditions similar to space.
   (must / test)

4. Zero gravity _____ underwater as well as on the ISS.
   (can / experience)

5. Underwater living space _____ by Aquatics Laboratory.
   (will / provide)

6. A lot more astronauts _____ there for training.
   (may / send)

7. Skills for Moon missions _____ also _____ underwater.
   (could / develop)

C | *Find and correct five mistakes.*

The new spacesuits are going to be testing underwater today. They've got to been improved before they can be used on the Moon or Mars. Two astronauts are going to be wearing them while they're working, and they'll watched by the engineers. This morning communication was lost with the Earth's surface, and all decisions had to be make by the astronauts themselves. It was a very realistic situation. This crew will got to be very well prepared for space travel. They're going to the Moon in a few years.

STEP 1 GRAMMAR IN CONTEXT

Before You Read

Look at the photos on this page and the next. Discuss the questions.

1. Which forms of body art do you think are attractive?
2. Does body art have any disadvantages? What are they?

Read

Read the article from a fashion magazine.

Body Art

Each culture has a different ideal of beauty, and throughout the ages,[1] men and women have done amazing things to achieve the ideal. They have **had *their hair* shaved**, **cut**, **colored**, **straightened**, and **curled**; and they have **had *their bodies* decorated** with painting and tattoos. Here are some of today's many options:

———— HAIR ————

Getting *your hair* done is the easiest way to change your appearance. Today, both men and women **have *their hair* permed**. This chemical procedure[2] can curl hair or just give it more body.[3] If your hair is long, you can, of course, **get *it* cut**. But did you know that you can also **have *short hair* lengthened** with hair extensions[4]? Of course you can **have *your hair* colored** and become a blonde, brunette, or redhead. But you can also **have *it* bleached** white or **get *it* dyed** blue, green, or orange!

(continued on next page)

---
[1]***throughout the ages:*** during different periods of time
[2]***chemical procedure:*** a technique that uses chemicals (for example, hydrogen peroxide) to change the appearance or texture of something
[3]***body:*** hair thickness
[4]***hair extensions:*** pieces of hair (natural or synthetic) that people have attached to their own hair to make it longer

Body Art

PIERCING

Pierced ears are an old favorite, but lately the practice of piercing has expanded.[6] Many people now **are getting *their noses*, *lips*, *or other parts of the body* pierced** for jewelry. Piercing requires even more caution than tattooing, and aftercare is very important to avoid infection.

TATTOOS

This form of body art was created many thousands of years ago. Today, tattoos have again become popular. More and more people are **having *them* done**. However, caution is necessary. Although nowadays you can **get *a tattoo* removed** with less pain and scarring[5] than before, **having *one* applied** is still a big decision.

BODY PAINT

If a tattoo is not for you, you can **have *ornaments* painted** on your skin instead. Some people **have *necklaces and bracelets* painted** on their neck and arms or **get *a butterfly mask* applied** to their face for a special event. Sports fans often get their face painted with their team's colors or the name of their favorite player. Body paintings can be large, but unlike tattoos, they can be washed off.

COSMETIC SURGERY

You can **get *your nose* shortened**, or **have *your chin* lengthened**. You can even **have *the shape of your body* changed**. There is always some risk involved, so the decision to have cosmetic surgery requires a lot of thought.

Some of the ways of changing your appearance may be cheap and temporary. However, others are expensive and permanent. So, think before you act, and don't let today's choice become tomorrow's regret.

—By Debra Santana

---

[5]***scarring:*** the creation of a permanent mark on the skin as a result of an accident, or a cosmetic or medical procedure
[6]***expand:*** to become larger

After You Read

A | **Vocabulary:** *Complete the sentences with the words from the box.*

| appearance | event | option | permanent | remove | risk |

1. Dana and Nasir's wedding was a wonderful _____. The whole town attended.

2. Getting a tattoo isn't (an) _____ if you're under 16. It's illegal at that age.

3. Piercing can be attractive, but there's always the _____ of infection.

4. You won't recognize Elsa! She's completely changed her _____.

5. Carly hates her new hair color. It's a good thing it isn't _____.

6. Can a dry cleaner _____ this stain? Coffee is hard get out.

B | **Comprehension:** *Check (✓)* **True, False,** *or* **?** *(the information isn't in the article).*

	True	False	?
1. Most people have the same idea about beauty.	☐	☐	☐
2. There are many ways people can change their hair.	☐	☐	☐
3. Many men change their hair color.	☐	☐	☐
4. Tattoos are a modern invention.	☐	☐	☐
5. Tattoos are permanent.	☐	☐	☐
6. Body paint is a temporary alternative to tattoos.	☐	☐	☐
7. Body piercing has more risks than tattooing.	☐	☐	☐
8. You can have cosmetic surgery to lengthen your nose.	☐	☐	☐
9. It's always easy to change back to the way you looked before.	☐	☐	☐

THE PASSIVE CAUSATIVE

Statements

Subject	*Have / Get*	Object	Past Participle	(*By* + Agent)	
She	**has**	*her hair*	cut	*by André*	every month.
He	**has had**	*his beard*	trimmed		before.
I	**get**	*my nails*	done		at André's.
They	**are going to get**	*their ears*	pierced.		

Yes / No Questions

Auxiliary Verb	Subject	*Have / Get*	Object	Past Participle	(*By* + Agent)	
Does	she	**have**	*her hair*	cut	*by André*?	
Has	he	**had**	*his beard*	trimmed		before?
Do	you	**get**	*your nails*	done		at André's?
Are	they	**going to get**	*their ears*	pierced?		

Wh- Questions

Wh- Word	Auxiliary Verb	Subject	*Have / Get*	Object	Past Participle	(*By* + Agent)	
How often	**does**	she	**have**	*her hair*	cut	*by André*?	
Where	**did**	he	**get**	*his beard*	trimmed		before?
When	**do**	you	**get**	*your nails*	done		at André's?
Why	**are**	they	**going to get**	*their ears*	pierced?		

GRAMMAR NOTES

<table>
<tr>
<td>**1**</td>
<td>Form the **passive causative** with the appropriate form of *have* or *get* + **object** + **past participle**. *Have* and *get* have the same meaning.

You can use the **passive causative** with:
- **all verb tenses**
- **modals**
- **gerunds**
- **infinitives**</td>
<td>
- I **have** *my hair* **cut** by André.
  OR
- I **get** *my hair* **cut** by André.

- I **had** *the car* **washed** yesterday.
- You **should get** *the oil* **changed**.
- I love **having** *my hair* **done**.
- I want **to get** *it* **colored**.</td>
</tr>
<tr>
<td>**2**</td>
<td>Use the **passive causative** to talk about **services** that you arrange for someone to do for you.

BE CAREFUL! Do **NOT confuse** the passive causative with *had* with the **past perfect**.</td>
<td>
- I used to color my own hair, but I've started to **have** *it* **colored**.
- André is going to **get** *his hair salon* **remodeled** by a local architect.

PASSIVE CAUSATIVE WITH *HAD*:
- I **had** *it* **colored** last week.
  (Someone did it for me.)

PAST PERFECT:
- I **had colored** it before.
  (I did it myself.)</td>
</tr>
<tr>
<td>**3**</td>
<td>Use *by* when it is necessary to mention the **agent** (the person doing the service).
Do **NOT use** *by* when it is clear who is doing the service.</td>
<td>
- This week Lynne **is getting her hair done** *by a new stylist*.
  NOT: Where does Lynne get her hair done by a hair stylist?</td>
</tr>
</table>

REFERENCE NOTE

For information on when to include the **agent**, see Unit 18, page 293.

EXERCISE 1: Discover the Grammar

Read the conversations. Decide if the statement that follows each conversation is **True (T)** *or* **False (F).**

1. **JAKE:** Have you finished writing your article on body art?

    DEBRA: Yes. I'm going to get it copied and then take it to the post office.

    _F_ Debra is going to copy the article herself.

2. **DEBRA:** I'm glad that's done. Now I can start planning for our party.

    JAKE: Me too. I'm going to get my hair cut tomorrow for the big event.

    _____ Jake cuts his own hair.

3. **JAKE:** Speaking about hair—Amber, *your* hair's getting awfully long.

    AMBER: I know, Dad. I'm cutting it tomorrow.

    _____ Amber cuts her own hair.

4. **AMBER:** Mom, why didn't you get your nails done last time you went to the hairdresser?

    DEBRA: Because I did them just before my appointment.

    _____ Debra did her own nails.

5. **AMBER:** I was thinking of painting a butterfly on my forehead for the party.

    DEBRA: A butterfly! Well, OK. As long as it's not permanent.

    _____ Someone is going to paint a butterfly on Amber's forehead for her.

6. **DEBRA:** Jake, do you think we should get the floors waxed before the party?

    JAKE: I think they look OK. We'll get them done afterward.

    _____ Debra and Jake are going to hire someone to wax their floors after the party.

7. **DEBRA:** I'm going to watch some TV and then go to bed. What's on the agenda for tomorrow?

    JAKE: I have to get up early. I'm getting the car washed before work.

    _____ Jake is going to wash the car himself.

8. **DEBRA:** You know, I think it's time to change the oil too.

    JAKE: You're right. I'll do it this weekend.

    _____ Jake is going to change the oil himself.

EXERCISE 2: Statements

(Grammar Notes 1–2)

Today is February 15. Look at the Santanas' calendar and write sentences about when they **had/got things done**, and when they are **going to have/get things done**. Use the correct form of the words in parentheses.

FEBRUARY						
SUNDAY	MONDAY	TUESDAY	WEDNESDAY	THURSDAY	FRIDAY	SATURDAY
1	2	3	4	5	6	7 Deb– hairdresser
8	9	10	11	12 Jake– barber	13 carpets	14 dog groomer
15 TODAY'S DATE	16 windows	17	18	19	20 food and drinks	21 party!! family pictures
22	23	24	25 Amber– ears pierced	26	27	28

1. (The Santanas / have / family pictures / take)

   The Santanas are going to have family pictures taken on the 21st.

2. (Debra / get / her hair / perm)

   _____

3. (Amber / have / the dog / groom)

   _____

4. (They / get / the windows / wash)

   _____

5. (They / have / the carpets / clean)

   _____

6. (Amber / have / her ears / pierce)

   _____

7. (Jake / get / his hair / cut)

   _____

8. (They / have / food and drinks / deliver)

   _____

Debra and Jake are going to have a party. Complete the conversations with the passive
causative of the appropriate verbs in the box.

color	cut	dry clean	paint	remove	repair	~~shorten~~	wash

1. **AMBER:** I bought a new dress for the party, Mom. What do you think?

   DEBRA: It's pretty, but it's a little long. Why don't you _____*get it shortened*_____?

   AMBER: OK. They do alterations at the cleaners. I'll take it in tomorrow.

2. **AMBER:** By the way, what are *you* planning to wear?

   DEBRA: My white silk suit. I'm glad you reminded me. I'd better _____.

   It has a stain on the sleeve.

   AMBER: I can drop it off at the cleaners with my dress.

3. **JAKE:** The house is ready, except for the windows. They look pretty dirty.

   DEBRA: Don't worry. We _____ tomorrow.

4. **DEBRA:** Amber, your hair is getting really long. I thought you were going to cut it.

   AMBER: I decided not to do it myself this time. I _____ by André.

5. **DEBRA:** My hair's getting a lot of gray in it. Should I _____?

   JAKE: Well, I guess that's an option. But it looks fine to me the way it is.

6. **AMBER:** Mom, I've been thinking about getting a butterfly tattoo instead of having one painted.

   I can always _____ if I decide I don't like it.

   DEBRA: No! That's *not* an option! There are too many risks involved in the procedure.

7. **AMBER** Someone's at the door, and it's only 12 o'clock!

   DEBRA: No, it's not. The clock stopped again.

   JAKE: Oh no, not again. I don't believe it! I _____ already

   _____ twice this year, and it's only February!

8. **GUEST:** The house looks beautiful, Jake. I love the color. _____ you

   _____?

   JAKE: No, actually we did it ourselves last summer.

EXERCISE 4: Editing

Read Amber's Facebook post. There are seven mistakes in the use of the passive causative. The first mistake is already corrected. Find and correct six more.

February 21: The party was tonight. It went really well! The house looked great.

Last week, Mom and Dad had the floors waxed and all the windows ~~clean~~ *cleaned* professionally so everything

sparkled. And of course we had the whole house painted ourselves last summer. (I'll never forget that.

It took us two weeks!) I wore my pink dress that I have

shortened by Bo, and my best friend, Alicia, wore her new

black gown. Right before the party, I got cut my hair by André.

He did a great job. There were a lot of guests at the party. We

had almost 50 people invited, and they almost all showed up

for our family event! The food was great too. Mom made most

of the main dishes herself, but she had the rest of the food

prepare by a caterer. Mom and Dad had hired a professional

photographer, so at the end of the party we took our pictures.

As you can see, they look great!

EXERCISE 5: Listening

A | *Amber has just gone to college. Read the statements. Then listen to her conversation with her father. Listen again and circle the words to complete each statement.*

1. Amber walks / (drives) / takes the bus to school.

2. Amber does not have a new car / apartment / roommate.

3. Her neighborhood is old / safe / noisy.

4. Her apartment needed cleaning / carpeting / painting.

5. Amber didn't have to buy a computer / a computer desk / lamps.

6. Amber didn't change the appearance of her hair / face / hands.

B | *Listen again to the conversation. Check (✓) the correct column.*

Amber . . .	Did the job herself	Hired someone to do the job
1. change the oil in her car	☐	☑
2. change the locks	☐	☐
3. paint the apartment	☐	☐
4. put up bookshelves	☐	☐
5. bring new furniture to the apartment	☐	☐
6. paint her hands	☐	☐
7. cut her hair	☐	☐
8. color her hair	☐	☐

EXERCISE 6: Pronunciation

A | *Read and listen to the Pronunciation Note.*

Pronunciation Note

We often **contract *have*** in sentences in the **present perfect**.

EXAMPLES: She **has cut** her hair. ➔ "She**'s cut** her hair."
She **has had** her hair cut. ➔ "She**'s had** her hair cut."

But we do **NOT contract *have*** in sentences that use the **passive causative** in the **simple present**.

EXAMPLES: She **has** her hair **cut**. NOT: "~~She's~~ her hair cut."
They **have** their taxes **done**. NOT: "~~They've~~ their taxes done."

B | *Listen to the short conversations. Complete the sentences. Write contractions if the speakers use them.*

1. **A:** Marta's hair looks great.

   B: Yes. She _____.

2. **A:** Do you do your own taxes or do you have them done?

   B: I _____.

3. **A:** Is Anton's car OK now?

   B: Yes. He _____.

4. **A:** Does Amy wash her own car?

   B: She _____ once a month.

5. **A:** What color is your new apartment?

   B: I _____ green.

6. **A:** Your hair looks different!

   B: Yes. I _____.

C | *Listen again to the conversations and repeat the answers. Then practice the conversations with a partner.*

EXERCISE 7: Making Plans

A | *Work in small groups. Imagine that you are taking a car trip together to another country. You'll be gone for several weeks. Decide where you're going. Then make a list of things you have to do and arrange before the trip. Use the ideas below and ideas of your own.*

- passport and visa
- car (oil, gas, tires, brake fluid)
- home (pets, plants, mail, newspaper delivery)
- personal (clothing, hair)
- medical (teeth, eyes, prescriptions)
- *Other:* _____

EXAMPLE: **A:** I have to get my passport renewed.
   B: Me too. And we should apply for visas right away.

B | *Now compare your list with that of another group. Did you forget anything?*

EXERCISE 8: Compare and Contrast

A | *Work in pairs. Look at the **Before** and **After** pictures of a fashion model. You have five minutes to find and write down all the things she had done to change her appearance.*

Before

After

> **EXAMPLE:** She had her nose shortened.

B | *When the five minutes are up, compare your list with that of another pair. Then look at the pictures again to check your answers.*

C | *Do you think the woman looks better? Why or why not?*

> **EXAMPLE:** **A:** I don't know why she had her nose fixed.
> **B:** Neither do I. I think it looked fine before.

EXERCISE 9: Cross-Cultural Comparison

Work in small groups. Think about other cultures. Discuss the types of things people do or get done in order to change their appearance. Report back to your class.

Some procedures to think about:

- **eyes:** lengthening eyelashes, coloring eyebrows
- **teeth:** straightening, whitening
- **face:** shortening nose, plumping lips
- **hair:** coloring, lengthening, styling, curling, straightening, braiding
- **skin:** whitening, tanning, tattooing, painting
- **hands / feet:** painting nails, painting hands or soles of feet

Hand painting in India

> **EXAMPLE:** **A:** In India, women get their hands painted for special occasions. I think it looks nice.
> **B:** In Japan, . . .

EXERCISE 10: Writing

A | *Write an email to someone you know. Describe your activities. Include things that you have recently done or have had done. Also talk about things you are going to do or are going to have done. Use the passive causative.*

EXAMPLE: Hi Sara,

I've just moved into a new apartment. I've already had it painted, but there are still so many things that I have to get done! . . .

B | *Check your work. Use the Editing Checklist.*

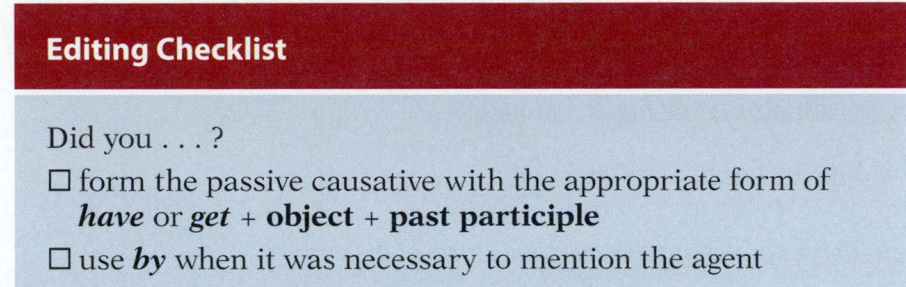

Editing Checklist

Did you . . . ?

☐ form the passive causative with the appropriate form of
have or ***get*** + **object** + **past participle**

☐ use ***by*** when it was necessary to mention the agent

UNIT **20** **Review**

Check your answers on page UR-5.
Do you need to review anything?

A | *Circle the correct words to complete the sentences.*

1. I don't cut my own hair. I <u>have it cut / have cut it</u>.

2. My friend has her hair <u>did / done</u> every week.

3. We should <u>get / gotten</u> the house painted again this year.

4. Did you have <u>painted your house / your house painted</u>?

5. I want to have the job done <u>by / from</u> a professional.

B | *Complete each sentence with the correct passive causative form of the verb in parentheses and a pronoun.*

1. My computer stopped working. I have to _____.
   (repair)

2. I don't clean the windows myself. I _____ once a year.
   (clean)

3. Your pants are too long. You should _____.
   (shorten)

4. Does Monica color her own hair or does she _____?
   (color)

5. I can't fix this vacuum cleaner myself. I'll have to _____.
   (fix)

6. Todd used to have a tattoo, but he _____ last year.
   (remove)

7. My passport is going to expire soon. I need to _____.
   (renew)

8. The car has been making a strange noise. I _____ tomorrow.
   (check)

C | *Find and correct seven mistakes.*

I'm going on vacation next week. I'd like to have done some work in my office, and this seems like a good time for it. Please have my carpet clean while I'm gone. And could you have my computer and printer looked at? It's been quite a while since they've been serviced. Ted wants to have my office painted by a painter while I'm gone. Please tell him any color is fine except pink! Last week, I had designed some new brochures by Perfect Print. Please call the printer and have them delivered directly to the sales reps. And could you get made up more business cards too? When I get back, it'll be time to plan the holiday party. I think we should have it catered this year from a professional. While I'm gone, why don't you call around and get some estimates from caterers? Has the estimates sent to Ted. Thanks.

PART VIII

From Grammar to Writing
CHANGING THE FOCUS WITH THE PASSIVE

Reports often **focus on the results of an action** rather than the people who performed the action. Use the **passive** to focus on the results.

> **EXAMPLE:** Artists **carved** many wooden statues for the temple. (*active*)
> Many wooden statues **were carved** for the temple. (*passive*)

1 | *Read about a famous building in Korea. Underline the passive forms and their subjects.*

Two Buddhist monks built Haeinsa Temple in the year 802. The king gave them the money to build the temple after the two monks saved his queen's life. Haeinsa burned down in 1817, but <u>the Main Hall was rebuilt</u> in 1818 on its original foundations. Today, Haeinsa is composed of several large, beautiful buildings. It contains many paintings and statues. Someone carved three of the statues from a single ancient tree. Behind the Main Hall is a steep flight of stone stairs that leads to the Storage Buildings. These buildings, which escaped the fire, were constructed in 1488 in order to store wooden printing blocks of Buddhist texts. It was believed that these printing blocks could protect the country against invaders. Monks carved the 81,258 wooden blocks in the 13th century. A century later, nuns carried them to Haeinsa for safekeeping. Architects designed the Storage Buildings to preserve the wooden blocks. For more than 500 years, the blocks have been kept in perfect condition because of the design of these buildings. Haeinsa, which means *reflection on a smooth sea*, is also known as the Temple of Teaching because it houses the ancient printing blocks.

2 | *Find five sentences in Exercise 1 that would be better expressed in the passive. Rewrite them.*

1. *Haeinsa Temple was built by two Buddhist monks in the year 802.* _____

2. _____

3. _____

4. _____

5. _____

3 | *Answer these questions about Haeinsa Temple.*

1. When was it built?

   _____

2. Who built it?

   _____

3. Why was it built?

   _____

4. What are some of its features?

   _____

5. What is it famous for?

   _____

4 | *Before you write . . .*

1. Choose a famous building to write about. Do some research in the library or on the Internet. Answer the questions in Exercise 3.

2. Work with a partner. Ask and answer questions about your topic.

5 | *Write a research report about the building you researched. Use the passive where appropriate. If possible, include a photograph or drawing of the building.*

6 | *Exchange paragraphs with a different partner. Answer the following questions.*

1. Did the writer answer all the questions in Exercise 3?_____

2. What interested you the most about the building?_____

3. What would you like to know more about?_____

4. Did the writer use the passive appropriately?_____

5. Are the past participles correct?_____

7 | *Work with your partner. Discuss each other's editing questions from Exercise 6. Then rewrite your report and make any necessary corrections.*

PART IX

CONDITIONALS

Before You Read

Look at the title of the article and the picture on this page. Discuss the questions.

1. What is a cyber mall?
2. Have you ever purchased something online?
3. What are some steps people should take to shop safely online?

Read

🎧 *Read the article about cyber malls.*

Pick and Click Shopping @ Home
By E. Buyer

Where is the largest mall[1] in the world? **If you think it's in Alberta, Canada, you're wrong!** It's in cyberspace![2] And you can get there from home on your very own computer.

Cyber shopping is fast, convenient, and often less expensive. **It doesn't matter if it's a book or a diamond necklace**—with just a click of your mouse, you can buy anything without getting up from your chair. **If you're looking for the best price, you can easily compare prices and read other buyers' reviews of products**. Shopping online can save you time and money—but you need to surf[3] and shop safely. Here are some tips to make your trip to the cyber mall a good one:

🔒 **You are less likely to have a problem if you shop with well-known companies**.

🔒 **If you don't know the company, ask them to send you information**. What is their address? Their phone number?

🔒 **Always pay by credit card if you can. If you are unhappy with the product (or if you don't receive it), then you can dispute the charge**.

---

[1]*mall:* a very large building or outdoor area with a lot of stores in it
[2]*cyberspace:* all the connections between computers in different places (people think of it as a real place where information, messages, pictures, etc. exist)
[3]*surf:* to go quickly from one website to another in order to find information that interests you

Pick and Click Shopping @ Home

🔒 Only enter your credit card information on a secure site. **If you see a closed lock (🔒) or complete key (🔑) symbol at the bottom of your screen, the site is secure**. Also, the web address will change from http://www to https://www. This means that your credit card number will be encrypted (changed so that others can't read it). **If the site isn't secure, don't enter your credit card information**.

🔒 **If you have kids, don't let them give out personal information**.

🔒 **If you have any doubts about a site's security, contact the store by phone or email**.

🔒 Find out the return policy. **What happens if you don't like the product?**

🔒 Print out and save a record of your purchase. **If there is a problem, the receipt gives you proof of purchase**.

🔒 **If you change your mind about an order, contact the company immediately**.

As you can see, many of these steps are similar to the ones you follow in a "store with doors." Just use common sense. **If you take some basic precautions, you shouldn't have any problems**.

Internet shopping has literally[4] brought a world of opportunity to consumers. Today we can shop 24 hours a day, 7 days a week in stores that are halfway around the globe without ever having to leave home or stand in line. As with many things in life, there are some risks. Just remember that online or off, **if an offer seems too good to be true, it probably is**. Happy cyber shopping!

_____
[4]*literally:* (used to emphasize that something is actually true)

SHOPPING ON LINE IS CONVENIENT... BUT I MISS PUSHING AND SHOVING AND GRABBING SALE ITEMS FROM OTHER SHOPPER'S HANDS!

McLemore 5-04

After You Read

A | Vocabulary: *Complete the statements with the words from the box.*

consumer	dispute	policy	precaution	secure	site

1. You should ask about a store's return _____policy_____.

2. A smart _____consumer_____ always compares prices before making a purchase.

3. As a safety _____precaution_____, you should never give your password to anyone.

4. My friend never shops online. He doesn't think it's _____secure_____ enough.

5. I don't like that store's online _____site_____. It's very confusing.

6. I need to _____dispute_____ that charge. I ordered one sweater, but they charged me for two.

Present Real Conditionals **341**

B | Comprehension: *Circle the letter of the word or phrase that best completes each statement.*

1. The largest mall in the world is in _C_.

   a. Canada

   b. the United States

   c. cyberspace

2. Cyber shopping is often _b_ than shopping in a store with walls.

   a. slower

   b. cheaper

   c. more dangerous

3. It's a good idea to shop with a company that has _b_.

   a. a nice website

   b. a name you know

   c. products for children

4. If possible, you should pay for Internet purchases _a_.

   a. by credit card

   b. by check

   c. with cash

5. A closed lock at the bottom of the computer screen means _b_.

   a. you can't make a purchase

   b. it's safe to enter your credit card information

   c. the site doesn't have the product you want

6. In some ways, shopping online is _b_ _c_ shopping in a "store with doors."

   a. exactly the same as

   b. totally different from

   c. similar to

7. One of the biggest advantages of shopping online is _a_.

   a. convenience

   b. quality

   c. safety

PRESENT REAL CONDITIONALS

Statements	
If Clause	Result Clause
If I **shop** online,	I **save** time.
If the mall **is** closed,	I **can shop** online.

Statements	
Result Clause	*If* Clause
I **save** time	*if* I **shop** online.
I **can shop** online	*if* the mall **is** closed.

Yes / No Questions	
Result Clause	*If* Clause
Do you **save** time	*if* you **shop** online?
Can you **shop** online	*if* the mall **is** closed?

Short Answers			
Affirmative		Negative	
Yes,	I **do**.	No,	I **don't**.
	I **can**.		I **can't**.

Wh- Questions	
Result Clause	*If* Clause
What **happens**	*if* I **don't like** it?

GRAMMAR NOTES

1	Use **present real conditional** sentences for **general truths**. The *if* clause talks about the **condition**, and the **result clause** talks about **what happens** if the condition occurs. Use the **simple present** in both clauses. **USAGE NOTE:** We often use *even if* when the **result is surprising**.	IF CLAUSE RESULT CLAUSE • *If* it**'s** a holiday, the store **is** closed. PRESENT PRESENT • *If* you **use** a credit card, it**'s** faster. • *Even if* it's a holiday, this store stays open.
2	You can also use **real conditional** sentences for **habits** and things that happen again and again. Use the **simple present** or **present progressive** in the *if* clause. Use the **simple present** in the **result clause**.	• *If* Bill **shops** online, he **uses** a credit card. PRESENT PRESENT • *If* I **surf** the Web, I **use** Google. PRESENT PROGRESSIVE PRESENT • *If* I**'m surfing** the Web, I **use** Google.

(continued on next page)

Present Real Conditionals **343**

3	You can use **modals** (*can*, *should*, *might*, *must* . . .) in the **result clause**.	• If you don't like the product, you ***can* return** it. • If you have children, you ***shouldn't* let** them shop online.
	USAGE NOTE: We sometimes use ***then*** to **emphasize the result** in real conditional sentences with modals.	• If you don't like the product, ***then*** you **can return** it. • If you have children, ***then*** you **shouldn't let** them shop online.
4	Use the **imperative** in the **result clause** to give **instructions**, **commands**, and **invitations** that depend on a certain condition.	IMPERATIVE • If you change your mind, **call** the company. • If a site isn't secure, **don't enter** your credit card information.
	USAGE NOTE: We sometimes use ***then*** to **emphasize the result** in real conditional sentences with imperatives.	• If you change your mind, ***then*** **call** the company. • If a site isn't secure, ***then*** **don't enter** your credit card information.
5	You can **begin conditional sentences** with the ***if* clause** or **the result clause**. The meaning is the same.	• ***If* I shop online,** I save time. OR • I save time ***if* I shop online**. NOT: I save time~~,~~ if I shop online.
	BE CAREFUL! Use a **comma** between the two clauses only when the ***if* clause comes first**.	
6	A **conditional sentence** does not always have ***if***. You can often use ***when*** instead of ***if***.	• ***When*** Bill **shops** online, he **uses** a credit card. • I **use** Google ***when*** I'**m surfing** the Web.
	Notice that both clauses can use the **present progressive** to describe actions that happen at the same time.	• ***When*** stores **are opening** in Los Angeles, they **are closing** in Johannesburg.

EXERCISE 1: Discover the Grammar

Read these shopping tips. In each real conditional sentence, underline once the result clause. Underline twice the clause that talks about the condition.

SHOP SMART

You're shopping in a foreign city. Should you pay full price, or should you bargain? If you don't know the answer, you can pay too much or miss a fun experience. Bargaining is one of the greatest shopping pleasures if you know how to do it. The strategies are different in different places. Check out these tips before you go.

Hong Kong

Hong Kong is one of the world's greatest shopping cities. If you like to bargain, you can do it anywhere except the larger department stores. The trick is not to look too interested. If you see something you want, pick it up along with some other items and ask the prices. Then make an offer below what you are willing to pay. If the seller's offer is close to the price you want, then you should be able to reach an agreement quickly.

Italy

Bargaining in Italy is appropriate at outdoor markets and with street vendors. In stores, you can politely ask for a discount if you want to bargain. Take your time. Make conversation if you speak Italian. Show your admiration for the object by picking it up and pointing out its wonderful features. When you hear the price, look sad. Make your own offer. Then end the bargaining politely if you can't agree.

Mexico

In Mexico, people truly enjoy bargaining. There are some clear rules, though. You should bargain only if you really are interested in buying the object. If the vendor's price is far more than you want to pay, then politely stop the negotiation. If you know your price is truly reasonable, walking away will often bring a lower offer.

Remember, bargaining is always a social interaction, not an argument. And it can still be fun even if you don't get the item you want at the price you want to pay.

EXERCISE 2: Conditional Statements: Modals and Imperatives   (Grammar Notes 1–4)

*Read this Q and A about shopping around the world. Write conditional sentences to
summarize the advice. Start with the **if** clause and use appropriate punctuation.*

1. Hong Kong

Q: I want to buy some traditional crafts. Any ideas?

A: You ought to visit the Western District on Hong Kong Island. It's famous for its crafts.

*If you want to buy some traditional crafts, (then) you ought to visit the Western District
on Hong Kong Island.*

2. Barcelona

Q: I'd like to buy some nice but inexpensive clothes. Where can I go?

A: Take the train to outdoor markets in towns *outside* of the city. They have great stuff.

if You'd like to buy some nice but inexpensive clothes
take the train to outdoor markets in towns.

3. Istanbul

Q: I want to go shopping in the Grand Bazaar. Is it open on Sunday?

A: You have to go during the week. It's closed on Sunday.

if you want to go shopping in the Grand B
you have to go during the week.

4. Bangkok

Q: My son wants to buy computer games. Where should he go?

A: He should try the Panthip Plaza. The selection is huge.

if your son wants to buy computer games,
He should try the Panthip plaza.

5. Mexico City

Q: I plan to buy some silver jewelry in Mexico. Any tips?

A: Try bargaining. That way, you'll be able to get something nice at a very good price.

if you plan to buy some silver jewelry in Mexico
try bargaining, that way.

6. London

Q: I'd like to find some nice secondhand clothing shops. Can you help me?

A: Try the Portobello market on the weekend. Happy shopping!

EXERCISE 3: Conditional Statements

(Grammar Notes 1–3, 5)

Complete the interview with Claudia Leggett, a fashion buyer. Combine the two sentences in parentheses to make a real conditional sentence. Keep the same order and decide which clause begins with **if**. *Make necessary changes in capitalization and punctuation.*

INTERVIEWER: Is understanding fashion the most important thing for a career as a buyer?

LEGGETT: It is. *If you don't understand fashion, you don't belong in this field.*
1. **(You don't understand fashion. You don't belong in this field.)**

But buyers need other skills too.

INTERVIEWER: Such as?

LEGGETT: _____
2. **(You can make better decisions. You have good business skills.)**

INTERVIEWER: "People skills" must be important too.

LEGGETT: True. _____
3. **(A buyer needs great interpersonal skills. She's negotiating prices.)**

INTERVIEWER: Do you travel in your business?

LEGGETT: A lot! _____
4. **(There's a big international fashion fair. I'm usually there.)**

INTERVIEWER: Why fashion fairs?

LEGGETT: Thousands of professionals attend. _____

_____
5. **(I go to a fair. I can see hundreds of products in a few days.)**

INTERVIEWER: You just got back from the Leipzig fair, didn't you?

LEGGETT: Yes, and I went to Paris and Madrid too. _____

_____
6. **(I usually stay two weeks. I'm traveling to Europe.)**

INTERVIEWER: Does your family ever go with you?

LEGGETT: Often. _____
7. **(My husband can come. He and our son, Pietro, do things together.)**

_____
8. **(Pietro comes to the fair with me. My husband can't get away.)**

Next week, we're all going to Hong Kong.

INTERVIEWER: What do you do when you're not at a fashion fair?

LEGGETT: _____
9. **(I always go shopping. I have free time.)**

EXERCISE 4: Conditional Statements with *When*

(Grammar Note 6)

*Look at the map. Write sentences about the cities with clocks. Use the words in parentheses and **when**. Note: The light clocks show daylight hours; the shaded clocks show evening or nighttime hours.*

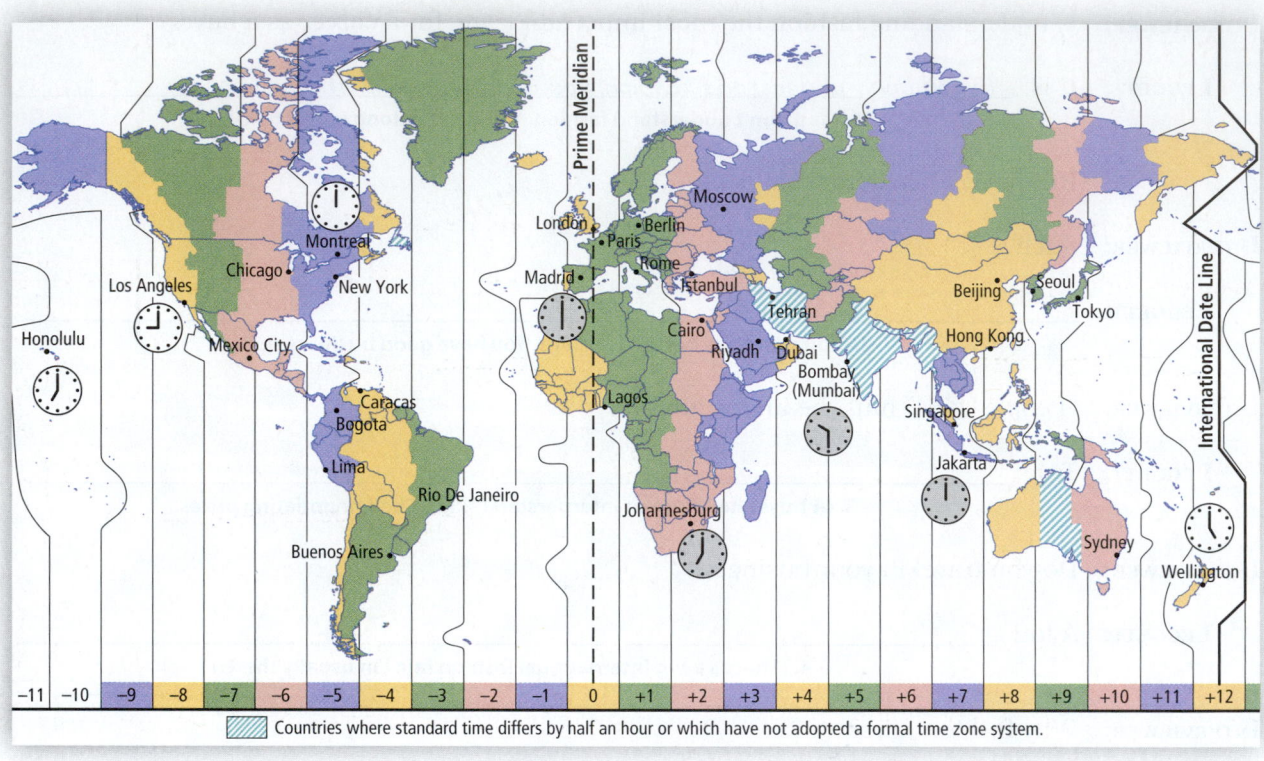

1. When it's noon in Montreal, it's midnight in Jakarta.

   (be noon / be midnight)

2. When stores are opening in Los Angeles, they're closing in Johannesburg.

   (stores open / stores close)

3. _____

   (people watch the sun rise / people watch the sun set)

4. _____

   (be midnight / be 6:00 P.M.)

5. _____

   (people eat lunch / people eat dinner)

6. _____

   (people get up / people go to bed)

7. _____

   (be 7:00 A.M. / be 7:00 P.M.)

8. _____

   (be 5:00 A.M. / be 9:00 A.M.)

EXERCISE 5: Editing

Read Claudia's email message. There are eight mistakes in the use of present real conditionals. The first mistake is already corrected. Find and correct seven more. Don't forget to check punctuation.

Tomorrow I'm flying to Hong Kong for a fashion show! My son, Pietro, is flying with me, and

                                                             like

my husband is already there. Whenever Pietro's off from school, I ~~liked~~ to take him on trips with

me. If my husband comes too, they are going sightseeing during the day. Our plane leaves Los

Angeles around midnight. If we flew at night, we can sleep on the plane. (At least that's the plan!)

I love Hong Kong. We always have a great time, when we will go there. The shopping is really

fantastic. When I'm not working I'm shopping.

I'll call you when I arrive at the hotel (around 7:00 A.M.). When it will be 7:00 A.M. in Hong

Kong, it's midnight in London. Is that too late to call? If you want to talk, just calling.

And, of course you can always email me.

STEP 4 COMMUNICATION PRACTICE

EXERCISE 6: Listening

A | *Claudia and her 10-year-old son, Pietro, are flying from Los Angeles to Hong Kong by way of Taipei. Read the statements. Then listen to each announcement. Listen again and circle the correct words to complete each statement.*

1. The airline's policy allows passengers to take (one)/ two / no piece(s) of luggage on the plane.

2. Flight 398 makes one / two / no stop(s) before Taipei.

3. Passengers need to show their boarding passes / passports / boarding passes and passports

   before getting on the plane.

4. The plane has six flight attendants / emergency exits / captains.

5. The plane will probably arrive early / on time / late.

6. The temperature in Taipei is cool / warm / very hot.

B | *Read the statements. Then listen to each announcement and check (✓) **True** or **False** for the statement with the same number.*

	True	False
1. Claudia has two pieces of carry-on luggage, and Pietro has one. They can take them on the plane.	☐	☑
2. Look at their boarding passes. They can board now.	☐	☐

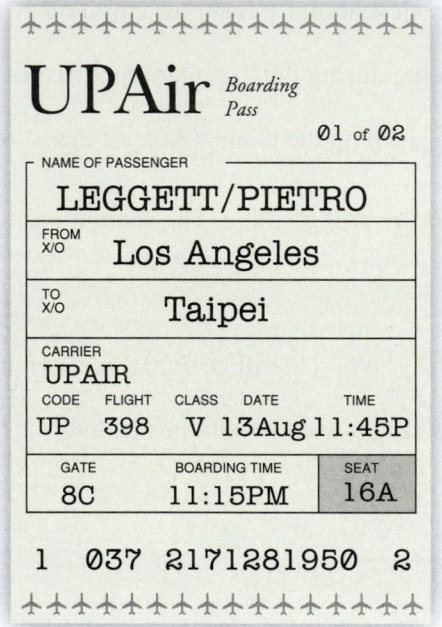

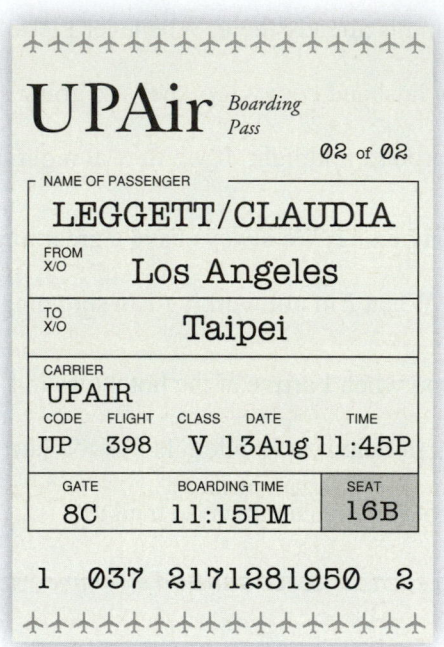

	True	False
3. Look at their boarding passes again. They can board now.	☐	☐
4. Pietro is only 10 years old. Claudia should put his oxygen mask on first.	☐	☐
5. Claudia is sitting in a left-hand window seat. She can see the lights of Tokyo.	☐	☐
6. Claudia needs information about their connecting flight. She can get this information on the plane.	☐	☐

Passengers on Flight 398 to Taipei

EXERCISE 7: Pronunciation

A | *Read and listen to the Pronunciation Note.*

B | *Listen to each sentence and add a comma where you hear the pause.*

1. If I have time I like to go to the mall.

2. I pay by cash if my purchase isn't expensive.

3. If I like something I sometimes buy two.

4. When I shop online I only use secure sites.

5. I usually read reviews when I shop online.

6. I always check the return policy when I buy something.

7. If I don't like something I return it.

8. When I shop with friends I always buy more.

9. If the mall is crowded I don't stay long.

10. I often stop at the food court when I'm at the mall.

C | *Listen again to each sentence and repeat. Notice the intonation and the pause (if any).*

EXERCISE 8: Reaching Agreement

A | *Work with a partner. You are going to buy some T-shirts for a friend—an 18-year-old male or female. Look at part of a store's website, and discuss the selections. Agree on a purchase. Think about these issues:*

- color
- style
- price
- size
- quantity
- shipping

NEW! UNISEX T-SHIRTS

| short-sleeves, crew neck $15.00 | short-sleeves, V-neck $15.00 | long-sleeves, crew neck $18.00 | long-sleeves, V-neck $18.00 |

Available in:
tangerine   hot pink   cherry red   ivory   ebony   ink blue   turquoise

All T-shirts available in Small, Medium, Large
Buy 1, get the second at 50% off! Buy today, take another 10% off!

Return/Exchange Policy: Return by mail (within 45 days of purchase): $6.00 fee
Exchange by mail (within 45 days of purchase): free

EXAMPLE:
A: Let's get a cherry red T-shirt.
B: What if she doesn't like red?
A: Well, if she doesn't like it, she can always exchange it for another color.
B: OK. If we decide today, ...

B | *With your partner, complete the order form for the item(s) you decided on.*

	Quantity	Color	Size
short-sleeved, crew neck T			○ S ○ M ○ L
short-sleeved, V-neck T			○ S ○ M ○ L
long-sleeved, crew neck T			○ S ○ M ○ L
long-sleeved, V-neck T			○ S ○ M ○ L

Shipping Method   ○ Standard: 5–9 business days $5.00
○ Express: 2 business days $10.00

EXERCISE 9: Cross-Cultural Comparison

Work with a partner. Compare shopping in a place you've lived in or one you have visited. Choose two different places and consider these questions:

- What days and hours are stores open?
- What kinds of stores are there: malls? small stores? indoor or outdoor markets?
- Do people bargain?
- How do people pay?
- What are some special products sold in that country?
- Is there a sales tax for clothing? If yes, how much is it?
- Do stores allow refunds or exchanges?

EXAMPLE: **A:** If you're in a small city or town in Mexico, stores are usually open from Monday to Friday between 9:00 A.M. and 2:00 or 4:00 P.M.

B: In South Korean cities, stores usually stay open until 10:00 P.M. And if you want to go shopping after that, you can find many stores that are open 24 hours.

EXERCISE 10: Discussion

Work in small groups. Discuss what you do when you want to make an important purchase (a gift, a camera, a car).

EXAMPLE: **A:** If I want to buy a camera, I check prices online.

B: When I buy a camera, I always ask friends for recommendations.

C: I always . . .

EXERCISE 11: For or Against

Look at the cartoon. What are some of the differences between shopping in a "store with doors" and shopping online? What are the advantages and disadvantages of each? Discuss these questions with your classmates.

EXAMPLE: **A:** If you shop for clothes in a store, you can try them on first.

B: And you can feel the material. That's important.

C: But you have a lot more choices if you shop online.

EXERCISE 12: Writing

A | *Work with a partner. Imagine that you are preparing an information sheet for tourists about your city or town. Write a list of tips for visitors. Include information on shopping. Use present real conditional sentences.*

EXAMPLE: • If you like to shop, Caterville has the biggest mall in this part of the country.
   • If you enjoy swimming or boating, you should visit Ocean Park.

B | *Compare your list with another pair's.*

EXAMPLE: **A:** If you're interested in history, there's a lot to see in Caterville.
   B: If golf is your sport, Ames has several beautiful golf courses.

C | *Check your work. Use the Editing Checklist.*

Editing Checklist

Did you use . . . ?
☐ the simple present in both clauses for general truths
☐ the simple present or present progressive in the ***if / when*** clause for habits and things that happen again and again
☐ a comma between the two clauses when the ***if / when*** clause comes first

---

Check your answers on page UR-6.

Do you need to review anything?

A | Complete the present real conditional sentences in the conversation with the correct form of the verbs in parentheses.

A: What ___do___ you ___do___ when you ___are___ too busy to shop?
1. (do)   2. (be)

B: It depends. If a store ___is___ open late, I ___shop___ in the evening.
3. (be)   4. (shop)

A: What ___happens___ if a store ___doesn't stay___ open late?
5. (happen)   6. (not stay)

B: If it ___closes___ early, I ___go___ to its website. It's really easy.
7. (close)   8. (go)

A: Great idea! When I ___feel___ rushed, I never ___think___ of that.
9. (feel)   10. (think)

B | Combine each pair of sentences to make a present real conditional sentence. Keep the same order.

1. It's 7:00 A.M. in Honolulu. What time is it in Mumbai?

   if it's 7:00 AM in Honolulu. what time is it in Mumbai?

2. You love jewelry. You should visit an international jewelry show.

   if you love jewelry you should visit an international jewelry show.

3. A tourist might have more fun. She tries bargaining.

   A tourist might have more fun, if she tries bargaining

4. You're shopping at an outdoor market. You can always bargain for a good price.

   When you are shopping at an outdoor market, You can always bargain For a good price.

5. But don't try to bargain. You're shopping in a big department store.

   But don't try to bargain, if you're shopping in a big department store

C | Find and correct five mistakes. Remember to check punctuation.

1. If I don't like something I bought online, then I returned it.

2. Don't buy from an online site, if you don't know anything about the company.

3. When he'll shops online, Frank always saves a lot of time.

4. I always fell asleep if I fly at night. It happens every time.

5. Isabel always has a wonderful time, when she visits Istanbul.

Future Real Conditionals
CAUSE AND EFFECT

Before You Read

Look at the pictures. Discuss the questions.

1. What is a superstition? Can you give an example of one?
2. Do you believe in any superstitions?
3. Do you wear or carry things that make you feel lucky?

Read

 *Read the magazine article about superstitions.*

KNOCK ON WOOD!

❀ **If you knock on wood, you'll keep bad luck away.**

❀ **You'll get a good grade on the test if you wear your shirt inside out.**

❀ **You'll get a bad grade unless you use your lucky pen.**

Superstitions may sound silly to some, but millions of people all over the world believe in their power to bring good luck or prevent bad luck. Different cultures share many similar superstitions:

❀ **If you break a mirror, you'll have seven years of bad luck.**

❀ **If the palm of your hand itches, you're going to get some money.**

❀ **If it rains when you move to a new house, you'll get rich.**

All superstitions are based on a cause and effect relationship: **If X happens, then Y will also happen**. However, in superstitions, the cause is magical and unrelated to the effect. In our scientific age, why are these beliefs so powerful and widespread? The Luck Project, an online survey of superstitious behaviors, gives us some fascinating insight. Read some of their findings on the next page.

❦ Emotions can influence superstitions, especially in uncertain situations where people do not have control. **People will react more superstitiously if they are worried. They will feel less superstitious if they aren't feeling a strong need for control.**

❦ We make our own luck. **If you believe you're lucky, you will carry out superstitions that make you feel good** (crossing your fingers for luck, for example). As a result, you probably won't fear bad luck superstitions, and you might perform better in stressful situations. In contrast, **if you think you're unlucky, you will anticipate the worst and look for bad luck superstitions that confirm your belief.** Your attitude makes a difference.

❦ More people than you might think believe in superstitions. Of the 4,000 people surveyed, 84 percent knocked on wood for good luck. Almost half feared walking under a ladder. And 15 percent of the people who studied or worked in the sciences feared the number 13.

Clearly, education doesn't eliminate superstition— college students are among the most superstitious people. Other superstitious groups are performers, athletes, gamblers,[1] and stock traders. People in these groups often have lucky charms[2] or personal good luck rituals.[3]

Deanna McBrearty, a New York City Ballet member, has lucky hair bands. **"If I have a good performance when I'm wearing one, I'll keep wearing it,"** she says. Baseball player Wade Boggs would only eat chicken before a game. Brett Gallagher, a stock trader, believes **he'll be more successful if he owns pet fish.** "I had fish for a while, and after they died, the market didn't do so well," he points out.

Will you do better on the test if you use your lucky pen? Maybe. **If the pen makes you feel more confident, you might improve your score.** So go ahead and use it. But don't forget: **Your lucky pen will be powerless unless you study.** The harder you work, the luckier you'll get.

---

[1]**gambler:** someone who risks money in a game or race (cards, horse race) because he or she might win more money
[2]**lucky charm:** a very small object worn on a chain that will bring good luck (horseshoe, four-leaf clover, etc.)
[3]**ritual:** a set of actions always done in the same way

After You Read

A | Vocabulary: *Match the words with their definitions.*

_____ 1. **widespread**　　　　**a.** to expect that something will happen

_____ 2. **insight**　　　　　　　**b.** sure

_____ 3. **percent**　　　　　　　**c.** a way of thinking about something

_____ 4. **confident**　　　　　　**d.** the ability to understand something clearly

_____ 5. **anticipate**　　　　　　**e.** happening in many places

_____ 6. **attitude**　　　　　　　**f.** equal to a certain amount in every hundred

good luck charm
تعويذة

B | Comprehension: *Check (✓)* **True** *or* **False.** *Correct the false sentences. Use information from the article.*

	True	False
1. Not many people are superstitious.	☐	☐
2. If you are worrying about something, you might act less superstitiously.	☐	☐
3. If you feel lucky, you'll have more good luck superstitions.	☐	☐
4. If you study science, you won't be superstitious.	☐	☐
5. If you don't study, your good luck pen won't work.	☐	☐

STEP 2 GRAMMAR PRESENTATION

FUTURE REAL CONDITIONALS

Statements

If Clause: Present	Result Clause: Future
If she **studies,**	she **won't fail** the test. she **'s going to pass** the test.
If she **doesn't study,**	she **'ll fail** the test. she **isn't going to pass** the test.

Yes / No Questions

Result Clause: Future	*If* Clause: Present
Will she **pass** the test	*if* she **studies?**
Is she **going to pass** the test	

Short Answers

Affirmative		Negative	
Yes,	she **will.** she **is.**	**No,**	she **won't.** she **isn't.**

Wh- Questions

Result Clause: Future	*If* Clause: Present
What **will** she **do**	*if* she **passes** the test?
What **is** she **going to do**	

datebases ← current Events and issues

1 Use **future real conditional** sentences to talk about what **will happen under certain conditions.**

The **if clause** gives the **condition.** The **result clause** gives the **probable or certain result.**

Use the **simple present** in the **if clause.** Use the **future** with **will** or **be going to** in the **result clause.**

BE CAREFUL! Even though the **if clause** refers to the future, use the **simple present.**

IF CLAUSE	RESULT CLAUSE

- **If** I **use** this pen, I**'ll pass** the test.
  (It's a real possibility that I will use this pen.)

SIMPLE PRESENT	FUTURE

- **If** you **feel** lucky, you**'ll expect** good things.
- **If** you **feel** unlucky, you**'re going to expect** bad things to happen.

- **If** she **gets** an A on her test, she will stop worrying.
  Nᴏᴛ: If she ~~will get~~ an A on her test, she will stop worrying.

2 You can also use **modals** (*can, should, might, must . . .*) in the **result clause.**

USAGE NOTE: We sometimes use **then** to **emphasize the result** in future real conditionals with **modals** or **will.**

- If she studies hard, she **might get** an A.
- If she has questions, she **should ask** her teacher.

- If she studies hard, **then** she **might get** an A.
- If she studies hard, **then** she**'ll get** an A.

3 You can **begin conditional sentences** with the **if clause or the result clause.** The meaning is the same.

BE CAREFUL! Use a **comma** between the two clauses only when the **if clause comes first.**

- **If she uses that pen,** she'll feel lucky.
  ᴏʀ
- She'll feel lucky **if she uses that pen.**

4 You can use **if** and **unless** in conditional sentences, but their <u>meanings are very different</u>.

Use **unless** to state a **negative condition.**

Unless often means **if . . . not.**

- **If** he studies, he will pass the test.

- **Unless** he studies, he will fail the test.
  (If he doesn't study, he will fail the test.)

- **Unless** you're superstitious, you won't be afraid of black cats.
  ᴏʀ
- **If** you are**n't** superstitious, you won't be afraid of black cats.

pornographie

EXERCISE 1: Discover the Grammar   unless

A | *Match the conditions with the results.*

	Condition		Result
d	**1.** If I lend someone my baseball bat,	**a.**	you could have an allergy.
e	**2.** If it rains,	**b.**	people might laugh at you.
f	**3.** If I give my boyfriend a new pair of shoes,	**c.**	I'll get 100 percent on the test.
a	**4.** If the palm of your hand itches,	**d.**	I won't hit a home run.
c	**5.** If I use my lucky pen,	**e.**	I'm going to get wet.
b	**6.** If you wear your sweater backwards,	**f.**	he'll walk out of the relationship.

B | *Now write the sentences that are superstitions.*

1. _If I lend someone my baseball bat, I won't hit a home run._

2. _if I use my lucky pen, I'll get 100 percent on the test._

3. _if I give my boyfriend a new pair of shoes, he'll walk out of the relationship._

EXERCISE 2: *If* or *Unless*   (Grammar Note 4)

Two students are talking about a test. Complete their conversations with **if** *or* **unless.**

YUKI: It's midnight. ___Unless___ we get some sleep, we won't do well tomorrow.
1.

EVA: But I won't be able to sleep ___unless___ I stop worrying about the test.
2.

YUKI: Here's my lucky charm. ___if___ you wear it, you'll do fine!
3.

EVA: I found my blue shirt! ___if___ I wear my blue shirt today, I'm confident
4.

that I'll pass!

YUKI: Great. Now ___unless if___ we just clean up the room, we can leave for school.
5.

EVA: We can't clean up! There's a Russian superstition that says ___if___ you
6.

clean your room, you'll get a bad test grade!

YUKI: ___if___ we finish the test by noon, we can go to the job fair.
7.

EVA: I want to get a job, but nobody is going to hire me ___unless___ I pass this test.
8.

EVA: I'm looking for my lucky pen. ___Unless___ I find it, I won't pass the test!
9.

YUKI: Don't worry. ___if___ you use the same pen that you used to study with,
10.

you'll do great! The pen will remember the answers.

EVA: I was so nervous without my lucky pen. It'll be a miracle[1] _____if_____ I pass.

YUKI: That's the wrong attitude! There aren't any miracles. _____if_____ you study,
you'll do well. It's that simple.

EVA: Do you think a company like ZY3, Inc. will offer me a job _____if_____ I fill out
an application?

YUKI: Only _____if_____ you use your lucky pen. I'm kidding! You won't know
_____unless_____ you try!

[1] *miracle:* something lucky that happens when you didn't think it was possible

EXERCISE 3: Simple Present or Future

(Grammar Note 1)

Complete these superstitions from all over the world. Use the correct form of the verbs in parentheses.

RUSSIA: If you _____spill_____ salt at the table, you _____'ll have_____ an argument.
1. (spill)   2. (have)

ENGLAND: If a cat _____washes_____ behind its ears, it _____will rain_____.
3. (wash)   4. (rain)

CANADA: If you _____walk_____ under a ladder, you _____will have_____ bad luck.
5. (walk)   6. (have)

CHINA: If you _____sweep_____ the dirt and dust out of your house through the front door,
7. (sweep)
you _____will sweep_____ away your family's good luck.
8. (sweep)

GREECE: If your right hand _____is_____ itchy, you _____'ll get_____ money. If your left
9. (be)   10. (get)
hand _____itches_____, you _____'ll give_____ someone money.
11. (itch)   12. (give)

ICELAND: If somebody _____throws_____ away a dead mouse, the wind _____will start_____ to
13. (throw)   14. (start)
blow from that direction.

SLOVAKIA: If you _____sit_____ at the corner of the table, you _____'ll not get_____ married.
15. (sit)   16. (not get)

MEXICO: If you _____throw_____ red beans at a newly married couple, they _____'ll have_____
17. (throw)   18. (have)
good luck.

TURKEY: If you _____drop_____ food on your clothing while you're eating, you
19. (drop)
_____will have_____ guests that day.
20. (have)

BRAZIL: If you _____put_____ a broom behind the front door, you _____'ll keep away_____
21. (put)   22. (keep away)
bad visits.

JAPAN: If you _____put_____ a snake skin in your wallet, you _____'ll become_____ rich.
23. (put)   24. (become)

KOREA: If you _____cut_____ your hair, you _____'ll grow_____ taller.
25. (cut)   26. (grow)

EXERCISE 4: Statements

(Grammar Notes 1, 3)

Eva is thinking of working for a company called ZY3, Inc. Her friend Don, who used to work there, thinks it's a terrible idea and is explaining the consequences. Write his responses. Use the words in parentheses and future real conditional sentences.

1. **Eva:** If I work for ZY3, I'm going to be happy. I'm sure of it.

   Don: *If you work for ZY3, you're not going to be happy. You're going to be miserable.*
   (miserable)

2. **Eva:** You have such a pessimistic attitude! I'll have the chance to travel a lot if I take this job.

   Don: Not true. _____
   (never leave the office)

3. **Eva:** But I'll get a raise every year if I stay at ZY3.

   Don: _____
   (every two years)

4. **Eva:** Well, if I join ZY3, I'm going to have wonderful health care benefits.

   Don: Stay healthy!_____
   (terrible health care benefits)

5. **Eva:** I don't believe you! If I accept ZY3's offer, it'll be the best career move of my life.

   Don: Believe me, _____
   (the worst)

EXERCISE 5: Statements

(Grammar Notes 1–2)

*Yuki Tamari is not sure whether to go to law school. She made a decision tree to help her decide. In the tree, arrows connect the conditions and the results. Write future real conditional sentences about her decision. Use **may, might,** or **could** if the result is uncertain. Remember to use commas where necessary.*

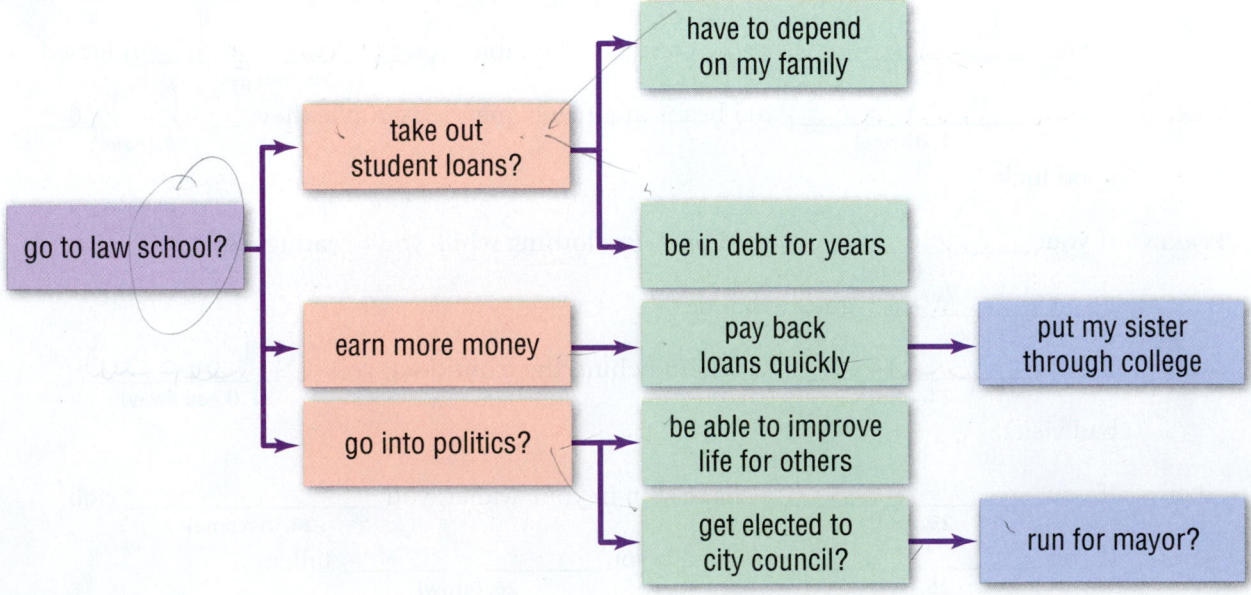

1. <u>If I go to law school, I might take out student loans.</u>

2. <u>I'll be in debt for years if I take out student loans.</u>

3. <u>If I take up student loan, I may have to depend my family.</u>

4. <u>If I take out student loans, I might be in debt for years.</u>

5. <u>If I earn more money, I will pay back loans quickly.</u>

6. <u>If I go into politics, I could be able to improve life for others.</u>

7. <u>If I go into politics, I'll/might get selected for city council.</u>

8. <u>If I pay back loan quickly, I will</u>

9. _____

10. _____

EXERCISE 6: Editing

Read Yuki's journal entry. There are seven mistakes in the use of future real conditionals. The first mistake is already corrected. Find and correct six more. Don't forget to check punctuation.

October 1

    Should I campaign for student council president? I'll have to decide
soon if I ~~wanted~~ ^{want} to run. If I'll be busy campaigning, I won't have much
time to study. That's a problem because I'm not going to get into law
school ^{unless} if I get good grades this year. On the other hand, the problems in
this school are widespread, and nothing ^{will get} is getting done if Todd Laker
becomes president again. I'm 100 percent certain of that, and most
people agree with me. But will I know what to do if ^{I get} I'll get the job?
Never mind. I shouldn't anticipate difficulties. I really need to have a
better attitude. I'll deal with that problem, if I win. I know what I'll do.
If I become president, I ^{will} cut my hair. That always brings me good luck!

EXERCISE 7: Listening

A | *Yuki is talking about her campaign platform. Read the list of issues. Then listen to the interview. Listen again and check (✓) the things that Yuki promises to work for if she is elected.*

- ☑ **1.** have contact with a lot of students
- ☐ **2.** improve the student council's newsletter
- ☐ **3.** publish teacher evaluations on the student council's website
- ☐ **4.** get the college to provide a bus service between the airport and the college
- ☐ **5.** get the college to offer a major in environmental science
- ☐ **6.** reduce tuition costs

B | *Read the statements. Then listen again to the interview and check (✓) True or False. Correct the false statements.*

	True	False
1. If Yuki gets elected, she'll have ~~formal~~ *informal* meetings with students.	☐	☑
2. Yuki wants to improve the student council's website.	☐	☐
3. She thinks student council representatives should have their phone numbers on the website.	☐	☐
4. She believes the college should have free bus service between the airport and the college at the beginning and end of every semester.	☐	☐
5. She wants the college to offer more majors.	☐	☐
6. She wants to meet with students to discuss college costs.	☐	☐
7. Yuki wears a lucky charm for good luck.	☐	☐
8. She anticipates winning the election.	☐	☐

EXERCISE 8: Pronunciation

A | *Read and listen to the Pronunciation Note.*

Pronunciation Note

As with other questions, in **conditional questions**:

The voice usually **rises** at the **end of *yes/no* questions**.

EXAMPLES: If you win the election, will you work with the president?

Will you work with the president if you win the election?

The voice usually **falls** at the **end of *wh-* questions**.

EXAMPLES: What will you do if you win the election?

If you win the election, what will you do?

B | *Listen to the short conversations. Draw a rising arrow (↗) or a falling arrow (↘) over the end of each question to show if the voice rises or falls.*

1. **A:** What will you do if you win the election?
    B: I'll go out and celebrate.

2. **A:** Will you take out a loan if you go to law school?
    B: Yes, I'll have to.

3. **A:** If you can't get a loan, what will you do?
    B: I'll get a part-time job.

4. **A:** Will you buy a new car if you get a raise?
    B: No, I'll get a used car.

5. **A:** If your computer stops working, will you buy a new one?
    B: Yes. It's too old to repair.

6. **A:** Where will you go if you have to find a new apartment?
    B: I'll move back to my parent's house.

C | *Listen again to the conversations and repeat the questions. Then practice the conversations with a partner.*

EXERCISE 9: Problem Solving

Work in small groups. Read these problems and discuss possible solutions. Use **if,** **if . . . not,** *or* **unless.**

1. Your neighbors are always playing music so loudly that you can't fall asleep.

   EXAMPLE: **A:** What will you do if they don't stop?
   B: If they don't stop, I'll call the police.
   C: Unless they stop, I'll call the landlord.
   D: I'll consider moving if they continue to bother me.

2. You've had a headache every day for a week. You can't concentrate.

3. You keep phoning your parents, but there's no answer. It's now midnight.

4. You like your job, but you just found out that other workers are making much more money than you are.

5. You live in an apartment building. It's winter, and the building hasn't had any heat for a week. You're freezing.

6. You're 10 pounds overweight. You've been trying for months to lose weight, but so far you haven't lost a single pound.

7. You bought a radio at a local store. It doesn't work, but when you tried to return it, the salesperson refused to take it back.

8. Your roommates don't clean up after they cook. You've already reminded them several times, but they always "forget."

9. You paid for a parking space near school or work. For the past week the same car has taken your space.

EXERCISE 10: Cross-Cultural Comparison

Here are some superstitions about luck. Work in small groups and discuss similar superstitions that you know about.

- If you cross your fingers, you'll have good luck.

   EXAMPLE: **A:** In Germany, people believe that if you press your thumbs together, you will have good luck.
   B: In Mexico, . . .
   C: In Russia, . . .

- If you touch blue, your dreams will come true.

- If you break a mirror, you will have seven years of bad luck.

- If you put a piece of clothing on inside out, you will have good luck.

- If your palm itches, you're going to find some money soon.

EXERCISE 11: Writing

A | *Imagine you are running for class or school president. Write a short speech. Include five campaign promises with* **will** *or* **be going to**. *List problems that* **may, might,** *or* **could** *happen if you are not elected. In small groups, give your speeches and elect a candidate. Then hold a general class election.*

EXAMPLE: If I become school president, I will ask for 10 new computers . . .
If I'm not elected, classroom conditions might . . .

B | *Check your work. Use the Editing Checklist.*

Editing Checklist

Did you use . . . ?

☐ the simple present in the *if* clause

☐ the future with ***will*** or ***be going to*** in the result clause for probable results

☐ ***may***, ***might***, or ***could*** in the result clause for possible results

☐ ***unless*** to state a negative condition

☐ a comma between the two clauses when the *if* or *unless* clause comes first

A | Match the cause and effect.

Cause	Effect
_d_ **1.** If it rains,	**a.** I'll answer it.
_f_ **2.** Unless you study,	**b.** I'll pay you back tomorrow.
_a_ **3.** If the phone rings,	**c.** you should ask the teacher.
_c_ **4.** If you have questions,	**d.** I'll take an umbrella.
_b_ **5.** If you lend me $10,	**e.** you can't drive.
_e_ **6.** If you don't have a license,	**f.** you won't pass.

B | Complete the future real conditional sentences in these conversations with the correct form of the verbs in parentheses.

- **A:** Are you going to take the bus?

  B: No. If I ___take___ the bus, I _'ll be_ late.
    1. (take)   2. (be)

- **A:** What ___do___ you ___do___ if you _'ll not get_ the job?
                3. (do)   4. (not get)

  B: I ___stay___ in school unless I _'ll get_ the job.
        5. (stay)   6. (get)

- **A:** If I ___pas___ the test, I _'ll celebrate_
        7. (pass)   8. (celebrate)

  B: Good luck, but I'm sure you'll pass. You've studied really hard for it.

  A: Thanks!

C | Find and correct six mistakes. Remember to check punctuation.

It's been a hard week, and I'm looking forward to the weekend. If the weather will be

nice tomorrow Marco and I are going to go to the beach. The ocean is usually too cold for

swimming at this time of year, so I probably don't go in the water unless it's really hot outside.

But I love walking along the beach and breathing in the fresh sea air.

If Marco has time, he might makes some sandwiches to bring along. Otherwise, we'll just

get some pizza. I hope it'll be a nice day. I just listened to the weather report, and there may be

some rain in the afternoon. Unless it rains, we probably go to the movies instead. That's our

Plan B. But I really want to go to the beach, so I'm keeping my fingers crossed!

STEP 1 GRAMMAR IN CONTEXT

Before You Read

Read the first sentence of the story and look at the picture. Discuss these questions.

1. Is this a true story? What makes you think so?
2. How do fairy tales begin in your culture?

Read

Read this version of a famous fairy tale.

The Fisherman and His Wife

Once upon a time there was a poor fisherman and his wife who lived in a pigpen[1] near the sea. Every day the man went to fish. One day, after waiting a very long time, he caught a very big fish. To his surprise, the fish spoke and said, "Please let me live. I'm not a regular[2] fish. **If you knew my real identity, you wouldn't kill me**. I'm an enchanted prince."

"Don't worry. I won't kill you," responded the kind-hearted fisherman. With these words, he threw the fish back into the clear water and went home to his wife.

"Husband," said the wife, "didn't you catch anything today?"

"I caught a fish, but it said it was an enchanted prince, so I let it go."

"You mean you didn't wish for anything?" asked the wife.

"No," said the fisherman. "What do I need to wish for?"

"Just look around you," said the wife. "We live in a pigpen. **I wish we had a nice little cottage.**[3] **If we had a cottage, I would be a lot happier**. You saved the prince's life. He's sure to grant your wish. Go back and ask him."

(continued on next page)

[1]*pigpen:* a small building where pigs are kept
[2]*regular:* ordinary
[3]*cottage:* a small house, usually in the country

"I'm not going to ask for a cottage! **If I asked for a cottage, the fish might get angry.**" But in the end, he consented because he was much more afraid of his wife's anger.

When he got to the sea, it was all green and yellow. "**My wife wishes we had a cottage,**" said the fisherman. "Just go on back," said the fish. "She already has it."

When he returned home, the fisherman found his wife sitting outside a lovely little cottage. The kitchen was filled with food and all types of cooking utensils.[4] Outside was a little garden with vegetables, fruit trees, hens, and ducks.

Things were fine for a week or two. Then the wife said, "This cottage is much too crowded. **I wish we lived in a bigger house. If we lived in a big stone castle, I would be much happier.** Go and ask the fish for it."

The fisherman didn't want to go, but he did. When he got to the sea, it was dark blue and gray. "**My wife wishes we lived in a big stone castle,**" he said to the fish.

"Just go on back. She's standing in front of the door," said the fish.

When he returned home, the fisherman found his wife on the steps of a great big stone castle. The inside was filled with beautiful gold furniture, chandeliers,[5] and carpets. There were servants everywhere.

The next morning the wife woke up and said, "**I wish I were King of all this land.**"

"**What would you do if you were King?**" asked her husband. "**If I were King, I would own all this land.** Go on back and ask the fish for it."

This time, the sea was all blackish gray, and the water was rough and smelled terrible. "What does she want now?" asked the fish.

"She wants to be King," said the embarrassed fisherman.

"Just go on back. She already is."

When the fisherman returned home, he found an enormous palace.[6] Everything inside was made of marble and pure gold, and it was surrounded by soldiers with drums and trumpets. His wife was seated on a throne, and he said to her, "How nice for you that you are King. Now we won't need to wish for anything else."

But his wife was not satisfied. "I'm only King of *this* country," she said. "**I wish I were Emperor of the whole world. If I were Emperor, I would be the most powerful ruler on Earth.**"

"Wife, now be satisfied," responded the fisherman. "You're King. You can't be anything more."

The wife, however, wasn't convinced. She kept thinking and thinking about what more she could be. "**If I were Emperor, I could have anything—and you wouldn't have to ask the fish for anything more.** Go right now and tell the fish that I want to be Emperor of the whole world."

"Oh, no," said the fisherman. "The fish can't do that. **If I were you, I wouldn't ask for anything else.**" But his wife got so furious that the poor fisherman ran back to the fish. There was a terrible storm, and the sea was pitch black[7] with waves as high as mountains. "Well, what does she want now?" asked the fish.

"**She wishes she were Emperor of the whole world,**" said the fisherman.

"Just go on back. She's sitting in the pigpen again."

And they are still sitting there today.

---

[4]*utensil:* a tool used for cooking or preparing food
[5]*chandelier:* a large structure that hangs from the ceiling and holds many lights or candles
[6]*palace:* a very large house where the ruler of a country lives
[7]*pitch black:* the color of coal or tar; very dark black

A | **Vocabulary:** *Circle the letter of the word or phrase that best completes each sentence.*

1. If something is **enchanted**, it has been _a_.

    a. changed by magic

    b. broken

    c. stolen

2. When you **consent**, you _b_ to do something.

    a. refuse

    b. agree

    c. like

3. Someone who is **furious**, is very _c_.

    a. kind-hearted

    b. poor

    c. angry

4. Someone who is **embarrassed** feels _a_.

    a. uncomfortable

    b. powerful

    c. frightened

5. If you **grant** something, you _a_ to do it.

    a. want

    b. refuse

    c. agree

6. When you **respond**, you _b_ a question.

    a. ask

    b. answer

    c. forget

B | **Comprehension:** *Check (✓)* **True** *or* **False**. *Correct the false statements.*

	True	False
1. Before the man caught the fish, he and his wife lived in a nice little cottage.	☐	✓
2. At first, the fish believed that the man was going to kill him.	✓	☐
3. The man didn't want to ask for the first wish because he didn't want to make the fish angry.	☐	✓
4. The wife was satisfied with the stone castle.	☐	✓
5. The man advised his wife not to ask to be Emperor of the whole world.	✓	☐
6. The fish granted the wife's wish to be the most powerful ruler on Earth.	☐	✓

melt

PRESENT AND FUTURE UNREAL CONDITIONALS

Statements		Contractions		
If Clause: Simple Past	**Result Clause: *Would* (*not*) + Base Form**			
If Mia **had** money,	she **would live** in a palace.	I would	=	**I'd**
If she **were*** rich,	she **wouldn't live** in a cottage.	you would	=	**you'd**
		he would	=	**he'd**
If Mia **didn't have** money,	she **wouldn't live** in a palace.	she would	=	**she'd**
If she **weren't** rich,	she **would live** in a cottage.	we would	=	**we'd**
		they would	=	**they'd**
		would not	=	**wouldn't**

*With the verb *be*, use *were* for all subjects.

Yes / No Questions		Short Answers	
Result Clause	**If Clause**	**Affirmative**	**Negative**
Would she **live** here	*if* she **had** money?	**Yes**, she **would**.	**No**, she **wouldn't**.
	if she **were** rich?		

Wh- Questions	
Result Clause	**If Clause**
What **would** she **do**	*if* she **had** money?
	if she **were** rich?

GRAMMAR NOTES

1 | Use **present and future unreal conditional** sentences to talk about **unreal conditions and their results**. A condition and its result may be untrue, imagined, or impossible.

The *if* **clause** gives the **unreal condition**, and the **result clause** gives the **unreal result** of that condition.

The sentence can be about:
• the **present**

• the **future**

IF CLAUSE   RESULT CLAUSE
• *If* I **had** more time, I **would read** fairy tales.
  (But I don't have time, so I don't read fairy tales.)

IF CLAUSE   RESULT CLAUSE
• *If* I **lived** in a palace *now*, I **would give** parties.
  (I don't live in a palace. I don't give parties.)

IF CLAUSE   RESULT CLAUSE
• *If* I **moved** *next month*, I **would buy** a car.
  (I won't move. I won't buy a car.)

2   Use the **simple past** in the *if* clause.
Use *would* + **base form** in the **result clause**.

- *If* he **had** a nice house, he **wouldn't move**.

BE CAREFUL!
- The *if* clause uses the simple past, but the **meaning is NOT past**.
- Do **NOT use** *would* in the *if* clause.

- *If* I **had** more money *now*, I would take a trip around the world.
- *If* she **knew** the answer, she would tell you.
  Noᴛ: If she ~~would know~~ the answer . . .

- Use *were* for **all subjects** when the verb in the *if* clause is a form of *be*.

- *If* she **were** prime minister, she would deal with this problem.

USAGE NOTE: Some people use *was* with *I*, *he*, *she*, and *it*. However, this is usually considered incorrect, especially in formal or written English.

Noᴛ: If she ~~was~~ prime minister . . .

---

3   You can also use *might* or *could* in the **result clause**, but the meaning is different from *would*.

a. Use *would* if the result is **certain**.
Do NOT use *will* in unreal conditional sentences.

- They love to travel. If they had time, they ***would take*** a trip next summer.
  Noᴛ: If they had time, they ~~will~~ take a trip . . .

b. Use *might* or *could* if the result is **not certain**.
Do NOT use *may* or *can*.

- If they took a trip, they ***might go*** to Japan.
  Noᴛ: If they took a trip, they ~~may~~ go to Japan.
- If they took a trip, they ***could go*** to Japan.
  Noᴛ: If they took a trip, they ~~can~~ go to Japan.

You can also use *could* in the result clause to express **ability**.

- You don't know Japanese. If you knew Japanese, you ***could* translate** this article for them.

---

4   You can **begin conditional sentences** with the *if* **clause** or **the result clause**. The meaning is the same.

- *If* **I had more money,** I would move.
  OR
- I would move *if* **I had more money**.

BE CAREFUL! Use a **comma** between the two clauses only when the *if* **clause comes first**.

Noᴛ: I would move ✗ if I had more money.

---

5   Use *If I were you,* . . . to give **advice**.

- *If I were you,* I wouldn't ask for anything else.

---

6   Use *wish* + **simple past** to talk about things that you **want to be true** now, but that are **not true**.

- I *wish* I **lived** in a castle.
  (I don't live in a castle now, but I want to.)

BE CAREFUL!
- Use *were* instead of *was* after *wish*.

- I **wish** I ***were*** a child again.
  Noᴛ: I wish I ~~was~~ a child again.

- Use *could* or *would* after *wish*.
  Do NOT use *can* or *will*.

- I **wish** I ***could* buy** a car.
  Noᴛ: I wish I ~~can~~ buy a car.
- I **wish** she ***would* call** tomorrow.
  Noᴛ: I wish she ~~will~~ call tomorrow.

EXERCISE 1: Discover the Grammar

*Read the numbered statements. Decide if the sentences that follow are **True (T)** or **False (F)**.*

1. If I had time, I would read fairy tales in English.

   __F__ **a.** I have time.

   __F__ **b.** I'm going to read fairy tales in English.

2. If it weren't so cold, I would go fishing.

   __T__ **a.** It's cold.

   __F__ **b.** I'm going fishing.

3. If I caught an enchanted fish, I would make three wishes.

   __F__ **a.** I believe I'm going to catch an enchanted fish.

   __F__ **b.** I'm going to make three wishes.

4. If I had three wishes, I wouldn't ask for a palace.

   __F__ **a.** I have three wishes.

   __T__ **b.** I don't want a palace.

5. If my house were too small, I would try to find a bigger one.

   __F__ **a.** My house is big enough.

   __T__ **b.** I'm not looking for a bigger house right now.

6. If I got a raise, I could buy a new car.

   __F__ **a.** I recently got a raise.

   __T__ **b.** I want a new car.

7. If we didn't earn enough money, I might train for a better job.

   __F__ **a.** We don't earn enough money.

   __F__ **b.** I'm training for a better job.

8. Your friend tells you, "If I were you, I wouldn't change jobs."

   __T__ **a.** Your friend is giving you advice.

   __T__ **b.** Your friend thinks you shouldn't change jobs.

9. I wish I were a princess.

   __F__ **a.** I'm a princess.

   __T__ **b.** I want to be a princess.

10. I wish I lived in a big house.

    __T__ **a.** I want to live in a big house.

    __T__ **b.** I don't live in a big house.

Complete this article from a popular psychology magazine. Use the correct form of the verbs in parentheses to form unreal conditional sentences.

Marty Hijab has always wanted to invite his whole family over for the holidays, but his apartment is small, his family is very large, and he doesn't want to feel embarrassed. "If I _____invited_____ them all for
1. (invite)
dinner, there _____wouldn't be_____ enough room for everyone to sit
2. (not be)
down," he told a friend. If Marty _____were_____ a complainer,
3. (be)
he _would moan_ about the size of his apartment and spend
4. (moan)
the holiday at his parents' house. But Marty is a problem solver.

This year he is hosting an open house. People can drop in at different times during the day, and there will be room for everyone.

"If life _____were_____ a fairy tale, we _could wish_ problems away," noted
5. (be) **6. (can / wish)**
therapist Joel Grimes. "What complainers are really saying is, 'If I _____had_____ a magical
7. (have)
solution, I _wouldn't have to deal_ with this myself.' I wish it _____were_____ that
8. (not have to deal) **9. (be)**
easy," says Grimes. He gives an example of a very wealthy client who is convinced that he has

almost no time for his family. "He's waiting for a miracle to give him the time he needs. But

he _____could fin__ the time if he _____thought_____ about the problem creatively,"
10. (can / find) **11. (think)**
says Grimes.

Even the rich have limited time, money, and space. If complainers _realized_ this,
12. (realize)
then they _would understand_ that there will always be problems. Then they
13. (understand)
could stop complaining and try to find possible solutions. Marty, who is still in college,

might have to wait for years before inviting his family over if he _____insisted_____
14. (may / have to wait) **15. (insist)**
on a bigger apartment for his party. Instead, he is creatively solving his problems right now.

There's an old saying: "If wishes _____were_____ horses, then beggars _could ride_.
16. (be) **17. (can / ride)**
But wishes aren't horses. We have to learn to create our own good fortune and not wait for a

genie with three wishes to come along and solve our problems.

EXERCISE 3: Statements

Psychologist Joel Grimes hears all types of excuses from his clients. Rewrite each excuse as a present unreal conditional sentence. Keep the same order and decide which clause begins with **if**. Use commas where necessary.

1. I'm so busy. That's why I don't read bedtime stories to my little girl.

   If I weren't so busy, I would read bedtime stories to my little girl.

2. My husband won't ask for a raise. It's because he's not ambitious.

   If My husband were ambitious, he would ask for a raise

3. I don't play sports. But only because I'm not in shape.

   I would play sport if I were in shape.

4. I don't have enough time. That's why I'm not planning to study for the exam.

   if I had enough time I would study for the exam.

5. I'm too old. That's why I'm not going back to school.

   If I were not too old, I would go back to school.

6. I can't do my job. The reason is, my boss doesn't explain things properly.

   If I would do my job if my boss explained things properly

7. I'm not good at math. That's why I don't balance my checkbook.

   If I were good at math, I would balance my checkbook,

8. I can't stop smoking. The problem is, I feel nervous all the time.

   If I could stop smoking, I would not feel nervous all the time

9. I'm so tired. That's why I get up so late.

   If I were not so tired, I would not wake up so late

EXERCISE 4: Wishes About the Present

(Grammar Note 6)

Remember the fish from the fairy tale on pages 369–370? Read the things the fish would like to change. Then write sentences with **wish**.

1. I'm a fish. _I wish I weren't a fish._

2. I'm not a handsome prince. I wish I were a handsome prince

3. I live in the sea. I wish I didn't live in the sea.

4. I don't live in a castle. I wish I would live in a castle.

5. I'm not married to a princess. I wish I were married to a princess.
   wouldn't

376 UNIT 23

6. The fisherman comes here every day. _He wish He didn't come there every day._

7. His wife always wants more. _I wish, she didn't want more._

8. She isn't satisfied. _I wish, she were satisfied_

9. They don't leave me alone. _I wish They left me alone_

10. I can't grant my own wishes. _I wish I could grant my own wishes_

EXERCISE 5: Questions

(Grammar Notes 1–4)

Marty is having his open-house holiday party. His nieces and nephews are playing a fantasy question game. Write questions using the words in parentheses and the present unreal conditional. Use commas where necessary. Keep the same order.

1. (what / you / do / if / you / be a millionaire)

   What would you do if you were a millionaire?

2. (if / you / be the leader of this country / what / you / do)

   what would you do if you were the leader of this county?

3. (how / you / feel / if / you / never need to sleep)

   how would you feel if you never needed to sleep?

4. (what / you / do / if / you / have more free time)

   what would do you do if you had more free time?

5. (if / you / have three wishes / what / you / ask for)

   what would you ask For if you had three wishes?

6. (what / you / do / if / you / not have to work)

   what would you do if you didn't have to work

7. (if / you / have a ticket for anywhere in the world / where / you / travel)

   where you would have if you had a ticket for anywhere

8. (if / you / can build anything / what / it / be)

   what would

9. (if / you / can meet a famous person / who / you / want to meet)

   who would you wanted to meet if you could meet a famous person

10. (who / you / have dinner with / if / you can invite three famous people)

    who would you have dinner with if you could invite three famous people.

EXERCISE 6: Editing

Read part of a book report that Marty's niece wrote. There are eight mistakes in the use of the present unreal conditional. The first mistake is already corrected. Find and correct seven more.

NAME: Laila Hijab   CLASS: English 4

The Disappearance

What would happen to the women if all the men in the world ~~would disappear~~ *disappeared*? What would happen to the men when there were no women in the world? Philip Wylie's 1951 science-fiction novel, *The Disappearance*, addresses these fascinating questions. The answers show us how society has changed since the 1950s.

According to Wylie, if men and women live [lived] in different worlds, the results would be a disaster. In Wylie's vision, men are too aggressive to survive on their own, and women are too helpless. If women didn't control them, men will [would] start more wars. If men aren't [were not] there to pump gas and run the businesses, women wouldn't be able to manage.

If Wylie is [were] alive today, would he write the same novel? Today, a lot of men take care of their children, and a lot of women run businesses. In 1951, Wylie couldn't imagine these changes because of his opinions about men and women. I wish that Wylie was [were] here today. If he were, then he might learns [learn] that men are not more warlike than women, and women are not more helpless than men. His story might be very different.

EXERCISE 7: Listening

A | *Read the sentences. Then listen to a modern fairy tale about Cindy, a clever young girl, and a toad. Listen again and circle the correct answers.*

1. Cindy loses her soccer (ball) / game.

2. A toad wants to <u>marry / play soccer with</u> Cindy.

3. The toad tells Cindy about his amazing <u>modern laboratory / magic powers</u>.

4. The toad agrees to turn Cindy into a <u>princess / scientist</u>.

5. Cindy <u>went to a lot of ceremonies / worked in her laboratory</u>.

6. The toad became a good <u>king / magician</u>.

B | *Read the statements. Listen again to the fairy tale, and check (✓) **True** or **False**. Correct the false statements.*

	True	False
1. Cindy wishes she ~~had a new~~ soccer ball. *could find her*	☐	☑
2. The toad wishes Cindy would marry him.	☐	☐
3. If Cindy married the toad, he would become a prince again.	☐	☐
4. Cindy wishes she could become a beautiful princess.	☐	☐
5. If Cindy became a princess, she'd have plenty of time to study science.	☐	☐
6. The toad doesn't know how to use his powers to help himself.	☐	☐
7. Cindy wants to become a scientist and help the prince.	☐	☐
8. Cindy and the prince get married and live happily ever after.	☐	☐

EXERCISE 8: Pronunciation

A | *Read and listen to the Pronunciation Note.*

Pronunciation Note

In **conversation**, we usually pronounce *would* "d" after pronouns in **conditional sentences** and after *wish*.

EXAMPLES: If you came, we **would** drive you.   →   "If you came, we**'d** drive you."
I wish you **would** come.   →   "I wish you**'d** come."

We usually **drop the final "t"** in *wouldn't* before words beginning with a **consonant** sound.

EXAMPLES: I wish they **wouldn't** call so late.   →   "I wish they **wouldn'** call so late."
If I were you, I **wouldn't** pick it up.   →   "If I were you, I **wouldn'** pick it up."

But do NOT use *wouldn'* in **writing**. Use *wouldn't*.

B | *Listen to these short conversations. Circle the words you hear.*

1. **A:** I want to give one big party this year.

   B: If I were you, I <u>'d / wouldn't</u> give it during the holidays.

2. **A:** Karen's soccer team has a big game today.

   B: I know. I wish she <u>'d / wouldn't</u> play.

3. **A:** Is Don coming over?

   B: Probably not. If he came, he <u>'d / wouldn't</u> stay for dinner.

4. **A:** She always looks upset. Does she tell you what's wrong?

   B: No. But if she told me, I <u>'d / wouldn't</u> be able to help.

5. **A:** I hate to keep reminding Debra about her homework.

   B: If you didn't remind her, she <u>'d / wouldn't</u> remember by herself.

6. **A:** The kids don't read enough.

   B: If I were you, I <u>'d / wouldn't</u> read to them.

C | *Listen again to the conversations and repeat the responses. Then practice the conversations with a partner. Use the short forms.*

EXERCISE 9: What About You?

Work in small groups. Answer the questions in Exercise 5. Discuss your answers with the whole class.

EXAMPLE: **A:** What would you do if you were a millionaire?
B: If I were a millionaire, I'd donate half my money to charity.
C: With half the money, you could . . .

EXERCISE 10: Problem Solving

Work in small groups. One person describes a problem. Group members give advice with **If I were you, I would / wouldn't . . .** Use the problems below and write three more.

1. You need $500 to pay this month's rent. You only have $300.

   EXAMPLE: **A:** I can't pay the rent this month. I only have $300, and I need $500. I wish I knew what to do.
   B: If I were you, I'd try to borrow the money.
   C: If I were you, I'd call the landlord right away.

2. You're lonely. You work at home and never meet new people.

3. You never have an opportunity to practice English outside of class.

4. You've been invited to dinner. The main dish is going to be shrimp. You hate shrimp.

5. _____

6. _____

7. _____

EXERCISE 11: Discussion

A In fairy tales, people are often given three wishes. Imagine that you had just three wishes. What would they be? Write them down.

EXAMPLE: **1.** I wish I were famous.
2. I wish I spoke perfect English.
3. I wish I knew how to fly a plane.

B Discuss your wishes with a partner.

EXAMPLE: **A:** I wish I were famous.
B: What would you do if you were famous?
A: I would. . . .

C There is an old saying: "Be careful what you wish for; it may come true." Look at your wishes again. Discuss the results—negative as well as positive—that might happen if they came true.

EXAMPLE: **A:** If I were famous, I might not have enough free time. I wouldn't have a private life because . . .
B: Yes, but if you were famous, maybe you could travel a lot and meet a lot of interesting people.

EXERCISE 12: Writing

A | *If you had one wish, what would you wish for your own life or for society? Write two paragraphs. In the first paragraph, explain your wish with examples. In the second paragraph, describe the changes that might occur if your wish came true.*

EXAMPLE: In Philip Wylie's book, men and women live in separate societies. I don't wish that men and women lived separately, but sometimes I think that boys and girls would learn better if they went to separate schools. For example, when I was in middle school, boys and girls were embarrassed to make mistakes in front of each other . . .

   If boys and girls went to separate schools, they might feel more comfortable about speaking in class. They could . . .

B | *Check your work. Use the Editing Checklist.*

Editing Checklist

Did you use . . . ?

☐ present and future unreal conditional sentences

☐ simple present in the *if* clause

☐ *would* + **base form** of the verb in the result clause if the result is certain

☐ *might* or *could* + **base form** of the verb in the result clause if the result is possible

☐ *wish* + **simple past**, *could*, or *would* for wishes about the present

☐ *were* for all subjects in *if* clauses and after *wish*

Check your answers on page UR-6.

Do you need to review anything?

A | *Circle the correct words to complete the conversation.*

A: If I lived in another city, I 'd feel / 'm feeling much happier.
1.

B: Then if I am / were you, I'd move.
2.

A: I wish I can / could move, but that's just impossible right now.
3.

B: Would it be impossible if you found / 'll find a job somewhere else?
4.

A: No, I think Harry can / could help me find a job if I asked him. But I hate to ask.
5.

B: If he isn't / weren't an old friend, he might not want to help. But he's been your friend for ages.
6.

A: That's true. You know, I thought that if I talked to you, I 'll / 'd get some good ideas.
7.

B | *Complete the present and future unreal conditional sentences in this paragraph with the correct form of the verbs in parentheses.*

What _____ you _____ if you _____ a wallet in
                         1. (do)   **2. (find)**

the street? _____ you _____ the money if you _____
                           3. (take)   **4. (know)**

no one would ever find out? When Lara faced that situation, she first said to herself, "Our life

_____ a lot easier if I just _____ this money in my
     5. (become)   **6. (put)**

pocket." Then she brought the wallet to the police. Her family needed the money, but she's not

sorry. "If we _____ bad choices, our kids _____ the
             7. (make)   **8. (learn)**

wrong lessons," she told reporters. "So we always try to do the right thing."

C | *Find and correct five mistakes.*

1. Pablo wishes he can speak German.

2. If he had the time, he'll study in Germany. But he doesn't have the time right now.

3. He could get a promotion when he spoke another language.

4. His company may pay the tuition if he took a course.

5. What would you do if you are in Pablo's situation?

Past Unreal Conditionals
ALTERNATE HISTORIES

STEP 1 GRAMMAR IN CONTEXT

Before You Read

Look at the first cartoon and the title of the article. Discuss the questions.

1. What in the cartoon is different from reality? Describe it.
2. Do you ever ask *What if* questions?
3. Do you think *What if* questions are useful?

Read

 Read the article on alternate history.

What would have happened if I had stayed in my own country? What would have happened if I had never met my husband? It's human nature to wonder how **life would have been different if certain events had (or had not) occurred**. There's even a name for the stories we create to answer these *What if* questions—alternate histories. Scientists, historians, fiction writers, and everyday people are always asking *What if* questions. Here are some examples.

Science

More than 65 million years ago, dinosaurs roamed[1] our planet. Then, a meteor[2] hit the Earth, changing the climate, causing the complete extinction[3] of most types of dinosaurs and making the development of other kinds of animals possible. But **what if the meteor had missed?** Phil Currie, a scientist from the University of Alberta, Canada, believes that **if the meteor had not struck the Earth, some types of dinosaurs would have continued to develop and would have become more intelligent**. They **would have gone on to dominate[4] the world** the way humans do today. **Would humans have been able to develop alongside these "supersaurs"?** If yes, **what would our lives have been like if most types of dinosaurs had survived?**

JUST THINK IF THAT METEOR HAD NEVER HIT PLANET EARTH 65 MILLION YEARS AGO...

POLLY WANTS A CRACKER!

2935

OLSEN

A dinosaur* and his pet human

*Today most scientists believe that birds are really a type of dinosaur.

[1] ***roam:*** to travel freely over a wide area
[2] ***meteor:*** a rock that falls from space into the Earth's atmosphere
[3] ***extinction:*** the disappearance of a whole group of animals so that no more animals of that kind exist any more
[4] ***dominate:*** to have power and control over other people, animals, or things

What if . . . ?

History

Many alternate history questions are about wars. One of the most common is, **What would have happened if Adolph Hitler had never been born or if the assassination[5] attempt on his life had been successful?** Many people believe that **World War II could have been avoided or at least might have been shortened**.

But **there are many other famous events that would have had different outcomes if just one fact had been different**. Take the case of the *Titanic*, for example. The largest luxury ship in the world, the *Titanic* hit an iceberg and sank on April 15, 1912, taking with it the lives of more than 1,500 people. **Could the event have been avoided or could more lives have been saved?** Yes, say historians. **If the *Titanic's* lookout had seen the iceberg earlier, the ship wouldn't have hit it**. Or, **if the *Titanic* had had more lifeboats, more people would have been saved**.

Everyday Life

A woman rushes to catch a subway train. Just as she gets there, the doors close. The train pulls away, leaving her on the platform. **What would have happened if she had gotten on the train?** The film *Sliding Doors* explores this question by showing us two parallel stories: the life of the woman **if she had gotten on the train**, and the life of the same woman **if she had missed the train**. In one version of the story, the woman meets a man on the train, and the two end up falling in love. In the other, she gets mugged[6] while running to catch a taxi and has to go to the hospital. The results of this everyday occurrence—catching or

missing a train—show us how a single ordinary moment can change the direction of our lives.

Some people argue that there is no way of ever really knowing **what would have happened if a single event had been different**. To those people, speculating about the past is just a game, an amusing way to pass the time. Yet to others it is obvious that alternate histories have a lot to offer. To them, while we can never know exactly how **a small change could have affected an outcome**, exploring the results of an alternate past—in books, movies, or our own lives—can teach us important lessons.

Big or small—the choices we make and the accidents that occur can change the course of history—for the whole world or for us as individuals.

---

[5] **assassination:** the murder of an important person, usually for political reasons

[6] **get mugged:** to be attacked and robbed in a public place

A | Vocabulary: *Match the words with their definitions.*

_____	**1. alternate**	**a.**	to happen
_____	**2. intelligent**	**b.**	one person's description of an event
_____	**3. occur**	**c.**	smart
_____	**4. outcome**	**d.**	happening at the same time
_____	**5. parallel**	**e.**	different
_____	**6. version**	**f.**	a result

B | Comprehension: *Circle the words or phrases that complete the sentences.*

1. Alternate histories answer *What if* questions about the <u>present / past / future</u>.

2. Most types of dinosaurs became extinct as a result of <u>an accident / a decision / a human plan</u>.

3. Alternative histories are often about <u>the weather / military events / movies</u>.

4. Many people believe that avoiding World War II was <u>possible / impossible / dangerous</u>.

5. Historians think that the *Titanic* disaster was NOT <u>avoidable / necessary / major</u>.

6. In *Sliding Doors*, a woman's life changes because of a <u>missed train / train crash / bad choice</u>.

STEP 2 GRAMMAR PRESENTATION

PAST UNREAL CONDITIONALS

Statements	
If Clause: Past Perfect	**Result Clause: *Would (not) have* + Past Participle**
If I **had missed** the train,	I **would have been** late. I **wouldn't have come** on time.
If I **had not gotten** that job,	I **would have felt** very bad. I **wouldn't have met** my wife.

Yes / No Questions	
Result Clause	***If* Clause**
Would you **have walked**	**if** you **had had** the time?

Short Answers	
Affirmative	**Negative**
Yes, I **would have**.	No, I **wouldn't have**.

Wh- Questions	
Result Clause	***If* Clause**
What **would** you **have done**	**if** you **had missed** the train?

Contractions
would have = **would've**
would not have = **wouldn't have**

GRAMMAR NOTES

1 Use **past unreal conditional** sentences to talk about **past unreal conditions and their results**. A condition and its result may be untrue, imagined, or impossible.
The *if clause* gives the **unreal condition**, and the **result clause** gives the **unreal result** of that condition.

IF CLAUSE	RESULT CLAUSE

- *If* he **had missed** the train, he **would have been** late.
  (But he didn't miss the train, so he wasn't late.)
- *If* he **hadn't taken** that job, he **wouldn't have met** his wife.
  (But he took the job, so he met his wife.)

2 Use the **past perfect** in the *if clause*. Use *would have* + **past participle** in the **result clause**.

USAGE NOTE: Sometimes speakers use *would have* in the *if* clause. However, this is often considered incorrect, especially in formal or written English.

PAST PERFECT	WOULD HAVE + PAST PARTICIPLE

- *If* it **had won** an award, it **would have become** a famous movie.
- *If* I **had owned** a DVD player, I **would have watched** the movie.
  NOT: If I ~~would have~~ owned . . .

3 You can also use *might have* or *could have* in the **result clause**, but the meaning is different from *would have*.

a. Use *would have* if the result is **certain**. Do NOT use *will* in unreal conditional sentences.

b. Use *might have* or *could have* if the result is **not certain**. Do NOT use *may* or *can*.

You can also use *could have* in the result clause to express **ability**.

- If Glen had gone to college, he *would have studied* hard.
  NOT: . . . he ~~will~~ have studied hard.

- If Glen had gone to college, he *might have become* a history teacher.
  NOT: . . . he ~~may~~ have become . . .
- If Glen had gone to college, he *could have become* a history teacher.
  NOT: . . . he ~~can~~ have become . . .

- If Glen had become a history teacher, he *could have taught* here.

4 You can **begin conditional sentences** with the *if clause* or the **result clause**. The meaning is the same.

BE CAREFUL! Use a **comma** between the two clauses only when the *if clause comes first*.

- *If he had won a million dollars,* he would have traveled around the world. OR
- He would have traveled around the world *if he had won a million dollars.*

5 **Past unreal conditionals** are often used to **express regret** about what really **happened in the past**.

- *If* I **had been** free, I **would have gone** to the movies with you.
  (I regret that I didn't go to the movies.)

6 Use *wish* + **past perfect** to express **regret or sadness** about things in the past that you **wanted to happen but didn't**.

- Glen *wishes* he **had studied** history.
  (He didn't study history, and now he thinks that was a mistake.)

EXERCISE 1: Discover the Grammar

*Read the numbered statements. Decide if the sentences that follow are **True (T)** or **False (F)**.*

1. If a girl hadn't stepped in front of her, Helen wouldn't have missed her train.

    __T__ **a.** A girl stepped in front of Helen.

    __T__ **b.** Helen missed her train.

2. If she had gotten on the train, she would've met James.

    _____ **a.** She met James.

    _____ **b.** She got on the train.

3. She wouldn't have gotten her new job if James hadn't told her about it.

    _____ **a.** She got a new job.

    _____ **b.** James didn't tell her about it.

4. If I had gotten home before 10:00, I could've watched the movie *Sliding Doors*.

    _____ **a.** I got home before 10:00.

    _____ **b.** I didn't watch the movie.

5. I would have recorded the movie if my DVD player hadn't stopped working.

    _____ **a.** I recorded the movie.

    _____ **b.** My DVD recorder broke.

6. If I hadn't had a history test the next day, I wouldn't have gone to bed so late.

    _____ **a.** I had a history test the next day.

    _____ **b.** I went to bed late.

7. I wish I had studied hard for the test.

    _____ **a.** I studied hard for the test.

    _____ **b.** I feel bad about not studying hard.

8. Ana would've helped me if I had asked.

    _____ **a.** Ana helped me.

    _____ **b.** I asked Ana for help.

9. If I had studied more, I might have gotten a good grade.

    _____ **a.** I definitely would have gotten a good grade.

    _____ **b.** I possibly would have gotten a good grade.

10. If I had gotten a good grade, I would've been happy.

    _____ **a.** I didn't get a good grade.

    _____ **b.** I wasn't happy.

EXERCISE 2: *If* and Result Clauses: Verb Forms

(Grammar Notes 1–3)

George is a character from the movie It's a Wonderful Life. *Complete his thoughts about the past. Use the correct form of the verbs in parentheses.*

1. I didn't go into business with my friend Sam. If I _____ had gone _____ into business
   (go)

   with him, I _____ might have become _____ a success.
   (may / become)

2. I couldn't go into the army because I was deaf in one ear. I _____ into
   (go)

   the army if I _____ the hearing in that ear.
   (not lose)

3. Mary and I weren't able to go on a honeymoon. We _____ away if my
   (can / go)

   father _____ sick.
   (not get)

4. My uncle lost $8,000 of the company's money. I _____ so desperate if
   (not feel)

   he _____ the money.
   (find)

5. I'm so unhappy about losing my father's business. I wish I _____

   never _____ born.
   (be)

6. Clarence showed me how the world would look without me.

   I _____ that I was so important if
   (not know)

   he _____ me.
   (not show)

7. If I _____ my little brother, Harry,
   (not rescue)

   he _____ all those lives, later on,
   (not save)

   when he was a soldier.

8. My old boss once almost made a terrible mistake in his

   shop. If I _____ him, my old boss
   (not help)

   _____ to jail.
   (may / go)

George with his angel, Clarence

9. Mary _____ happy if she _____ me.
   (not be)   **(not meet)**

10. Life here really _____ worse if I _____ born.
    (be)   **(not be)**

EXERCISE 3: Affirmative and Negative Statements

(Grammar Notes 1–3)

A | *The movie* The Curious Case of Benjamin Button *explores how simple actions can change lives. Read the information below.*

Events that occurred

- someone's shoelace broke
- a delivery truck moved
- a package wasn't wrapped on time
- a girl broke up with her boyfriend
- a man forgot to set his alarm clock and got up five minutes late
- a taxi driver stopped for a cup of coffee
- a woman forgot her coat and took a later taxicab
- Daisy and her friend didn't cross the street
- the taxi didn't drive by
- Daisy was hit by the taxi

Daisy

B | *Daisy, a dancer and the love of Benjamin Button's life, was in a serious accident. Look at the information in Part A. Complete Benjamin's story from the movie. Use the correct form of the verbs in parentheses. Choose between affirmative and negative.*

"Sometimes we're on a collision course,[1] and we just don't know it. Whether it's by accident or by design,[2] there's not a thing we can do about it. . . . And if only one thing

____ *had happened* ____ differently: If that shoelace _____;
    1. (happen)   **2. (not break)**

or that delivery truck _____ moments earlier; or that package
                 3. (not move)

_____ wrapped and ready because the girl _____
4. (be)   **5. (not break up)**

with her boyfriend; or that man _____ his alarm and
                             6. (set)

_____ five minutes earlier; or that taxi driver _____
7. (get up)   **8. (not stop)**

for a cup of coffee; or that woman _____ her coat, and
                       9. (remember)

_____ into an earlier cab, Daisy and her friend _____
10. (get)   **11. (cross)**

the street, and the taxi _____ by. But life being what it is—a series
                 12. (drive)

of intersecting lives[3] and incidents, out of anyone's control—that taxi did not go by, and that

driver was momentarily distracted, and that taxi hit Daisy, and her leg was crushed."

_____
[1] *collision course:* a direction that leads to a crash
[2] *by design:* according to a plan
[3] *intersecting lives:* lives that cross each other

EXERCISE 4: Regrets About the Past

(Grammar Note 6)

These characters from the movie Sliding Doors *feel bad about things that happened.*
Read their regrets. Then write their wishes.

1. **HELEN:** I took supplies from my office. My boss fired me.

   I wish I hadn't taken supplies from my office. I wish my boss hadn't fired me.

2. **HELEN:** I didn't catch my train. I had to find a taxi.

3. **TAXI DRIVER:** She got mugged near my taxi. She needed to go to the hospital.

4. **GERRY** *(Helen's old boyfriend)*: Helen saw me with Lydia. Helen left me.

5. **LYDIA** *(Gerry's old girlfriend)*: I started seeing Gerry again. I didn't break up with him.

6. **JAMES** *(Helen's new boyfriend)*: I didn't tell Helen about my wife. I lost her trust.

7. **HELEN:** James didn't call me. I got so depressed.

8. **ANNA** *(Helen's best friend)*: James lied to Helen. He hurt her.

Helen and James after their first meeting

EXERCISE 5: Negative and Affirmative Statements

(Grammar Notes 1–4)

Read these stories from an Internet message board about how people met their wives, husbands, boyfriends, or girlfriends. Using the words in parentheses, combine each pair of sentences to make one past unreal conditional sentence.

1. My temp became permanent. I'd already planned this great vacation to Jamaica when my boss cancelled my time off. "Sorry," she told me, "I'm going to be away, but I'll hire a temp to help you out." I was so furious that I almost quit right on the spot. I thought,

If she had planned ahead, we wouldn't have needed that temp .

a. She didn't plan ahead. We needed that temp. (would)

Now I know that _____ .

b. She didn't plan ahead. I met the love of my life. (might)

When Vlad, the temp, walked in that first morning, I nearly ran into her office to thank her.

_____ .

c. She was so disorganized. My next trip to Jamaica was for my honeymoon. (would)

2. She knocked me off my feet.[1] I was skiing with some friends in Colorado. I met my wife when she knocked me down on a ski slope. It's a good thing I was OK because

_____ .

a. I didn't break my leg. I accepted her dinner invitation. (could)

Actually, I only accepted because she felt so bad about the accident. But after the first few minutes, I knew I had to see her again. She was pretty, funny, and really intelligent.

_____ .

b. I went skiing that day. She knocked me over. (would)

And _____ !

c. She knocked me over. We got married. (would)

3. Best in the universe. I met my boyfriend online. We write stories on a *Star Trek* fan site.

_____ .

a. He was such a good writer. I thought about contacting him. (would)

because I'm very careful about online privacy. In fact, I didn't even know he was a guy!

_____ .

b. I didn't know. I was brave enough to write to him. (might)

But I thought he was another Isaac Asimov,[2] so I wanted to discuss his writing. We just emailed for a long time. Then we decided to meet at a Star Trek conference. I'm really glad we waited. He isn't the most handsome Klingon[3] in the universe, but to me he's Mr. Right.

_____ .

c. We didn't meet right away. I realized that. (might)

[1] *knock someone off his/her feet:* to make a very big impression on someone
[2] *Isaac Asimov:* a famous science fiction writer
[3] *Klingon:* in *Star Trek* stories, a race of people from another planet

EXERCISE 6: Editing

Read the student's book report. There are eleven mistakes in the use of the past unreal conditional. The first mistake is already corrected. Find and correct ten more.

Have you ever had a small accident that made a big difference in your life? If it ~~haven't~~ *hadn't*
happened, would your life have been much different? A lot of people think so. They wish they were
avoided a mistake. Or they worry that today's good luck *was* just a mistake. Isaac Asimov's short
story, *What If* – suggests another way to look at life. Norman and Livvy are traveling to New York
to celebrate their fifth wedding anniversary. The two met on a streetcar when Livvy accidentally
fell into Norman's lap. Although they're happy, Livvy always thinks about other possible outcomes
of their lives. Now, on the train to New York, she asks her favorite question: "Norman, what if you
would have been one minute later on the streetcar corner and had taken the next car? What do you
suppose would had happened?" Minutes later, a man carrying a box sits in the seat across from
them. He takes out a piece of glass that looks like a TV screen and shows them the answers to
Livvy's question.

Sadly, the couple sees that if Livvy hadn't fallen, the two wouldn't connected that day. Then
the screen shows Norman's marriage—to Livvy's friend Georgette. Upset, Livvy now thinks
Norman only married her because she fell into his lap. "If I hadn't, you would have married
Georgette. If she hasn't wanted you, you would have married somebody else. You would have
marry *anybody*." However, the couple next sees a New Year's Eve party with a very unhappily
married Norman and Georgette. The truth is clear: Norman could never have forgotten Livvy, even
if they did not married. But will Norman and Georgette have stayed together? Now *Norman* needs
to know! What would they be doing right now, he wonders: "This very minute! If I have married
Georgette." In the final scene, the couple sees themselves, married (after Norman and Georgette's
divorce), and traveling on the same train, at the same time, headed for their honeymoon in New
York. If Livvy hadn't fallen into Norman's lap, nothing would have changes! At the end, Livvy
sees that her *What if* questions have caused pain, and that ". . . all the possibles are none of our
business. The real is enough."

EXERCISE 7: Listening

A | *Read the sentences. Then listen to the conversations. Listen again and circle the words that complete the sentences.*

1. The man is describing why he was (late) / injured.

2. The woman is explaining how she got sick / became a teacher.

3. The man is telling how he found a(n) bookstore / apartment.

4. The man / woman is expressing regret.

5. The man lost / found a wallet on the train.

6. The man and his wife opened a bank / café.

B | *Read the statements. Then listen again to the conversations and check (✓)* **True** *or* **False***. Correct the false statements.*

	True	False
1. The man ~~was~~ *wasn't* injured in a train accident.	☐	☑
2. The woman became a teacher as a result of her friend's illness.	☐	☐
3. The man found an apartment when he was lost.	☐	☐
4. The woman enjoyed the movie.	☐	☐
5. The man had definitely planned on calling the police.	☐	☐
6. The man doesn't regret losing his job.	☐	☐

EXERCISE 8: Pronunciation

A | *Read and listen to the Pronunciation Note.*

> ### Pronunciation Note
>
> In **conversation** when we use the **past unreal conditional**,
>
> - we usually pronounce *have* like the word "**of**"
> - we use the **contractions** "**'d**" for *had* and "**hadn't**" for *had not*
> - we use the **contractions** "**wouldn't**" for *would not* and "**couldn't**" for *could not*
>
> | **EXAMPLES:** | If **I had** been on the train, I **could have** been injured. | → | "If **I'd** been on the train, I **could of** been injured." |
> |---|---|---|---|
> | | If I **had not** caught it, I **would not have** arrived on time. | → | "If I **hadn't** caught it, I **wouldn't of** arrived on time." |
> | | If he **had been** injured, he **could not have** called you. | → | "If **he'd been** injured, he **couldn't of** called you." |
>
> In **writing**, use *would have*, *wouldn't have*, *could have*, and *couldn't have*, NOT would ~~of~~, wouldn't ~~of~~, could ~~of~~, and couldn't ~~of~~.

B | *Listen to the short conversations. Circle the words you hear in each response.*

1. **A:** Did Mike go to the movie with you?

   B: No, but if his cousin <u>had / hadn't</u> been in town, he would've gone.

2. **A:** Did you get to the theater by 8:00?

   B: Well, if I'd taken a different train, I <u>could've / couldn't have</u> done it.

3. **A:** What's the matter? You look upset.

   B: I wish <u>I'd / I hadn't</u> invited Jason to go with us.

4. **A:** Did you like the movie?

   B: Not really. If I'd understood more of the English, I <u>could've / would've</u> enjoyed it.

5. **A:** I called you at 11:00, but there was no answer.

   B: Well, I would've been home if <u>I'd / I hadn't</u> walked.

6. **A:** What would you have done instead?

   B: I <u>would've / wouldn't have</u> taken a taxi.

C | *Listen again to the conversations and check your answers. Then practice the conversations with a partner.*

EXERCISE 9: What About You?

Work in small groups. Tell your classmates how a single decision or event changed your life or the life of someone you know. What would have happened if that decision or event hadn't occurred?

> EXAMPLE: I had just moved to a new town. I didn't know anyone, and I was lonely and depressed. One day, I *forced* myself to go out for a walk. (All I really wanted to do was stay in my room and read). I was sitting near the lake when this guy came over and asked me if I had a watch. We started to talk. He was funny, handsome, and seemed really intelligent. If I hadn't gone for that walk, I never would've met him. Six months later we were married!

EXERCISE 10: Problem Solving

Work in small groups. Read the following situations. Did the person make the right decision? What would you have done in each situation? Why? What might have or could have happened as a result?

1. Zeke started his business making and selling energy bars[1] when he was a teenager. Ten years later, a large company offered to buy the business. Zeke turned the offer down because he wanted to make sure Zeke's Bars were always very high quality. If he had accepted, he could have retired rich by age 35. What would you have done?

   > EXAMPLE: **A:** I wouldn't have rejected the offer. I would've sold the business.
   > **B:** If he'd sold the business, he could've started a new one.
   > **C:** He might've . . .

2. A man was walking down the street when he found ten $100 bills lying on the ground. There was no one else around. He picked them up and put them in his pocket.

3. A woman came home late and found her apartment door unlocked. She was sure she had locked it. No one else had the keys. She went inside.

---

[1] *energy bar:* food that gives you energy and that is in the shape of a candy bar

EXERCISE 11: Discussion

With a partner, discuss a situation in your life that you regret. Describe the situation and talk about what you wish had happened and why.

> EXAMPLE: **A:** Someone asked me to go to a party the night before a test. I didn't like the course, and I didn't feel like studying, so I decided to go.
> **B:** What happened? Did you do OK on the test?
> **A:** No. I failed it.
> **B:** Oh, that's too bad.
> **A:** It's even worse than that. I had to repeat the course! I wish I hadn't gone to the party. If I'd stayed home, I'd have studied for the test. If I'd been prepared, I would've passed.

EXERCISE 12: Writing

A | *Write one or two paragraphs about an event that changed your life or the life of someone you know. If the event hadn't happened, what would have been different?*

EXAMPLE: Two years ago, I was in a serious car accident that changed my life. I was in the hospital for a long time, and my friends and family were always there for me. If I hadn't been so badly injured, I might never have realized what good friends and family I had. . . .

B | *Check your work. Use the Editing Checklist.*

Editing Checklist

Did you use . . . ?

☐ the past perfect in the *if* clause

☐ *would have*, *might have*, or *could have* + **past participle** in the result clause

☐ a comma between the two clauses when the *if* clause comes first

☐ *wish* + **past perfect** to express a regret

Check your answers on page UR-6.

Do you need to review anything?

A | Circle the correct words to complete the sentences.

1. If you <u>didn't tell / hadn't told</u> us about the movie, we wouldn't have seen it.

2. I wish I <u>had / hadn't</u> gone to the movie too. I hear it's great.

3. We <u>had been / would have been</u> late if we had taken the bus.

4. <u>If / When</u> you had called me, I might have driven you there.

5. I would've <u>gone / went</u> to the movies if I had had the time.

B | Complete the past unreal conditional sentences in these conversations with the correct form of the verbs in parentheses.

- **A:** Sorry I'm late. I _____ on time if I _____ my train.

1. (be)   2. (not miss)

  B: Well, if you _____ on time, I _____ that great café.

3. (be)   4. (not discover)

- **A:** I wish I _____ this job offer.

5. (not accept)

  B: But, if you _____ another job instead, we _____!

6. (take)   7. (not meet)

- **A:** It's hard to believe that birds are a type of dinosaur!

  B: I know. If I _____ that science program on TV, I _____ it.

8. (not see)   9. (not believe)

C | Find and correct six mistakes.

Tonight we watched the movie *Back to the Future* starring Michael J. Fox. I might never had seen it if I hadn't read his autobiography, *Lucky Man*. His book was so good that I wanted to see his most famous movie. Now I wish I saw it in the theater when it first came out, but I hadn't even been born yet! It would have been better if we would have watched it on a big screen. Fox was great. He looked really young—just like a teenager. But I would have recognized him even when I hadn't known he was in the film.

In real life, when Fox was a teenager, he was too small to become a professional hockey player. But if he hadn't looked so young, he can't have gotten his role in the TV hit series *Family Ties*. In Hollywood, he had to sell his furniture to pay his bills, but he kept trying to find an acting job. If he wouldn't have, he might never have become a star.

From Grammar to Writing
SHOWING CAUSE AND EFFECT

One way to develop a topic is to discuss its causes and effects. **To show cause and effect**, you can

- **connect sentences** with *as a result* and *therefore*
- **connect clauses** with *so*, *because*, or *if*

	CAUSE	EFFECT
EXAMPLE:	*I was shy*	*I didn't talk in class.* ➔

I was shy. **As a result**, I didn't talk in class.

I was shy. **Therefore**, I didn't talk in class.

I was shy, **so** I didn't talk in class.

Because I was shy, I didn't talk in class.

If I hadn't been shy, I would have talked in class.

Notice the use of a **comma**: 1) after *as a result* and *therefore*, 2) before *so*, 3) after a clause beginning with *because* or *if* when it comes before the main clause.

---

1 | *Read this essay. Underline once sentences or clauses that show a cause.*
Underline twice sentences or clauses that show an effect. Circle the connecting words.

(Almost) No More Fear of Talking

My biggest problem in school is my fear of talking in class. My hands always shake if I answer a question or present a paper. If it is a big assignment, I even feel sick to my stomach.

There are several reasons for my problem, but my family's attitude is the most important. My family motto is, "Children should be seen, but not heard." Because my parents never ask for our opinions, we never give them. I can feel my mother's disapproval if a talkative friend visits. In addition, my parents classify their children. My older brother is the "Smart One." I am the "Creative One." I think I would do better in school if they expected more, but they don't expect much. Therefore, I have not tried very hard.

Recently I decided to do something about my problem. I discovered that I feel less nervous about giving a speech in class if I role-play my presentation with a friend. I have also joined a discussion club. As a result, I get a lot of practice talking. My problem has causes, so it must have solutions!

2 | *Connect the pairs of sentences. Use the word(s) in parentheses.*

1. Mr. Stewart didn't help me. I never spoke in class. (if)

   <u>If Mr. Stewart hadn't helped me, I never would have spoken in class.</u>

2. He believed in me. I became more courageous. (because)

   _____

3. We worked in groups. I got used to talking about ideas with classmates. (so)

   _____

4. I have gotten a lot of practice. I feel more confident. (as a result)

   _____

5. Sena didn't understand the question. She didn't raise her hand. (therefore)

   _____

3 | *Before you write . . .*

1. Work with a partner. Discuss the causes of a strong feeling that you have.

   EXAMPLE: I usually feel excited at the beginning of the school year.

2. Complete this outline for a cause and effect essay.

   Paragraph I   The feeling you are going to write about: _____

   One or two examples: _____

   Paragraph II   The causes and effects of the feeling:

   A. _____

   B. _____

   C. _____

   Paragraph III   How you deal with the feeling:

   A. _____

   B. _____

4 | *Write a three-paragraph essay about the causes and effects of a feeling that you have. Use your outline to organize your writing.*

5 | *Exchange essays with a different partner. Outline your partner's essay. Write questions about anything that is not clear.*

6 | *Work with your partner. Discuss each other's questions from Exercise 5. Then rewrite your own essay and make any necessary corrections.*

INDIRECT SPEECH AND EMBEDDED QUESTIONS

Direct and Indirect Speech
TRUTH AND LIES

STEP 1 GRAMMAR IN CONTEXT

Before You Read

Look at the title of the article and the photo, and read what the woman is saying. Discuss the questions.

1. Do you think the woman's hair looks great?
2. Is it ever all right to tell a lie?
3. If so, in what situations?

Read

Read the magazine article about lying.

THE TRUTH ABOUT LYING

BY JENNIFER MORALES

At 9:00, a supervisor from Rick Spivak's bank called and **said Rick's credit card payment was late.** **"The check is in the mail,"** Rick **replied** quickly. At 11:45, Rick left for a 12 o'clock meeting across town. Arriving late, Rick **told his client that traffic had been bad.** That evening, Rick's fiancée, Ann, came home with a new haircut. Rick hated it. **"It looks great,"** he **said.**

Three lies in one day! Does Rick have a problem? Or is he just an ordinary guy? Each time, he **told himself that sometimes the truth causes too many problems.** Like Rick, most of us tell white lies—harmless untruths that help us avoid trouble. In fact, one social psychologist[1] estimates that the average American tells about 200 lies a day! He **says that lying is a habit**, and we are often not even aware that we are doing it. When we do notice, we justify the lie by **telling ourselves it was for a good purpose.**

He **said my hair looked great this way!**

These are our six most common excuses:

◆ To be polite: **"I'd love to go to your party, but I have to work."**

◆ To protect someone else's feelings: **"Your hair looks great that way!"**

◆ To feel better about yourself: **"I'm looking better these days."**

◆ To appear more interesting to others: **"I run a mile every day."**

◆ To get something more quickly: **"I have to have that report today."**

◆ To avoid uncomfortable situations: **"I tried to call you, but your cell phone was turned off."**

[1]*social psychologist:* a psychologist who studies how social groups affect the way people behave

How do we get away with all those white lies? First of all, it's difficult to recognize a lie because body language usually doesn't reveal dishonesty. But even when we suspect[2] someone is lying, we often don't want to know the truth. If an acquaintance **says she's fine**, but she clearly isn't, a lot of people find it easier to take her statement at face value.[3] And when someone **tells you, "You did a great job!"** you probably don't want to question the compliment!

Is telling lies a new trend? In one survey, the majority of people who answered **said that people were more honest in the past**. Nevertheless, lying wasn't really born yesterday. In the 18th century, the French philosopher[4] Vauvenargues told the truth about lying when he **wrote, "All men are born truthful and die liars."**

---

[2]*suspect:* to think that something is probably true
[3]*take something at face value:* to accept the obvious meaning of words and not look for hidden meanings
[4]*philosopher:* someone who thinks a lot and questions the meaning of life and ideas about the world

After You Read

A **Vocabulary:** *Circle the letter of the word or phrase that best completes each sentence.*

1. I was an **average** student. I ___ every semester.
   a. got B's and C's
   b. failed a couple of courses
   c. was at the top of my class

2. Ed was **aware** that Sid lost his job. He ___ it.
   a. suspected
   b. didn't know about
   c. knew about

3. Some people **justify** lying. They ___ it.
   a. always avoid
   b. find good reasons for
   c. never recognize

4. The **majority** of people are honest. ___ of them don't tell lies.
   a. None
   b. All
   c. Most

5. Hamid **revealed** his plans yesterday. He ___ about them.
   a. refused to say anything
   b. told his friends and family
   c. didn't tell the truth

B | Comprehension: *Find the situations in the article. Check (✓) the person's exact words.*

1. The supervisor at Rick's bank (to Rick):
   - ☐ "His credit card payment was late."
   - ☑ "Your credit card payment is late."

2. Rick (to his client):
   - ☐ "Traffic had been bad."
   - ☑ "Traffic was bad."

3. You (to a new friend):
   - ☐ "You run a mile every day."
   - ☑ "I run a mile every day."

4. An acquaintance (to you):
   - ☐ "She's fine."
   - ☑ "I'm fine."

5. People answering a survey question:
   - ☐ "That people were more honest 10 years ago."
   - ☑ "People were more honest 10 years ago."

STEP 2 GRAMMAR PRESENTATION

DIRECT AND INDIRECT SPEECH

Direct Speech			
Direct Statement	**Subject**	**Reporting Verb**	**Noun / Pronoun**
"The check **is** in the mail," "The haircut **looks** great," "The traffic **was** bad,"	he	**told**	the bank. Ann. her.
		said.	

Indirect Speech				
Subject	**Reporting Verb**	**Noun / Pronoun**	**Indirect Statement**	
He	**told**	the bank Ann her	(that)	the check **was** in the mail. the haircut **looked** great. the traffic **had been** bad.
	said			

GRAMMAR NOTES

1	**Direct speech** states the <u>exact words</u> that a speaker used.	• **"The check is in the mail,"** he said. • **"I like that tie,"** she told him.
	In **writing**, put **quotation marks** before and after the speech you are quoting. That speech (called the **quotation**) can go at the **beginning** or at the **end** of the sentence.	• **"The traffic is bad,"** he said. OR • He said**, "The traffic is bad."**
	Use a **comma** to separate the quotation from the rest of the sentence.	

2	**Indirect speech** (also called *reported speech*) reports what a speaker said <u>without using the exact words</u>.	• He said **the check was in the mail**. • She told him **she liked that tie**.
	The word *that* can introduce indirect speech.	• He said *that* **the check was in the mail**. • She told him *that* **she liked that tie**.
	BE CAREFUL! Do **NOT** use **quotation marks** when writing indirect speech.	• She said **that she had to work**. Not: She said that ~~"she had to work."~~

3	**Reporting verbs** (such as *say* and *tell*) are usually in the **simple past** for both direct and indirect speech.	**DIRECT SPEECH:** • "It's a great haircut," he **said**. • "I'm sorry to be late," Rick **told** Ann. **INDIRECT SPEECH:** • He **said** it was a great haircut. • Rick **told** Ann that he was sorry to be late.
	Use *say* when you **do not mention the listener**.	• "It's a great haircut," he **said**. • He **said** it was a great haircut.
	Use *tell* when you **mention the listener**.	• "It's a great haircut," he **told** *Ann*. • He **told** *her* that it was a great haircut.
	BE CAREFUL! Do **NOT** use *tell* when you don't mention the listener.	• He **said** he had been sick. Not: He ~~told~~ he had been sick.

4	When the **reporting verb** is in the **simple past** (*said, told*), we often **change the verb tense** in the indirect speech statement.	
	The **simple present** in direct speech becomes the **simple past** in indirect speech.	• "I only *buy* shoes on sale," she **said**. • She **said** she only *bought* shoes on sale.
	The **simple past** in direct speech becomes the **past perfect** in indirect speech.	• "I *found* a great store," she **said**. • She **said** she *had found* a great store.

(continued on next page)

5 You do **NOT have to change the tense** when you report:

a. something that was **just said**

> **A:** I'**m** tired from all this shopping.
> **B:** What did you say?
> **A:** I **said** I'**m** tired. OR
>   I **said** I **was** tired.

b. something that is **still true**

- Rick **said** the bank **wants** a check. OR
- Rick **said** the bank **wanted** a check.

c. a **general truth** or **scientific law**

- Mrs. Smith **told** her students that water **freezes** at 0° Celsius. OR
- Mrs. Smith **told** her students that water **froze** at 0° Celsius.

6 When the **reporting verb** is in the **simple present**, do **NOT change the verb tense** in the indirect speech statement.

USAGE NOTE: In newspapers, magazines, and on the TV and radio news, **reporting verbs** are often in the **simple present**.

- "I **run** a mile every day," **says** Ann.
- Ann **says** that she **runs** a mile every day.
  NOT: Ann says that she ~~ran~~ a mile every day.

- The majority of women **say** that they never **lie**.

7 In **indirect speech**, make necessary changes in **pronouns** and **possessives** to keep the speaker's <u>original meaning</u>.

- Rick told Ann, "**I** like **your** haircut."

- Rick told Ann that **he** liked **her** haircut.

REFERENCE NOTES

For **punctuation rules for direct speech**, see Appendix 27 on page A-13.
For additional **tense changes in indirect speech**, see Unit 26, page 420.
For a list of **reporting verbs**, see Appendix 14 on page A-5.

EXERCISE 1: Discover the Grammar

Read the magazine article about lying on the job. Circle the reporting verbs. Underline once the examples of direct speech. Underline twice the examples of indirect speech. Go to Appendix 14 on page A-5 for help with reporting verbs.

"Lying during a job interview is risky business," says Martha Toledo, director of the management consulting firm Maxwell. "The truth has a funny way of coming out." Toledo tells the story of one woman applying for a job as an office manager. The woman told the interviewer that she had a B.A. degree. Actually, she was eight credits short. She also said that she had made $50,000 at her last job. The truth was $10,000 less. "Many firms really do check facts," warns Toledo. In this case, a call to the applicant's company revealed the truth. "She was a strong applicant," says Toledo, "and most of the information on the resume was true. Nevertheless, those details cost her the job."

Toledo relates a story about another job applicant, George. During an interview, George reported that he had quit his last job. George landed the new job and was doing well until the company hired another employee, Pete. George and Pete had worked at the same company. Pete later told his boss that his old company had fired George. After George's supervisor became aware of the lie, he stopped trusting George, and their relationship became difficult. Eventually, George quit.

EXERCISE 2: *Said* and *Told*; Verb and Pronoun Changes   (*Grammar Notes 2–5, 7*)

Complete the student's essay with the correct words.

Once when I was a teenager, I went to my Aunt Leah's house. Aunt Leah collected pottery, and as soon as I got there, she _____told_____ me she _____wanted_____ to show me
        1. (said / told)   **2. (wants / wanted)**

_____her_____ lovely new bowl. She _____told / said_____ she _____had_____ just
3. (my / her)   **4. (said / told)**   **5. (has / had)**

bought it. When Aunt Leah left the room, she handed me the bowl. As I was looking at it, it

slipped and broke on the floor. When she came back, I _____said_____ the cat had broken
        6. (said / told)

_____her_____ bowl. She _____told_____ me that it _____wasn't_____ important.
7. (her / your)   **8. (said / told)**   **9. (isn't / wasn't)**

I didn't sleep at all that night, and the next morning I called my aunt and _____told_____
                10. (said / told)

her that I had broken the bowl. I apologized and _____said_____ that I _____felt_____
        11. (said / told)   **12. (feel / felt)**

terrible. She laughed and said _____she_____ had known all along. We still laugh about it.
        13. (I / she)

EXERCISE 3: Indirect Speech

(Grammar Notes 2–4, 7)

*Look at the pictures. Rewrite the statements as indirect speech. Use **said** as the reporting verb and make all necessary changes in the verbs and pronouns.*

1.

    a. *She said it was her own recipe.*

    b. *He said it looked great.*

2.

    a. He told Mr. Brown th, this car had Broken down

    b. _____

3.

    a. _____

    b. _____

4.

    a. _____

    b. _____

5.

    a. _____

    b. _____

6.

    a. _____

    b. _____

Rewrite Lisa and Ben's conversation using indirect speech. Use the reporting verbs in parentheses. Make necessary changes in the verbs and pronouns.

1. **LISA:** I just heard about a job at a scientific research company.

   (tell) _She told him she had just heard about a job at a scientific research company._

2. **BEN:** Oh, I majored in science at Florida State.

   (say) _He said that he had majored in science at Florida State._

3. **LISA:** They didn't mention the starting salary.

   (say) _She said that They had not mentioned the starting salary._

4. **BEN:** I need a lot of money to pay off my student loans.

   (say) _He said that he needed a lot of money to pay off his student_

5. **LISA:** They want someone with some experience as a programmer.

   (say) _she said that she wanted some_

6. **BEN:** Well, I work as a programmer for Data Systems.

   (tell) _he told her, he worked as a programmer For DataSyste_

7. **LISA:** Oh—they need a college graduate.

   (say) _she said that they needed a college graduate_

8. **BEN:** Well, I graduated from Florida State.

   (tell) _He told her, that He had graduated From Floridasta_

9. **LISA:** But they don't want a recent graduate.

   (say) _she said that they didn't want a recent graduate_

10. **BEN:** I got my degree four years ago.

    (tell) _He told her, He had gotten his degree four years before previously_

11. **LISA:** Great—I wasn't aware of that.

    (tell) _she told him, she had not been aware of that_

12. **BEN:** I really appreciate the information.

    (say) _He said that he really appreciated the information._

13. **LISA:** My boss just came in, and I have to go.

    (tell) _she told him, that her boss just had come in, and she had have to go_

EXERCISE 5: Editing

Read the article. There are nine mistakes in the use of direct and indirect speech. The first mistake is already corrected. Find and correct eight more.

WARNING!!!! THIS MESSAGE IS A HOAX!!!!!

Everyone gets urgent email messages. They tell you that Bill Gates
now ~~wanted~~ *wants* to give away his money—to YOU! They say you that
a popular floor cleaner kills family pets. They report that your
computer monitor had taken photographs of you. Before I
became aware of Internet hoaxes, I used to forward these emails
to all my friends. Not long ago, a very annoyed friend explains
that the story about killer bananas was a hoax (an untrue story).
He said me "that the majority of those scary emails were hoaxes."
He told me about these common telltale signs of hoaxes:

! The email always says that it was very urgent. It has lots of
exclamation points.

! It tells that it is not a hoax and quotes important people.
(The quotations are false.)

! It urges you to send the email to everyone you know.

He also told that a lot of Internet sites reveal information about
Internet hoaxes. With this information, you can avoid the
embarrassment of forwarding all your friends a false warning.
So, before *you* announce that sunscreen had made people blind,
check out the story on a reliable website.

STEP 4 COMMUNICATION PRACTICE

EXERCISE 6: Listening

A | *Read the sentences. Then listen to Lisa's conversations. Listen again and circle the correct word or phrase to complete each sentence.*

1. **a.** Alex told Lisa that he'd found a new Armenian / (vegetarian) restaurant.

   b. He probably thinks that Lisa is going to go out with her parents / Ben on Saturday.

2. **a.** Lisa told Ben that she loves to work / work out too.

   b. Ben probably thinks that Lisa will miss / attend her next aerobics class.

3. **a.** Lisa told Mark that she needed the report on Monday / Tuesday.

   b. Mark thought the staff meeting was on Monday / Tuesday.

4. **a.** Chris said she wanted Lisa's opinion of / recipe for the sauce.

   b. She probably thinks that Lisa will / won't cook the sauce in the future.

B | *Now read Lisa's weekly planner. Lisa wasn't always honest in her conversations. Listen to the conversations again and notice the differences between what Lisa said and the truth. Then write sentences about Lisa's white lies.*

SATURDAY

Morning

Afternoon

Evening — 6:00 date with Ben!

SUNDAY

Morning — sleep late! 9:00 ~~aerobics class~~

Afternoon

Evening

MONDAY

Morning

Afternoon

Evening — 6:00 Vegetarian Society meeting

7:30 dinner with Chris

TUESDAY

Morning

Afternoon — 4:00 weekly staff meeting – present sales report

Evening

1. _She said her parents were in town, but she actually has a date with Ben._

2. _____

3. _____

4. _____

EXERCISE 7: Pronunciation

A | *Read and listen to the Pronunciation Note.*

> ### Pronunciation Note
>
> As you learned in Unit 9, the **way we say something** can express our **feelings** about it. For example:
>
> We can say *He said he had to work late.* and mean that we **believe** that he had to work late. But we can also say *He said he had to work late.* and mean that we **don't believe** he had to work late.
>
> When we **don't believe** what the person said, we usually **give extra stress** to the **reporting verb** and our **voice falls** when we say it.
>
> **EXAMPLE:** He said he had to work.
>
> When we **believe** what the person said, we usually **don't give extra stress** to the **reporting verb** and our **voice doesn't fall** when we say it.
>
> **EXAMPLE:** He said he had to work.

B | *Listen to the short conversations. Notice the stress and intonation. Decide if the speaker* **believes** *or* **doesn't believe** *what he is reporting. Check (✓) the correct box.*

The speaker . . .	Believes	Doesn't believe
1. A: We haven't received Bob Miller's rent check yet.		
B: He said he mailed it last week.	☐	☑
2. A: Didn't you go out with Lisa Saturday night?		
B: No, she said her parents were in town this weekend.	☑	☐
3. A: Anton went skiing this weekend.		
B: And he said he had to work all weekend.	☐	☑
4. A: I saw Karen in the Chinese takeout place last night.		
B: She told us she'd cooked everything herself.	☐	☑
5. A: Ben looks very fit.		
B: He told me he exercises every day.	☑	☐
6. A: Guess how old Kellan is.		
B: Well, he says he's twenty-two.	☐	☑

EXERCISE 8: Discussion

Review the six excuses for lying described in "The Truth About Lying" on page 402. Work in small groups. Is it OK to lie in these circumstances? Give examples from your own experience to support your ideas.

EXAMPLE: **A:** Once my friend told me that my haircut looked great, but it really looked awful. I know she wanted to protect my feelings, but I think she should have told me the truth. Now it's hard for me to believe anything she says.

B: I think at times it's OK to lie to protect someone's feelings. Once I told my friend that . . .

C: I think . . .

EXERCISE 9: Questionnaire: Honesty

A | *Complete the questionnaire. Check (✓) your answers.*

	Always	Usually	Sometimes	Rarely	Never
1. I tell the truth to my friends.					
2. I tell the truth to my family.					
3. It's OK to lie on the job.					
4. "White lies" protect people's feelings.					
5. Most people are honest.					
6. It's best to tell the truth.					
7. I tell people my real age.					
8. My friends are honest with me.					
9. It's difficult to tell a convincing lie.					
10. Politicians are honest.					
11. Doctors tell patients the whole truth.					
12. I answer questionnaires honestly.					

B | *Work in small groups and compare your answers. Summarize your group's results and report them to the rest of the class.*

EXAMPLE: **A:** Five of us said that we usually told the truth.

B: Only one of us said it was always best to tell the truth.

C: Everyone in our group said that they tell people their real age.

EXERCISE 10: Game: To Tell the Truth

A | *Work in groups of three. Each student tells an interesting fact about his or her life. Each fact is <u>true for only one student</u>. The group chooses one of the facts to tell the class.*

EXAMPLE: **ALICIA:**   Once I climbed a mountain that was 7,000 meters high.
        BERNARDO: I speak four languages.
           CHEN: I scored the winning point for my soccer team at a big tournament.

B | *The group goes to the front of the class. Each student states the same fact, but <u>only one</u> student is telling the truth.*

EXAMPLE:

C | *The class asks the three students questions to find out who is telling the truth.*

EXAMPLES: **A:** Alicia, how long did it take you?
           B: Bernardo, who did you climb the mountain with?
           C: Chen, did you train for a long time?

D | *As a class, decide who was telling the truth. Explain your reasons.*

EXAMPLES: **A:** I didn't believe Alicia. She said it had taken two weeks to climb the mountain.
           B: I think Bernardo was lying. He told us he'd climbed the mountain alone.
           C: I think Chen was telling the truth. She said that she'd trained for several months.

EXERCISE 11: Quotable Quotes

*Work in small groups. Discuss these famous quotations about lying. Do you agree with them? Give examples to support your opinion. Use **says** to report the proverbs and **said** to report the ideas of individuals.*

1. All men are born truthful and die liars.
    —Vauvenargues (French philosopher, 1715–1747)

EXAMPLE: **A:** Vauvenargues said that all men are born truthful and die liars.
           B: I agree because babies don't lie, but children and adults do.
           C: I don't believe that *everyone* lies . . .

2. A half truth is a whole lie.
   —*Jewish proverb*

3. A little inaccuracy saves tons of explanation.
   —*Saki (British short story writer, 1870–1916)*

4. A liar needs a good memory.
   —*Quintilian (first-century Roman orator)*

5. The man who speaks the truth is always at ease.
   —*Persian proverb*

6. The cruelest lies are often told in silence.
   —*Robert Louis Stevenson (Scottish novelist, 1850–1894)*

EXERCISE 12: Writing

A | *Read the conversation between Rick and Ann. Then write a paragraph reporting what they said. Use direct and indirect speech. At the end of your paragraph, say who you think is lying and why.*

> **RICK:** Hi, honey. Sorry I'm late.
>
> **ANN:** That's all right. I made liver and onions. It's almost ready.
>
> **RICK:** *(looking upset)* It smells great, honey. It's one of my favorites.
>
> **ANN:** You look upset!
>
> **RICK:** I'm OK. I had a rough day at work. Oh, I stopped and bought some frog legs for dinner tomorrow. It's my turn to cook.
>
> **ANN:** *(looking upset)* That's interesting. I look forward to trying them.

EXAMPLE: Rick came home and said he was sorry he was late. Ann said that was all right.

B | *Check your work. Use the Editing Checklist.*

Editing Checklist

Did you use . . . ?
☐ quotation marks before and after direct speech
☐ a comma to separate direct speech from the rest of the sentence
☐ *say* when you didn't mention the listener
☐ *tell* when you mentioned the listener
☐ the correct verb tenses and pronouns in indirect speech

A | *Circle the correct words to complete the sentences.*

1. My friend Bill always <u>says / tells</u> that white lies are OK.

2. When Trish invited him to dinner, he said, <u>"I'd love to."</u> / <u>"That he'd love to."</u>

3. Then Trish told him that she <u>plans / planned</u> to cook a Chinese meal.

4. Bill said that <u>he / I</u> loved Chinese food. That was a white lie—he really dislikes it.

5. Trish served a wonderful meal. She told Bill that she <u>'d / 'll</u> cooked it all herself.

6. Bill really liked it! When he finished dinner, he <u>told / said</u> Trish, "That was great."

7. After they got married, Trish told Bill that the Chinese meal <u>is / had been</u> takeout.

8. Today, Bill always says it was the best meal of <u>my / his</u> life—and that's the truth.

B | *Rewrite each direct statement as an indirect statement. Keep the original meaning. (The direct statement was said <u>one week ago</u>.)*

Direct Speech	Indirect Speech
1. "I always get up early."	She said _____.
2. "Water boils at 100 degrees Celsius. "	He told them _____.
3. "I like your haircut."	He told me _____.
4. "I loved the pasta."	She said _____.
5. "It's my own recipe."	He said _____.
6. "I mailed you the check."	She told him _____.
7. "My boss liked my work."	He said _____.

C | *Find and correct five mistakes.*

1. A psychologist I know often tells me "that people today tell hundreds of lies every day."

2. Yesterday Marcia's boyfriend said her that he liked her new dress.

3. When she heard that, Marcia said she didn't really believe you.

4. I didn't think that was so bad. I said that her boyfriend tells her a little white lie.

5. But Marcia hates lying. She said that to me, all lies were wrong.

Indirect Speech: Tense Changes
EXTREME WEATHER

Before You Read

Look at the map and the photos on this page and the next. Discuss the questions.

1. What was happening and where?
2. What do you think the title of the article means?

Read

Read *the news article about a flood.*

Read

THE FLOOD OF THE CENTURY

Central Europe

Juuly was hot and dry. Then, in August, the skies opened. Writing from Berlin on August 13, 2002, journalist John Hooper reported **that it had been raining for more than 24 hours straight**. A huge weather system was dumping rain on eastern and central Europe. Berliners worried not only about their own city but also about Prague and Dresden, the homes of priceless treasures

indirect

of art and architecture.[1] The journalist noted **that people were already evacuating Prague and were just beginning to leave Dresden**.

As Hooper wrote his story, about 50,000 residents were streaming[2] out of Prague.

---

[1]*architecture:* the style of buildings in a particular country or at a particular time in history
[2]*stream:* to move in a continuous flow in the same direction, like water in a river

(continued on next page)

THE FLOOD OF THE CENTURY

The city's 16th century Charles Bridge was in danger of collapsing. Still, Mayor Igor Nemec told reporters **that the historic Old Town should remain safe**. Dr. Irena Kopencova wasn't that optimistic. She was sloshing[3] through the National Library of the Czech Republic in big rubber boots, grabbing old manuscripts.[4] She told Hooper sadly **that many original copies of the most treasured poems in the Czech language had been lost**.

A few days later, Dresden was battling its worst flood since 1501. All over the city, museum employees rushed items to the top floors. Egyptian stone tablets lay mixed together with some Roman statues, and masterpieces[5] by Rembrandt were piled on top of paintings by Rubens. The museum director, Martin Rohl, was still worried. He told reporter Julian Coman of the *News Telegraph* **that with another few feet of water, nothing would be safe**.

Heiko Ringel stopped stacking sandbags to talk to Coman. Ringel didn't live in Dresden anymore, but he said **he was back in his hometown that summer to help**. Why? He couldn't stand seeing all that history swept away.[6] He said **it would have been too cruel to bear**. "Dresden and Prague are the twin jewels of Central Europe."

The danger didn't stop tourism. "Flood tourists" moved from city to city gaping[7] at the flood of the century. One speculated **that it might even be the flood of the millennium**. John Hooper didn't agree. He thought climate change was causing these events, and believed that they would get worse. His headline announced **that the summer of 2002 would go down in history as the time when the weather had changed forever**.

Was Hooper right? Were the floods of 2002 just the beginning of worse and worse disasters? Or were they "normal disasters" that we should expect only once every 100 years? Right after the floods, statistical studies claimed **that floods were not getting worse**, **but that flood damage was increasing**. They concluded **that people ought to stop building so close to water**. Then, in 2003, thousands died in Europe in a heat wave that even statistics could not call "normal." And in 2006, while buildings damaged in the 2002 flood were still being restored, the Elbe flooded again —even higher than the 2002 "flood of the century." Just four years later, in the summer of 2010, more floods hit Central Europe. Poland suffered the most. Prime Minister Donald Tuck called it "the worst natural disaster in the nation's history."

Today more and more scientists are warning **that governments have to do something about climate change**. Recent events have already shown us how much we could lose if we don't listen.

---

[3]**slosh:** to walk noisily through water or mud
[4]**manuscript:** a document, often old and valuable, that is written by hand
[5]**masterpiece:** a work of art that is considered the best of its kind
[6]**sweep away:** to remove or destroy completely
[7]**gape:** to look at something for a long time, usually with your mouth open, because you are shocked

After You Read

A | Vocabulary: *Complete the sentences with the words from the box.*

| bear | collapse | damage | evacuate | optimistic | restore |

1. The mayor of the city was very ___optimistic___ during the storm. She believed things would turn out well.

2. Many people had to ___evacuate___ the city. Some left by car and some left by public transportation.

3. I couldn't ___bear___ to leave my grandmother's painting behind. It was too important to me.

4. Did the bridge ___collapse___ during the storm, or is it still standing?

5. A professional can ___restore___ this old painting so that it looks almost like it did when it was first painted.

6. The ___damage___ to the building was not too bad. They were able to fix most of it.

B | Comprehension: *Check (✓) the exact words that people from the article said.*

1. John Hooper said:
   - ☐ "It had been raining for more than 24 hours."
   - ☑ "It has been raining for more than 24 hours."

2. Dr. Irena Kopencova said:
   - ☐ "Many treasured poems in the Czech language had been lost."
   - ☑ "Many treasured poems in the Czech language have been lost."

3. Heiko Ringel said:
   - ☑ "I'm back in my hometown this summer to help."
   - ☐ "He's back in his hometown this summer to help."

4. Martin Rohl said:
   - ☐ "With another few feet of water, nothing was safe."
   - ☑ "With another few feet of water, nothing will be safe."

5. Scientists said:
   - ☑ "Governments have to do something about climate change."
   - ☐ "Governments had to do something about climate change."

INDIRECT SPEECH: TENSE CHANGES

Direct Speech			Indirect Speech				
Subject	**Reporting Verb**	**Direct Statement**	**Subject**	**Reporting Verb**	**Noun / Pronoun**	**(that)**	**Indirect Statement**
He	said,	"I **live** in Dresden." "I **moved** here in June." "I'**m looking** for an apartment." "I'**ve started** a new job." "I'**m going to stay** here." "I'**ll invite** you for the holidays." "We **can go** to the museums." "I **may look** for a roommate." "I **should get back** to work." "I **have to finish** my report." "You **must come** to visit." "We **ought to see** each other more."	He	told / said	Jim me you him her us them	(that)	he **lived** in Dresden. he **had moved** there in June. he **was looking** for an apartment. he **had started** a new job. he **was going to stay** there. he **would invite** me for the holidays. we **could go** to the museums. he **might look** for a roommate. he **should get back** to work. he **had to finish** his report. I **had to come** to visit. we **ought to see** each other more.

GRAMMAR NOTES

1 As you learned in Unit 25, when the **reporting verb** is in the **simple past**, we often **change the verb tense** in the indirect speech statement.

DIRECT SPEECH		INDIRECT SPEECH
Simple present	→	Simple past
Present progressive	→	Past progressive
Simple past	→	Past perfect
Present perfect	→	Past perfect

DIRECT SPEECH	INDIRECT SPEECH
He said, "It'**s** cloudy."	He said it **was** cloudy.
She said, "A storm **is coming**."	She said that a storm **was coming**.
He said, "Klaus **called**."	He said that Klaus **had called**.
She told him, "I'**ve heard** the news."	She told him that she'**d heard** the news.

2 **Modals often change** in indirect speech.

DIRECT SPEECH		INDIRECT SPEECH
will	→	*would*
can	→	*could*
may	→	*might*
must	→	*had to*

DIRECT SPEECH	INDIRECT SPEECH
I said, "The winds **will be** strong."	I said the winds **would be** strong.
"You **can stay** with me," he told us.	He told us that we **could stay** with him.
He said, "The storm **may cause** severe damage."	He said that the storm **might cause** severe damage.
"You **must leave**," he told us.	He told us that we **had to leave**.

3 The following **do NOT change** in indirect speech:

a. *should*, *could*, *might*, and *ought to*

b. the **past perfect**

c. the **present** and **past unreal conditional**

d. past modals

DIRECT SPEECH	INDIRECT SPEECH
"You **should listen** to the news," he told us.	He told us that we **should listen** to the news.
"I **had moved** here a week before the flood," he said.	He said he **had moved** here a week before the flood.
"If I **knew**, I **would tell** you," said Jim.	Jim said if he **knew**, he **would tell** me.
"If I **had known**, I **would have told** you," said Jim.	He said that if he **had known**, he **would have told** me.
"I **should have left**."	He said that he **should have left**.
"We **couldn't have known**."	They said they **couldn't have known**.

4 **Change time words** in indirect speech to keep the speaker's <u>original meaning</u>.

DIRECT SPEECH	→	INDIRECT SPEECH
now	→	*then*
today	→	*that day*
tomorrow	→	*the next day*
yesterday	→	*the day before*
this week / month / year	→	*that week / month / year*
last week / month / year	→	*the week / month / year before*
next week / month / year	→	*the following week / month / year*

Uta to Klaus:
- "I just got home **yesterday**. I'll start cleaning up **tomorrow**."

Klaus to Heiko (a few days later):
- Uta told me she had just gotten home **the day before**. She said she would start cleaning up **the next day**.

Lotte to her mother (right after the storm):
- "Our electricity won't be restored until **next week**."

The family newsletter (two months later):
- Lotte reported that their electricity wouldn't be restored until **the following week**.

(continued on next page)

5 Change *here* and *this* in indirect speech to keep the speaker's <u>original meaning</u>.

DIRECT SPEECH		INDIRECT SPEECH
here	→	*there*
this	→	*that*

Jim (in Athens) to Erica (in Berlin):
- "I love it **here**. **This** climate is great."

Erica to Susan (both in Berlin):
- Jim said he loved it ***there***. He told me that ***that*** climate was great.

REFERENCE NOTES

For a list of **reporting verbs**, see Appendix 14 on page A-5.

For **punctuation rules for direct speech**, see Appendix 27 on page A-13.

STEP 3 FOCUSED PRACTICE

EXERCISE 1: Discover the Grammar

Read each numbered sentence (indirect speech). Circle the letter of each sentence (direct speech) that is similar in meaning.

1. The local weather forecaster said that it was going to be a terrible storm.
   a. "It was going to be a terrible storm."
   (b.) "It's going to be a terrible storm."
   c. "It was a terrible storm."

2. She said the winds might reach 60 kilometers per hour.
   a. "The winds reached 60 kilometers per hour."
   b. "The winds would reach 60 kilometers per hour."
   (c.) "The winds may reach 60 kilometers per hour."

3. She said there would be more rain the next day.
   a. "There will be more rain the next day."
   b. "There would be more rain tomorrow."
   (c.) "There will be more rain tomorrow."

4. She told people that they should try to leave the area.
   (a.) "You should try to leave the area."
   b. "You should have tried to leave the area."
   c. "You would leave the area."

5. She reported that people were evacuating the city.
   (a.) "People are evacuating the city."
   b. "People were evacuating the city."
   c. "People evacuated the city."

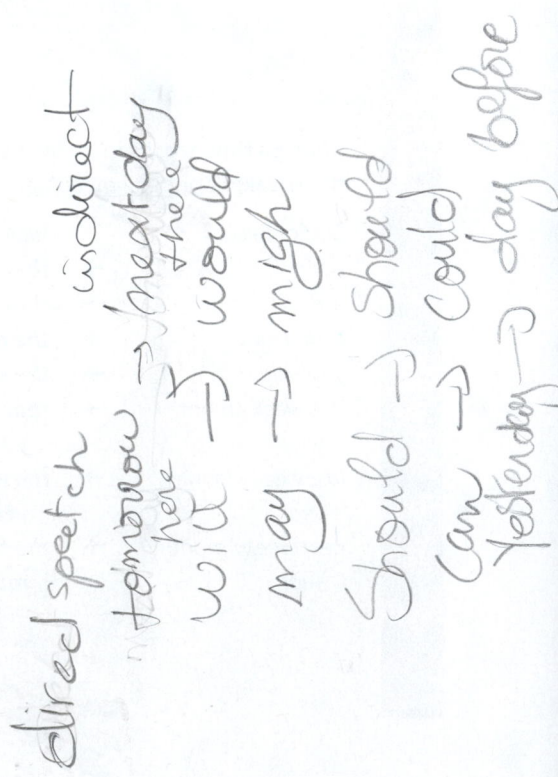

6. She said that they could expect a lot of damage.

   a. "We could expect a lot of damage." .

   b. "We could have expected a lot of damage."

   c. "We can expect a lot of damage."

7. She said that the floods were the worst they had had there.

   a. "The floods are the worst we have here."

   b. "The floods are the worst we have had here."

   c. "The floods are the worst we have had there."

8. She told them that the emergency relief workers had arrived the day before.

   a. "Emergency relief workers arrived the day before."

   b. "Emergency relief workers arrived yesterday."

   c. "Emergency relief workers arrived today."

9. She reported that the president would be there to inspect the damage.

   a. "The president will be here to inspect the damage."

   b. "The president will be there to inspect the damage."

   c. "The president would be there to inspect the damage."

10. She said that if they hadn't had time to prepare, the danger would have been even greater.

   a. "If we hadn't had time to prepare, the danger would have been even greater."

   b. "If we don't have time to prepare, the danger will be even greater."

   c. "If we didn't have time to prepare, the danger would be even greater."

EXERCISE 2: Indirect Statements and Tense Changes

(Grammar Notes 1–5)

You are in Berlin. Imagine you heard these rumors yesterday about the storm in Europe. Use **They said** *to report the rumors.*

1. "The storm changed direction last night."

   They said that the storm had changed direction the night before.

2. "It's going to pass north of here."

   They said that it was going to pass north of here.

3. "The bridge collapsed this afternoon."

   They said that the bridge had collapsed that afternoon

4. "It's not really a hurricane, just a big storm."

   They said that it was not really a hurricane, just a big storm

(continued on next page)

5. "People in Dresden are evacuating."

They said that people in Dresden were evacuating

6. "They won't restore the electricity until tomorrow."

They said that they wouldn't → _following day_

7. "They can't reopen the schools because of the damage."

They said that they couldn't reopen the schools
because of the damage

8. "You ought to use bottled water for a few days."

they said that they ought to use bottled water
for a few days.

EXERCISE 3: Indirect Statements and Tense Changes (Grammar Notes 1–3)

A | *Read the interview between radio station WWEA and meteorologist Dr. Ronald Myers.*

WWEA: Exactly how common are floods?

MYERS: Floods are the most common of all natural disasters except fire. They are also the most widespread. They occur everywhere.

WWEA: What causes them?

MYERS: Usually they are the result of intense, heavy rainfall. But they can also be caused by melting snow. Another cause is unusually high tides in coastal areas. Then, of course, there are tsunamis, like the one that struck Japan in 2011. These tremendous waves are often caused by earthquakes.

WWEA: And what causes these high tides?

MYERS: Severe winds over the ocean surface cause high tides. Often these winds are part of a hurricane.

WWEA: What is a *flash flood*? Is it just a very bad flood?

MYERS: No. A flash flood comes with little or no warning. Because of this, it's the most dangerous type of flood. In fact, flash floods cause almost 75 percent of all flood-related deaths.

WWEA: That's terrible. Is there anything that can be done?

MYERS: We've made progress in predicting floods. But we must get better at predicting flash floods.

WWEA: Is there anything that can be done to actually prevent floods?

MYERS: People must improve their protection of the Earth and the environment. When we replace grass and soil with roads and buildings, the ground loses its ability to absorb rainfall. This can lead to flooding. We should restore these "green" areas. In addition, many scientists believe that global warming is causing an increase in the number of floods.

WWEA: So the answer lies in better prediction and better treatment of the Earth?

MYERS: Exactly. We can't completely stop floods from happening. It's part of nature. But I'm optimistic that we *can* predict them better and prevent flood damage from increasing.

B | *Now read the following statements. For each statement write* **That's right** *or* **That's wrong** *and report what Dr. Myers said.*

1. Floods are not very common.

   That's wrong. He said floods were the most common of all natural disasters except fire.

2. They are very widespread. → everywhere

   that's true, He said that they were also the most widespread. intense

3. Floods are usually caused by melting snow.

   that's wrong, He said that they were result of heavy rain fall, melting snow

4. Tsunamis are often caused by high tides.

   that's wrong He said that the Tsunamis were often caused by earthquakes.

5. A flash flood is just a very bad flood.

   wrong He said that Flash Flash came with little or no warning

6. A flash flood is the most dangerous type of flood.

   that's right, He said that it was the most dangerous type of flood.

7. Flash floods cause 25 percent of all flood-related deaths.

   that's wrong, He said that it caused Almost 75%

8. We have made progress in predicting floods.

   right He said that we had made progress in predicting Floods.

9. People are doing a good job of protecting the Earth and the environment.

   wrong, He said that people had to impro

10. Restoring green areas can lead to flooding.

    wrong, He said that we should restore the green areas.

11. Many scientists believe that global warming is causing an increase in the number of floods.

    true. He said that they believed that global warming, was causing an increase in the

12. We can completely stop floods from happening.

    wrong, He said that we couldn't completely s

13. It's possible to prevent flood damage from increasing.

    true it was possible.

EXERCISE 4: Direct Speech

(Grammar Notes 1–5)

John and Eva live in Germany. Read the information that John got during the day. Then write what people said. Use direct speech.

> John's mother called. She told him that she was listening to the weather report. She said that she was worried about John and Eva. She told him that if they weren't so stubborn they'd pack up and leave right then.

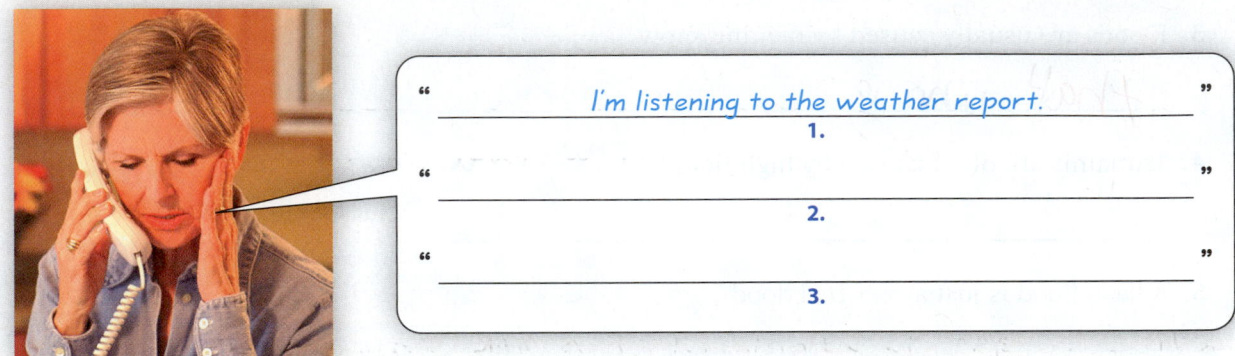

"   I'm listening to the weather report.   "
1.

"   "
2.

"   "
3.

> John's father gave him some good advice. He said he'd had some experience with floods. He said John and Eva had to put sandbags in front of their doors. He also told John that they ought to fill the sinks and bathtubs with clean water. He said they should buy a lot of batteries.

"   "
4.

"   "
5.

"   "
6.

"   "
7.

> John's brother, Steve, called. He and Uta are worried. Their place is too close to the river. He said that they couldn't stay there, and he told John that they wanted to stay with him and Eva. He said they were leaving that night. Steve told John that he and Uta should have called sooner.

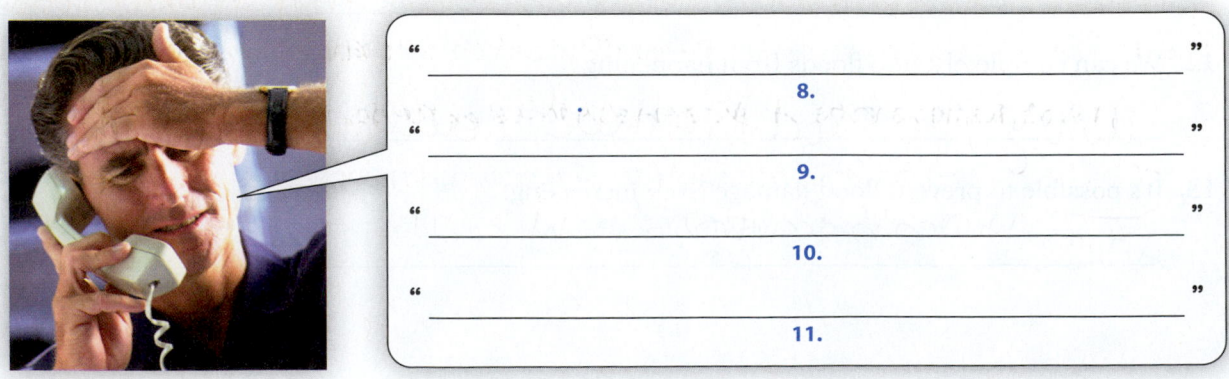

"   "
8.

"   "
9.

"   "
10.

"   "
11.

John listened to the storm warning in the afternoon. The forecaster said the storm would hit that night. She warned that the rainfall was going to be very heavy, and she said that the storm might last for several hours.

"_____
12.

"_____
13.

"_____
14.

EXERCISE 5: Editing

Read this student's report. There are ten mistakes in the use of indirect speech. The first mistake is already corrected. Find and correct nine more.

What is it like to live through a flood? For my report, I interviewed the Nemec family, who experienced last month's floods in our city. They reported that ~~we~~ *they* had experienced fear and sadness. On September 14, the family went to a movie. Jerzy, a high school student, said they can't drive the car home because their street was flooded. He told it had happened in only three hours. Mrs. Nemec said that all their belongings were ruined, but that their cat has gone to an upstairs bedroom. They were sad about losing so many valuable items, but she said she will have been much sadder to lose the family pet. Jerzy's father also said their home had been a complete mess and that the family had worked all this week to clean out the house. Anna, who is in junior high school, wanted to keep her old dollhouse. It had belonged to her mother and her mother's mother. At first, her father told her that she can't keep it because seeing it would just make her sad. Anna replied that she saw memories in that dollhouse—not just broken wood. She said I couldn't bear to throw it away. In the end, they kept it. Mr. Nemec said he and Anna are able to restore the dollhouse a few weeks later. Mrs. Nemec said that Anna had taught them something important today.

EXERCISE 6: Listening

A | *Read the sentences. Then listen to the winter storm warning. Listen again and circle the word or phrase that best completes each sentence.*

1. A foot of snow <u>will fall</u> / (<u>has fallen</u>) this morning.

2. <u>Schools / Roads</u> may remain closed tomorrow.

3. Snow and high winds are causing dangerous <u>conditions / accidents</u> on the roads.

4. If you must drive, you should bring extra clothes and have plenty of <u>food / gas</u>.

5. The post office is <u>closed / open</u> now.

6. You can buy food and other necessary items until this <u>afternoon / evening</u>.

7. Driving probably <u>will / won't</u> be easier tomorrow.

B | *Work in small groups. Listen again to the winter storm warning and check (✓) the correct information. It's all right to leave something blank.*

Schools

1. Today schools:	✓ closed at 10:00	☐ will close at 1:00
2. Students and teachers:	☐ should stay at school	☐ should go home immediately
3. Tomorrow schools:	☐ will open	☐ may stay closed

Roads

4. Road conditions:	☐ are safe	☐ are dangerous
5. Drivers must:	☐ drive slowly	☐ pick up passengers
6. Everyone should:	☐ avoid driving	☐ continue driving

Public Offices

7. Libraries:	☐ will stay open	☐ will close at 1:00
8. Post offices:	☐ will stay open until 5:00	☐ will close early
9. Government offices:	☐ will be closed tomorrow	☐ will remain open tomorrow

Businesses

10. Banks:	☐ will close at noon	☐ will stay open until 3:00
11. Gas stations:	☐ will close at noon	☐ will stay open until evening
12. Supermarkets:	☐ are open now	☐ are closed now

C | *Now compare your information with what other group members heard. Complete any missing information in your chart. Then listen again and check your answers.*

> **EXAMPLE:** **A:** She said that schools would close at 1:00.
> **B:** That's not right. She said that schools had closed at 10:00.

EXERCISE 7: Pronunciation

A | *Read and listen to the Pronunciation Note.*

Pronunciation Note

When we speak, we usually **stress content words**.

Content words are the words in a sentence that **carry the most information**.

Some types of content words:

Nouns (*Tom, storm, gas, camera*)   **Main Verbs** (*say, tell, look, get*)

Adjectives (*big, dangerous, careful*)   **Adverbs** (*always, carefully, later, yesterday*)

Wh- question words (*what, when, who*)   **Negatives** (*no, not, didn't, weren't*)

EXAMPLES: He **said** he'd **call** us **soon**.

Jorge said we should **listen** to the **news**.

Emma told me she **never works late**.

They **told** us that the **storm** was **coming**.

B | *Listen to the short conversations. Listen again and put a dot (●) over the words that are stressed in the answers.*

1. **A:** Will Debra and Tom leave soon?

   B: Tom said they would leave tomorrow.

2. **A:** How are the roads?

   B: He said they weren't dangerous.

3. **A:** Has Jorge called?

   B: No. He told me he'd call us later.

4. **A:** What did they say on the weather report?

   B: They said that the storm could start soon.

5. **A:** Is there enough gas in the car?

   B: No. I told you we needed some yesterday.

6. **A:** Did you pack the camera?

   B: Definitely. You told me that I should pack it.

7. **A:** What did your father tell you?

   B: He told me to drive carefully.

C | *Listen again to the conversations and repeat the answers. Then practice the conversations with a partner.*

EXERCISE 8: Game: Telephone

Work in small groups. Student A whispers something in the ear of Student B. Student B reports (in a whisper) to Student C what he or she heard. Each student reports to the next student in a whisper and may only say the information once. The last student tells the group what he or she heard. Expect surprises.

EXAMPLE: **A:** There won't be any class tomorrow.
                  B: He said that there wouldn't be any class tomorrow.
                  C: She said that there wouldn't be any gas tomorrow.

EXERCISE 9: Interview

Use the questions below to interview three classmates. Report your findings to the class.

- Have you ever experienced extreme weather conditions such as the following?

  a hurricane or a tornado   a flood

  a heat wave   a sandstorm or a dust storm

  a blizzard   wildfires

  a drought   *Other:* _____

- How did you feel?

- What did you do to protect yourself?

- What advice would you give to someone in the same situation?

EXAMPLE: Arielle told me she had experienced a heat wave when temperatures reached over 40 degrees Celsius (That's 104 degrees Fahrenheit). She told me that she had felt sick a lot of the time. She said she had stayed indoors until evening every day. Arielle told me that everyone should move slowly and drink a lot of liquids in hot weather.

EXERCISE 10: Writing

A | *Write a paragraph reporting someone else's experiences with extreme weather. Use information from your interview in Exercise 9, or interview another person. Use indirect speech.*

EXAMPLE: My friend Julie told me about a dust storm in Australia. She said that one afternoon, the sky had gotten very dark, and the wind had started to blow hard. Her mother told her that they all had to go inside right away and close all the windows. Then . . .

B | *Check your work. Use the Editing Checklist.*

Editing Checklist

In indirect speech, did you make necessary changes in . . . ?
- ☐ verb tenses
- ☐ modals
- ☐ time words (to keep the speaker's original meaning)
- ☐ *here* and *this* (to keep the speaker's original meaning)

A | Circle the correct words to complete the indirect speech sentences.

Direct Speech	Indirect Speech
"It's cloudy."	She said it <u>was / were</u> cloudy. **1.**
"You should take an umbrella to work."	He told me <u>she / I</u> should <u>take / have taken</u> an umbrella **2.** **3.** to work.
"The temperature may drop."	She said the temperature <u>must / might</u> drop. **4.**
"Tomorrow will be nice."	He said yesterday that <u>tomorrow / today</u> <u>will / would</u> be nice. **5.** **6.**
"We can expect a lot of damage here in Florida."	She said they <u>can / could</u> expect a lot of damage **7.** <u>here / there</u> in Florida. *(reported a week later in Texas)* **8.**

B | Rewrite each direct statement as an indirect statement. Keep the original meaning.
(The direct statement was said to you <u>two months ago</u>).

Direct Speech	Indirect Speech
1. "It's going to rain."	She said _____.
2. "It could be the worst storm this year."	He said _____.
3. "It's going to start soon."	She said _____.
4. "We should buy water."	He said _____.
5. "We must leave right now."	He told me _____.
6. "I'll call you tomorrow."	She said _____.

C | Find and correct six mistakes.

What a storm! They told it is going to be bad, but it was terrible. They said it will last two

days, but it lasted four. On the first day of the storm, my mother called and told me that we

should have left the house right now. (I still can hear her exact words: "You should leave the

house *right now*!") We should have listened to her! We just didn't believe it was going to be so

serious. I told her last night that if we had known, we would had left right away. We're lucky we

survived. I just listened to the weather forecast. Good news! They said tomorrow should be

sunny.

STEP 1 GRAMMAR IN CONTEXT

Before You Read

Look at the photo. Discuss the questions.

1. What time is it? Where is the man?
2. How does the man feel? Why does he feel that way?

Read

Read the transcript of a radio interview with the director of a sleep clinic.

HERE'S TO YOUR HEALTH

THE SNOOZE NEWS

CONNIE: Good morning! This is Connie Sung, bringing you "Here's to Your Health," a program about today's health issues. This morning, we've invited Dr. Thorton Ray **to talk to us about insomnia**. As you probably know, insomnia is a problem with getting to sleep or staying asleep. Dr. Ray is the director of the Sleep Disorders[1] Clinic, so he should have some good information for us. Welcome to the show!

DR. RAY: Thanks, Connie. It's great to be here.

CONNIE: Your book *Night Shift*[2] will be coming out soon. In it, you tell people **to pay more attention to sleep disorders**. But why is losing a little sleep such a big problem?

DR. RAY: I always tell people **to think of the worst industrial disaster**[3] **they've ever heard about**. Usually it was caused at least in part by sleep deprivation.[4] Then I ask them **to think about what can happen if they drive when they're tired**. Every year, more than 100,000 automobile accidents in this country are caused by sleepy drivers.

---

[1] *disorder:* a physical or mental problem that can affect health for a long period of time
[2] *shift:* a work period, especially in a factory (the night shift is often midnight to 8:00 A.M.)
[3] *industrial disaster:* an accident in a factory that causes a great deal of damage and loss of life
[4] *deprivation:* not having something that you need or want

HERE'S TO YOUR HEALTH

THE SN☯☯ZE NEWS

CONNIE: Wow! That *is* a big problem.

DR. RAY: And a costly one. Recently, a large study of workers' fatigue reported that the problem costs U.S. employers around $136.4 billion a year in lost work time.

CONNIE: That's astonishing! But now let's talk about how individuals can deal with insomnia. For example, if I came to your clinic, what would you advise me **to do**?

DR. RAY: First, I would find out about some of your habits. If you drank coffee or cola late in the day, I would tell you **to stop**. The caffeine in these drinks interferes with sleep.

CONNIE: What about old-fashioned remedies like warm milk?

DR. RAY: Actually, a lot of home remedies do make sense. We tell patients **to have a high-carbohydrate[5] snack like a banana before they go to bed**. Warm milk helps too. But I'd advise you **not to eat a heavy meal before bed**.

CONNIE: My doctor told me **to get more exercise**, but when I run at night, I have a hard time getting to sleep.

DR. RAY: It's true that if you exercise regularly, you'll sleep better. But we always tell patients **not to exercise too close to bedtime**.

CONNIE: My mother always told me just **to get up and scrub the floor when I couldn't sleep**.

DR. RAY: That works. I advised one patient **to balance his checkbook**. He went right to sleep, just to escape from the task.

"I couldn't sleep."

CONNIE: Suppose I try these remedies and they don't help?

DR. RAY: If the problem persists, we often ask patients **to come and spend a night at our sleep clinic**. Our equipment monitors the patient through the night. In fact, if you're really interested, we can invite you **to come to the clinic for a night**.

CONNIE: Maybe I should do that.

---

[5] **high-carbohydrate:** containing a great deal of sugar or starch (for example fruit, potatoes, and rice)

After You Read

A | Vocabulary: *Circle the letter of the word or phrase that best completes each sentence.*

1. An **astonishing** fact is very _____.
   a. frightening
   b. surprising
   c. uninteresting

2. **Fatigue** is a feeling of extreme _____.
   a. excitement
   b. pain
   c. tiredness

3. If someone **interferes** with your success, he or she _____ it.
   a. enjoys
   b. prevents
   c. causes

4. Hank's parents **monitored** his homework by _____ it every night.
   a. checking
   b. doing
   c. copying

5. My grandparents use traditional **remedies**. Those old _____ fascinate me.
   a. recipes
   b. stories
   c. treatments

6. After Jerry took pain medication, his headache **persisted**. It _____ for days.
   a. stopped
   b. continued
   c. improved

B | Comprehension: *Check (✓) the things Dr. Ray suggests for people with insomnia.*

☐ 1. Stop drinking coffee and cola late in the day.

☐ 2. Eat a heavy meal before going to bed.

☐ 3. Get more exercise.

☐ 4. Exercise right before bedtime.

☐ 5. Get up from bed and balance your checkbook.

☐ 6. Spend the night at the sleep clinic.

INDIRECT INSTRUCTIONS, COMMANDS, REQUESTS, AND INVITATIONS

Direct Speech		
Subject	**Reporting Verb**	**Direct Speech**
He	said,	"**Drink** warm milk." "**Don't drink** coffee." "Can you **turn out** the light, please?" "Why don't you **visit** the clinic?"

Indirect Speech			
Subject	**Reporting Verb**	**Noun / Pronoun**	**Indirect Speech**
He	told advised asked	Connie her	**to drink** warm milk. **not to drink** coffee. **to turn out** the light.
	said		
	invited	her	**to visit** the clinic.

GRAMMAR NOTES

1 In **indirect speech**, use an **infinitive** (**to** + **base form** of the verb) for:

- **instructions**

- **commands**

- **requests**

- **invitations**

DIRECT SPEECH	INDIRECT SPEECH
"**Come** early," said the doctor.	The doctor said **to come** early.
The doctor told her, "**Lie down**."	The doctor told her **to lie down**.
"Could you please **arrive** by 8:00?"	He asked Connie **to arrive** by 8:00.
"Could you **join** me for lunch?"	He invited us **to join** him for lunch.

2 Use a **negative infinitive** (**not** + **infinitive**) for:

- **negative instructions**

- **negative commands**

- **negative requests**

DIRECT SPEECH	INDIRECT SPEECH
"**Don't eat** after 9:00 P.M.," he said.	He told me **not to eat** after 9:00 P.M.
Mrs. Bartolotta told me, "**Don't wake** Cindy!"	Mrs. Bartolotta told me **not to wake** Cindy.
Jean said, "Please **don't set** the alarm."	Jean asked me **not to set** the alarm.

REFERENCE NOTES

For a list of **reporting verbs**, see Appendix 14 on page A-5.

For **punctuation rules for direct speech**, see Appendix 27 on page A-13.

EXERCISE 1: Discover the Grammar

Connie Sung decided to write an article about her visit to Dr. Ray's clinic. Read her notes for the article. Underline the indirect instructions, commands, requests, and invitations. Circle the reporting verbs that introduce them.

A Dream Job

2/18 11:00 A.M. The clinic called and (asked) me <u>to arrive at 8:30 tonight</u>. They told me to bring my nightshirt and toothbrush. They told me people also like to bring their own pillow, but I decided to travel light.

8:30 P.M. I arrived on schedule. My room was small but cozy. Only the video camera and cable told me I was in a sleep clinic. Juan Estrada, the technician for the night shift, told me to relax and watch TV for an hour.

9:30 P.M. Juan came back and got me ready for the test. He pasted 12 small metal disks to my face, legs, and stomach. I asked him to explain, and he told me that the disks, called electrodes, would be connected to a machine that records electrical activity in the brain. I felt like a character in a science fiction movie.

11:30 P.M. Juan came back and asked me to get into bed. After he hooked me up to the machine, he instructed me not to leave the bed that night. I fell asleep easily.

2/19 7:00 A.M. Juan came to awaken me and to disconnect the wires. I told him that I didn't think insomnia was my problem—those electrodes hadn't interfered with my sleep at all! He invited me to join him in the next room, where he had spent the whole night monitoring the equipment. I looked at the pages of graphs and wondered aloud whether Juan and Dr. Ray would be able to read my weird dream of the night before. Juan laughed and told me not to worry. "Those just show electrical impulses," he assured me.

8:00 A.M. Dr. Ray reviewed my data with me. He told me I had healthy sleep patterns, except for some leg movements during the night. He told me to get more exercise, and I promised I would.

EXERCISE 2: Indirect Instructions: Affirmative and Negative
(Grammar Notes 1–2)

Read the questions to Helen, a newspaper columnist who writes about health issues. Report her instructions using the verbs in parentheses.

Q: Do you have a remedy for insomnia? I have trouble getting to sleep.—MIKE LANDERS, DETROIT

A: Don't drink anything with caffeine after 2:00 P.M. Try exercising regularly, early in the day.

1. (tell) _She told him not to drink anything with caffeine after 2:00 P.M._

2. (say) _She said to try exercising regularly, early in the day._

Q: What can I do to soothe a sore throat? I never take medicine unless I have to.—ANNE BLY, TROY

A: One remedy is hot herbal tea with honey. But don't drink black tea. It will make your throat dry.

3. (say) _____

4. (tell) _____

Q: I get leg cramps at night. They wake me up, and I can't get back to sleep.—LOU RICH, DALLAS

A: The next time you feel a cramp, do this: Pinch the place between your upper lip and your nose. The cramp should stop right away. Sounds simple, but it's astonishing how well this works.

5. (say) _____

Q: Do you know of an inexpensive way to remove stains on teeth?—PETE LEE, BROOKLYN

A: Make a toothpaste of one tablespoon of baking soda and a little water. Brush as usual.

6. (tell) _____

7. (say) _____

Q: What can I do to ease an itchy poison ivy rash?—MARVIN SMITH, HARTFORD

A: Spread cool, cooked oatmeal over the rash. Also, try soaking the rash in a cool bath with a quarter cup of baking soda. Don't scratch the rash. That will make it worse.

8. (tell) _____

9. (say) _____

10. (tell) _____

Q: Bugs love me. They bite me all the time.—ED SMALL, TULSA

A: There are a few things you can do to keep bugs away. Eat onions or garlic every day. Your skin will have a slight odor that bugs hate. Or ask your doctor about a vitamin B supplement.

11. (say) _____

12. (tell) _____

IMPORTANT: A PROBLEM THAT PERSISTS MIGHT NEED MEDICAL TREATMENT. CALL YOUR DOCTOR ABOUT ANY CONDITION THAT DOESN'T IMPROVE OR GETS WORSE.

EXERCISE 3: Direct and Indirect Speech

(Grammar Notes 1–2)

A | *Connie had a dream at the sleep clinic. She wrote about it in her journal. Read her account of the dream and underline the indirect instructions, commands, requests, and invitations.*

I dreamed that an extraterrestrial came into my room. He told me <u>to get up</u>. Then he said to follow him. There was a spaceship outside the clinic. It was an astonishing sight! The creature from outer space invited me to come aboard. I asked him to lead the way! Juan, the lab technician, was on the ship. Suddenly, Juan told me to pilot the ship. He ordered me not to leave the controls. Then he went to sleep. Next, Dr. Ray was at my side giving me instructions. He told me to slow down. Then he said to point the ship toward the Earth. There was a loud knocking noise as we hit the ground, and I told everyone not to panic. Then I heard Juan tell me to wake up. I opened my eyes and saw him walking into my room at the sleep clinic.

B | *Complete the cartoon by writing what each character said.*

EXERCISE 4: Editing

Read this entry in a student's journal. There are twelve mistakes in the use of indirect instructions, commands, requests, and invitations. The first mistake is already corrected. Find and correct eleven more. Don't forget to check punctuation. Mistakes with quotation marks count as one mistake for the sentence.

In writing class today, the teacher asked Juan ^to read one of his stories. Juan, who works in a sleep clinic, read a story about someone with insomnia. It was wonderful, and everyone in class enjoyed it a lot. After class, the teacher invited me read a story in class next week. I don't feel ready to do this. I asked her no to call on me next week because I'm having trouble getting ideas. She told me that not to worry, and she said to wait for two weeks. I was still worried about coming up with an idea, so I decided to talk to Juan after class. I asked him tell me the source for his ideas. He was really helpful. He said that they came from his dreams. I was astonished—I'd never thought of using my dreams! He said me to keep a dream journal for ideas. Then he invited me "to read some of his journal." It was very interesting, so I asked him to give me some tips on remembering dreams. (Juan says that everyone dreams, but many people, like me, just don't remember their dreams in the morning.) Again, Juan was very helpful. He said getting a good night's sleep because the longer dreams came after a long period of sleep. He also tell me to keep my journal by the bed and to write as soon as I wake up. He said to no move from the sleeping position. He also told me not think about the day at first. (If you think about your day, you might forget your dreams.) Most important: Every night he tells himself that to remember his dreams. These all sound like great ideas, and I want to try them out right away. The only problem is, I'm so excited about this, I'm not sure I'll be able to fall asleep!

EXERCISE 5: Listening

A | *Read the statements. Then listen to Juan's conversation with Ann. Listen again and check (✓)* **True** *or* **False** *for each statement. Correct the false statements.*

	True	False

1. Juan just got back from a ~~sleep~~ *headache* clinic. ☐ ☑

2. At the clinic, they said that too much sleep causes headaches. ☐ ☐

3. Juan thinks the night shift interferes with his sleep. ☐ ☐

4. Ann advised him not to use painkillers right now. ☐ ☐

5. She suggested massaging around his eyes. ☐ ☐

6. At the clinic, they said to eat several large meals every day. ☐ ☐

7. Ann has been working at a headache clinic for a long time. ☐ ☐

B | *Listen again to the conversation. Check (✓) the correct column to show what the doctors at the clinic told Juan to do, what they told him not to do, and what they didn't mention.*

	Do	Don't Do	Not Mentioned
1. Get regular exercise.	☑	☐	☐
2. Get eight hours of sleep.	☐	☐	☐
3. Take painkillers.	☐	☐	☐
4. Use an ice pack.	☐	☐	☐
5. Massage around the eyes.	☐	☐	☐
6. Eat three big meals a day.	☐	☐	☐
7. Eat chocolate.	☐	☐	☐
8. Avoid cheese.	☐	☐	☐

EXERCISE 6: Pronunciation

🎧 **A** | *Read and listen to the Pronunciation Note.*

Pronunciation Note

As you learned in Unit 26, **content words** are usually **stressed**.

In **affirmative** indirect instructions, commands, requests, and invitations, in addition to other content words in the sentence, we usually **stress**:

- the **reporting verb**
- the **base form** of the verb in the infinitive (*to* isn't stressed)

EXAMPLES: The doctor **invited** her to **visit** the sleep clinic.

They **asked** us to **arrive** by 8:00.

In **negative** instructions, commands, requests, and invitations, we also **stress** *not*.

EXAMPLES: They **told** him **not** to **eat** a big meal.

They **said not** to **watch** TV before bedtime.

🎧 **B** | *Listen to the short conversations. Circle the words you hear.*

1. **A:** What did the doctor say?

   B: She told me <u>to eat / not to eat</u> a lot of cheese.

2. **A:** What time are you going to the sleep clinic?

   B: Well, they asked me <u>to arrive / not to arrive</u> before 8:00.

3. **A:** How can I remember my dreams?

   B: I'd advise you <u>to sleep / not to sleep</u> for a long time, if possible.

4. **A:** Is Ella jogging with us today?

   B: No. Her doctor told her <u>to exercise / not to exercise</u> in the morning.

5. **A:** This article says that vinegar is good for a sunburn.

   B: Really? My mother always said <u>to use / not to use</u> that.

6. **A:** Did you tell your boss you needed a new schedule?

   B: Yes. I asked him <u>to put / not to put</u> me on the night shift.

🎧 **C** | *Listen again to the conversations and repeat the answers. Then practice the conversations with a partner. Use the correct stress.*

EXERCISE 7: Problem Solving

A | *What advice have you heard for the following problems? Work in pairs and talk about what to do and what not to do for them.*

- minor kitchen burns
- insomnia
- insect bites
- headaches
- snoring
- hiccups

- a cold
- blisters
- poison ivy
- a sore throat
- a tooth ache
- *Other:* _____

> **EXAMPLE:** **A:** My mother always told me to hold a burn under cold water.
> **B:** They say not to put butter on a burn.

B | *Choose two problems. Take turns reporting to the class.*

> **EXAMPLE:** **A:** My mother always told me to hold a burn under cold water.
> **B:** For insomnia, my grandparents said to . . .

EXERCISE 8: Picture Discussion

Jeff's parents went out for the evening and left a list of instructions for him. Work in pairs. Read the list and look at the picture on the next page. Talk about which instructions Jeff followed and which ones he didn't follow. Use indirect instructions.

> Dear Jeff,
>
> We'll be home late. Here are a few things to remember:
>
> Don't stay up after 10:00.
> Don't drink any cola —it keeps you awake. Drink some milk instead.
> Have some cake, but please save some for us.
> Please take the garbage out. Also, wash the dishes and put
>   them away.
> And please let the cat in —then close and lock the back door.
> Do your homework.
> Don't watch any horror movies. (They give you nightmares—remember?)
> Don't invite your friends over tonight.
>
>   Love,
>   Mom and Dad

> **EXAMPLE:** **A:** His parents told him not to stay up after 10:00, but it's 11:30 and he's not in bed— he's asleep on the couch and having a nightmare.
> **B:** They also said to . . .

EXERCISE 9: Writing

A | *Write a paragraph about a dream you had or one that someone has told you about. You can even invent a dream. Use the paragraph from Connie's journal in Exercise 3 as a model. Use indirect instructions, commands, requests, and invitations.*

> **EXAMPLE:** One night I dreamed that I was in my grandmother's kitchen. In my dream, I saw a beautiful, carved wooden door. My grandmother invited me to open the door. She said that there were a lot of rooms in the house, and she invited me to explore them with her.

B | *Exchange your paragraph with a partner. Draw a sketch of your partner's dream and write the direct speech in speech bubbles. Discuss your sketch with your partner to make sure you understood the story and the indirect speech in your partner's dream. Make any changes necessary in your paragraph to make your writing clearer.*

C | *Check your work. Use the Editing Checklist.*

Editing Checklist

Did you use . . . ?

☐ affirmative infinitives to report affirmative indirect instructions, commands, requests, and invitations

☐ negative infinitives to report negative indirect instructions, commands, and requests

---

A | *Circle the correct words or punctuation mark to complete the sentences.*

1. I arrived at 8:00 because the doctor asked me to come early **. / ?**

2. Mr. Vance's class asked him to **give / gave** a test on Friday.

3. The teacher said, **"To sit down." / "Please sit down."**

4. Johannes advised us **don't / not to** worry.

5. Some experts **say / tell** to eat a snack before bedtime.

6. At the sleep clinic, the technician **told / said** me to relax and watch TV.

7. My neighbors **invited / advised** me to have dinner at their new home.

B | *Rewrite the direct speech as an indirect instruction, command, request, or invitation. Use an appropriate reporting verb (**advise**, **ask**, **invite**, or **tell**). Use pronouns.*

1. Officer David Zhu to Anita: "Please show me your license."

   _____

2. Doctor Sue Rodriguez to Sam: "You ought to get more exercise."

   _____

3. Ms. Carson to her students: "Please come to the English Department party."

   _____

4. Robert to Nina: "Could you turn on the light, please?"

   _____

5. Lisa to Nina and Paulo: "Why don't you hang out at my house?"

   _____

C | *Find and correct eight mistakes. Remember to check punctuation.*

My teacher, Mr. Wong, told to sleep well before the test. He said to don't stay up late studying. He always invites we to ask him questions. He says, "Not to be shy." I'm glad my friend Tom advised me taking his class. He said me to register early, and he warned me "that the class filled up fast every semester." I told him don't to worry. I said I'd already registered.

Indirect Questions
JOB INTERVIEWS

STEP 1 GRAMMAR IN CONTEXT

Before You Read

Look at the photo and the title of the article. Discuss the questions.

1. What are the people doing?
2. Are the man's questions typical in this situation? What is the woman's reaction?
3. What do you think a *stress interview* is?

Read

Read the excerpt from an article about job interviews.

The **STRESS**
Interview
By Miguel Vega

Why can't you work under pressure? Have you cleaned out your car recently? Who wrote your application letter for you?

Do I really want this job?

A few weeks ago, Melissa Morrow had an unusual job interview. First, the interviewer asked **why she couldn't work under pressure**. Before she could answer, he asked **if she had cleaned out her car recently**. Right after that he wanted to know **who had written her application letter for her**. Melissa was shocked, but she handled herself well. She asked the interviewer **whether he was going to ask her serious questions**. Then she politely ended the interview.

Melissa had had a *stress interview*, a type of job interview that features tough, tricky questions, long silences, and negative evaluations of the job candidate. To the unhappy candidate, this may seem unnecessarily nasty on the interviewer's part. However, some positions require an ability to handle just this kind of pressure. If there is an accident in an oil well near the coast, for example, the oil company's public relations officer[1] must remain calm when hostile[2] reporters ask **how the accident could have occurred**.

(*continued on next page*)

---
[1]*public relations officer:* someone hired by a company to explain to the public what the company does, so that the public will understand it and approve of it
[2]*hostile:* angry and unfriendly

The STRESS Interview

The uncomfortable atmosphere[3] of a stress interview gives the potential employer a chance to watch a candidate react to pressure. In one case, the interviewer ended each interview by saying, "We're really not sure that you're the right person for this job." One excellent candidate asked the interviewer angrily **if he was sure he knew how to conduct an interview**. She clearly could not handle the pressure she would encounter as a TV news reporter—the job she was interviewing for.

Stress interviews may be appropriate for some jobs, but they can also work against a company. Some excellent candidates may refuse the job after a hostile interview. Melissa Morrow handled her interview extremely well, but she later asked herself **if she really wanted to work for that company**. Her answer was *no*.

A word of warning to job candidates: Not all tough questioning is legitimate.[4] In some countries, certain questions are illegal unless the answers are directly related to the job. If an interviewer asks **how old you are, whether you are married**, or **how much money you owe**, you can refuse to answer. If you think a question isn't appropriate, then ask the interviewer **how the answer specifically relates to that job**. If you don't get a satisfactory explanation, you don't have to answer the question. And remember: Whatever happens, don't lose your cool.[5] The interview will be over before you know it!

DID YOU KNOW . . . ?

In some countries, employers must hire only on the basis of skills and experience. In Canada, most countries in Europe, and in the United States, for example, an interviewer cannot ask an applicant certain questions unless the information is related to the job. Here are some questions an interviewer may NOT ask:

✗ How old are you?

✗ What is your religion?

✗ Are you married?

✗ What does your husband (or wife) do?

✗ Have you ever been arrested?

✗ How many children do you have?

✗ How tall are you?

✗ Where were you born?

---

[3]*atmosphere:* the feeling that you get from a situation or a place
[4]*legitimate:* proper and allowable
[5]*lose your cool:* to get excited and angry

After You Read

A | **Vocabulary:** *Circle the letter of the word or phrase that best completes each sentence.*

1. A job **evaluation** gives a worker _____.
   a. more money
   b. more vacation time
   c. comments on his or her work

2. A bad way to **handle** an interview is to _____.
   a. say the right things
   b. get angry
   c. ask good questions

3. A **candidate** for a job promotion _____ get a better position.
   a. may
   b. will
   c. can't

4. A job with a lot of **pressure** _____.
   a. pays well
   b. is easy
   c. is difficult

5. Sara's behavior was **appropriate**. She did the _____ thing.
   a. right
   b. wrong
   c. easiest

6. A **potential** problem is one that _____.
   a. is very serious
   b. may happen
   c. has an easy solution

B | **Comprehension:** *Check (✓) the questions the interviewer asked Melissa Morrow.*

☐ **1.** "Does she really want to work for this company?"

☐ **2.** "Have you cleaned out your car recently?"

☐ **3.** "Is he going to ask me serious questions?"

☐ **4.** "How can the accident have occurred?"

☐ **5.** "Why can't you work under pressure?"

☐ **6.** "Are you sure you know how to conduct an interview?"

INDIRECT QUESTIONS

Direct Speech: *Yes / No* Questions		
Subject	**Reporting Verb**	**Direct Question**
He	asked,	"**Do you have** any experience**?**" "**Can you create** spreadsheets**?**" "**Will you stay** for a year**?**"

Indirect Speech: *Yes / No* Questions				
Subject	**Reporting Verb**	**(Noun / Pronoun)**	**Indirect Question**	
He	asked	(Melissa) (her)	*if* *whether (or not)*	**she had** any experience. **she could create** spreadsheets. **she would stay** for a year.

Direct Speech: *Wh-* Questions About the Subject		
Subject	**Reporting Verb**	**Direct Question**
He	asked,	"***Who* told** you about the job**?**" "***What* happened** on your last job**?**" "***Which company* hired** you**?**"

Indirect Speech: *Wh-* Questions About the Subject				
Subject	**Reporting Verb**	**(Noun / Pronoun)**	**Indirect Question**	
He	asked	(Bob) (him)	*who*	**had told** him about the job.
			what	**had happened** on his last job.
			which company	**had hired** him.

Direct Speech: *Wh-* Questions About the Object		
Subject	**Reporting Verb**	**Direct Question**
He	asked,	"***Who* do you work** for**?**" "***What* do you do** there**?**" "***Which job* did you accept?**"

Indirect Speech: *Wh-* Questions About the Object				
Subject	**Reporting Verb**	**(Noun / Pronoun)**	**Indirect Question**	
He	asked	(Melissa) (her)	*who*	**she worked** for.
			what	**she did** there.
			which job	**she had accepted**.

Direct Speech: *Wh-* Questions with *When*, *Where*, *Why*, and *How*

Subject	Reporting Verb	Direct Question
He	asked,	"*When* **did you start** your new job?" "*Where* **do you work** now?" "*Why* **have you changed** jobs?" "*How much* **did you earn** there?"

Indirect Speech: *Wh-* Questions with *When*, *Where*, *Why*, and *How*

Subject	Reporting Verb	(Noun / Pronoun)	Indirect Question	
He	asked	(Melissa) (her)	*when*	**she had started** her new job.
			where	**she worked** now.
			why	**she had changed** jobs.
			how much	**she had earned** there.

GRAMMAR NOTES

1 We often use **indirect speech** to report **questions**.
The most common **reporting verb** for both direct and indirect questions is *ask*.
We also use other **expressions** such as *want to know*.

- "Did you find a new job?" she *asked*.
  She *asked* if I had found a new job.
- "Where do you work?" she *wanted to know*.
  She *wanted to know* where I worked.

REMEMBER: When the **reporting verb** is in the **simple past**, the verb tense in the **indirect question** often **changes**. For example:
The **simple present** in direct speech becomes the **simple past** in indirect speech.
The **simple past** in direct speech becomes the **past perfect** in indirect speech.

- "**Do** you **like** your new job?" he asked.
  He asked me if I **liked** my new job.
- "**Did** you **find** it online?" he wanted to know.
  He wanted to know if I **had found** it online.

2 Use *if* or *whether* in **indirect yes / no questions**.

DIRECT QUESTION	INDIRECT QUESTION
"Can you type?" she asked.	She asked me *if* I could type.
"Do you know how to use a scanner?" he asked.	He wanted to know *whether* I knew how to use a scanner.

USAGE NOTES:

- *Whether* is more formal than *if*.

- We often use *whether or not* to report *yes / no* questions.

- My boss wants to know *whether* the report **is ready yet**.
- He wanted to know *whether or not* the report **was ready yet**.

3 Use **question words** in **indirect wh- questions**.

DIRECT QUESTION	INDIRECT QUESTION
"Where is your office?" I asked.	I asked *where* **his office was**.
I asked, "How much is the salary?"	I asked *how much* **the salary was**.

(continued on next page)

4 Use **statement word order** (**subject** + **verb**), not question word order, for all indirect questions:

SUBJECT   VERB
They hired Li.

DIRECT QUESTION	INDIRECT QUESTION
"Did he hire Li?"	I asked **if he had hired** Li.

a. indirect *yes / no* questions

b. indirect *wh-* questions about the **subject**

DIRECT QUESTION	INDIRECT QUESTION
"Who hired Li?"	I asked **who had hired** Li.

c. indirect *wh-* questions about the **object**

DIRECT QUESTION	INDIRECT QUESTION
"Who did he hire?"	I asked **who he had hired**.

d. indirect *wh-* questions with *when*, *where*, *why* and *how* or *how much / many*.

DIRECT QUESTION	INDIRECT QUESTION
"Why did they hire Li?"	I asked **why they had hired** Li.

BE CAREFUL! If a direct question about the subject has the form **question word** + *be* + **noun**, then the indirect question has the form **question word** + **noun** + *be*.

"**Who** *is* **the boss**?"	I asked them **who the boss** *was*.
	Not: I asked them who ~~was the boss~~.

5 In **indirect questions**:

DIRECT QUESTION	INDIRECT QUESTION
"Why did you leave?"	She asked me *why* **I had left**.

• Do **NOT use** the auxiliary *do*, *does*, or *did*.

Not: She asked me why ~~did I leave~~.

• Do **NOT end with a question mark** (end with a period).

Not: She asked me why I had left~~?~~

REFERENCE NOTES

The same **verb tense changes and other changes** occur in both indirect questions and indirect statements (see Units 25 and 26).

For a list of **reporting verbs** in questions, see Appendix 14 on page A-5.

For **punctuation rules for direct speech**, see Appendix 27, on page A-13.

STEP 3 FOCUSED PRACTICE

EXERCISE 1: Discover the Grammar

A *Melissa Morrow is telling a friend about her job interview. Underline the indirect questions in the conversation.*

DON: So, how did the interview go?

MELISSA: It was very strange.

DON: What happened?

MELISSA: Well, it started off OK. He asked me how much experience I'd had, and I told him I'd been a public relations officer for 10 years. Let's see . . . He also asked what I would change about my current job. That was a little tricky.

Don: What did you say?

Melissa: Well, I didn't want to say anything negative, so I told him that I was ready to take on a lot more responsibility.

Don: Good. What else did he ask?

Melissa: Oh, you know, the regular things. He asked what my greatest success had been, and how much money I was making.

Don: Sounds like a normal interview to me. What was so strange about it?

Melissa: Well, at one point, he just stopped talking for a long time. Then he asked me all these questions that weren't even related to the job. I mean, *none* of them were appropriate.

Don: Like what?

Melissa: He asked me if I'd cleaned out my car recently.

Don: You're kidding.

Melissa: No, I'm not. Then he asked me why my employer didn't want me to stay.

Don: That's crazy. I hope you told him that you hadn't been fired.

Melissa: Of course. In fact, I told him I'd never even gotten a negative evaluation. Oh, and then he asked me if I was good enough to work for his company.

Don: What did you tell him?

Melissa: I told him that with my skills and experience I was one of the best in my field.

Don: That was a great answer. It sounds like you handled yourself very well.

Melissa: Thanks. But now I'm asking myself if I really want this job.

Don: Take your time. This job is a potential opportunity for you. Don't make any quick decisions.

B | *Now check (✓) the direct questions that the interviewer asked Melissa.*

☐ **1.** How much experience have you had?

☐ **2.** What would you change about your current job?

☐ **3.** Are you ready for more responsibility?

☐ **4.** What was your greatest success?

☐ **5.** How much are you making now?

☐ **6.** Was it a normal interview?

☐ **7.** Have you cleaned out your car recently?

☐ **8.** Have you been fired?

☐ **9.** Are you good enough to work for this company?

☐ **10.** Do you ever make quick decisions?

EXERCISE 2: Word Order

(Grammar Notes 1–4)

Jaime has an interview next week. His neighbor, Claire, wants to know all about it. Report Claire's questions using the words in parentheses in the correct order. Use **ask** *or* **want to know** *to report the questions.*

1. **CLAIRE:** I heard you're going on an interview next week. What kind of job is it?

   JAIME: It's for a job as an office assistant.

   <u>*She asked what kind of job it was.*</u>
   (kind of job / what / was / it)

2. **CLAIRE:** Oh, really? When is the interview?

   JAIME: It's on Tuesday at 9:00.

   _____
   (the interview / was / when)

3. **CLAIRE:** Where's the company?

   JAIME: It's downtown on the west side.

   _____
   (was / where / the company)

4. **CLAIRE:** Do you need directions?

   JAIME: No, I know the way.

   _____
   (needed / if / he / directions)

5. **CLAIRE:** How long does it take to get there?

   JAIME: About half an hour.

   _____
   (to get there / it / takes / how long)

6. **CLAIRE:** Are you going to drive?

   JAIME: I think so. It's probably the fastest way.

   _____
   (was going to / if / he / drive)

7. **CLAIRE:** Who's going to interview you?

   JAIME: Um. I'm not sure. Probably the manager of the department.

   _____
   (was going to / his / who / interview)

8. **CLAIRE:** Well, good luck. When will they let you know?

   JAIME: It will take a while. They have a lot of candidates.

   _____
   (his / they / would / when / let / know)

EXERCISE 3: Indirect Questions: Verb and Pronoun Changes

(Grammar Notes 1–5)

Read the questions that were asked during Jaime's interview. Jaime asked some of the questions, and the manager, Ms. Stollins, asked others. Decide who asked each question. Then rewrite each question as indirect speech.

1. "What type of training is available for the job?"

   Jaime asked (Ms. Stollins) what type of training was available for the job.

2. "What kind of experience do you have?"

   _____

3. "Is there opportunity for promotion?"

   _____

4. "Are you interviewing with other companies?"

   _____

5. "What will my responsibilities be?"

   _____

6. "How is job performance rewarded?"

   _____

7. "What was your starting salary at your last job?"

   _____

8. "Did you get along well with your last employer?"

   _____

9. "When does the job start?"

   _____

10. "Why did you apply for this position?"

   _____

EXERCISE 4: Editing

Read the memo an interviewer wrote after an interview. There are seven mistakes in the use of indirect questions. The first mistake is already corrected. Find and correct six more. Don't forget to check punctuation. Mistakes with quotation marks count as one mistake for the sentence.

May 15, 2012

TO: Francesca Giuffrida

FROM: Ken Marley

SUBJECT: Interview with Carlos Lopez

This morning I interviewed Carlos Lopez for the administrative
assistant position. Since this job requires a lot of contact with the
public, I did some stress questioning. I asked Mr. Lopez why
he couldn't
~~couldn't he~~ work under pressure. I also asked him why his
supervisor disliked him. Finally, I inquired when he would quit the
job with our company?

Mr. Lopez remained calm throughout the interview. He answered all
my questions, and he had some excellent questions of his own. He
asked "if we expected changes in the job." He also wanted to know
how often do we perform employee evaluations. I was quite
impressed when he asked why did I decide to join this company.

Mr. Lopez is an excellent candidate for the job, and I believe he will
handle the responsibilities well. At the end of the interview, Mr.
Lopez inquired when we could let him know our decision? I asked
him if whether he was considering another job, and he said he was.
I think we should act quickly in order not to lose this excellent
potential employee.

EXERCISE 5: Listening

A | *You are going to hear a job interview that takes place in Canada. Read the checklist. Then listen to the interview. Listen again and check (✓) the topics that the interviewer asks about.*

Possible Job Interview Topics

OK to Ask

☐ Name
☐ Address
☐ Work experience
☑ Reason for leaving job
☐ Reason for seeking position
☐ Salary
☐ Education
☐ Professional affiliations
☐ Convictions[1] for crimes
☐ Skills
☐ Job performance
☐ Permission to work in Canada

Not OK to Ask[2]

☐ Age
☐ Race
☐ Sex
☐ Religion
☐ National origin
☐ Height or weight
☐ Marital status
☐ Information about spouse
☐ Arrest record
☐ Physical disabilities
☐ Children
☐ Citizenship
☐ English language skill
☐ Financial situation

_____

[1]*conviction:* a court's decision that a person is guilty of a crime
[2]*not OK to ask:* illegal to ask if not related to the job

B | *Listen again to the interview and write the illegal questions the interviewer asks.*

1. *How old are you?*

2. _____

3. _____

4. _____

5. _____

6. _____

7. _____

C | *Now report the illegal questions to the class.*

EXAMPLE: He asked her how old she was.

EXERCISE 6: Pronunciation

A | *Read and listen to the Pronunciation Note.*

> **Pronunciation Note**
>
> In **direct *yes / no* questions**, the voice usually **rises at the end**.
>
> **EXAMPLES:**   Do you have a lot of experience?
>
>   Will you be able to start next week?
>
> In **indirect *yes / no* questions**, the voice usually **falls at the end**.
>
> **EXAMPLES:**   He asked if I had a lot of experience.
>
>   She wanted to know if I'd be able to start next week.

B | *Listen to parts of a conversation. Notice how the voice rises (↗) or falls (↘) at the end of the direct and indirect questions. Draw a rising arrow or a falling arrow over the end of each direct or indirect question.*

1. **A:** So, **did the interview go OK**?

   B: I think so. The interviewer asked me **if she could call my old employer.**

2. **A: Did you say yes?**

   B: Of course. And she also wanted to know **whether I could start next month.**

3. **A:** Sounds good. **Did you ask any questions?**

   B: Yes. I asked her **if she liked working there.**

4. **A:** Great question. So, **does she like working there?**

   B: She said yes. But **was she telling the truth?**

5. **A:** Never mind. Just ask yourself **if you want the job.**

   B: I don't know. **Can we talk about something else?**

6. **A:** Sure. I forgot to ask you **if you wanted to eat out tonight.**

   B: Sounds good. **Do you want to try that new Japanese restaurant?**

C | *Listen again. Then practice the conversation with a partner.*

EXERCISE 7: Role Play: A Job Interview

A | *Read the résumé and the job advertisement. Work in groups to write questions for a job interview. Half of the group should write questions to ask the candidate. The other half should write questions to ask the interviewer. Write at least three questions for each.*

Pat Rogers
215 West Hill Drive
Baltimore, MD 21233
Telephone: (410) 555-7777
Fax: (410) 555-7932
progers@email.com

EDUCATION	**Taylor Community College** Associate's degree (Business) 2010 **Middlesex High School** High school diploma, 2008
EXPERIENCE 2010–Present **Patients Plus** **Baltimore, MD**	**Medical receptionist** Responsibilities: Greet patients, make appointments, answer telephones, update computer records
2008–2010 **Union Hospital** **Baltimore, MD**	**Admitting clerk, hospital admissions office** Responsibilities: Interviewed patients for admission, input information in computer, answered telephones

MEDICAL RECEPTIONIST for busy doctor's office. Mature individual needed to answer phones, greet patients, make appointments. Some filing and billing. Similar experience preferred. Computer skills necessary.

EXAMPLES: **To ask the candidate:**   Why did you leave your job at Union Hospital?
 To ask the interviewer: How many doctors work here?

B | *Select two people to act out the interview for the class.*

C | *Discuss each group's role-play interview as a class. Use these questions to guide your discussion. Support your ideas by reporting questions that were asked in the interview.*

1. Was it a stress interview? Why or why not?

2. Did the interviewer ask any illegal questions? Which ones were illegal?

3. Which of the candidate's questions were the most useful in evaluating the job? Why do you think so?

4. Which of the interviewer's questions gave the clearest picture of the candidate? Why do you think so?

5. If you were the interviewer, would you hire this candidate? Why or why not?

6. If you were the candidate, would you want to work for this company? Why or why not?

EXAMPLE: **A:** I think it was a stress interview because the interviewer asked him why he couldn't find a new job.
 B: The interviewer asked two illegal questions. She asked when the candidate was born. She also asked . . .
 C: The candidate's most useful questions were . . .

EXERCISE 8: Questionnaire: Work Values

A | *Your values are the things that are most important to you. Take this work values quiz on your own. (If none of the answers match your values, add your own.) Then work with a partner. Ask your partner three of the questions and discuss your answers. Then answer the other three questions and discuss your answers.*

Work Values Questionnaire

1. Why do you want to work?

- To make a lot of money.
- To help people.
- To become well known.
- Other: _____

2. Where do you prefer to work?

- I'd like to travel.
- In an office.
- At home.
- Other: _____

3. When do you want to work?

- 9–5 every day.
- On a changing schedule.
- On my own schedule.
- Other: _____

4. What kind of routine do you like?

- The same type of task all day.
- A variety of tasks every day.
- Tasks that change often.
- Other: _____

5. How much job pressure can you handle?

- I like a high-pressure job.
- I can handle some, but not a lot.
- Just enough to keep me awake.
- Other: _____

6. Who would you like to work with?

- I work best with a team.
- I like to work by myself.
- I enjoy working with the public.
- Other: _____

B | *Get together with another pair and report your conversations.*

EXAMPLE: **A:** Sami asked me how much job pressure I could handle. I told him . . .
 B: Ella asked why I wanted to work. I said that . . .

EXERCISE 9: What About You?

In small groups, discuss a personal experience with a school or job interview. (If you do not have a personal experience, use the experience of someone you know.) Talk about these questions:

- What did the interviewer want to find out?

- What was the most difficult question to answer? Why?

- Were there any questions that you didn't want to answer? What did you say?

- What did you ask the interviewer?

EXAMPLE: **A:** The interviewer asked me if I was married.
                  B: That isn't legal, is it?
                  C: What did you say?
                  A: I asked him. . . .

EXERCISE 10: Writing

A | *Before you look for work, it's a good idea to talk to people who are already working in jobs that might interest you. In these kinds of "informational interviews" you can ask what the tasks in that job are, why people like or dislike the work, or how much you can expect to be paid. Write a list of questions to ask in an informational job interview.*

EXAMPLE: Do you like your job?
                 How much vacation time do you get?

B | *Now interview someone and write a report about the interview. Use indirect questions.*

EXAMPLE: I interviewed Pete Ortiz, who is an assistant in the computer lab. I wanted to talk to him because I'm interested in applying for a job in the lab. I asked Pete if he liked working there, and he told me he liked it most of the time . . .

C | *Check your work. Use the Editing Checklist.*

Editing Checklist

Did you use . . . ?
- ☐ *if* or ***whether*** in indirect ***yes*** / ***no*** questions
- ☐ question words in indirect ***wh-*** questions
- ☐ statement word order for all indirect questions
- ☐ a period at the end of indirect questions

Check your answers on page UR-7.

Do you need to review anything?

A | *Circle the correct punctuation mark or words to complete the sentences.*

1. She asked what my name was <u>. / ?</u>

2. He asked me <u>if / do</u> I had work experience.

3. I asked them where <u>was their office / their office was</u>.

4. They asked where <u>I lived / did I live</u>.

5. They asked me why <u>had I / I had</u> left my last job.

B | *Rewrite the direct questions in parentheses as indirect questions. (The direct questions were asked <u>a few months ago</u>).*

1. They asked _____
   (Who did the company hire?)

2. He asked me _____
   (Did you take the job?)

3. She wanted to know _____
   (Do you like your present job?)

4. He asked me _____
   (Who is your boss?)

5. I asked _____
   (How many employees work here?)

6. They wanted to know _____
   (Why do you want to change jobs?)

7. I asked _____
   (What's the starting salary?)

8. They wanted to know _____
   (Can you start soon?)

C | *Find and correct seven mistakes. Remember to check punctuation.*

They asked me so many questions! They asked me where did I work. They asked who was my boss. They asked why I did want to change jobs. They asked how much money I made. They ask me who I have voted for in the last election. They even asked me what my favorite color was? Finally, I asked myself whether or no I really wanted that job!

STEP 1 GRAMMAR IN CONTEXT

Before You Read

Look at the cartoon. Discuss the questions.

1. What is unusual about the vending machine?
2. What is the man worried about?

Read

Read the interview about tipping from World Travel (WT) *magazine.*

THE TIP: Who? When? and How much?

In China it used to be illegal, in New Zealand it's uncommon, but in Germany it's included in the bill. In the United States and Canada it's common, but it isn't logical: You tip the person who delivers flowers, but not the person who delivers a package.

Do *you* often wonder **what to do** about tipping? *We* do, so to help us through the tipping maze[1] we interviewed author Irene Frankel. Her book, *Tips on Tipping: The Ultimate Guide to **Who**, **When**, and **How Much to Tip*** answers all your questions about this complicated practice.

"I wonder **how much we should give**."

WT: Tell me **why you decided to write a book about tipping**.

IF: I began writing it for people from cultures where tipping isn't a custom. But when I started researching, I found that Americans were also unsure **how to tip**, so *Tips* became a book to clarify tipping practices for people traveling to the U.S. *and* for people living here.

[1]*maze:* something that is complicated and hard to understand

(continued on next page)

THE TIP: Who? When? and How much?

WT: Does your book explain **who to tip?**

IF: Oh, absolutely. It tells you **who to tip**, **how much to tip**, and **when to tip**. And equally important, it tells you **when not to tip**.

WT: That *is* important. Suppose[2] I don't know **whether to tip someone**, and I left your book at home. Is it OK to ask?

IF: Sure. If you don't know **whether to leave a tip**, the best thing to do is ask. People usually won't tell you **what to do**, but they *will* tell you **what most customers do**.

WT: I always wonder **what to do when I get bad service**. Should I still tip?

IF: Don't tip the ordinary amount, but tip *something* so that the service person doesn't think that you just forgot to leave a tip.

WT: That makes sense. Here's another thing I've always wondered about.

Is there any reason **why we tip a restaurant server but we don't a flight attendant**?

IF: Not that I know. The rules for tipping in the United States aren't very logical, and there are often contradictions in who we tip.

WT: Another thing—I've never really understood **why a restaurant tip depends on the amount of the bill rather than on the amount of work involved in serving the meal**. After all, bringing out a $20 dish of food involves the same amount of work as carrying out a $5 plate.

IF: You're right. It makes no sense. That's just the way it is.

WT: One last question. Suppose I'm planning a trip to Egypt. Tell me **how I can learn about tipping customs in that country**.

IF: There are a number of Internet sites where you can learn **what the rules are for tipping in each country**. The *World Travel* site is always reliable. You can also find that information in travel books for the country you're planning to visit.

WT: Well, thanks for all the good tips! I know our readers will find them very helpful. *I* certainly did.

IF: Thank *you*.

---

[2]*suppose:* to imagine that something is true and its possible results; a way to ask "What if . . . ?"

After You Read

A | Vocabulary: *Match the words with their definitions.*

_____ 1. **clarify**   **a.** not unusual

_____ 2. **custom**   **b.** reasonable and sensible

_____ 3. **ultimate**   **c.** a traditional way of doing something

_____ 4. **logical**   **d.** to make clear

_____ 5. **ordinary**   **e.** to be affected by

_____ 6. **depend on**   **f.** best

B | Comprehension: *Circle the word or phrase that best completes each sentence.*

1. *Tips on Tipping* is a guide to tipping customs in <u>restaurants / Egypt / the United States</u>.

2. A question that is NOT mentioned in the interview is: "<u>How much / Who / Why</u> should I tip?"

3. If you're not sure whether to tip, it's OK to ask <u>Irene Frankel / the server / a customer</u>.

4. When you get bad service, Frankel says to leave <u>no / a smaller / the normal</u> tip.

5. In the U.S., tipping customs are <u>logical / required by law / often not logical</u>.

6. To learn about tipping customs in Mexico, read *Tips on Tipping* / <u>a travel website /</u>

   <u>this interview</u>.

STEP 2 GRAMMAR PRESENTATION

EMBEDDED QUESTIONS

Direct *Yes / No* Question	Main Clause	Embedded *Yes / No* Question
Did I leave the right tip?	I don't know	*if* **I left** the right tip.
	Can you tell me	*if* **I left** the right tip?
Was five dollars enough?	I wonder	*whether* (*or not*) **five dollars was** enough.
	Do you know	*whether* (*or not*) **five dollars was** enough?
Should we leave a tip?	We're not sure	*whether* (*or not*) **to leave** a tip.

Direct *Wh*- Question	Main Clause	Embedded *Wh*- Question
Who is our server?	I don't know	*who* **our server is**.
	Can you tell me	*who* **our server is**?
Why didn't he leave a tip?	I wonder	*why* **he didn't leave** a tip.
	Do you know	*why* **he didn't leave** a tip?
How much should we give the taxi driver?	We're not sure	*how much* **to give** the taxi driver.

GRAMMAR NOTES

1 | **Embedded questions** are questions that are inside another sentence. An embedded question can be:
- inside a **statement**
- inside **another question**

BE CAREFUL! If the embedded question is inside a **statement**, use a **period** at the end of the sentence.
If the embedded question is inside a **question**, use a **question mark** at the end of the sentence.

- I don't know **who our server is**.
- Do you remember **who our server is?**

- I wonder **if that's our server**.
  NOT: I wonder if that's our server☓

- Do you know **if that's our server?**

2 | Use **embedded questions** to:

- **express** something you **do not know**

- **ask** for **information** in a **more polite** way

DIRECT QUESTION	EMBEDDED QUESTION
Why didn't he tip her?	I don't know **why he didn't tip her**.
Is the tip included?	Can you tell me **if the tip is included?**

3 | There are **two kinds of embedded questions**.

a. embedded *yes / no* questions
The direct questions are *yes / no* questions.

Begin **embedded *yes / no* questions** with *if*, *whether*, or *whether or not*.

USAGE NOTE: *Whether* is more **formal** than *if*.

DIRECT QUESTION	EMBEDDED QUESTION
Did they *deliver* the pizza?	I don't know **if they delivered the pizza**.

- Do you know **if they delivered the pizza?**

- Do you know **whether they delivered the pizza?** OR
- Do you know **whether or not they delivered the pizza?**

b. embedded *wh-* questions
The direct questions are *wh-* questions.

Begin **embedded *wh-* questions** with a *wh-* word (*who, what, which, whose, when, where, why, how, how many, how much*).

DIRECT QUESTION	EMBEDDED QUESTION
Who delivered the pizza?	I don't know **who delivered the pizza**.

- I wonder **who our server is**.
- Do you know **when the restaurant closes?**
- Many tourists wonder **how much they should tip their restaurant server**.

4

Use **statement word order** (**subject** + **verb**), not question word order, for all embedded questions:

a. embedded *yes / no* questions

b. embedded *wh-* questions about the **subject**

c. embedded *wh-* questions about the **object**

d. embedded *wh-* questions with *when*, *where*, *why*, *how*, *how much*, or *how many*

REMEMBER: Do NOT use question word order and auxiliary verbs *do*, *does*, or *did* in embedded questions.
Do NOT leave out *if* or *whether* in embedded *yes / no* questions.

BE CAREFUL! If a direct question about the subject has the form *be* + **noun**, then the embedded question has the form **noun** + **be**.

	SUBJECT	VERB
	Eva ordered pizza.	

DIRECT QUESTION	EMBEDDED QUESTION
Did Eva order pizza?	Do you know *if* **Eva ordered** pizza?
Who ordered pizza?	I can't remember *who* ordered pizza.
What does it cost?	Can you tell me *what* it costs?
When do they open?	Do you know *when* they open?

- I wonder *why* **they ordered** pizza.
  NOT: I wonder why ~~did they order~~ pizza.

- I don't know *if* **they ordered** pizza.
  NOT: I don't know ~~did they order~~ pizza.

DIRECT QUESTION	EMBEDDED QUESTION
Who *is* **our server**?	Do you know who **our server** *is*?
	NOT: Do you know who ~~is our server~~?
Is **our order** ready?	Do you know if **our order** *is* ready?
	NOT: Do you know ~~is our order~~ ready?

5

In embedded questions, you can also use:

- **question word** + **infinitive**

- *whether* + **infinitive**

BE CAREFUL! Do **NOT use the infinitive** after *if* or *why*.

- Let's ask where we should leave the tip. OR
- Let's ask *where* **to leave** the tip.

- I wonder whether I should leave a tip. OR
- I wonder *whether* **to leave** a tip.

- I don't understand *why* **I should tip**.
  NOT: I don't understand why ~~to tip~~.

6

Embedded questions often **follow these phrases**:

STATEMENTS:

I don't know . . .	*I'm not sure . . .*
I don't understand . . .	*I wonder . . .*
I'd like to know . . .	*Let's ask . . .*

QUESTIONS:

Do you know . . . ?	*Can you tell me . . . ?*
Can you remember . . . ?	*Could you explain . . . ?*

- ***I don't know*** what the name of the restaurant is.
- ***I wonder*** what time the restaurant closes.
- ***Let's ask*** what today's specials are.

- ***Do you know*** how much the shrimp costs?
- ***Could you explain*** what that sign means?

REFERENCE NOTE

For a list of **phrases introducing embedded questions,** see Appendix 16 on page A-5.

EXERCISE 1: Discover the Grammar

Read the advertisement for Tips on Tipping. *Underline the embedded questions.*

This book is for you if . . .

- you've ever avoided a situation just because you didn't know <u>how much to tip</u>.
- you've ever realized (too late) that you were supposed to offer a tip.
- you've ever given a huge tip and then wondered if a tip was necessary at all.
- you've ever needed to know how to calculate the right tip instantly.
- you're new to the United States and you're not sure who you should tip here.
- you'd like to learn how tipping properly can get you the best service for your money.

What readers are saying . . .

"Essential, reliable information—I can't imagine how I got along without it."
 —*Chris Sarton, Minneapolis, Minnesota*

"Take *Tips* along if you want a stress-free vacation."
 —*Midori Otaka, Osaka, Japan*

"I took my fiancée to dinner at Deux Saisons and knew exactly how to tip everyone!"
 —*S. Prasad, San Francisco, California*

"You need this book—whether you stay in hostels or five-star hotels."
 —*Cuno Pumpin, Bern, Switzerland*

Send for the ultimate guide to tipping and get all the answers to your tipping questions.

Yes! I want to learn who to tip, when to tip, and how much to tip. Please send me additional information on *Tips on Tipping*. I understand that the book will be $4.95 plus $2.00 postage and handling for each copy. (New York residents: Add sales tax.) Contact Martin Unlimited, Inc. at dmifdmif@yahoo.com.

EXERCISE 2: Embedded Questions

(Grammar Notes 1–4, 6)

Complete this travel column about tipping customs around the world. Change the direct questions in parentheses to embedded questions. Use correct punctuation.

Tipping customs vary, so travelers should find out who, where, and how much to tip. Here are some frequently asked questions.

Q: Can you tell me whether *I should tip in Canada?*

1. (Should I tip in Canada?)

A: Yes. Tipping practices in Canada are similar to those in the United States.

Q: I know that most restaurants and cafés in France include a service charge. Could you explain

_____

2. (How can I tell if the tip is included in the bill?)

A: Look for the phrase *service compris* (service included) on the bill.

Q: I'm going to China next month. I understand that tipping used to be illegal there. Do you know

_____

3. (Will restaurant servers accept tips now?)

A: It depends on where you are. In large cities, you can leave 3 percent in a restaurant. In small cities, your tip may not be accepted.

Q: On a recent trip to Iceland, I found that most service people refused tips. Could you explain

_____

4. (Why did this happen?)

A: In Iceland, people often feel insulted by tips. Just say thank you—that's enough.

Q: I'm going on an eco tour[1] of Costa Rica. The guides are professional naturalists.[2] I'm not sure

_____

5. (Should I offer them a tip or not?)

A: Professional guides should get $10–$15 per day. Remember, your guide's knowledge will turn an ordinary experience into an extraordinary one.

Q: My husband and I are planning a trip to several cities in Australia and New Zealand. Please tell us

_____

6. (Who expects a tip and who doesn't?)

A: Restaurant servers expect a tip of 10 percent, but you don't need to tip taxi drivers.

Q: I'm moving to Japan, and I have a lot of luggage. I'm finding some contradictions on travel websites. One says not to tip in Japan, but another says to tip airport porters. Could you tell me

_____

7. (Is it the custom to tip airport and train porters?)

A: There's a fixed fee[3] per bag for airport porters, not a tip. Most train stations don't have porters. We recommend shipping your luggage from the airport. I hope that clarifies things!

---

[1] *eco tour:* a trip to see natural places such as rainforests and the animals and plants there
[2] *naturalist:* a professional who studies nature
[3] *fixed fee:* a price that does not change

EXERCISE 3: Embedded Questions

(Grammar Notes 1–4, 6)

Two foreign exchange students are visiting Rome, Italy. Complete their conversations.
Choose the appropriate questions from the list and change them to embedded questions.
Use correct punctuation.

- How much are we supposed to tip the taxi driver?
- Could we rent a car and drive there?
- Do they have tour buses that go there?
- How much does the subway cost?
- How far are you going?
- How are we going to choose?
- How much does a bus tour cost?
- What did they put in the sauce?
- Where is the Forum?
- ~~Where is it?~~

Rome: the Forum

DRIVER: Where do you want to go? The airport?

MARTINA: The Hotel Forte. Do you know *where it is?* _____
                                                                          1.

DRIVER: Sure. Get in and I'll take you there.

MARTINA: (*whispering*) Do you know _____
                                                                          2.

MIUKI: According to the book, the custom is to leave 10 to 15 percent. I've got it.

★ ★ ★ ★ ★

MARTINA: There's so much to see in Rome. I don't know _____
                                                                          3.

MIUKI: We could take a bus tour of the city first, and then decide.

MARTINA: Does the guidebook say _____
                                                                          4.

MIUKI: Yeah. About $15 per person, plus tips for the guide and the driver.

★ ★ ★ ★ ★

MARTINA: That was delicious.

MIUKI: Let's try to find out _____
                                                                          5.

MARTINA: It tasted like it had a lot of garlic and basil. I'll ask the server.

★ ★ ★ ★ ★

MARTINA: Excuse me. Can you tell me _____
                                                                          6.

OFFICER: Sure. Just turn right and go straight.

★ ★ ★ ★ ★

MIUKI: Let's take the subway. Do you know _____

7.

MARTINA: It's not expensive. I don't think it depends on _____

8.

★ ★ ★ ★ ★

MARTINA: I'd like to visit Ostia Antica. It's supposed to be like the ruins at Pompeii.

MIUKI: I wonder _____

9.

MARTINA: I really don't want to go with a big group of people. What about you? Do you know

_____

10.

MIUKI: Sure! It would be nice to drive around and see some of the countryside too.

EXERCISE 4: Question Word + Infinitive

(Grammar Note 5)

Complete the conversation between Martina and Miuki. Use a question word and the infinitive form of the verbs from the box.

| figure out | get | go | invite | leave | ~~wear~~ |

MARTINA: I can't decide _____ *what to wear* _____ Friday night.

1.

MIUKI: Your red dress. You always look great in it. By the way, where are you going?

MARTINA: Trattoria da Luigi. It's Janek's birthday, so I wanted to take him someplace special—not

just the ordinary places we usually go to. We're meeting there at 8:00.

MIUKI: Great! You know _____ there, don't you?

2.

MARTINA: Yes, but I'm not sure _____.

3.

MIUKI: Leave at 7:30. That'll give you enough time.

MARTINA: I'd like to take Janek someplace for dessert afterward, but I don't know

_____.

4.

MIUKI: The desserts at da Luigi's are supposed to be pretty good.

MARTINA: Oh. By the way, since it's Janek's birthday, I'm paying. But I'm still not quite sure

_____ the tip.

5.

MIUKI: Service is usually included in Italy. The menu should tell you. So, who else is going?

MARTINA: Well, I thought about asking a few people to join us, but I really didn't know

_____.

6.

MIUKI: Don't worry. I'm sure it will be fine with just the two of you.

EXERCISE 5: Editing

Read this post to a travelers' website. There are ten mistakes in the use of embedded questions. The first mistake is already corrected. Find and correct nine more. Don't forget to check punctuation.

Tipping at the Hairdresser's in Italy

✉ [Email this page to someone!](#) | New Topic | | Post a Poll | | Post Reply |

Subject: Tipping at the Hairdresser's in Italy
Posted April 10 by Jenna Thompson

I wonder ~~if~~ you can help clarify some tipping situations for me. I never know what doing at the hairdresser's. I don't know if I should tip the person who washes my hair? What about the person who cuts it, and the person who colors it? And what happens if the person is the owner. Do you know do I still need to tip him or her? That doesn't seem logical. (And often I'm not even sure who is the owner!) Then I never know how much to tip or where should I leave the tip? Do I leave it on the counter or in the person's hands? What if somebody's hands are wet or have hair color on them? Can I just put the tip in his or her pocket? It all seems so complicated! I can't imagine how do customers figure all this out? What's the custom? I really need to find out what to do—and FAST! My hair is getting very long and dirty.

Please help!

470   UNIT 29

EXERCISE 6: Listening

A | *A travel agent is being interviewed on a call-in radio show about tipping. Read the sentences. Then listen to the callers' questions. Listen again and check (✓) **True** or **False** for each statement. Correct the false statements.*

	True	False
1. Where Caller One comes from, people usually ~~leave a 10%~~ tip. *don't leave a tip*	☐	✓
2. Caller Two thinks that she often tips taxi drivers too much.	☐	☐
3. Caller Three wants to know how much to tip the server.	☐	☐
4. Caller Four plans to go to the theater in France.	☐	☐
5. Caller Five is annoyed about the service he got in a restaurant.	☐	☐
6. Caller Six wants to know whether to tip the person who washes her hair.	☐	☐
7. Caller Seven needs cultural information for his business trip.	☐	☐
8. Caller Eight is planning to order a pizza after he hangs up.	☐	☐

B | *Listen again to the callers' questions. Then circle the letter of the correct response to each caller's question.*

1. **Caller One**
   a. between 15 and 20 percent of the bill
   b. the server

2. **Caller Two**
   a. about 15 percent of the fare
   b. only if you are happy with the ride

3. **Caller Three**
   a. before you leave
   b. on the table

4. **Caller Four**
   a. the person who takes you to your seat
   b. one euro for one person; two euros for two or more people

5. **Caller Five**
   a. the manager
   b. don't leave a tip

6. **Caller Six**
   a. one dollar
   b. at the cashier

7. **Caller Seven**
   a. Look it up on the Internet.
   b. It's included in the bill.

8. **Caller Eight**
   a. at least three dollars
   b. the person who delivers your food

EXERCISE 7: Pronunciation

A | *Read and listen to the Pronunciation Note.*

> **Pronunciation Note**
>
> In **direct *wh-* questions**, the voice usually **falls** at the end.
>
> **EXAMPLE:**   How much should we tip?
>
> When a ***wh-* question** is **embedded inside a *yes / no* question**, the voice usually **rises** at the end.
>
> **EXAMPLE:**   Do you know how much we should tip?

B | *Listen to the short conversations. Draw a rising arrow (↗) or a falling arrow (↘) over the end of each question.*

1. **BRAD:** Do you know when Lily's birthday is?

   EMMA: I think it's next week.

2. **BRAD:** Where should we take her?

   EMMA: Let's take her to True Blue Café.

3. **EMMA:** Can you remember where you took me last year?

   BRAD: I think it was Rustica. I bet she'd love that place.

4. **LILY:** What's the soup of the day?

   SERVER: Today it's tomato soup.

5. **LILY:** Do you know which salad you're going to order?

   BRAD: They make a great vegetable salad here.

6. **EMMA:** Could you tell me what's in the hollandaise sauce?

   SERVER: Certainly. It's made with egg yolks, butter, and lemon juice.

7. **EMMA:** Why is our server taking so long?

   BRAD: Here he comes now!

EXERCISE 8: Information Gap: Eating Out

*Work in groups of three. Students A and B are customers in a restaurant. Student C is the server. **Students A and B**, look at the menu. **Student C**, go to page 476 and follow the instructions there.*

Trattoria da Luigi

English version

Appetizers

Bruschetta	€1.25
Roasted vegetables	3.25

FIRST COURSE

Soup of the day (*please ask*)	€2.95
Caesar salad	3.25
Luigi's salad	2.95
Linguine with clam sauce	10.80
Spaghetti da Luigi	12.90

SECOND COURSE

Chicken

Chicken da Luigi	€7.95
Half roasted chicken	6.95

Beef

Veal parmigiano	€15.90
Steak frites	12.90

Fish

Catch of the day (*please ask*)	price varies
Shrimp marinara	€15.80
Filet of sole with sauce Dijon	13.90

Side Dishes

Vegetable of the day	€2.50
Roasted potatoes	2.50

Desserts

Fruit tart (in season)	€4.30
Ice cream	3.40
Chocolate cake	2.50
Fresh fruit	2.95
Dessert of the day (*please ask*)	price varies

Service Charge Not Included

Student A, *you are allergic to tomatoes and dairy products.* **Student B,** *you don't eat meat or chicken. Discuss the menu with your partner. Then ask your server about items on the menu and order a meal. When you get the check, figure out a 20 percent tip.*

EXAMPLE: **A:** Do you know what's in a Caesar salad?
B: Not really. We'll have to ask the server. Excuse me. Can you tell us what's in the Caesar salad?
C: Sure. It has lettuce, parmesan cheese, and croutons.

EXERCISE 9: Discussion

Work in small groups. Discuss these questions.

1. Do you think tipping is a good system? Why or why not?
2. Were you ever in a situation where you didn't know what to do about a tip? What did you do?
3. How do people tip in your country and in other countries you know?

EXAMPLE: **A:** I'm not sure whether tipping is good or not. I think people should get paid enough so that they don't have to count on tips to live.
B: I wonder if you would still get good service if the tip were included.
C: Sure you would. A service charge is included in a lot of countries, and the service is still good.

EXERCISE 10: What About You?

A | *Think about the first time you did something—such as the following:*

- traveled to a foreign country
- went on a job interview
- drove a car
- became a parent

B | *Work in pairs. Discuss what problems you had.*

EXAMPLE: **A:** I remember the first time I went to a restaurant in Italy. I didn't know how to get the server's attention.
B: I didn't know whether to tip or not.

EXERCISE 11: Role Play: Information Please!

Work in pairs (A and B). **Student A,** *you are a desk clerk at a hotel.* **Student B,** *you are a guest at the hotel. Use embedded questions to find out information about the following:*

- restaurants
- interesting sights
- transportation
- entertainment
- banks
- shopping
- tipping
- laundry

EXAMPLE: **A:** Can I help you?
B: Yes. Could you tell me where to find a good, inexpensive restaurant around here?
A: There are some nice restaurants around the university.

EXERCISE 12: Writing

A | *Write a paragraph about a situation that confused or surprised you. It could be a time when you were traveling or another unfamiliar situation. Use embedded questions.*

EXAMPLE: When I was an exchange student in China, my Chinese friends always wanted to know how old I was. I couldn't understand why my new friends needed to know my age. I wasn't sure whether to tell the truth, because I was younger than them . . .

B | *Check your work. Use the Editing Checklist.*

Editing Checklist
Did you use . . . ?
☐ *if*, *whether (or not)*, or a *wh-* word to begin an embedded question
☐ statement word order (**subject** + **verb**) for embedded questions
☐ correct punctuation at the end of sentences with embedded questions

Student C, read the notes about today's menu.

Trattoria da Luigi

Appetizers

Bruschetta (toasted bread with chopped tomatoes, garlic, olive oil)
Roasted vegetables (onions, red pepper, zucchini, eggplant)

FIRST COURSE

Soup of the day
Monday: vegetable soup (carrots, peas, string beans in a tomato broth)
Tuesday: tomato soup
Wednesday: pea soup
Thursday: onion soup
Friday: fish soup
Saturday: potato soup (includes cream)

Caesar salad (lettuce, parmesan cheese,
croutons—cubes of bread toasted in olive oil and garlic)
Luigi's salad (spinach, mushrooms, tomatoes, onions)
Spaghetti da Luigi (spaghetti with spinach, fresh
tomatoes, and mushrooms in a light cream sauce)

SECOND COURSE

Chicken da Luigi (chicken baked in a tomato sauce
with olives and basil)
Steak frites (steak cooked in pan with butter,
served with french fried potatoes)
Catch of the day: grilled flounder—€6.95
Shrimp marinara (shrimp in tomato sauce)
Filet of sole with sauce Dijon (mustard sauce)

Side Dishes

Vegetable of the day: broccoli

Desserts

Fruit tart (cherry, apple, blueberry)
Ice cream (chocolate, strawberry, vanilla)
Fresh fruit (apples, bananas, strawberries)
Dessert of the day: strawberry shortcake (yellow cake
with fresh strawberries and whipped cream—€3.25)

Answer your customers' questions. When they are done ordering, look at the menu on
page 473. Write up a check. Include the items ordered and the prices. Use your own paper.

EXAMPLE: **A:** Do you know what's in a Caesar salad?
B: Not really. We'll have to ask the server. Excuse me. Can you tell us what's in the
Caesar salad?
C: Sure. It has lettuce, parmesan cheese, and croutons.

UNIT 29 Review

Check your answers on page UR-8.
Do you need to review anything?

A | Circle the correct words and punctuation marks to complete the sentences.

1. I wonder whether <u>should we / we should</u> tip the driver.

2. Do you remember who <u>is our server / our server is</u>?

3. I don't know why she ordered pizza <u>? / .</u>

4. Let's ask how <u>can we / to</u> get to the museum.

5. I wonder if <u>to / I should</u> take a taxi.

6. Can you tell me whether I need to tip the owner of a hair salon <u>? / .</u>

7. I'm not sure <u>whether / did</u> they read the tipping book.

B | Rewrite the questions in parentheses to complete the embedded questions. Use correct punctuation.

1. Can you remember _____
   (Where is the restaurant?)

2. I don't know _____
   (Does the subway go to the museum?)

3. We're not sure _____
   (Should we tip the porter?)

4. I can't imagine _____
   (Why didn't we buy the book on tipping?)

5. Let's ask _____
   (How much should we tip the tour guide?)

6. I'd like to know _____
   (Do you have any travel books?)

7. Could you explain _____
   (What does this sign say?)

C | Find and correct six mistakes. Remember to check punctuation.

A: Hi. Is this a good time to call? I wasn't sure what time you have dinner?

B: This is fine. I didn't know were you back from your trip.

A: We got back two days ago. I can't remember did I email you some photographs.

B: Yes. They were great. Can you tell me where took you that picture of the lake? I want to go!

A: Hmm. I'm not sure which one was that. We saw a lot of lakes in Switzerland.

B: I'll show it to you. I'd really like to find out where is it.

From Grammar to Writing
USING DIRECT AND INDIRECT SPEECH

A letter of complaint often includes both direct and indirect speech to describe a problem. We use **direct speech** only when it is important (**for 100 percent accuracy**) to report someone's exact words or to communicate a speaker's attitude. Otherwise, we use indirect speech.

1 | *Read this letter of complaint. Underline once examples of indirect speech. Underline twice examples of direct speech.*

Computer Town, Inc.
Customer Service Department
One Swell Way
Dallas, TX 75201

Dear Customer Service Manager:

In September 2012, I purchased a computer from your company. After the one-year warranty expired, I bought an extended service contract every year. I always received a renewal notice in the mail that told me that my policy was going to expire in a few weeks. This year, however, I did not receive the notice, and, as a result, I missed the deadline.

Upon realizing this mistake, I immediately called your company and asked if I could renew the service contract. The representative said, "It's too late, Miss." He said that if I wanted to extend my contract, the company would have to send someone to my home to inspect my computer. He also told me I would have to pay $160 for this visit. He said that my only other option was to ship my computer back to the company for inspection. I told him that neither of these options was acceptable.

When I asked him why I hadn't been notified that my contract was going to expire, he said, "We don't send notices out anymore." I said that I wanted to make a complaint. He said, "Don't complain to me. I don't even park the cars of the people who make these decisions." I think that your representatives should be more polite when speaking to customers. I also think that your customers should have been told that they would no longer receive renewal notices in the mail. That way, I would not have missed the deadline. I would, therefore, greatly appreciate it if I could have my service contract renewed without having to go through the inconvenience and expense of having my computer inspected.

Thank you for your attention.

Sincerely yours,

Anne Marie Clarke

Anne Marie Clarke
Customer No. 5378593

---

2 | *Look at the letter in Exercise 1. Circle the correct words to complete these sentences. Give an example of each item.*

1. The word *that* often introduces direct / (indirect) speech.

   He told me that my policy was going to expire in a few weeks.

2. Use quotation marks for direct / indirect speech.

   _____

3. Put final punctuation inside / outside the quotation marks.

   _____

4. Don't use a comma before direct / indirect speech.

   _____

5. Capitalize the first word of direct / indirect speech.

   _____

6. You can leave out the word *that* / question word when it introduces an indirect statement.

   _____

7. The writer used direct / indirect speech to show that the representative was rude.

   _____

3 | *Before you write . . .*

1. Think of an incident you would like to complain about, or make one up.

2. Work with a partner. Discuss each other's incidents and ask questions. Talk about where to use direct speech most effectively.

4 | *Write your letter of complaint. Remember to use indirect speech, and, if appropriate, direct speech. Be sure to capitalize and punctuate correctly.*

5 | *Exchange letters with a different partner. Then answer the following questions.*

	Yes	No
1. Do you understand the writer's complaint?	☐	☐
2. Did the writer choose direct speech to show the other person's attitude?	☐	☐
3. Did the writer choose direct speech for 100 percent accuracy?	☐	☐
4. Did the writer use quotation marks for direct speech only?	☐	☐
5. Is the direct speech punctuated correctly?	☐	☐

6 | *Work with your partner. Discuss each other's editing questions from Exercise 5. Then rewrite your own letter and make any necessary corrections.*

1 Irregular Verbs

Base Form	Simple Past	Past Participle	Base Form	Simple Past	Past Participle
arise	arose	arisen	hang	hung*/hanged**	hung*/hanged**
awake	awoke	awoken	have	had	had
be	was/were	been	hear	heard	heard
beat	beat	beaten/beat	hide	hid	hidden
become	became	become	hit	hit	hit
begin	began	begun	hold	held	held
bend	bent	bent	hurt	hurt	hurt
bet	bet	bet	keep	kept	kept
bite	bit	bitten	kneel	knelt/kneeled	knelt/kneeled
bleed	bled	bled	knit	knit/knitted	knit/knitted
blow	blew	blown	know	knew	known
break	broke	broken	lay	laid	laid
bring	brought	brought	lead	led	led
build	built	built	leap	leaped/leapt	leaped/leapt
burn	burned/burnt	burned/burnt	leave	left	left
burst	burst	burst	lend	lent	lent
buy	bought	bought	let	let	let
catch	caught	caught	lie (lie down)	lay	lain
choose	chose	chosen	light	lit/lighted	lit/lighted
cling	clung	clung	lose	lost	lost
come	came	come	make	made	made
cost	cost	cost	mean	meant	meant
creep	crept	crept	meet	met	met
cut	cut	cut	pay	paid	paid
deal	dealt	dealt	prove	proved	proved/proven
dig	dug	dug	put	put	put
dive	dived/dove	dived	quit	quit	quit
do	did	done	read /rid/	read /rɛd/	read /rɛd/
draw	drew	drawn	ride	rode	ridden
dream	dreamed/dreamt	dreamed/dreamt	ring	rang	rung
drink	drank	drunk	rise	rose	risen
drive	drove	driven	run	ran	run
eat	ate	eaten	say	said	said
fall	fell	fallen	see	saw	seen
feed	fed	fed	seek	sought	sought
feel	felt	felt	sell	sold	sold
fight	fought	fought	send	sent	sent
find	found	found	set	set	set
fit	fit/fitted	fit	sew	sewed	sewn/sewed
flee	fled	fled	shake	shook	shaken
fling	flung	flung	shave	shaved	shaved/shaven
fly	flew	flown	shine (intransitive)	shone/shined	shone/shined
forbid	forbade/forbid	forbidden	shoot	shot	shot
forget	forgot	forgotten	show	showed	shown
forgive	forgave	forgiven	shrink	shrank/shrunk	shrunk/shrunken
freeze	froze	frozen	shut	shut	shut
get	got	gotten/got	sing	sang	sung
give	gave	given	sink	sank/sunk	sunk
go	went	gone			
grind	ground	ground			
grow	grew	grown			

* hung = *hung an object*
** hanged = *executed by hanging*

(continued on next page)

Base Form	Simple Past	Past Participle		Base Form	Simple Past	Past Participle
sit	sat	sat		swim	swam	swum
sleep	slept	slept		swing	swung	swung
slide	slid	slid		take	took	taken
speak	spoke	spoken		teach	taught	taught
speed	sped/speeded	sped/speeded		tear	tore	torn
spend	spent	spent		tell	told	told
spill	spilled/spilt	spilled/spilt		think	thought	thought
spin	spun	spun		throw	threw	thrown
spit	spit/spat	spat		understand	understood	understood
split	split	split		upset	upset	upset
spread	spread	spread		wake	woke	woken
spring	sprang	sprung		wear	wore	worn
stand	stood	stood		weave	wove/weaved	woven/weaved
steal	stole	stolen		weep	wept	wept
stick	stuck	stuck		win	won	won
sting	stung	stung		wind	wound	wound
stink	stank/stunk	stunk		withdraw	withdrew	withdrawn
strike	struck	struck/stricken		wring	wrung	wrung
swear	swore	sworn		write	wrote	written
sweep	swept	swept				

2 Non-Action Verbs

EMOTIONS	MENTAL STATES		WANTS AND PREFERENCES	SENSES AND PERCEPTION	APPEARANCE AND VALUE	POSSESSION AND RELATIONSHIP
admire	agree	imagine	desire	feel	appear	belong
adore	assume	know	hope	hear	be	come from (*origin*)
appreciate	believe	mean	need	notice	cost	contain
care	consider	mind	prefer	observe	equal	have
detest	disagree	presume	want	perceive	look (*seem*)	own
dislike	disbelieve	realize	wish	see	matter	possess
doubt	estimate	recognize		smell	represent	
envy	expect	remember		sound	resemble	
fear	feel (*believe*)	see (*understand*)		taste	seem	
hate	find (*believe*)	suppose			signify	
like	forget	suspect			weigh	
love	guess	think (*believe*)				
miss	hesitate	understand				
regret	hope	wonder				
respect						
trust						

3 Verbs Followed by Gerunds (Base Form of Verb + *-ing*)

acknowledge	celebrate	endure	give up (*stop*)	permit	quit	resist
admit	consider	enjoy	go	postpone	recall	risk
advise	delay	escape	imagine	practice	recommend	suggest
allow	deny	excuse	justify	prevent	regret	support
appreciate	detest	explain	keep (*continue*)	prohibit	report	tolerate
avoid	discontinue	feel like	mention	propose	resent	understand
ban	discuss	finish	mind (*object to*)			
can't help	dislike	forgive	miss			

= postpone =
after put

put it off

4 Verbs Followed by Infinitives (*To* + Base Form of Verb)

afford	can('t) afford	expect	hurry	neglect	promise	volunteer
agree	can't wait	fail	intend	offer	refuse	wait
appear	choose	grow	learn	pay	request	want
arrange	consent	help	manage	plan	seem	wish
ask	decide	hesitate	mean (*intend*)	prepare	struggle	would like
attempt	deserve	hope	need	pretend	swear	yearn

5 Verbs Followed by Object + Infinitive

advise	challenge	encourage	help*	order	remind	urge
allow	choose*	expect*	hire	pay*	request	want*
ask*	convince	forbid	instruct	permit	require	warn
beg*	dare*	force	invite	persuade	teach	wish*
cause	enable	get*	need*	promise*	tell	would like*

*These verbs can also be followed by an infinitive without an object (EXAMPLE: *ask to leave* or *ask someone to leave*).

6 Verbs Followed by Gerunds or Infinitives

begin	forget*	love	start
can't stand	hate	prefer	stop*
continue	like	remember*	try

*These verbs can also be followed by either a gerund or an infinitive, but there is a big difference in meaning.

7 Verb + Preposition Combinations

admit to	choose between	feel like/about	pay for	talk about
advise against	complain about	go along with	plan on	thank s.o. for
apologize for	deal with	insist on	rely on	think about
approve of	decide on	look forward to	resort to	wonder about
believe in	dream about/of	object to	succeed in	worry about

8 Adjective + Preposition Combinations

accustomed to	awful at	concerned about	fed up with	known for	sad about	sorry for/about
afraid of	bad at	content with	fond of	nervous about	safe from	surprised at/about/by
amazed at/by	bored with/by	curious about	glad about	opposed to	satisfied with	terrible at
angry at	capable of	different from	good at	pleased about	shocked at/by	tired of
ashamed of	careful of	excited about	happy about	ready for	sick of	used to
aware of	certain about	famous for	interested in	responsible for	slow at/in	worried about

I can't stand doing Dishes.

A-3

9 Adjectives Followed by Infinitives

afraid	ashamed	difficult	easy	glad	pleased	reluctant	surprised
alarmed	curious	disappointed	embarrassed	happy	prepared	right	touched
amazed	delighted	distressed	encouraged	hesitant	proud	sad	upset
angry	depressed	disturbed	excited	likely	ready	shocked	willing
anxious	determined	eager	fortunate	lucky	relieved	sorry	wrong

10 Nouns Followed by Infinitives

attempt	desire	offer	price	right
chance	dream	opportunity	promise	time
choice	failure	permission	reason	trouble
decision	need	plan	request	way

11 Irregular Comparisons of Adjectives, Adverbs, and Quantifiers

ADJECTIVE	ADVERB	COMPARATIVE	SUPERLATIVE
bad	badly	worse	the worst
far	far	farther/further	the farthest/furthest
good	well	better	the best
little	little	less	the least
many/a lot of	—	more	the most
much*/a lot of	much*/a lot	more	the most

*Much is usually only used in questions and negative statements.

12 Adjectives that Form the Comparative and Superlative in Two Ways

ADJECTIVE	COMPARATIVE	SUPERLATIVE
common	commoner/more common	commonest/most common
cruel	crueler/more cruel	cruelest/most cruel
deadly	deadlier/more deadly	deadliest/most deadly
friendly	friendlier/more friendly	friendliest/most friendly
handsome	handsomer/more handsome	handsomest/most handsome
happy	happier/more happy	happiest/most happy
likely	likelier/more likely	likeliest/most likely
lively	livelier/more lively	liveliest/most lively
lonely	lonelier/more lonely	loneliest/most lonely
lovely	lovelier/more lovely	loveliest/most lovely
narrow	narrower/more narrow	narrowest/most narrow
pleasant	pleasanter/more pleasant	pleasantest/most pleasant
polite	politer/more polite	politest/most polite
quiet	quieter/more quiet	quietest/most quiet
shallow	shallower/more shallow	shallowest/most shallow
sincere	sincerer/more sincere	sincerest/most sincere
stupid	stupider/more stupid	stupidest/most stupid
true	truer/more true	truest/most true

13 Participial Adjectives

-ed	-ing	-ed	-ing	-ed	-ing
alarmed	alarming	disturbed	disturbing	moved	moving
amazed	amazing	embarrassed	embarrassing	paralyzed	paralyzing
amused	amusing	entertained	entertaining	pleased	pleasing
annoyed	annoying	excited	exciting	relaxed	relaxing
astonished	astonishing	exhausted	exhausting	satisfied	satisfying
bored	boring	fascinated	fascinating	shocked	shocking
confused	confusing	frightened	frightening	surprised	surprising
depressed	depressing	horrified	horrifying	terrified	terrifying
disappointed	disappointing	inspired	inspiring	tired	tiring
disgusted	disgusting	interested	interesting	touched	touching
distressed	distressing	irritated	irritating	troubled	troubling

14 Reporting Verbs

STATEMENTS				**INSTRUCTIONS, COMMANDS, REQUESTS, AND INVITATIONS**		**QUESTIONS**
acknowledge	complain	note	state	advise	invite	ask
add	conclude	observe	suggest	ask	order	inquire
admit	confess	promise	tell	caution	say	question
announce	declare	remark	warn	command	tell	want to know
answer	deny	repeat	whisper	demand	urge	wonder
argue	exclaim	reply	write	instruct	warn	
assert	explain	report	yell			
believe	indicate	respond				
claim	maintain	say				
comment	mean	shout				

15 Time Word Changes in Indirect Speech

DIRECT SPEECH		INDIRECT SPEECH
now	→	then
today	→	that day
tomorrow	→	the next day OR the following day OR the day after
yesterday	→	the day before OR the previous day
this week/month/year	→	that week/month/year
last week/month/year	→	the week/month/year before
next week/month/year	→	the following week/month/year

16 Phrases Introducing Embedded Questions

I don't know . . .
I don't understand . . .
I wonder . . .
I'm not sure . . .
I can't remember . . .
I can't imagine . . .
It doesn't say . . .

I'd like to know . . .
I want to understand . . .
I'd like to find out . . .
We need to find out . . .
Let's ask . . .

Do you know . . . ?
Do you understand . . . ?
Can you tell me . . . ?
Could you explain . . . ?
Can you remember . . . ?
Would you show me . . . ?
Who knows . . . ?

17 Verbs and Expressions Used Reflexively

allow yourself	be proud of yourself	enjoy yourself	keep yourself (busy)	remind yourself
amuse yourself	behave yourself	feel sorry for yourself	kill yourself	see yourself
ask yourself	believe in yourself	forgive yourself	look after yourself	take care of yourself
avail yourself of	blame yourself	help yourself	look at yourself	talk to yourself
be hard on yourself	cut yourself	hurt yourself	prepare yourself	teach yourself
be yourself	deprive yourself of	imagine yourself	pride yourself on	tell yourself
be pleased with yourself	dry yourself	introduce yourself	push yourself	treat yourself

18 Transitive Phrasal Verbs

(s.o. = someone   s.t. = something)
- **Separable phrasal verbs** show the object between the verb and the particle: **call** s.o. **up**.
- **Verbs that must be separated** have an asterisk (*): **do** s.t. **over***
- **Inseparable phrasal verbs** show the object after the particle: **carry on** s.t.

REMEMBER: You can put a **noun object** between the verb and the particle of **separable** two-word verbs (*call Jan up* OR *call up Jan*). You <u>must</u> put a **pronoun object** between the verb and the particle of separable verbs (*call her up* NOT ~~call up her~~).

PHRASAL VERB	MEANING	PHRASAL VERB	MEANING
ask s.o. **over***	*invite to one's home*	**draw** s.t. **together**	*unite*
block s.t. **out**	*stop from passing through (light/ noise)*	**dream** s.t. **up**	*invent*
		drink s.t. **up**	*drink completely*
blow s.t. **out**	*stop burning by blowing air on it*	**drop** s.o. or s.t. **off**	*take someplace*
blow s.t. **up**	1. *make explode*	**drop out of** s.t.	*quit*
	2. *fill with air (a balloon)*	**empty** s.t. **out**	*empty completely*
	3. *make something larger (a photo)*	**end up with** s.t.	*have an unexpected result*
bring s.t. **about**	*make happen*	**fall for** s.o.	*feel romantic love for*
bring s.o. or s.t. **back**	*return*	**fall for** s.t.	*be tricked by, believe*
bring s.o. **down***	*depress*	**figure** s.o. or s.t. **out**	*understand (after thinking about)*
bring s.t. **out**	*introduce (a new product/book)*	**fill** s.t. **in**	*complete with information*
bring s.o. **up**	*raise (children)*	**fill** s.t. **out**	*complete (a form)*
bring s.t. **up**	*bring attention to*	**fill** s.t. **up**	*fill completely*
build s.t. **up**	*increase*	**find** s.t. **out**	*learn information*
burn s.t. **down**	*burn completely*	**fix** s.t. **up**	*redecorate (a home)*
call s.o. **back***	*return a phone call*	**follow through with** s.t.	*complete*
call s.o. **in**	*ask for help with a problem*	**get** s.t. **across**	*get people to understand an idea*
call s.t. **off**	*cancel*	**get off** s.t.	*leave (a bus/a train)*
call s.o. **up**	*contact by phone*	**get on** s.t.	*board (a bus/a train)*
carry on s.t.	*continue*	**get out of** s.t.	*leave (a car/taxi)*
carry s.t. **out**	*conduct (an experiment/a plan)*	**get** s.t. **out of** s.t.*	*benefit from*
cash in on s.t.	*profit from*	**get through with** s.t.	*finish*
charge s.t. **up**	*charge with electricity*	**get to** s.o. or s.t.	1. *reach s.o. or s.t.*
check s.t. **out**	*examine*		2. *upset s.o.*
cheer s.o. **up**	*cause to feel happier*	**get together with** s.o.	*meet*
clean s.o. or s.t. **up**	*clean completely*	**give** s.t. **away**	*give without charging money*
clear s.t. **up**	*explain*	**give** s.t. **back**	*return*
close s.t. **down**	*close by force*	**give** s.t. **out**	*distribute*
come off s.t.	*become unattached*	**give** s.t. **up**	*quit, abandon*
come up with s.t.	*invent*	**go after** s.o. or s.t.	*try to get or win, pursue*
count on s.o. or s.t.	*depend on*	**go along with** s.t.	*support*
cover s.o. or s.t. **up**	*cover completely*	**go over** s.t.	*review*
cross s.t. **out**	*draw a line through*	**hand** s.t. **in**	*submit, give work (to a boss/teacher)*
cut s.t. **down**	1. *bring down by cutting (a tree)*		
	2. *reduce*	**hand** s.t. **out**	*distribute*
cut s.t. **off**	1. *stop the supply of*	**hang** s.t. **up**	*put on a hook or hanger*
	2. *remove by cutting*	**help** s.o. **out**	*assist*
cut s.t. **out**	*remove by cutting*	**hold** s.t. **on**	*keep attached*
cut s.t. **up**	*cut into small pieces*	**keep** s.o. or s.t. **away**	*cause to stay at a distance*
do s.t. **over***	*do again*	**keep** s.t. **on***	*not remove (a piece of clothing/jewelry)*
do s.o. or s.t. **up**	*make more beautiful*		

PHRASAL VERB	MEANING	PHRASAL VERB	MEANING
keep s.o. or s.t. **out**	prevent from entering	**show up on** s.t.	appear
keep up with s.o. or s.t.	go as fast as	**shut** s.t. **off**	stop (a machine/light)
lay s.o. **off**	end employment	**sign** s.o. **up** (for s.t.)	register
lay s.t. **out**	1. arrange according to a plan	**start** s.t. **over***	start again
	2. spend money	**stick with/to** s.o. or s.t.	not quit, not leave, persevere
leave s.t. **on**	1. not turn off (a light/radio)	**straighten** s.t. **up**	make neat
	2. not remove (a piece of clothing/jewelry)	**switch** s.t. **on**	start (a machine/light)
		take s.t. **away**	remove
leave s.t. **out**	omit, not include	**take** s.o. or s.t. **back**	return
let s.o. **down**	disappoint	**take** s.t. **down**	remove
let s.o. or s.t. **in**	allow to enter	**take** s.t. **in**	1. notice, understand, and remember
let s.o. **off**	1. allow to leave (a bus/car)		2. earn (money)
	2. not punish	**take** s.t. **off**	remove
let s.o. or s.t. **out**	allow to leave	**take** s.o. **on**	hire
light s.t. **up**	illuminate	**take** s.t. **on**	agree to do
look after s.o. or s.t.	take care of	**take** s.t. **out**	borrow from a library
look into s.t.	research	**take** s.t. **up**	begin a job or activity
look s.o. or s.t. **over**	examine	**talk** s.o. **into***	persuade
look s.t. **up**	try to find (in a book/on the Internet)	**talk** s.t. **over**	discuss
		team up with s.o.	start to work with
make s.t. **up**	create	**tear** s.t. **down**	destroy
miss out on s.t.	lose the chance for something good	**tear** s.t. **up**	tear into small pieces
		think back on s.o. or s.t.	remember
move s.t. **around***	change the location	**think** s.t. **over**	consider
pass s.t. **out**	distribute	**think** s.t. **up**	invent
pass s.o. or s.t. **up**	decide not to use	**throw** s.t. **away/out**	discard, put in the trash
pay s.o. or s.t. **back**	repay	**touch** s.t. **up**	improve by making small changes
pick s.o. or s.t. **out**	1. choose		
	2. identify	**try** s.t. **on**	put clothing on to see if it fits
pick s.o. or s.t. **up**	lift	**try** s.t. **out**	use to see if it works
pick s.t. **up**	1. buy, purchase	**turn** s.t. **around***	change the direction so the front is at the back
	2. get (an idea/an interest)		
	3. answer the phone	**turn** s.o. **down**	reject
point s.o. or s.t. **out**	indicate	**turn** s.t. **down**	1. lower the volume (a TV/radio)
put s.t. **away**	put in an appropriate place		2. reject (a job/an idea)
put s.t. **back**	return to its original place	**turn** s.t. **in**	submit, give work (to a boss/teacher)
put s.o. or s.t. **down**	stop holding		
put s.o. **off**	discourage	**turn** s.o. or s.t. **into***	change from one form to another
put s.t. **off**	delay	**turn** s.o. **off***	[slang] destroy interest
put s.t. **on**	cover the body (with clothes or jewelry)	**turn** s.t. **off**	stop (a machine), extinguish (a light)
put s.t. **together**	assemble	**turn** s.t. **on**	start (a machine/light)
put s.t. **up**	erect	**turn** s.t. **over**	turn something so the top side is at the bottom
run into s.o.	meet accidentally		
see s.t. **through***	complete	**turn** s.t. **up**	make louder (a TV/radio)
send s.t. **back**	return	**use** s.t. **up**	use completely, consume
send s.t. **out**	mail	**wake** s.o. **up**	awaken
set s.t. **off**	cause to explode	**watch out for** s.o. or s.t.	be careful about
set s.t. **up**	1. prepare for use	**work** s.t. **off**	remove by work or activity
	2. establish (a business/an organization)	**work** s.t. **out**	solve, understand
		write s.t. **down**	write on a piece of paper
settle on s.t.	choose s.t. after thinking about many possibilities	**write** s.t. **up**	write in a finished form
show s.o. or s.t. **off**	display the best qualities		

Phrasal Verb	Meaning	Phrasal Verb	Meaning
act up	cause problems	go away	leave a place or person
blow up	explode	go back	return
break down	stop working (a machine)	go down	become less (price, number), decrease
break out	happen suddenly		
burn down	burn completely	go off	explode (a gun/fireworks)
call back	return a phone call	go on	continue
catch on	1. become popular	go out	leave
	2. understand	go over	succeed with an audience
cheer up	make happier	go up	1. be built
clean up	clean completely		2. become more (price, number), increase
clear up	become clear		
close down	stop operating	grow up	become an adult
come about	happen	hang up	end a phone call
come along	come with, accompany	hold on	1. wait
come around	happen		2. not hang up the phone
come back	return	keep away	stay at a distance
come down	become less (price)	keep on	continue
come in	enter	keep out	not enter
come off	become unattached	keep up	go as fast as
come out	appear	lie down	recline
come up	arise	light up	illuminate
dress up	wear special clothes	look out	be careful
drop in	visit by surprise	make up	end a disagreement, reconcile
drop out	quit	miss out	lose the chance for something good
eat out	eat in a restaurant		
empty out	empty completely	pay off	be worthwhile
end up	1. do something unexpected or unintended	pick up	improve
		play around	have fun
	2. reach a final place or condition	run out	not have enough of
		show up	appear
fall off	become detached	sign up	register
find out	learn information	sit down	take a seat
follow through	complete	slip up	make a mistake
fool around	act playful	stand up	rise
get ahead	make progress, succeed	start over	start again
get along	have a good relationship	stay up	remain awake
get back	return	straighten up	make neat
get by	survive	take off	depart (a plane)
get off	1. leave (a bus, the Internet)	turn out	have a particular result
	2. end a phone conversation	turn up	appear
get on	enter, board (a bus, a train)	wake up	stop sleeping
get through	finish	watch out	be careful
get together	meet	work out	1. be resolved
get up	rise from bed, arise		2. exercise
give up	quit		

20 Modals and Their Functions

A. SOCIAL MODALS AND EXPRESSIONS

FUNCTION	MODAL OR EXPRESSION	TIME	EXAMPLES
Ability	can can't	Present	• Sam **can swim**. • He **can't skate**.
	could couldn't	Past	• We **could swim** last year. • We **couldn't skate**.
	be able to* not be able to*	All Verb Forms	• Lea **is able to run** fast. • She **wasn't able to run** fast last year.
Advice	should shouldn't ought to had better** had better not**	Present or Future	• You **should study** more. • You **shouldn't miss** class. • We **ought to leave**. • We**'d better go**. • We**'d better not stay**.
Advisability in the Past and **Regret or Blame**	should have shouldn't have ought to have could have might have	Past	• I **should have become** a doctor. • I **shouldn't have wasted** time. • He **ought to have told** me. • She **could have gone** to college. • You **might have called**. I waited for hours.
Necessity	have to* not have to*	All Verb Forms	• He **has to go** now. • He **doesn't have to go** yet. • I **had to go** yesterday. • I **will have to go** soon.
	have got to* must	Present or Future	• He**'s got to leave**! • You **must use** a pen for the test.
Permission	can	Present or Future	• **Can** I **sit** here? • **Can** I **call** tomorrow? • Yes, you **can**.
	can't could may		• No, you **can't**. Sorry. • **Could** he **leave** now? • **May** I **borrow** your pen? • Yes, you **may**.
	may not		• No, you **may not**. Sorry.
Prohibition	must not can't	Present or Future	• You **must not drive** without a license. • You **can't drive** without a license.
Requests	can	Present or Future	• **Can** you **close** the door, please? • Sure, I **can**.
	can't could will would		• Sorry, I **can't**. • **Could** you please **answer** the phone? • **Will** you **wash** the dishes, please? • **Would** you please **mail** this letter?

 * The meaning of this expression is similar to the meaning of a modal. Unlike a modal, it has *-s* for third-person singular.
** The meaning of this expression is similar to the meaning of a modal. Like a modal, it has no *-s* for third-person singular.

Function	Modal or Expression	Time	Examples
Conclusions and Possibility	**must** **must not** **have to*** **have got to***	Present	• This **must be** her house. Her name is on the door. • She **must not be** home. I don't see her car. • She **has to know** him. They went to school together. • He**'s got to be** guilty. We saw him do it.
	may **may not** **might** **might not** **could**	Present or Future	• She **may be** home now. • It **may not rain** tomorrow. • Lee **might be sick** today. • He **might not come** to class. • They **could be** at the library. • It **could rain** tomorrow.
	may have **may not have** **might have** **might not have** **could have**	Past	• They **may have left** already. I don't see them. • They **may not have arrived** yet. • He **might have called.** I'll check my phone messages. • He **might not have left** a message. • She **could have forgotten** to mail the letter.
Impossibility	**can't**	Present or Future	• That **can't be** Ana. She left for France yesterday. • It **can't snow** tomorrow. It's going to be too warm.
	couldn't	Present	• He **couldn't be** guilty. He wasn't in town when the crime occurred. • The teacher **couldn't give** the test tomorrow. Tomorrow's Saturday.
	couldn't have	Past	• You **couldn't have failed**. You studied so hard.

*The meaning of this expression is similar to the meaning of a modal. Unlike a modal, it has *-s* for third-person singular.

21 Irregular Plural Nouns

Singular	Plural	Singular	Plural	Singular	Plural	Singular	Plural
analysis	analyses	half	halves	person	people	deer	deer
basis	bases	knife	knives	man	men	fish	fish
crisis	crises	leaf	leaves	woman	women	sheep	sheep
hypothesis	hypotheses	life	lives	child	children		
		loaf	loaves	foot	feet		
		shelf	shelves	tooth	teeth		
		wife	wives	goose	geese		
				mouse	mice		

22 Spelling Rules for the Simple Present: Third-Person Singular (*He, She, It*)

1. Add *-s* for most verbs.

work	works
buy	buys
ride	rides
return	returns

2. Add *-es* for verbs that end in *-ch*, *-s*, *-sh*, *-x*, or *-z*.

watch	watches
pass	passes
rush	rushes
relax	relaxes
buzz	buzzes

3. Change the *y* to *i* and add *-es* when the base form ends in a **consonant** + *y*.

study	studies
hurry	hurries
dry	dries

   Do not change the *y* when the base form ends in a vowel + *y*. Add *-s*.

play	plays
enjoy	enjoys

4. A few verbs are irregular.

be	**is**
do	**does**
go	**goes**
have	**has**

23 Spelling Rules for Base Form of Verb + *-ing* (Progressive and Gerund)

1. Add *-ing* to the base form of the verb.

read	reading
stand	standing

2. If the verb ends in a silent *-e*, drop the final *-e* and add *-ing*.

leave	leaving
take	taking

3. In **one-syllable verbs**, if the last three letters are a consonant-vowel-consonant combination (CVC), double the last consonant and add *-ing*.

   ```
   C V C
   ↓ ↓ ↓
   s i t    sitting

   C V C
   ↓ ↓ ↓
   p l a n  planning
   ```

4. In verbs of **two or more syllables** that end in a consonant-vowel-consonant combination, double the last consonant only if the last syllable is stressed.*

admít	admitting	*(The last syllable is stressed.)*
whísper	whispering	*(The last syllable is not stressed, so don't double the -r.)*

5. If the verb ends in *-ie*, change the *ie* to *y* before adding *-ing*.

die	dying
lie	lying

   ---

   *The symbol ′ shows main stress.

   Do not double the last consonant in verbs that end in *-w*, *-x*, or *-y*.

sew	sewing
fix	fixing
play	playing

24 Spelling Rules for Base Form of Verb + -ed (Simple Past and Past Participle of Regular Verbs)

1. If the verb ends in a consonant, add -ed.

   return   return**ed**
   help   help**ed**

2. If the verb ends in -e, add -d.

   live   live**d**
   create   create**d**
   die   die**d**

3. In **one-syllable verbs**, if the last three letters are a consonant-vowel-consonant combination (CVC), double the last consonant before adding -ed.

   C V C
   ↓ ↓ ↓
   h o p   hop**ped**

   C V C
   ↓ ↓ ↓
   p l a n   plan**ned**

   Do not double the last consonant of one-syllable words ending in -**w**, -**x**, or -**y**.

   bow   bow**ed**
   mix   mix**ed**
   play   play**ed**

4. In verbs of **two or more syllables** that end in a consonant-vowel-consonant combination, double the last consonant only if the last syllable is stressed.*

   preférer prefer   prefer**red**   *(The last syllable is stressed, so double the r.)*

   vísit   visit**ed**   *(The last syllable is not stressed, don't double the -**t**.)*

5. If the verb ends in **consonant + y**, change the y to i and add -ed.

   worry   worr**ied**
   carry   carr**ied**

6. If the verb ends in **vowel + y**, add -ed. (Do not change the y to i.)

   play   play**ed**
   annoy   annoy**ed**
   EXCEPTIONS: pay—p**ai**d
                    lay—l**ai**d
                    say—s**ai**d

*The symbol ′ shows main stress.

25 Spelling Rules for the Comparative (-er) and Superlative (-est) of Adjectives

1. With **one-syllable** adjectives add -er to form the comparative. Add -**est** to form the superlative.

   cheap   cheap**er**   cheap**est**
   bright   bright**er**   bright**est**

2. If the adjective ends in -e, add -r or -**st**.

   nice   nic**er**   nic**est**

3. If the adjective ends in a **consonant + y**, change y to i before you add -er or -**est**.

   pretty   prett**ier**   prett**iest**

   EXCEPTION:
   shy   shy**er**   shy**est**

4. In one-syllable adjectives, if the last three letters are a consonant-vowel-consonant combination (CVC), double the last consonant before adding -er or -**est**.

   C V C
   ↓ ↓ ↓
   b i g   big**ger**   big**gest**

   Do not double the consonant in words ending in -**w** or -**y**.

   slow   slow**er**   slow**est**
   gray   gray**er**   gray**est**

26 Spelling Rules for Adverbs Ending in -ly

1. Add -**ly** to the corresponding adjective.

nice	nice**ly**
quiet	quiet**ly**
beautiful	beautiful**ly**

2. If the adjective ends in **consonant** + *y*, change the *y* to *i* before adding -**ly**.

easy	eas**ily**

3. If the adjective ends in -**le**, drop the *e* and add -**y**.

possible	possib**ly**

Do not drop the *e* for other adjectives ending in -*e*.

extreme	extreme**ly**

EXCEPTION:

true	tru**ly**

4. If the adjective ends in -**ic**, add -**ally**.

basic	basic**ally**
fantastic	fantastic**ally**

27 Direct Speech: Punctuation Rules

Direct speech may either follow or come before the reporting verb.

When direct speech follows the reporting verb:

a. Put a comma after the reporting verb.
b. Use opening quotation marks (") before the first word of the direct speech.
c. Begin the quotation with a capital letter.
d. Use the appropriate end punctuation for the direct speech. It may be a period (.), a question mark (?), or an exclamation point (!).
e. Put closing quotation marks (") after the end punctuation of the quotation.

> **EXAMPLES:** He said, "I had a good time."
> She asked, "Where's the party?"
> They shouted, "Be careful!"

When direct speech comes before the reporting verb:

a. Begin the sentence with opening quotation marks (").
b. Use the appropriate end punctuation for the direct speech.
   If the direct speech is a statement, use a comma (,).
   If the direct speech is a question, use a question mark (?).
   If the direct speech is an exclamation, use an exclamation point (!).
c. Use closing quotation marks after the end punctuation for the direct speech (").
d. Begin the reporting clause with a lowercase letter.
e. Use a period at the end of the main sentence (.).

> **EXAMPLES:** "I had a good time," he said.
> "Where's the party?" she asked.
> "Be careful!" they shouted.

28 Pronunciation Table

These are the pronunciation symbols used in this text. Listen to the pronunciation of the key words.

	VOWELS				CONSONANTS		
Symbol	Key Word	Symbol	Key Word	Symbol	Key Word	Symbol	Key Word
i	beat, feed	ə	banana, among	p	pack, happy	ʃ	ship, machine, station,
ɪ	bit, did	ɚ	shirt, murder	b	back, rubber		special, discussion
eɪ	date, paid	aɪ	bite, cry, buy, eye	t	tie	ʒ	measure, vision
ɛ	bet, bed	aʊ	about, how	d	die	h	hot, who
æ	bat, bad	ɔɪ	voice, boy	k	came, key, quick	m	men, some
ɑ	box, odd, father	ɪr	beer	g	game, guest	n	sun, know, pneumonia
ɔ	bought, dog	ɛr	bare	tʃ	church, nature, watch	ŋ	sung, ringing
oʊ	boat, road	ɑr	bar	dʒ	judge, general, major	w	wet, white
ʊ	book, good	ɔr	door	f	fan, photograph	l	light, long
u	boot, food, student	ʊr	tour	v	van	r	right, wrong
ʌ	but, mud, mother			θ	thing, breath	y	yes, use, music
				ð	then, breathe	t̬	butter, bottle
				s	sip, city, psychology		
				z	zip, please, goes		

29 Pronunciation Rules for the Simple Present: Third-Person Singular *(He, She, It)*

1. The third-person singular in the simple present always ends in the letter -s. There are three different pronunciations for the final sound of the third-person singular.

/s/	/z/	/ɪz/
talks	loves	dances

2. The final sound is pronounced /s/ after the voiceless sounds /p/, /t/, /k/, and /f/.

top	tops
get	gets
take	takes
laugh	laughs

3. The final sound is pronounced /z/ after the voiced sounds /b/, /d/, /g/, /v/, /m/, /n/, /ŋ/, /l/, /r/, and /ð/.

describe	describes
spend	spends
hug	hugs
live	lives
bathe	bathes
seem	seems
remain	remains
sing	sings
tell	tells
lower	lowers

4. The final sound is pronounced /z/ after all **vowel sounds**.

agree	agrees
try	tries
stay	stays
know	knows

5. The final sound is pronounced /ɪz/ after the sounds /s/, /z/, /ʃ/, /ʒ/, and /tʃ/. /dʒ/ adds a syllable to the verb.

relax	relaxes
freeze	freezes
rush	rushes
massage	massages
watch	watches
judge	judges

6. *Do* and *say* have a change in vowel sound.

do	/du/	does	/dʌz/
say	/seɪ/	says	/sɛz/

30 Pronunciation Rules for the Simple Past and Past Participle of Regular Verbs

1. The regular simple past and past participle always ends in the letter -*d*. There are three different pronunciations for the final sound of the regular simple past and past participle.

/t/	/d/	/ɪd/
raced	lived	attended

2. The final sound is pronounced /t/ after the voiceless sounds /p/, /k/, /f/, /s/, /ʃ/, and /tʃ/.

hop	hopped
work	worked
laugh	laughed
address	addressed
publish	published
watch	watched

3. The final sound is pronounced /d/ after the voiced sounds /b/, /g/, /v/, /z/, /ʒ/, /dʒ/, /m/, /n/, /ŋ/, /l/, /r/, and /ð/.

rub	rubbed
hug	hugged
live	lived
surprise	surprised
massage	massaged
change	changed
rhyme	rhymed
return	returned
bang	banged
enroll	enrolled
appear	appeared
bathe	bathed

4. The final sound is pronounced /d/ after all **vowel sounds**.

agree	agreed
play	played
die	died
enjoy	enjoyed
row	rowed

5. The final sound is pronounced /ɪd/ after /t/ and /d/. /ɪd/ adds a syllable to the verb.

start	started
decide	decided

31 Capitalization and Punctuation Rules

	USE FOR . . .	EXAMPLES
capital letter	• the pronoun *I* • proper nouns • the first word of a sentence	Tomorrow **I** will be here at 2:00. His name is **Karl**. He lives in **Germany**. **When** does the train leave? **At** 2:00.
apostrophe (')	• possessive nouns • contractions	Is that **Marta's** coat? **That's** not hers. **It's** mine.
comma (,)	• after items in a list • before sentence connectors *and*, *but*, *or*, and *so* • after the first part of a sentence that begins with *because* • after the first part of a sentence that begins with a preposition • after the first part of a sentence that begins with a time clause or an *if* clause • before and after a non-identifying adjective clause in the middle of a sentence. • before a non-identifying adjective clause at the end of a sentence	He bought **apples, pears, oranges,** and **bananas**. They watched TV, **and** she played video games. **Because it's raining**, we're not walking to work. **Across from the post office**, there's a good restaurant. **After he arrived**, we ate dinner. ***If it rains***, we won't go. Tony, **who lives in Paris**, emails me every day. I get emails every day from Tony, **who lives in Paris**.
exclamation mark (!)	• at the end of a sentence to show surprise or a strong feeling	You're here! That's great! Stop! A car is coming!
period (.)	• at the end of a statement	Today is Wednesday.
question mark (?)	• at the end of a question	What day is today?

GLOSSARY OF GRAMMAR TERMS

action verb   A verb that describes an action.
- Alicia **ran** home.

active sentence   A sentence that focuses on the agent (the person or thing doing the action).
- **Ari kicked** the ball.

addition   A clause or a short sentence that follows a statement and expresses similarity or contrast with the information in the statement.
- Pedro is tall, **and so is Alex**.
- Trish doesn't like sports. **Neither does her sister**.

adjective   A word that describes a noun or pronoun.
- It's a **good** plan, and it's not **difficult**.

adjective clause   A clause that identifies or gives additional information about a noun.
- The woman **who called you** didn't leave her name.
- Samir, **who you met yesterday**, works in the lab.

adverb   A word that describes a verb, an adjective, or another adverb.
- She drives **carefully**.
- She's a **very** good driver.
- She drives **really** well.

affirmative   A statement or answer meaning Yes.
- He **works**. (affirmative statement)
- **Yes**, he **does**. (affirmative short answer)

agent   The person or thing doing the action in a sentence. In passive sentences, the word by is used before the agent.
- This magazine is published **by National Geographic**.

article   A word that goes before a noun. The **indefinite** articles are **a** and **an**.
- I ate **a** sandwich and **an** apple.

The **definite** article is **the**.
- I didn't like **the** sandwich. **The** apple was good.

auxiliary verb   (also called **helping verb**) A verb used with a main verb. Be, do, and have are often auxiliary verbs. Modals (can, should, may, must . . .) are also auxiliary verbs.
- I **am** exercising right now.
- I **should** exercise every day.
- **Do** you like to exercise?

base form   The simple form of a verb without any endings (-s, -ed, -ing) or other changes.
- **be**, **have**, **go**, **drive**

clause   A group of words that has a subject and a verb. A sentence can have one or more clauses.
- **We are leaving now.** (one clause)
- **If it rains, we won't go.** (two clauses)

common noun   A word for a person, place, or thing (but not the name of the person, place, or thing).
- Teresa lives in a **house** near the **beach**.

comparative   The form of an adjective or adverb that shows the difference between two people, places, or things.
- Alain is **shorter** than Brendan. (adjective)
- Brendan runs **faster** than Alain. (adverb)

conditional sentence   A sentence that describes a condition and its result. The sentence can be about the past, the present, or the future. The condition and result can be real or unreal.
- If it **rains**, I **won't go**. (future, real)
- If it **had rained**, I **wouldn't have gone**. (past, unreal)

continuous   See **progressive**.

contraction   A short form of a word or words. An apostrophe (') replaces the missing letter or letters.
- **she's** = she is
- **can't** = cannot

count noun   A noun that you can count. It has a singular and a plural form.
- one **book**, two **books**

definite article   *the*   This article goes before a noun that refers to a specific person, place, or thing.

- *Please bring me **the book** on **the table**. I'm almost finished reading it.*

dependent clause   (also called **subordinate clause**) A clause that needs a main clause for its meaning.

- ***If I get home early**, I'll call you.*

direct object   A noun or pronoun that receives the action of a verb.

- *Marta kicked **the ball**. I saw **her**.*

direct speech   Language that gives the exact words a speaker used. In writing, quotation marks come before and after the speaker's words.

- ***"I saw Bob yesterday,"** she said.*
- ***"Is he in school?"***

embedded question   A question that is inside another sentence.

- *I don't know **where the restaurant is**.*
- *Do you know **if it's on Tenth Street**?*

formal   Language used in business situations or with adults you do not know.

- *Good afternoon, Mr. Rivera. Please have a seat.*

gerund   A noun formed with verb + *-ing* that can be used as a subject or an object.

- ***Swimming** is great exercise.*
- *I enjoy **swimming**.*

helping verb   See **auxiliary verb**.

identifying adjective clause   A clause that identifies which member of a group the sentence is about.

- *There are 10 students in the class. The student **who sits in front of me** is from Russia.*

***if* clause**   The clause that states the condition in a conditional sentence.

- ***If I had known you were here**, I would have called you.*

imperative   A sentence that gives a command or instructions.

- ***Hurry!***
- ***Turn left on Main Street.***

indefinite article   *a* **or** *an*   These articles go before a noun that does not refer to a specific person, place, or thing.

- *Can you bring me **a book**? I'm looking for something to read.*

indefinite pronoun   A pronoun such as *someone, something, anyone, anything, anywhere, no one, nothing, nowhere, everyone,* and *everything.* An indefinite pronoun does not refer to a specific person, place, or thing.

- ***Someone** called you last night.*
- *Did **anything** happen?*

indirect object   A noun or pronoun (often a person) that receives something as the result of the action of the verb.

- *I told **John** the story.*
- *He gave **me** some good advice.*

indirect speech   Language that reports what a speaker said without using the exact words.

- *Ann said **she had seen Bob the day before**.*
- *She asked **if he was in school**.*

infinitive   *to* + base form of the verb.

- *I want **to leave** now.*

infinitive of purpose   *(in order) to* + base form. This form gives the reason for an action.

- *I go to school **(in order) to learn** English.*

informal   Language used with family, friends, and children.

- *Hi, Pete. Sit down.*

information question   See *wh-* **question**.

inseparable phrasal verb   A phrasal verb whose parts must stay together.

- *We **ran into** Tomás at the supermarket. (Not: We ~~ran Tomás into~~ . . .)*

intransitive verb   A verb that does not have an object.

- *She **paints**.*
- *We **fell**.*

irregular   A word that does not change its form in the usual way.

- ***good → well***
- ***bad → worse***
- ***go → went***

main clause   A clause that can stand alone as a sentence.
- *I called my friend Tom, who lives in Chicago.*

main verb   A verb that describes an action or state. It is often used with an auxiliary verb.
- *Jared is **calling**.*
- *Does he **call** every day?*

modal   A type of auxiliary verb. It goes before a main verb or stands alone as a short answer. It expresses ideas such as ability, advice, permission, and possibility. *Can, could, will, would, may, might, should,* and *must* are modals.
- ***Can** you swim?*
- *Yes, I **can**.*
- *You really **should** learn to swim.*

negative   A statement or answer meaning *No.*
- *He **doesn't** work. (negative statement)*
- ***No**, he **doesn't**. (negative short answer)*

non-action verb   (also called **stative verb**). A verb that does not describe an action. It describes such things as thoughts, feelings, and senses.
- *I **remember** that word.*
- *Chris **loves** ice cream.*
- *It **tastes** great.*

non-count noun   A noun you usually do not count (*air, water, rice, love . . .*). It has only a singular form.
- *The **rice** is delicious.*

nonidentifying adjective clause   (also called **nonrestrictive adjective clause**) A clause that gives additional information about the noun it refers to. The information is not necessary to identify the noun.
- *My sister Diana, **who usually hates sports**, recently started tennis lessons.*

nonrestrictive adjective clause   See **nonidentifying adjective clause**.

noun   A word for a person, place, or thing.
- *My **sister**, **Anne**, works in an **office**.*
- *She uses a **computer**.*

object   A noun or a pronoun that receives the action of a verb. Sometimes a verb has two objects.
- *Layla threw **the ball**.*
- *She threw **it** to **Tom**.*
- *She threw **him the ball**.*

object pronoun   A pronoun (*me, you, him, her, it, us, them*) that receives the action of the verb.
- *I gave **her** a book.*
- *I gave **it** to **her**.*

object relative pronoun   A relative pronoun that is an object in an adjective clause.
- *I'm reading a book **that** I really like.*

paragraph   A group of sentences, usually about one topic.

particle   A word that looks like a preposition and combines with a main verb to form a phrasal verb. It often changes the meaning of the main verb.
- *He looked the word **up**. (He looked for the meaning of the word in the dictionary.)*

passive causative   A sentence formed with *have* or *get* + object + past participle. It is used to talk about services that you arrange for someone to do for you.
- *She **had the car checked** at the service station.*
- *He's going to **get his hair cut** by André.*

passive sentence   A sentence that focuses on the object (the person or thing receiving the action). The passive is formed with *be* + past participle.
- ***The ball was kicked** by Ari.*

past participle   A verb form (verb + *-ed*). It can also be irregular. It is used to form the present perfect, past perfect, and future perfect. It can also be an adjective.
- *We've **lived** here since April.*
- *They had **spoken** before.*
- *She's **interested** in math.*

phrasal verb   (also called two-word verb) A verb that has two parts (verb + particle). The meaning is often different from the meaning of its separate parts.
- *He **grew up** in Texas. (became an adult)*
- *His parents **brought** him **up** to be honest. (raised)*

phrase   A group of words that forms a unit but does not have a main verb. Many phrases give information about time or place.
- ***Last year**, we were living **in Canada**.*

plural   A form that means *two or more.*
- *There **are** three **people** in the restaurant.*
- ***They are** eating dinner.*
- ***We** saw **them**.*

possessive   Nouns, pronouns, or adjectives that show a relationship or show that someone owns something.

- *Zach is **Megan's** brother.* (possessive noun)
- *Is that car **his**?* (possessive pronoun)
- *That's **his** car.* (possessive adjective)

predicate   The part of a sentence that has the main verb. It tells what the subject is doing or describes the subject.

- *My sister **works for a travel agency**.*

preposition   A word that goes before a noun or a pronoun to show time, place, or direction.

- *I went **to** the bank **on** Monday. It's **next to** my office.*

progressive   (also called **continuous**) The verb form *be* + verb + *-ing*. It focuses on the continuation (not the completion) of an action.

- *She**'s reading** the paper.*
- *We **were watching** TV when you called.*

pronoun   A word used in place of a noun.

- *That's my brother. You met **him** at my party.*

proper noun   A noun that is the name of a person, place, or thing. It begins with a capital letter.

- ***Maria** goes to **Central High School**.*
- *It's on **High Street**.*

punctuation   Marks used in writing (period, comma, . . .) that make the meaning clear. For example, a period **(.)** shows the end of a sentence. It also shows that the sentence is a statement, not a question.

quantifier   A word or phrase that shows an amount (but not an exact amount). It often comes before a noun.

- *Josh bought **a lot of** books last year.*
- *He doesn't have **much** money.*

question   See **yes / no question** and **wh- question**.

question word   See **wh- word**.

quoted speech   See **direct speech**.

real conditional sentence   A sentence that talks about general truths, habits, or things that happen again and again. It can also talk about things that will happen in the future under certain circumstances.

- *If it rains, he takes the bus.*
- *If it rains tomorrow, we'll take the bus with him.*

regular   A word that changes its form in the usual way.

- *play → played*
- *fast → faster*
- *quick → quickly*

relative pronoun   A word that connects an adjective clause to a noun in the main clause.

- *He's the man **who** lives next door.*
- *I'm reading a book **that** I really like.*

reported speech   See **indirect speech**.

reporting verb   A verb such as *said*, *told*, or *asked*. It introduces direct and indirect speech. It can also come after the quotation in direct speech.

- *She **said**, "I'm going to be late."* OR *"I'm going to be late," she **said**.*
- *She **told** me that she was going to be late.*

restrictive adjective clause   See **identifying adjective clause**.

result clause   The clause in a conditional sentence that talks about what happens if the condition occurs.

- *If it rains, **I'll stay home**.*
- *If I had a million dollars, **I would travel**.*
- *If I had had your phone number, **I would have called you**.*

sentence   A group of words that has a subject and a main verb.

- ***Computers are** very useful.*

separable phrasal verb   A phrasal verb whose parts can separate.

- *Tom **looked** the word **up** in a dictionary.*
- *He **looked** it **up**.*

short answer   An answer to a *yes / no* question.

   A: *Did you call me last night?*
   B: *No, I didn't.* OR *No.*

singular   A form that means *one*.

- *They have **a sister**.*
- ***She works** in **a hospital**.*

statement   A sentence that gives information. In writing, it ends in a period.

- *Today is Monday.*

stative verb   See **non-action verb**.

subject   The person, place, or thing that the sentence is about.

- *Ms. Chen teaches English.*
- *Her class is interesting.*

subject pronoun   A pronoun that shows the person (*I, you, he, she, it, we, they*) that the sentence is about.

- *I read a lot.*
- *She reads a lot too.*

subject relative pronoun   A relative pronoun that is the subject of an adjective clause.

- *He's the man who lives next door.*

subordinate clause   See **dependent clause**.

superlative   The form of an adjective or adverb that is used to compare a person, place, or thing to a group of people, places, or things.

- *Cindi is the shortest player on the team.* (adjective)
- *She dances the most gracefully.* (adverb)

tag question   A statement + tag. The **tag** is a short question at the end of the statement. Tag questions check information or comment on a situation.

- *You're Jack Thompson, aren't you?*
- *It's a nice day, isn't it?*

tense   The form of a verb that shows the time of the action.

- **simple present**: *Fabio talks to his friend every day.*
- **simple past**: *Fabio talked to his teacher yesterday.*

third-person singular   The pronouns *he, she,* and *it* or a singular noun. In the simple present, the third-person-singular verb ends in *-s*.

- *Tomás works in an office.* (Tomás = he)

three-word verb   A phrasal verb + preposition.

- *Slow down! I can't keep up with you.*

time clause   A clause that begins with a time word such as *when, before, after, while,* or *as soon as.*

- *I'll call you when I get home.*

transitive verb   A verb that has an object.

- *She likes apples.*

two-word verb   See **phrasal verb**.

unreal conditional sentence   A sentence that talks about unreal conditions and their unreal results. The condition and its result can be untrue, imagined, or impossible.

- *If I were a bird, I would fly around the world.*
- *If you had called, I would have invited you to the party.*

verb   A word that describes what the subject of the sentence does, thinks, feels, senses, or owns.

- *They run two miles every day.*
- *She loved that movie.*
- *He has a new camera.*

wh- question   (also called **information question**) A question that begins with a *wh-* word. You answer a *wh-* question with information.

- **A:** *Where are you going?*
- **B:** *To the store.*

wh- word   A question word such as *who, what, when, where, which, why, how,* and *how much.* It can begin a *wh-* question or an embedded question.

- *Who is that?*
- *What did you see?*
- *When does the movie usually start?*
- *I don't know how much it costs.*

yes/no question   A question that begins with a form of *be* or an auxiliary verb. You can answer a *yes/no* question with *yes* or *no*.

- **A:** *Are you a student?*
- **B:** *Yes, I am.* OR *No, I'm not.*

UNIT REVIEW ANSWER KEY

Note: In this answer key, where a short or contracted form is given, the full or long form is also correct (unless the purpose of the exercise is to practice the short or contracted forms).

UNIT 1

A
1. helps
2. is working
3. Do
4. understand
5. usually go

B
1. 'm looking for
2. think
3. isn't carrying
4. need
5. see
6. 's standing
7. 's waiting
8. sounds
9. don't believe
10. wants

C Hi Leda,

How ~~do you do~~ *are you doing* these days? We're all fine. I'm writing to tell you that we ~~not~~ *aren't* living in California anymore. We just moved to Oregon. Also, we ~~expect~~ *'re expecting* a baby! We're looking for an interesting name for our new daughter. Do you have any ideas? Right now, we're thinking about *Gabriella* because it~~'s having~~ *has* good nicknames. For example, *Gabby*, *Bree*, and *Ella* all seem good to us. How ~~are~~ *do* those nicknames sound to you? We hope you'll write soon and tell us your news. Love,
Samantha

UNIT 2

A
1. met
2. was working
3. saw
4. had
5. When
6. was thinking
7. gave

B
1. were . . . doing
2. met
3. were waiting
4. met
5. were studying
6. noticed
7. entered

C It was 2005. I ~~studied~~ *was studying* French in Paris ~~while~~ *when* I met Paul. Like me, Paul was from California. We were both taking the same 9:00 A.M. conversation class. After class we always ~~were going~~ *went* to a café with some of our classmates. One day, while we ~~was~~ *were* drinking café au lait, Paul ~~was asking~~ *asked* me to go to a movie with him. After that, we started to spend most of our free time together. We really got to know each other well, and we discovered that we had a lot of similar interests. When the course was over, we left Paris and ~~were going~~ *went* back to California together. The next year we got married!

UNIT 3

A
1. got
2. has been living
3. since
4. read
5. been playing
6. has
7. 've been studying

B
1. has been working OR has worked
2. discovered
3. didn't know
4. found out
5. did OR 'd done
6. 's gone OR 's been going
7. hasn't found
8. 's had OR 's been having

C A: How long ~~did~~ *have* you been doing adventure sports?

B: I~~'ve gotten~~ *got* interested five years ago, and I haven't stopped since then.

A: You're lucky to live here in Colorado. It's a great place for adventure sports. *Have you lived* OR *Have you been living* ~~Did you live~~ here long?

B: No, not long. I moved here last year. Before that, I~~'ve been living~~ *lived* in Alaska.

A: I haven't ~~go~~ *been* there yet, but I've heard it's great.

B: It *is* great. When you go, be sure to visit Denali National Park.

UNIT 4

A
1. had gotten
2. had been studying
3. had graduated
4. moved
5. hadn't given

B
1. had . . . been playing
2. joined
3. 'd decided
4. 'd been practicing
5. 'd taught
6. Had . . . come
7. 'd . . . moved
8. 'd been living
9. hadn't expected

C When five-year-old Sarah Chang enrolled in the Juilliard School of Music, she ~~has~~ *had* already been playing the violin for more than a year. Her parents, both musicians, had ~~been moving~~ *moved* from Korea to further their careers. They had ~~gave~~ *given* their daughter a violin as a fourth birthday present, and Sarah had

UR-1

been ~~practiced~~ *practicing* hard since then. By seven, she already performed with several local orchestras. A child prodigy, Sarah became the youngest person to receive the Hollywood Bowl's Hall of Fame Award.

She had already ~~been receiving~~ *received* several awards including the Nan Pa Award—South Korea's highest prize for musical talent.

UNIT 5

A
1. turn
2. Are
3. doing
4. is
5. is going to
6. 're
7. finishes

B
1. will . . . be doing OR are . . . going to be doing
2. is going to be leaving OR will be leaving
3. 'll be sitting OR 'm going to be sitting
4. won't be coming OR 're not going to be coming
5. Is . . . going to cause OR Will . . . cause
6. No . . . isn't. OR No . . . won't.
7. 's going to be OR 'll be
8. 'll see

C A: How long are you going to *be* staying in Beijing?

B: I'm not sure. I'll let you know just as soon as I ~~X~~ find out, OK?

A: OK. It's going to be a long flight. What will you ~~did~~ *do* OR *be doing* to pass the time?

B: I'll be ~~work~~ *working* a lot of the time. And I'm going to try to sleep.

A: Good idea. Have fun, and I~~'m emailing~~ *'ll email* you all the office news. I promise.

UNIT 6

A
1. have saved
2. get
3. have been exercising
4. 'll have read
5. By

B
1. 'll have been living
2. 'll have been studying
3. 'll have graduated
4. graduate
5. 'll have found
6. 'll have made
7. 'll have saved

C I'm so excited about your news! By the time you read this, you'll have already ~~moving~~ *moved* into your new house! And I have some good news too. By the end of this month, I will ~~have been saving~~ *have saved* $3,000. That's enough for me to buy a used car! And that means that by this time next year, I ~~drive~~ *'ll have driven* to California to visit you! I have more news too. By the time I ~~will~~ graduate, I will have ~~been~~ started my new part-time job. I hope that by this time next year, I'll also ~~had~~ *have* paid off some of my loans.

It's hard to believe that in June, we will have been ~~being~~ friends for 10 years. Time sure flies! And we'll have ~~been~~ stayed friends even though we live 3,000 miles apart. Isn't the Internet a great thing?

UNIT 7

A
1. isn't
2. Didn't
3. 've
4. it
5. Hasn't
6. she
7. Shouldn't

B
1. haven't
2. No, I haven't
3. Can't
4. are
5. Yes, I am
6. won't
7. Yes, you will

C A: Ken hasn't come back from Korea yet, has ~~Ken~~ *he*?

B: ~~No~~ *Yes*, he has. He got back last week. Didn't he call you when he got back?

A: No, he didn't. He's probably busy. There are a lot of things to do when you move, ~~isn't it~~ *aren't there*?

B: Definitely. And I guess his family ~~wanted~~ *will want* to spend a lot of time with him, won't they?

A: I'm sure they will. You know, I think I'll just call him. You have his phone number, ~~have~~ *don't* you?

B: Yes, I do. Could you wait while I get it off my computer? You're not in a hurry, ~~aren't~~ *are* you?

UNIT 8

A
1. does
2. So
3. isn't either
4. but
5. doesn't
6. too

B
1. I speak Spanish, and so does my brother. OR . . . and my brother does too.
2. Jaime lives in Chicago, but his brother doesn't.
3. Chicago is an exciting city, and so is New York. OR . . . and New York is too.
4. Chen doesn't play tennis, but his sister does.
5. Diego doesn't eat meat, and neither does Lila. OR . . . and Lila doesn't either.

C My friend Alicia and I have a lot in common. She comes from Los Angeles, and so ~~I do~~ *do I*. She speaks Spanish. I ~~speak~~ *do* OR *I speak Spanish* too. Her parents are both teachers, ~~but~~ *and* mine are too. (My mother teaches math, and her father ~~do~~ *does* too.) I don't have any brothers or sisters. ~~Either~~ *Neither* does she. There are some differences too. Alicia is very outgoing, ~~and~~ *but* I'm not. I like to spend more time alone. I don't enjoy sports, but she ~~doesn't~~ *does*. She's on several school teams, but ~~not I'm~~ *I'm not*.

UR-2

I just think our differences make things more

interesting, and so ~~my friend does~~! *(does my friend)*

A 1. to use
   2. (in order) to save
   3. ordering
   4. to relax
   5. to study OR study
   6. preparing
   7. Stopping
   8. to eat
   9. having
   10. Cooking

B 1. doesn't OR didn't remember eating

   2. wants OR wanted him to take

   3. wonders OR wondered about Chu's OR Chu eating

   4. didn't stop to have OR is going to stop to have

   5. forgot to mail

C **A:** I was happy to hear that the cafeteria is serving

   salads now. I'm eager ~~trying~~ them. *(to try)*

   B: Me too. Someone recommended eating more

   salads in order ~~for losing~~ weight. *(to lose)*

   A: It was that TV doctor, right? He's always urging

   ~~we~~ to exercise more too. *(us)*

   B: That's the one. He's actually convinced me to

   stop ~~to eat~~ meat. *(eating)*

   A: Interesting! It would be a hard decision for us

   ~~making~~, though. We love to barbecue. *(to make)*

A 1. helped
   2. had
   3. made
   4. let
   5. got

B 1. didn't OR wouldn't let me have

   2. got them to give

   3. made me walk

   4. had me feed

   5. didn't OR wouldn't help me take / to take

   6. got him to give

   7. let them have

C Lately I've been thinking a lot about all the people

who helped me ~~adjusting~~ to moving here when I was *(adjust OR to adjust)*

a kid. My parents got me ^to^ join some school clubs so

that I met other kids. Then my dad helped me

~~improves~~ my soccer game so I could join the team. *(improve OR to improve)*

And my mom never let me ✗ stay home. She made

me ✗ get out and do things. My parents also spoke

to my new teacher, and they had her ~~called~~ on me a *(call)*

lot so the other kids got to know me quickly. The

neighbors helped too. They got ~~I~~ to walk their dog *(me)*

Red, and Red introduced me to all her human

friends! The fact that so many people wanted to

help me made me ✗ realize that I was not alone.

Before long I felt part of my new school, my new

neighborhood, and my new life.

A 1. off
   2. it down
   3. ahead
   4. up
   5. away
   6. back
   7. it up

B 1. take down
   2. touch up
   3. settle on
   4. figure . . . out
   5. show up
   6. find out
   7. left . . . on
   8. turn . . . off

C **A:** This apartment is bringing me down. Let's do

   ~~over it~~. *(it over)*

   B: It *is* depressing. Let's put ~~around~~ a list and *(together)*

   figure out what to do first.

   A: OK. Write this down: Pick ~~on~~ new paint colors. *(out)*

   We can look at some online.

   B: The new streetlight shines into the bedroom.

   We need to block ~~up~~ the light somehow. *(out)*

   A: We could put ~~on~~ some dark curtains in that *(up)*

   room. That should take care of the problem.

A 1. f
   2. e
   3. a
   4. c
   5. b
   6. d
   7. g

B 1. woke Jason up
   2. pick it up
   3. count on her
   4. call me back
   5. got off the phone
   6. put my nightshirt on
   7. turned the lights off

C I'm so tired of telemarketers calling me up as

soon as I get ~~from work back~~ or just when I sit ~~up~~ for *(back from work)* *(down)*

a relaxing dinner! It's gotten to the point that I've

stopped picking ^up^ the phone when it rings between

6:00 to 8:00 P.M. ✗. I know I can count on it being a

telemarketer who will try to talk me into spending

money on something I don't want. But it's still

annoying to hear the phone ring, so sometimes I

turn ~~off it~~. Then, of course, I worry that it may be *(it off)*

someone important. So I end up checking caller ID

to find out. I think the Do Not Call list is a great idea.

Who thought ~~up it~~? I'm going to sign ~~for it up~~ *(it up)* *(up for it)*

tomorrow!

UNIT 13

A
1. are
2. whose
3. thinks
4. which
5. which
6. who

B
1. who OR that behave
2. who makes
3. which . . . convince
4. who OR that . . . speaks
5. that OR which hurt
6. which . . . upset
7. whose . . . is

C It's true that we are often attracted to people ~~whose~~ *who* OR *that* are very different from ourselves. An extrovert, ~~which~~ *whose* personality is very outgoing, will often connect with a romantic partner who ~~are~~ *is* an introvert. They are both attracted to someone that ~~have~~ *has* different strengths. My cousin Valerie, who is an extreme extrovert, recently married Bill, whose idea of a party is a Scrabble game on the Internet. Can this marriage succeed? Will Bill learn the salsa, ~~that~~ *which* is Valerie's favorite dance? Will Valerie start collecting unusual words? Their friends, ~~what~~ *who* care about both of them, are hoping for the best.

UNIT 14

A
1. whose
2. that
3. where
4. who
5. when
6. who

B
1. where
2. that OR which
3. that OR which
4. who(m) OR that
5. whose
6. who(m)
7. that OR which

C I grew up in an apartment building ~~who~~ *that* OR *which* my grandparents owned. There was a small dining room ~~when~~ *where* OR *in which* we had family meals and a kitchen ~~in that~~ *in which* OR *where* I ate my breakfast. My aunt, uncle, and cousin, in ~~who~~ *whose* home I spent a lot of my time, lived in an identical apartment on the fourth floor. I remember the time my parents gave me a toy phone set that we set up so I could talk to my cousin. There weren't many children in the building, but I often visited the building manager, ~~who's~~ *whose* son I liked. I enjoyed living in the apartment, but for me it was a happy day ~~where~~ *when* OR *that* we moved into our own house.

UNIT 15

A
1. get
2. may
3. 've got
4. can't
5. help
6. might
7. post
8. must not
9. be able to

B
1. 'd better not OR shouldn't OR ought not to give
2. 'd better OR 've got to OR must register
3. must not be

4. has got to OR must get
5. can't OR must not eat
6. may OR might OR could come

C
1. Could that ~~being~~ *be* Amelie in this photograph?
2. No, that's impossible. It doesn't look anything like Amelie. It ~~doesn't have to~~ *can't* OR *couldn't* be her.
3. I don't know this person. I guess I'd ~~not better~~ *better not* accept him as a friend on my Facebook page.
4. With MySpace, I ~~must not~~ *don't have to* call to keep in touch with friends. It's just not necessary.
5. ~~May~~ *Will* hi5 be as popular as Facebook someday?

UNIT 16

A
1. have
2. ought
3. could
4. given
5. shouldn't
6. should I

B
1. I should've studied for the math test.
2. You could've shown me your class notes.
3. I shouldn't have stayed up so late the night before the test.
4. John ought to have called you.
5. You might've invited me to join the study group.

C I shouldn't have ~~stay~~ *stayed* up so late. I overslept and missed my bus. I ought *to* have asked Erik for a ride. I got to the office late, and my boss said, "You might ~~had~~ *have* called." She was right. I ~~shouldn't~~ *should* have called. At lunch my co-workers went out together. They really could ~~of~~ *have* invited me to join them. Should ~~have I~~ *I have* said something to them? Then, after lunch, my mother called. She said, "Yesterday was Aunt Em's birthday. You could've ~~sending~~ *sent* her a card!" I really think my mother might ~~has~~ *have* reminded me. Not a good day! I ~~shouldn't have~~ *should've* just stayed in bed.

UNIT 17

A
1. must
2. might not have
3. have
4. taken
5. may
6. have
7. couldn't

B
1. might OR may not have gotten my message
2. must not have studied
3. couldn't OR can't have forgotten our date
4. may OR might OR could have been at the movies
5. must have forgotten
6. must not have seen me

C Why did the Aztecs build their capital city in the middle of a lake? Could they ~~had~~ *have* wanted the protection of the water? They might have ~~been~~. Or the location may ~~has~~ *have* helped them to control nearby societies. At first it must have ~~being~~ *been* an awful place, full of mosquitoes and fog. But it must ~~no~~ *not* have been a bad idea—the island city became the center of a very powerful empire. To succeed, the Aztecs had to have ~~became~~ *become* fantastic engineers quite quickly. When the Spanish arrived, they couldn't have ~~expect~~ *expected* the amazing palaces, floating gardens, and well-built canals. Unfortunately, they destroyed the city anyway.

UNIT 18

A 1. Spanish is spoken in Bolivia.
2. They play soccer in Bolivia.
3. Reza Deghati took the photo.
4. The articles were translated into Spanish.
5. Quinoa is grown in the mountains.
6. They named the main street El Prado.

B 1. was discovered
2. is spoken
3. is grown
4. is exported
5. are OR have been employed
6. was made
7. has been performed
8. is attended

C Photojournalist Alexandra Avakian was born and ~~raise~~ *raised* in New York. Since she began her career, she has covered many of the world's most important stories. Her work ~~have~~ *has* been published in many newspapers and magazines including *National Geographic*, and her photographs have ~~being~~ *been* exhibited around the world. Avakian has also written a book, *Window of the Soul: My Journey in the Muslim World*, which was ~~been~~ published in 2008. It has not yet been translated ~~by translators~~ into other languages, but the chapter titles appear in both English and Arabic. Avakian's book ~~have be~~ *has been* discussed on international TV, radio, and numerous websites.

UNIT 19

A 1. done 3. could 5. be 7. has
2. be replaced 4. had 6. won't 8. are

B 1. should be trained
2. have to be given
3. must . . . be tested
4. can be experienced
5. will be provided
6. may be sent
7. could . . . be developed

C The new spacesuits are going to be ~~testing~~ *tested* underwater today. They've got to be ~~been~~ improved before they can be used on the Moon or Mars. Two astronauts are going to be wearing them while they're working, and they'll *be* watched by the engineers. This morning communication was lost with the Earth's surface, and all decisions had to be ~~make~~ *made* by the astronauts themselves. It was a very realistic situation. This crew ~~will got~~ *will have* OR *has got* to be very well prepared for space travel. They're going to the Moon in a few years.

UNIT 20

A 1. have it cut 4. your house painted
2. done 5. by
3. get

B 1. have OR get it repaired
2. have OR get them cleaned
3. have OR get them shortened
4. have OR get it colored
5. have OR get it fixed
6. had OR got it removed
7. have OR get it renewed
8. 'll have OR get OR 'm going to have OR 'm having OR getting it checked

C I'm going on vacation next week. I'd like to have ~~done some work~~ *some work done* in my office, and this seems like a good time for it. Please have my carpet ~~clean~~ *cleaned* while I'm gone. And could you have my computer and printer looked at? It's been quite a while since they've been serviced. Ted wants to have my office painted ~~by a painter~~ while I'm gone. Please tell him any color is fine except pink! Last week, I ~~had designed some new brochures~~ *had some new brochures designed* by Perfect Print. Please call the printer and have them delivered directly to the sales reps. And could you ~~get made up more business cards~~ *get more business cards made up* too? When I get back, it'll be time to plan the holiday party. I think we should have it catered this

UR-5

year ~~from~~ *by* a professional. While I'm gone, why don't you call around and get some estimates from

caterers? ~~Has~~ *Have* the estimates sent to Ted. Thanks.

UNIT 21

A 1. do . . . do   6. doesn't stay
2. are   7. closes
3. is   8. go
4. shop   9. feel
5. happens   10. think

B 1. When OR If it's 7:00 A.M. in Honolulu, what time is it in Mumbai?

2. If you love jewelry, you should visit an international jewelry show.

3. A tourist might have more fun if she tries bargaining.

4. If OR When you're shopping at an outdoor market, you can always bargain for a good price.

5. But don't try to bargain if OR when you're shopping in a big department store.

C 1. If I don't like something I bought online, then I ~~returned~~ *return* it.

2. Don't buy from an online site, if you don't know anything about the company.

3. When he shops online, Frank always saves a lot of time.

4. I always ~~fell~~ *fall* asleep if I fly at night. It happens every time.

5. Isabel always has a wonderful time, when she visits Istanbul.

UNIT 22

A 1. d   3. a   5. b
2. f   4. c   6. e

B 1. take

2. 'll be OR 'm going to be

3. will . . . do OR are . . . going to do

4. don't get

5. 'll stay OR 'm going to stay

6. get

7. pass

8. 'll celebrate OR 'm going to celebrate

C It's been a hard week, and I'm looking forward to

the weekend. If the weather ~~will be~~ *is* nice tomorrow, Marco and I are going to go to the beach. The ocean is usually too cold for swimming at this time of year,

so I probably ~~don't~~ *won't* go in the water unless it's really hot outside. But I love walking along the beach and breathing in the fresh sea air.

If Marco has time, he might ~~makes~~ *make* some sandwiches to bring along. Otherwise, we'll just get some pizza. I hope it'll be a nice day. I just listened to the weather report, and there may be some rain in

the afternoon. ~~Unless~~ *If* it rains, we'll probably go to the movies instead. That's our Plan B. But I really want to go to the beach, so I'm keeping my fingers crossed!

UNIT 23

A 1. 'd feel   5. could
2. were   6. weren't
3. could   7. 'd
4. found

B 1. would . . . do   5. would become
2. found   6. put
3. Would . . . take   7. made
4. knew   8. would learn

C 1. Pablo wishes he ~~can~~ *could* speak German.

2. If he had the time, he'~~ll~~*'d* study in Germany. But he doesn't have the time right now.

3. He could get a promotion ~~when~~ *if* he spoke another language.

4. His company ~~may~~ *might* pay the tuition if he took a course.

5. What would you do if you ~~are~~ *were* in Pablo's situation?

UNIT 24

A 1. hadn't told   4. If
2. had   5. gone
3. would have been

B 1. would've been

2. hadn't missed

3. had been

4. wouldn't have discovered

5. hadn't accepted

6. had taken

7. wouldn't have met

8. hadn't seen

9. wouldn't have believed

C Tonight we watched the movie *Back to the Future*

starring Michael J. Fox. I might never ~~had~~ *have* seen it if I hadn't read his autobiography, *Lucky Man*. His book was so good that I wanted to see his most famous

movie. Now I wish I ~~saw~~ *had seen* it in the theater when it first came out, but I hadn't even been born yet! It would

have been better if we ~~would have~~ *had* watched it on a big screen. Fox was great. He looked really young—

just like a teenager. But I would have recognized him even ~~when~~ *if* I hadn't known he was in the film.
In real life, when Fox was a teenager, he was too small to become a professional hockey player. But if he hadn't looked so young, he ~~can't~~ *couldn't* OR *wouldn't* have gotten his role in the TV hit series *Family Ties*. In Hollywood, he had to sell his furniture to pay his bills, but he kept trying to find an acting job. If he ~~wouldn't have~~ *hadn't*, he might never have become a star.

UNIT 25

A
1. says
2. "I'd love to."
3. planned
4. he
5. 'd
6. told
7. had been
8. his

B
1. (that) she always gets OR got up early.
2. (that) water boils OR boiled at 100 degrees Celsius.
3. (that) he liked OR likes my haircut.
4. (that) she loved OR 'd loved the pasta.
5. (that) it was OR is his own recipe.
6. (that) she mailed OR 'd mailed him the check.
7. (that) his boss had liked OR liked his work.

C
1. A psychologist I know often tells me ˣthat people today tell hundreds of lies every day. ˣ
2. Yesterday Marcia's boyfriend ~~said her~~ *said* OR *told her* that he liked her new dress.
3. When she heard that, Marcia said she didn't really believe ~~you~~ *him*.
4. I didn't think that was so bad. I said that her boyfriend ~~tells~~ *had told* OR *told* her a white lie.
5. But Marcia hates lying. She said that to ~~me~~ *her*, all lies are wrong.

UNIT 26

A
1. was
2. I
3. take
4. might
5. today
6. would
7. could
8. there

B
1. (that) it was going to rain
2. (that) it could be the worst storm this year
3. (that) it was going to start soon
4. (that) they should buy water
5. (that) they had to leave right then
6. (that) she would call me the next day

C What a storm! They ~~told~~ *said* it ~~is~~ *was* going to be bad, but it was terrible. They said it ~~will~~ *would* last two days, but it lasted four. On the first day of the storm, my mother called and told me that we should ~~have left~~ *leave* the house right ~~now~~ *then*. (I still can hear her exact words: "You should leave the house *right now*!") We should have listened to her! We just didn't believe it was going to be so serious. I told her last night that if we had known, we would ~~had~~ *have* left right away. We're lucky we survived. I just listened to the weather forecast. Good news! They said tomorrow should be sunny.

UNIT 27

A
1. . [*period*]
2. give
3. "Please sit down."
4. not to
5. say
6. told
7. invited

B
1. He told OR asked her to show him her license.
2. She advised OR told him to get more exercise.
3. She invited OR asked them to come to the English Department party.
4. He asked her to turn on the light.
5. She invited OR asked them to hang out at her house.

C My teacher, Mr. Wong, ~~told~~ *said* OR *told us* to sleep well before the test. He said ~~to don't~~ *not to* stay up late studying. He always invites ~~we~~ *us* to ask him questions. He says, "~~Not to~~ *Don't* be shy." I'm glad my friend Tom advised me ~~taking~~ *to take* his class. He ~~said me~~ *said* OR *told me* to register early, and he warned me ˣthat the class filled up fast every semester. ˣ I told him ~~don't~~ *not* to worry. I said I'd already registered.

UNIT 28

A
1. . [*period*]
2. if
3. their office was
4. I lived
5. I had

B
1. who the company had hired.
2. if OR whether I had taken the job.
3. if OR whether I liked my present job.
4. who my boss was.
5. how many employees worked there.
6. why I wanted to change jobs.
7. what the starting salary was.
8. if OR whether I could start soon.

C They asked me so many questions! They asked me
where ~~did I work~~ *I worked*. They asked who ~~was my boss~~ *my boss was*.
They asked why I ~~did want~~ *wanted* to change jobs. They
asked how much money I made. They ~~ask~~ *asked* me who I
~~have~~ *had* voted for in the last election. They even asked
me what my favorite color was ✗ *.* Finally, I asked
myself whether or ~~no~~ *not* I really wanted that job!

UNIT 29

A
1. we should
2. our server is
3. . [*period*]
4. to
5. I should
6. ? [*question mark*]
7. whether

B
1. where the restaurant is?
2. if OR whether the subway goes to the museum.
3. if OR whether we should tip the porter.
4. why we didn't buy the book on tipping.
5. how much we should tip the tour guide.
6. if OR whether you have any travel books.
7. what this sign says?

C
A: Hi. Is this a good time to call? I wasn't sure
what time you have dinner ✗ *.*
B: This is fine. I didn't know ~~were you~~ *if* OR *whether you were* back from
your trip.
A: We got back two days ago. I can't remember
~~did I email~~ *if* OR *whether I emailed* you some photographs.
B: Yes. They were great. Can you tell me where
~~took you~~ *you took* that picture of the lake? I want to go!
A: Hmm. I'm not sure which one ~~was that~~ *that was*. We
saw a lot of lakes in Switzerland.
B: I'll show it to you. I'd really like to find out
where ~~is it~~ *it is*.

INDEX

This index is for the full and split editions. All entries are in the full book. Entries for Volume A of the split edition are in black. Entries for Volume B are in red.

CREDITS